1972

Some Modern Writers

Selected and Edited by

ROBERT SCHOLES

New York

OXFORD UNIVERSITY PRESS

London 1971 Toronto

SOME MODERN WRITERS

Essays and Fiction by

CONRAD

DINESEN

LAWRENCE

ORWELL

FAULKNER

ELLISON

There is something of the essay in every work of fiction and something fictional in every essay.

Michel Butor

Library of Congress Catalogue Card Number: 79-82986

Printed in the United States of America

Acknowledgments

Selections from works by the following writers were made possible by the kind permission of their respective publishers.

JOSEPH CONRAD

Preface to *The Nigger of Narcissus*. Reprinted by permission of J. M. Dent & Sons, Ltd., and the Trustees of the Joseph Conrad Estate.

"Geography and Some Explorers" in *Late Essays*. Reprinted by permission of J. M. Dent & Sons, Ltd., and the Trustees of the Joseph Conrad Estate.

A Personal Record, Chapter 2. Reprinted by permission of J. M. Dent & Sons, Ltd., and the Trustees of the Joseph Conrad Estate.

"Heart of Darkness" in *Conrad's Heart of Darkness and the Critics*, edited by Bruce Harkness. © 1960 by Bruce Harkness. Reprinted by special permission of Mr. Harkness and the publisher, Wadsworth Publishing Company, Inc., and J. M. Dent & Sons, Ltd.

ISAK DINESEN

Out of Africa, pages 249–265, 279–283. Copyright 1937, renewed 1965 by Rungstedlundfonden. Reprinted by permission of Random House, Inc., and Putnam & Company.

"Sorrow Acre" in *Winter's Tales*. Copyright 1942 by Random House, Inc. Reprinted by permission of Random House, Inc., and Putnam & Company.

D. H. Lawrence

"Surgery for the Novel—or a Bomb," "Art and Morality," and "Why the Novel Matters" in *Phoenix: The Posthumous Papers of D. H. Lawrence*, edited by Edward D. Macdonald. Copyright 1936 by Frieda Lawrence, copyright © renewed 1964 by the Estate of Frieda Lawrence Ravagli. Reprinted by permission of The Viking Press, Inc., Laurence Pollinger, Ltd., and the Estate of the late Mrs. Frieda Lawrence Ravagli.

"Reflections on the Death of a Porcupine" in *Phoenix II*, edited by Warren Roberts and Harry T. Moore. Copyright 1925 by Centaur Press, renewed 1953 by Frieda Lawrence. Reprinted by permission of The Viking Press, Inc., Laurence Pollinger, Ltd., and the Estate of the late Mrs. Frieda Lawrence Ravagli.

"The Woman Who Rode Away" in *The Later D. H. Lawrence*, edited by William York Tindall. Copyright 1927 by Alfred A. Knopf, Inc., renewed 1955 by Frieda Lawrence Ravagli. Reprinted by permission of the publisher and the Estate of the late Mrs. Frieda Lawrence Ravagli.

George Orwell

"Politics and the English Language" and "Shooting an Elephant" in *Shooting an Elephant and Other Essays*. Copyright 1945, 1946, 1949, 1950 by Sonia Brownell Orwell. Reprinted by permission of Harcourt Brace Jovanovich, Inc., Secker and Warburg, and Miss Sonia Brownell.

The Road to Wigan Pier, Chapter I. Reprinted by permission of Harcourt Brace Jovanovich, Inc., Secker and Warburg, and Miss Sonia Brownell.

"The Ministry of Love" in *1984*. Copyright 1949 by Harcourt, Secker & Warburg, and Miss Sonia Brownell.

William Faulkner

Foreword to *The Faulkner Reader*. Copyright 1954 by William Faulkner. Reprinted by permission of Random House, Inc., and Curtis Brown, Ltd.

"Sunset" in *New Orleans Sketches*, edited by Carvel Collins. Copyright © 1958 by Carvel Collins. Reprinted by permission of Random House, Inc.

"Dry September" in *Collected Stories of William Faulkner*. Copyright 1930, renewed 1958 by William Faulkner. Reprinted by permission of Random House, Inc., and Curtis Brown, Ltd.

"The Old People" in *Go Down, Moses*. Copyright 1940, renewed 1968 by Estelle Faulkner and Jill Faulkner Summers. Copyright 1942 by William Faulkner. Reprinted by permission of Random House, Inc.

RALPH ELLISON

"Brave Words for a Startling Occasion" and "Hidden Name and Complex Fate" in *Shadow and Act*. Copyright © 1963, 1964 by Ralph Ellison. Reprinted by permission of Random House, Inc., and William Morris Agency, Inc.

Invisible Man, Prologue, Chapter 1, and Chapter 10. Copyright 1947, 1952 by Ralph Ellison. Reprinted by permission of Random House, Inc.

Contents

Editor's Introduction

The selections in this book are meant to provide substantial introductions to the work of six important modern writers. Why only six? Mainly so that they can be represented extensively both as essayists and writers of fiction. Why *these* six? That is a harder question. Why *not* certain others? That is harder still, but the answer to both these difficult questions has to do with the way that these six writers, and these selections from their work, fit together to make a book worth reading and studying.

To begin with, this collection includes only writers who work in the English language, so as to provide texts which are entirely suitable for close readings, with a concern for exact words and precise meanings which translated texts seldom admit. We are fortunate, of course, that gifted foreigners like Joseph Conrad and Isak Dinesen have chosen our language and enriched it with their writings. We are also fortunate that our language is used by Englishmen and Americans, with their quite different cultures and attitudes. And, in America, we can take some comfort in the fact that Blacks and Whites still find it possible to communicate in this common, international tongue. Thus the difference between Lawrence and Orwell—Englishmen of different backgrounds and classes—is as profound as that between Faulkner and Ellison—Americans of different colors. Each of these writers is, in fact, unique, offering us a particular perspective, a vision of the world framed in a special style, a way of using language which can be imitated but never duplicated. But the language is common—common to all of them and to all of us, enabling us to perform one of the most human of actions: sharing another's vision so as to see things we might not have discovered for ourselves.

These six writers also share a common concern—or a closely connected group of concerns—which the reader will find emphasized through this selection from their work. All six of them have experienced that violent shock which occurs when White Western culture encounters Asian, African, or American Indian cultures. In the writing of Conrad and Dinesen we get a glimpse of Blacks in an Africa which has been subdued by White imperialism. Faulkner and Ellison show us the Black transplanted to this alien American culture: slavery and the heritage of slavery. Orwell in Burma and Lawrence in Mexico reveal other aspects of that "White man's burden" which has become increasingly a burden of shame, guilt, and repression. Each of the six writers has reacted to this clash of cultures in a different way. But all six have responded with writing of a richness and power that demonstrates how truly relevant, how genuinely educative, literature at its best can be.

Another facet of the concern shared by these writers can be summed up in the word "politics"—if we take that word in its broadest sense. How men relate to one another, how they serve and rule one another—if these are political questions, then all six of these writers are highly political in their orientation. From the feudal estate of "Sorrow Acre" to the totalitarian torture chamber of *1984,* these writers present us with a full spectrum of political relationships, often complicated by matters of class, caste, and color. And beyond these human relationships they attend with extraordinary care to the other live things that populate this planet along with man. The politicians are only beginning to discover that ecology is a problem; writers have known it for a long time.

Literature is language in the service of vision. The greatest writers make us see the most, and the perspectives they offer us last the longest. In this volume the reader will find some selections in which they speak of themselves and their personal experience; as well as others which are more formal, more elaborate, more conspicuously creative. The selections from each writer have been arranged so as to begin with the more essayistic kinds of writing and close with an extended work of fiction. The balance of this arrangement varies from writer to writer, since some are highly essayistic in their total orientation while others have a way of turning everything into fiction. But the over-all effect should be to show each author approaching his subject matter through a variety of formal techniques and to reveal at least a glimpse of the range of styles and values that exist in his work as a whole.

Each separate selection in this book can be studied as a thing in itself. It is open to all the basic techniques of literary study: analysis of form, interpretation of meaning, critique of values. In connection with the other selections, however, each essay or story may be considered in a more elaborate way. The different works by a single author, for instance, offer opportunities to attempt at least a preliminary study of the values that inform that writer's work as a whole. Working in different forms, speaking through different voices, and considering life from different perspectives, a writer begins to reveal himself to us, to make himself knowable. The selections in this book should lead some students to pursue their studies further into the work of those writers whose minds most interest them.

More complex still is the comparative study of different authors. The selections in this volume have been made so as to afford the opportunity to consider the different ways these six writers approach similar situations and problems, especially problems and situations involving members of different species, different races, and different classes. Every kind of investigation, from the most precise and meticulous study of comparative styles to the broadest and most speculative weighing of comparative values, is open to the student of these works. The editor will not presume to formulate specific questions or problems for investigation. Imaginative instructors and their students will find appropriate subjects for consideration without editorial guidance.

Some Modern Writers

JOSEPH CONRAD

Jozef Teodor Konrad Nalecz Korzeniowski was born in Poland in 1857. The Korzeniowskis were a respected family of landed gentry, but Conrad's father was not typical of his class. A man of letters, he translated Shakespeare into Polish; a patriot, he worked for Polish independence and was condemned to exile in Russia. Young Joseph and his mother accompanied the head of their household into exile in 1862. Three years later the boy's mother died, and he was sent to live with an uncle in Poland.

Growing up inland, he formed the unaccountable desire to make his career on the sea. With misgivings his uncle allowed him to enter the French marine service at the age of eighteen. After a disastrous attempt to run guns from Marseilles to Spain in support of the romantic pretender Don Carlos, and an even more disastrous love affair which ended in a suicide attempt, he decided that he had exhausted the possibilities of France. He also wished to avoid the compulsary military service that would have been his lot in Poland or as a French citizen. Thus it was that at the age of twenty he left the Continent and sailed as an ordinary seaman on his first English ship.

A sympathetic biographer has described him at the end of his stay in France as "irresponsible, undisciplined, inconsiderate, sensitive, highly strung, passionate." His really generous and understanding uncle wrote him at the time to say, "Really, you have surpassed the limit of stupidity permitted to one of your age!" This apparently hopeless young man reached England knowing only a few words of the language. Two years later he had his third mate papers in the British Merchant Service, and six years after that, in 1886, he obtained his master's papers and his British citizenship. In two more years he had his first command at sea.

In 1890 he made a voyage up the Congo which provided him with the material for Heart of Darkness. *Around this time he began writing seriously in the English language. In 1895 his first novel,* Almayer's Folly, *was published, and he left the sea to pursue his career as a writer, under the simplified version of his name which he had adopted in the course of his nautical life. He died in 1924. On his tombstone at Canterbury are carved two lines spoken by Despair in Spenser's* Faerie Queene:

> Sleep after toyle, port after stormie seas,
> Ease after warre, death after life, does greatly please.

The best single collection of Conrad's work is still the Viking Portable Conrad, with its excellent critical introduction by the late M. D. Zabel. The standard biography (quoted from above) is Joseph Conrad *by Jocelyn Baines (McGraw-Hill, 1960). Some of his major novels are* Lord Jim *(1900)*, Nostromo *(1904)*, The Secret Agent *(1907), and* Victory *(1915)*.

The Condition of Art

This essay first appeared as the Preface to Conrad's third novel, The Nigger of the Narcissus *(1897).*

A work that aspires, however humbly, to the condition of art should carry its justification in every line. And art itself may be defined as a single-minded attempt to render the highest kind of justice to the visible universe, by bringing to light the truth, manifold and one, underlying its every aspect. It is an attempt to find in its forms, in its colours, in its light, in its shadows, in the aspects of matter, and in the facts of life what of each is fundamental, what is enduring and essential—their one illuminating and convincing quality—the very truth of their existence. The artist, then, like the thinker or the scientist, seeks the truth and makes his appeal. Impressed by the aspect of the world the thinker plunges into ideas, the scientist into facts—whence, presently, emerging they make their appeal to those qualities of our being that fit us best for the hazardous enterprise of living. They speak authoritatively to our common sense, to our intelligence, to our desire of peace, or to our desire of unrest; not seldom to our prejudices, sometimes to our fears, often to our egoism—but always to our credulity. And their words are heard with reverence, for their concern is with weighty matters: with the cultivation of our minds and the proper care of our bodies, with the attainment of our ambitions, with the perfection of the means and the glorification of our precious aims.

It is otherwise with the artist.

Confronted by the same enigmatical spectacle the artist descends within himself, and in that lonely region of stress and strife, if he be deserving and fortunate, he finds the terms of his appeal. His appeal is made to our less obvious capacities: to that part of our nature which, because of the warlike conditions of existence, is necessarily kept out of sight within the more resisting and hard qualities—like the vulnerable body within a steel armour. His appeal is less loud, more profound, less distinct, more stirring—and sooner forgotten. Yet its effect endures for ever. The changing wisdom of successive generations discards ideas, questions facts, demolishes theories. But the artist appeals to that part of our being which is not dependent on wisdom; to that in us which is a gift and not an acquisition—and, therefore, more permanently enduring. He speaks to our capacity for delight and wonder, to the sense of mystery surrounding our lives; to our sense of pity, and beauty, and pain; to the latent feeling of fellowship with all creation—and to the subtle but invincible conviction of solidarity that knits together the loneliness of innumerable hearts, to the solidarity in dreams, in joy, in sorrow, in aspirations, in illusions, in hope, in fear, which binds men to each other, which binds together all humanity—the dead to the living and the living to the unborn.

It is only some such train of thought, or rather of feeling, that can in a measure explain the aim of the attempt, made in the tale which follows, to present an unrestful episode in the obscure lives of a few individuals out of all the disregarded multitude of the bewildered, the simple, and the voiceless. For, if any part of truth dwells in the belief confessed above, it becomes evident that there is not a place of splendour or a dark corner of the earth that does not deserve, if only a passing glance of wonder and pity. The motive, then, may be held to justify the matter of the work; but this preface, which is simply an avowal of endeavour, cannot end here—for the avowal is not yet complete.

Fiction—if it at all aspires to be art—appeals to temperament. And in truth it must be, like painting, like music, like all art, the appeal of one temperament to all the other innumerable temperaments whose subtle and resistless power endows passing events with their true meaning, and creates the moral, the emotional atmosphere of the place and time. Such an appeal to be effective must be an impression conveyed through the senses; and, in fact, it cannot be made in any other way, because temperament, whether individual or collective, is not amenable to persuasion. All art, therefore, appeals primarily to the senses, and the artistic aim when expressing itself in written words must also make its appeal through the senses, if its high desire is to reach the secret spring of responsive emotions. It must strenuously aspire to the plasticity of sculpture, to the colour of painting, and to the magic suggestiveness of music—which is the art of arts. And it is only through complete, unswerving devotion to the perfect blending of form and substance; it is only through an unremitting never-discouraged care for the shape and ring of sentences that an approach can be made to plasticity, to colour, and that the light of magic suggestiveness may be brought to play for an evanescent instant over the commonplace surface of words: of the old, old words, worn thin, defaced by ages of careless usage.

The sincere endeavour to accomplish that creative task, to go as far on that road as his strength will carry him, to go undeterred by faltering, weariness, or reproach, is the only valid justification for the worker in prose. And if his conscience is clear, his answer to those who, in the fullness of a wisdom which looks for immediate profit, demand specifically to be edified, consoled, amused; who demand to be promptly improved, or encouraged, or frightened, or shocked, or charmed, must run thus: My task which I am trying to achieve is, by the power of the written word to make you hear, to make you feel—it is, before all, to make you see. That—and no more, and it is everything. If I succeed, you shall find there according to your deserts: encouragement, consolation, fear, charm—all you demand—and, perhaps, also that glimpse of truth for which you have forgotten to ask.

To snatch in a moment of courage, from the remorseless rush of time, a passing phase of life, is only the beginning of the task. The task approached in tenderness and faith is to hold up unquestioningly, without choice and without fear, the rescued fragment before all eyes in the light of a sincere mood. It is to show its vibration, its colour, its form; and through its movement, its form, and its colour, reveal the substance of its truth—disclose its inspiring secret: the stress and passion within the core of each convincing moment. In a single-minded attempt of that kind, if one be deserving and fortunate, one may perchance attain to such clearness of sincerity that at last the presented vision of regret or pity, of terror or mirth, shall awaken in the hearts of the beholders that feeling of unavoidable solidarity; of the solidarity in mysterious origin, in toil, in joy, in hope, in uncertain fate, which binds men to each other and all mankind to the visible world.

It is evident that he who, rightly or wrongly, holds by the convictions expressed above cannot be faithful to any one of the temporary formulas of his craft. The enduring part of them—the truth which each only imperfectly veils—should abide with him as the most precious of his possessions, but they all: Realism, Romanticism, Naturalism, even the unofficial sentimentalism (which, like the poor, is exceedingly difficult to get rid of), all these gods must, after a short period of fellowship, abandon him—even on the very threshold of the temple—to the stammerings of his conscience and to the outspoken consciousness of the difficulties of his work. In that uneasy solitude the supreme cry of Art for Art itself, loses the exciting ring of its apparent immorality. It sounds far off. It has ceased to be a cry, and is heard only as a whisper, often incomprehensible, but at times and faintly encouraging.

Sometimes, stretched at ease in the shade of a roadside tree, we watch the motions of a labourer in a distant field, and after a time, begin to wonder languidly as to what the fellow may be at. We watch the movements of his body, the waving of his arms, we see him bend down, stand up, hesitate, begin again. It may add to the charm of an idle hour to be told the purpose of his exertions. If we know he is trying to lift a stone, to dig a ditch, to uproot a stump, we look with a more real interest at his efforts; we are disposed to condone the jar of his agitation upon the restfulness of the landscape; and even, if in a brotherly frame of mind, we may bring ourselves to forgive his failure. We understood his object, and, after all, the fellow has tried, and perhaps he had not the strength—and perhaps he had not the knowledge. We forgive, go on our way—and forget.

And so it is with the workman of art. Art is long and life is short, and success is very far off. And thus, doubtful of strength to travel so far, we talk a little about the aim—the aim of art, which, like life itself, is inspiring, difficult—obscured by mists. It is not in the clear logic of a triumphant conclusion; it is not in the unveiling of one of those heartless secrets which are called the Laws of Nature. It is not less great, but only more difficult.

To arrest, for the space of a breath, the hands busy about the work of the earth, and compel men entranced by the sight of distant goals to glance for a moment at the surrounding vision of form and colour, of sunshine and shadows; to make them pause for a look, for a sigh, for a smile—such is the aim, difficult and evanescent, and reserved only for a very few to achieve. But sometimes, by the deserving and the fortunate, even that task is accomplished. And when it is accomplished—behold!—all the truth of life is there: a moment of vision, a sigh, a smile—and the return to an eternal rest.

Geography and Some Explorers

This work was included in the posthumously published volume, Last Essays *(1926).*

It is safe to say that for the majority of mankind the superiority of geography over geometry lies in the appeal of its figures. It may be an effect of the incorrigible frivolity inherent in human nature, but most of us will agree that a map is more fascinating to look at than a figure in a treatise on conic sections—at any rate for the simple minds which are all the equipment of the majority of the dwellers on this earth.

No doubt a trigonometrical survey may be a romantic undertaking, striding over deserts and leaping over valleys never before trodden by the foot of civilized man; but its accurate operations can never have for us the fascination of the first hazardous steps of a venturesome, often lonely, explorer jotting down by the light of his camp fire the thoughts, the impressions, and the toil of his day.

For a long time yet a few suggestive words grappling with things seen will have the advantage over a long array of precise, no doubt interesting, and even profitable figures. The earth is a stage, and though it may be an advantage, even to the right comprehension of the play, to know its exact configuration, it is the drama of human endeavour that will be the thing, with a ruling passion expressed by outward action marching perhaps blindly to success or failure, which themselves are often undistinguishable from each other at first.

Of all the sciences, geography finds its origin in action, and what is more, in adventurous action of the kind that appeals to sedentary people who like to dream of arduous adventure in the manner of prisoners dreaming behind bars of all the hardships and hazards of liberty dear to the heart of man.

Descriptive geography, like any other kind of science, has been built on the experience of certain phenomena and on experiments prompted by that unappeasable curiosity of men which their intelligence has elevated into a quite respectable passion for acquiring knowledge. Like other sciences it has fought its way to truth through a long series of errors. It has suffered from the love of the marvellous, from our credulity, from rash and unwarrantable assumptions, from the play of unbridled fancy.

Geography had its phase of circumstantially extravagant speculation which had nothing to do with the pursuit of truth, but has given us a curious glimpse of the mediæval mind playing in its ponderous childish way with the problems of our earth's shape, its size, its character, its products, its inhabitants. Cartography was almost as pictorial then as are some modern newspapers. It crowded its maps with pictures of strange pageants, strange trees, strange beasts, drawn with amazing precision in the midst of theoretically conceived continents. It delineated imaginary kingdoms of Monomotapa and of Prester John, the regions infested by lions or haunted by unicorns, inhabited by men with reversed feet, or eyes in the middle of their breasts.

All this might have been amusing if the mediæval gravity in the absurd had not been in itself a wearisome thing. But what of that! Has not the key science of modern chemistry passed through its dishonest phase of Alchemy (a portentous development of the confidence trick), and our knowledge of the starry sky been arrived at through the superstitious idealism of Astrology looking for men's fate in the depths of the infinite? Mere megalomania on a colossal scale. Yet, solemn fooling for solemn fooling of the scientific order, I prefer the kind that does not lay itself out to thrive on the fears and the cupidities of men.

From that point of view geography is the most blameless of sciences. Its fabulous phase never aimed at cheating simple mortals (who are a multitude) out of their peace of mind or their money. At the most it has enticed some of them away from their homes; to death may be, now and then to a little disputed glory, not seldom to contumely, never to high fortune. The greatest of them all, who has presented modern geography with a new world to work upon, was at one time loaded with chains and thrown into prison. Columbus remains a pathetic figure, not a sufferer in the cause of geography, but a victim of the imperfections of jealous human hearts, accepting his fate with resignation. Among explorers he appears lofty in his troubles and like a man of a kingly nature. His contribution to the knowledge of the earth was certainly royal. And if the discovery of America was the occasion of the greatest outburst of reckless cruelty and greed known to history we may say this at least for it, that the gold of Mexico and Peru, unlike the gold of alchemists, was really there, palpable, yet, as ever, the most elusive of the Fata Morgana that lure men away from their homes, as a moment of reflection will convince any one. For nothing is more certain than that there will never be enough gold to go round, as the Conquistadores found out by experience.

I suppose it is not very charitable of me, but I must say that to this day I feel a malicious pleasure at the many disappointments of those pertinacious searchers for El Dorado who climbed mountains, pushed through forests, swam rivers, floundered in bogs, without giving a single thought to the science of geography. Not for them the serene joys of scientific research, but infinite toil, in hunger, thirst, sickness, battle; with broken heads, unseemly squabbles, and empty pockets in the end. I cannot help thinking it served them right. It is an ugly tale, which has not much to do with the service of geography. The geographical knowledge of our day is of the kind that would have been beyond the conception of the hardy followers of Cortés and Pizarro; and of that most estimable of Conquerors who was called Cabeza de Vaca, who was high-minded and dealt humanely with the heathen nations whose territories he traversed in search of one more El Dorado. It is said they loved him greatly, but now the very memory of those nations is gone from the earth, while their territories, which they could not take with them, are being traversed many times every twenty-four hours by the trains of the Southern Pacific railroad.

The discovery of the New World marks the end of the fabulous geography, and it must be owned that the history of the Conquest contains at least one great moment—I mean a geographically great moment—when Vasco Núñez de Balboa, while crossing the Isthmus of

Panama, set his eyes for the first time upon the ocean, the immensity of which he did not suspect, and which in his elation he named the Pacific. It is anything but that; but the privileged Conquistador cannot be blamed for surrendering to his first impression.

The Gulf of Panama, which is what he really saw with that first glance, is one of the calmest spots on the waters of the globe. Too calm. The old navigators dreaded it as a dangerous region where one might be caught and lie becalmed for weeks with one's crew dying slowly of thirst under a cloudless sky. The worst of fates, this, to feel yourself die in a long and helpless agony. How much preferable a region of storms where man and ship can at least put up a fight and remain defiant almost to the last.

I must not be understood to mean that a tempest at sea is a delightful experience, but I would rather face the fiercest tempest than a gulf pacific even to deadliness, a prison-house for incautious caravels and a place of torture for their crews. But Balboa was charmed with its serene aspect. He did not know where he was. He probably thought himself within a stone's throw, as it were, of the Indies and Cathay. Or did he perhaps, like a man touched with grace, have a moment of exalted vision, the awed feeling that what he was looking at was an abyss of waters comparable in its extent to the view of the unfathomable firmament, and sown all over with groups of islands resembling the constellations of the sky?

But whatever spiritual glimpse of the truth he might have had, Balboa could not possibly know that this great moment of his life had added suddenly thousands of miles to the circumference of the globe, had opened an immense theatre for the human drama of adventure and exploration, a field for the missionary labours of, mainly, Protestant churches, and spread an enormous canvas on which armchair geographers could paint the most fanciful variants of their pet theory of a great southern continent.

I will not quarrel with the post-Columbian cartographers for their wild but, upon the whole, interesting inventions. The provocation to let one's self go was considerable. Geography militant, which had succeeded the geography fabulous, did not seem able to accept the idea that there was much more water than land on this globe. Nothing could satisfy their sense of the fitness of things but an enormous extent of solid earth which they placed in that region of the South where, as a matter of fact, the great white-crested seas of stormy latitudes will be free to chase each other all round the globe to the end of time. I suppose their landsmen's temperament stood in the way of their recognition that the world of geography, so far as the apportioning of space goes, seems to have been planned mostly for the convenience of fishes.

What is surprising to me is that the seamen of the time should have really believed that the large continents to the north of the Equator demanded, as a matter of good art or else of sound science, to be balanced by corresponding masses of land in the southern hemisphere. They were simple souls. The chorus of armchair people all singing the same tune made them blind to the many plain signs of a great open sea. Every bit of coast-line discovered, every mountaintop glimpsed in the distance, had to be dragged loyally into the scheme of the Terra Australis Incognita.

Even Tasman, the best seaman of them all before James Cook, the most accomplished of seventeenth-century explorers and navigators that went forth to settle the geography of the Pacific—even Tasman, after coming unexpectedly upon the North Island of New Zealand, and lingering long enough there to chart roughly a bit of the coast and lose a boat's crew in a sudden affray with the Maoris, seemed to take it for granted that this was the western limit of an enormous continent extending away towards the point of South America.

Mighty is the power of a theory, especially if based on such a common-sense notion as the balance of continents. And it must be remembered that it is difficult for us to realize not only the navigational dangers of unknown seas, but the awful geographical incertitudes of the first explorers in that new world of waters.

Tasman's journal, which was published not so very long ago, gives us some idea of their perplexing difficulties. The early navigators had no means of ascertaining their exact position on the globe. They could calculate their latitude, but the problem of longitude was a matter which bewildered their minds and often falsified their judgment. It had to be a matter of pure guesswork. Tasman and his officers, when they met on board the *Heemskirk*, anchored in Murderers' Bay, to consider their further course in the light of their instructions, did not know where any of the problematic places named in their instructions were, neither did they know where they themselves were.

Tasman might have sailed north or east, but in the end he decided to sail between the two, and, circling about, returned to Batavia, where he was received coldly by his employers, the honourable governor-general and the council in Batavia. Their final judgment was that Abel Tasman was a skilful navigator, but that he had shown himself "remiss" in his investigations, and that he had been guilty of leaving certain problems unsolved.

We are told that Tasman did not expect this armchair criticism; and indeed, even now, it seems surprising to an unprejudiced mind. It was the voyage during which, among other things, Tasman discovered the island by which his name lives on the charts, took first contact with New Zealand (which was not seen again till 130 years afterwards), sailed over many thousands of miles of uncharted seas, bringing back with him a journal which was of much value afterwards for his exploring successors.

It may be he was hurt by the verdict of the honourable council, but he does not seem to have been cast down by it, for it appears that shortly afterwards he asked for a rise of salary—and, what is still more significant, he got it. He was obviously a valuable servant, but I am sorry to say that his character as a man was not of the kind to cause governors and councils to treat him with particular consideration. Except in professional achievement he is not comparable to Captain Cook, a humble son of the soil like himself, but a modest man of genius, the familiar associate of the most learned in the land, medallist of the Royal Society, and a captain in the Royal Navy.

But there was a taint of an unscrupulous adventurer in Tasman. It is certain that at various times his patron, the Governor Anthony van Diemen, and the honourable council in Batavia, had employed him in some shady transactions of their own, connected with the Japan trade. There is also no doubt that once he had, on his own responsibility, kidnapped an influential Chinaman who stood in the way of some business negotiation Tasman was conducting with the Sultan of Achin.

The Chinaman may have been a worthless person, but one wonders what happened to him in the end; and, in any case, the proceeding is open to criticism. Then in his old age he got into some disreputable scrape which caused the congregation with which he worshipped to ask him to resign his membership. Even the honourable council was startled, and dismissed him from his employment, though characteristically enough not actually from their service. This action of the council fixes the character of the man better than any scandalous story. He was valuable, but compromising.

All these regrettable details came to my knowledge quite recently in a very amusing and interesting book, but I must confess that my early admiration for Tasman as one of the early fathers of militant geography has not been affected very much by it. Remiss or not, he had in the course of his voyages mapped 8,000 miles of an island which by common consent is called now a continent, a geologically very old continent indeed, but which is now the home of a very young commonwealth with all the possibilities of material and intellectual splendour still hidden in its future.

I like to think that in that portion the Elysian Fields set apart for great navigators, James Cook would not refuse to acknowledge the civilities of Abel Tasman, a fellow seaman who had first reported the existence of New Zealand in the perplexed, bewildered way of those times, 130 years before Captain Cook on his second voyage laid for ever the ghost of the Terra Australis Incognita and added New Zealand to the scientific domain of the geography triumphant of our day.

No shade of remissness nor doubtful motive rests upon the achievements of Captain Cook, who came out of a labourer's cottage to take his place at the head of the masters of maritime exploration who worked at the great geographical problem of the Pacific. *Endeavour* was the name of the ship which carried him on his first voyage, and it was also the watchword of his professional life. *Resolution* was the name of the ship he commanded himself on his second expedition, and it was the determining quality of his soul. I will not say that it was the greatest, because he had all the other manly qualities of a great man.

The voyages of the early explorers were prompted by an acquisitive spirit, the idea of lucre in some form, the desire of trade or the desire of loot, disguised in more or less fine words. But Cook's three voyages are free from any taint of that sort. His aims needed no disguise. They were scientific. His deeds speak for themselves with the masterly simplicity of a hard-won success. In that respect he seems to belong to the single-minded explorers of the nineteenth century, the late fathers of militant geography whose only object was the search for truth. Geography is a science of facts, and they devoted themselves to the discovery of facts in the configuration and features of the main continents.

It was the century of landsmen investigators. In saying this I do not forget the polar explorers, whose aims were certainly as pure as the air of those high latitudes where not a few of them laid down their lives for the advancement of geography. Seamen, men of science, it is difficult to speak of them without admirative emotion. The dominating figure among the seamen explorers of the first half of the nineteenth century is that of another good man, Sir John Franklin, whose fame rests not only on the extent of his discoveries, but on professional prestige and high personal character. This great navigator, who never returned home, served geography even in his death. The persistent efforts extending over ten years to ascertain his fate advanced greatly our knowledge of the polar regions.

As gradually revealed to the world this fate appeared the more tragic in this, that for the first two years the way of the *Erebus* and *Terror* expedition seemed to be the way to the desired and important success, while in truth it was all the time the way of death, the end of the darkest drama perhaps played behind the curtain of Arctic mystery.

The last words unveiling the mystery of the *Erebus* and *Terror* expedition were brought home and disclosed to the world by Sir Leopold McClintock, in his book, "The Voyage of the *Fox* in the Arctic Seas." It is a little book, but it records with manly simplicity the tragic ending of a great tale. It so happened that I was born in the year of its publication. Therefore, I may be excused for not getting hold of it till ten years afterwards. I can only account for it falling into my hands by the fact that the fate of Sir John Franklin was a matter of European interest, and that Sir Leopold McClintock's book was translated, I believe, into every language of the white races.

My copy was probably in French. But I have read the work many times since. I have now on my shelves a copy of a popular edition got up exactly as I remember my first one. It contains the touching facsimile of the printed form filled in with a summary record of the two ships' work, the name of "Sir John Franklin commanding the expedition" written in ink, and the pathetic underlined entry "All well." It was found by Sir Leopold McClintock under a cairn and it is dated just a year before the two ships had to be abandoned in their deadly ice-trap, and their crews' long and desperate struggle for life began.

There could hardly have been imagined a better book for letting in the breath of the stern romance of polar exploration into the existence of a boy whose knowledge of the poles of the earth had been till then of an abstract formal kind as mere imaginary ends of the imaginary axis upon which the earth turns. The great spirit of the realities of the story sent me off on the romantic explorations of my inner self; to the discovery of the taste of poring over maps; and revealed to me the existence of a latent devotion to geography which interfered with my devotion (such as it was) to my other schoolwork.

Unfortunately, the marks awarded for that subject were almost as few as the hours apportioned to it in the school curriculum by persons of no romantic sense for the real, ignorant of the great possibilities of active life; with no desire for struggle, no notion of the wide spaces of the world—mere bored professors, in fact, who were not only middle-aged but looked to me as if they had never been young. And their geography was very much like themselves, a bloodless thing with a dry skin covering a repulsive armature of uninteresting bones.

I would be ashamed of my warmth in digging up a hatchet which has been buried now for nearly fifty years if those fellows had not tried so often to take my scalp at the yearly examinations. There are things that one does not forget. And besides, the geography which I had discovered for myself was the geography of open spaces and wide horizons built up on men's devoted work in the open air, the geography still militant but already conscious of its approaching end with the death of the last great explorer. The antagonism was radical.

Thus it happened that I got no marks at all for my first and only paper on Arctic geography, which I wrote at the age of thirteen. I still think that for my tender years it was an erudite performance. I certainly did know something of Arctic geography, but what I was after really, I suppose, was the history of Arctic exploration. My knowledge had considerable gaps, but I managed to compress my enthusiasm into just two pages, which in itself was a sort of merit. Yet I got no marks. For one thing it was not a set subject. I believe the only comment made about it to my private tutor was that I seemed to have been wasting my time in reading books of travel instead of attending to my studies. I tell you, those fellows were always trying to take my scalp. On another occasion I just saved it by proficiency in map-drawing. It must have been good, I suppose; but all I remember about it is that it was done in a loving spirit.

I have no doubt that star-gazing is a fine occupation, for it leads you within the borders of the unattainable. But map-gazing, to which I became addicted so early, brings the problems of the great spaces of the earth into stimulating and directing contact with sane curiosity and gives an honest precision to one's imaginative faculty. And the honest maps of the nineteenth century nourished in me a passionate interest in the truth of geographical facts and a desire for precise knowledge which was extended later to other subjects.

For a change had come over the spirit of cartographers. From the middle of the eighteenth century on the business of map-making had been growing into an honest occupation, registering the hard-won knowledge, but also in a scientific spirit recording the geographical ignorance of its time. And it was Africa, the continent out of which the Romans used to say some new thing was always coming, that got cleared of the dull imaginary wonders of the dark ages, which were replaced by exciting spaces of white paper. Regions unknown! My imagination could depict to itself there worthy, adventurous and devoted men, nibbling at the edges, attacking from north and south and east and west, conquering a bit of truth here and a bit of truth there, and sometimes swallowed up by the mystery their hearts were so persistently set on unveiling.

Among them Mungo Park, of western Sudan, and Bruce, of Abyssinia, were, I believe, the first friends I made when I began to take notice—I mean geographical notice—of the continents of the world into which I was born. The fame of these two had already been for a long time European, and their figures had become historical by then. But their story was a very novel thing to me, for the very latest geographical news that could have been whispered to me in my cradle was that of the expedition of Burton and Speke, the news of the existence of Tanganyika and of Victoria Nyanza.

I stand here confessed as a contemporary of the Great Lakes. Yes, I could have heard of their discovery in my cradle, and it was only right that, grown to a boy's estate, I should have in the later sixties done my first bit of map-drawing and paid my first homage to the prestige of their first explorers. It consisted in entering laboriously in pencil the outline of Tanganyika on my beloved old atlas, which, having been published in 1852, knew nothing, of course, of the Great Lakes. The heart of its Africa was white and big.

Surely it could have been nothing but a romantic impulse which prompted the idea of bringing it up to date with all the accuracy of which I was capable. Thus I could imagine myself stepping in the very footsteps of geographical discovery. And it was not all wasted time. As a bit of prophetic practice it was not bad for me. Many years afterwards, as second officer in the Merchant Service, it was my duty to correct and bring up to date the charts of more than one ship, according to the Admiralty notices. I did this work conscientiously and with a sense of responsibility; but it was not in the nature of things that I should ever recapture the excitement of that entry of Tanganyika on the blank of my old atlas.

It must not be supposed that I gave up my interest in the polar regions. My heart and my warm participation swung from the frigid to the torrid zone, fascinated by the problems of each, no doubt, but more yet by the men who, like masters of a great art, worked each according to his temperament to complete the picture of the earth. Almost each day of my schoolboy life had its hour given up to their company. And to this day I think that it was a very good company.

Not the least interesting part in the study of geographical discovery lies in the insight it gives one into the characters of that special kind of men who devoted the best part of their lives to the exploration of land and sea. In the world of mentality and imagination which I was entering it was they and not the characters of famous fiction who were my first friends. Of some of them I had soon formed for myself an image indissolubly connected with certain parts of the world. For instance, western Sudan, of which I could draw the rivers and principal features from memory even now, means for me an episode in Mungo Park's life.

It means for me the vision of a young, emaciated, fair-haired man, clad simply in a tattered shirt and worn-out breeches, gasping painfully for breath and lying on the ground in the shade of an enormous African tree (species unknown), while from a neighbouring village of grass huts a charitable black-skinned woman is approaching him with a calabash full of pure cold water, a simple draught which, according to himself, seems to have effected a miraculous cure. The central Sudan, on the other hand, is represented to me by a very different picture, that of a self-confident and keen-eyed person in a long cloak and wearing a turban on his head, riding slowly towards a gate in the mud walls of an African city, from which an excited population is streaming out to behold the wonder—Doctor Barth, the protégé of Lord Palmerston, and subsidized by the British Foreign Office, approaching Kano, which no European eye had seen till then, but where forty years later my friend Sir Hugh Clifford, the Governor of Nigeria, travelled in state in order to open a college.

I must confess that I read that bit of news and inspected the many pictures in the illustrated papers without any particular elation. Education is a great thing, but Doctor Barth gets in the way. Neither will the monuments left by all sorts of empire builders suppress for me the memory of David Livingstone. The words "Central Africa" bring before my eyes an old man with a rugged, kind face and a clipped, gray moustache, pacing wearily at the head of a few black followers along the reed-fringed lakes towards the dark native hut on the Congo headwaters in which he died, clinging in his very last hour to his heart's unappeased desire for the sources of the Nile.

That passion had changed him in his last days from a great explorer into a restless wanderer refusing to go home any more. From his exalted place among the blessed of militant geography and with his memory enshrined in Westminster Abbey, he can well afford to smile without bitterness at the fatal delusion of his exploring days, a notable European figure and the most venerated perhaps of all the objects of my early geographical enthusiasm.

Once only did that enthusiasm expose me to the derision of my schoolboy chums. One day, putting my finger on a spot in the very middle of the then white heart of Africa, I declared that some day I would go there. My chums' chaffing was perfectly justifiable. I myself was ashamed of having been betrayed into mere vapouring. Nothing was further from my wildest hopes. Yet is it a fact that, about eighteen years afterwards, a wretched little stern-wheel steamboat I commanded lay moored to the bank of an African river.

Everything was dark under the stars. Every other white man on board was asleep. I was glad to be alone on deck, smoking the pipe of peace after an anxious day. The subdued thundering mutter of the Stanley Falls hung in the heavy night air of the last navigable reach of the Upper Congo, while no more than ten miles away, in Reshid's camp just above the Falls, the yet unbroken power of the Congo Arabs slumbered uneasily. Their day was over. Away in the middle of the stream, on a little island nestling all black in the foam of the broken water, a solitary little light glimmered feebly, and I said to myself with awe, "This is the very spot of my boyish boast."

A great melancholy descended on me. Yes, this was the very spot. But there was no shadowy friend to stand by my side in the night of the enormous wilderness, no great haunting memory, but only the unholy recollection of a prosaic newspaper "stunt" and the distasteful knowledge of the vilest scramble for loot that ever disfigured the history of human conscience and geographical exploration. What an end to the idealized realities of a boy's daydreams! I wondered what I was doing there, for indeed it was only an unforeseen episode, hard to believe in now, in my seaman's life. Still, the fact remains that I have smoked a pipe of peace at midnight in the very heart of the African continent, and felt very lonely there.

But never so at sea. There I never felt lonely, because there I never lacked company. The company of great navigators, the first grown-up friends of my early boyhood. The unchangeable sea preserves for one the sense of its past, the memory of things accomplished by wisdom and daring among its restless waves. It was those things that commanded my profoundest loyalty, and perhaps it is by the professional favour of the great navigators ever present to my memory that, neither explorer nor scientific navigator, I have been permitted to sail through the very heart of the old Pacific mystery, a region which even in my time remained very imperfectly charted and still remote from the knowledge of men.

It was in 1888, when in command of a ship loading in Sydney a mixed cargo for Mauritius, that, one day, all of a sudden, all the deep-lying historic sense of the exploring adventures in the Pacific surged up to the surface of my being. Almost without reflection I sat down and wrote a letter to my owners suggesting that, instead of the usual southern route, I should take the ship to Mauritius by way of Torres Strait. I ought to have received a severe rap on the knuckles, if only for wasting their time in submitting such an unheard-of proposition.

I must say I awaited the reply with some trepidation. It came in due course, but instead of beginning with the chiding words, "We fail to understand," etc., etc., it simply called my attention in the first paragraph to the fact that "there would be an additional insurance premium to pay for that route," and so on, and so on. And it ended like this: "Upon the whole, however, we have no objection to your taking the ship through Torres Strait if you are certain that the season is not too far advanced to endanger the success of your passage by the calms which, as you know, prevail at times in the Arafura Sea."

I read, and in my heart I felt compunctious. The season was somewhat advanced. I had not been scrupulously honest in my argumentation. Perhaps it was because I never expected it to be effective. And here it was all left to my responsibility. My letter must have struck a lucky day in Messrs. H. Simpson & Sons' offices—a romantic day. I won't pretend that I regret my lapse from strict honesty, for what would the memory of my sea life have been for me if it had not included a passage through Torres Strait, in its fullest extent, from the mouth of the great Fly River right on along the track of the early navigators.

The season being advanced, I insisted on leaving Sydney during a heavy southeast gale. Both the pilot and the tug-master were scandalized by my obstinacy, and they hastened to leave me to my own devices while still inside Sydney Heads. The fierce southeaster caught me up on its wings, and no later than the ninth day I was outside the entrance of Torres Strait, named after the undaunted and reticent Spaniard who, in the seventeenth century, first sailed that way without knowing where he was, without suspecting he had New Guinea on one side of him and the whole solid Australian continent on the other—he thought he was passing through an archipelago—the Strait whose existence for a century and a half had been doubted, argued about, squabbled over by geographers, and even denied by the disreputable but skilful navigator, Abel Tasman, who thought it was a large bay, and whose true contours were first laid down on the map by James Cook, the navigator without fear and without reproach, the greatest in achievement and character of the later seamen fathers of militant geography. If the dead haunt the scenes of their earthly exploits, then I must have been attended benevolently by those three shades—the inflexible Spaniard of such lofty spirit that in his report he disdains to say a single word about the appalling hardships and dangers of his passage; the pigheaded Hollander who, having made up his mind that there was no passage there, missed the truth by only fifty miles or so; and the great Englishman, a son of the soil, a great commander and a great professional seaman, who solved that question among many others and left no unsolved problems of the Pacific behind him. Great shades! All friends of my youth!

It was not without a certain emotion that, commanding very likely the first, and certainly the last, merchant ship that carried a cargo that way—from Sydney to Mauritius—I put her head at daybreak for Bligh's Entrance, and packed on her every bit of canvas she could carry. Windswept, sunlit empty waters were all around me, half-veiled by a brilliant haze. The first thing that caught my eye upon the play of green whitecapped waves was a black speck marking conveniently the end of a low sandbank. It looked like the wreck of some small vessel.

I altered the course slightly in order to pass close, with the hope of being able to read the letters on her stern. They were already faded. Her name was *Honolulu.* The name of the port I could not make out. The story of her life is known by now to God alone, and the winds must have drifted long ago around her remains a quiet grave of the very sand on which she had died. Thirty-six hours afterwards, of which about nine were spent at anchor, approaching the other end of the Strait, I sighted a gaunt, gray wreck of a big American ship lying high and dry on the southernmost of the Warrior Reefs. She had been there for years. I had heard of her. She was legendary. She loomed up, a sinister and enormous *memento mori* raised by the refraction of this serene afternoon above the far-away line of the horizon drawn under the sinking sun.

And thus I passed out of Torres Strait before the dusk settled on its waters. Just as a clear sun sank ahead of my ship I took a bearing of a little island for a fresh departure, an insignificant crumb of dark earth, lonely, like an advanced sentinel of that mass of broken land and water, to watch the approaches from the side of the Arafura Sea. But to me it was a hallowed spot, for I knew that the *Endeavour* had been hove to off it in the year 1762 for her captain, whose name was James Cook, to go ashore for half an hour. What he could possibly want to do I cannot imagine. Perhaps only to be alone with his thoughts for a moment. The dangers and the triumphs of exploration and discovery were over for that voyage. All that remained to do was to go home, and perhaps his great and equable soul, tempered in the incessant perils of a long exploration, wanted to commune with itself at the end of its task. It may be that on this dry crumb of the earth's crust which I was setting by compass he had tasted a moment of perfect peace. I could depict to myself the famous seaman navigator, a lonely figure in a three-cornered hat and square-skirted laced coat, pacing to and fro slowly on the rocky shore, while in the ship's boat, lying off on her oars, the coxswain kept his eyes open for the slightest sign of the captain's hand.

Thus the sea has been for me a hallowed ground, thanks to those books of travel and discovery which have peopled it with unforgettable shades of the masters in the calling which, in a humble way, was to be mine, too; men great in their endeavour and in hard-won successes of militant geography; men who went forth each according to his lights and with varied motives, laudable or sinful, but each bearing in his breast a spark of the sacred fire.

A Memorable Year

This is the second chapter of Conrad's volume of reminiscences, A Personal Record *(1912). The title used here has been supplied by the editor.*

As I have said, I was unpacking my luggage after a journey from London into Ukraine. The MS. of "Almayer's Folly"—my companion already for some three years or more, and then in the ninth chapter of its age—was deposited unostentatiously on the writing-table placed between two windows. It didn't occur to me to put it away in the drawer the table was fitted with, but my eye was attracted by the good form of the same drawer's brass handles. Two candelabra, with four candles each, lighted up festally the room which had waited so many years for the wandering nephew. The blinds were down.

Within five hundred yards of the chair on which I sat stood the first peasant hut of the village—part of my maternal grandfather's estate, the only part remaining in the possession of a member of the family; and beyond the village in the limitless blackness of a winter's night there lay the great unfenced fields—not a flat and severe plain, but a kindly, bread-giving land of low, rounded ridges, all white now, with the black patches of timber nestling in the hollows. The road by which I had come ran through a village with a turn just outside the gates closing the short drive. Somebody was abroad on the deep snow-track; a quick tinkle of bells stole gradually into the stillness of the room like a tuneful whisper.

My unpacking had been watched over by the servant who had come to help me, and, for the most part, had been standing attentive but unnecessary at the door of the room. I did not want him in the least, but I did not like to tell him to go away. He was a young fellow, certainly more than ten years younger than myself; I had not been—I won't say in that place but within sixty miles of it, ever since the year '67; yet his guileless physiognomy of the open peasant type seemed strangely familiar. It was quite possible that he might have been a descendant, a son or even a grandson, of the servants whose friendly faces had been familiar to me in my early childhood. As a matter of fact he had no such claim on my consideration. He was the product of some village near by and was there on his promotion, having learned the service in one or two houses as pantry-boy. I know this because I asked the worthy V—— next day. I might well have spared the question. I discovered before long that all the faces about the house and all the faces in the village: the grave faces with long moustaches of the heads of families, the downy faces of the young men, the faces of the little fair-haired children, the handsome, tanned, wide-browed faces of the mothers seen at the doors of the huts, were as familiar to me as though I had known them all from childhood, and my childhood were a matter of the day before yesterday.

The tinkle of the traveller's bells, after growing louder, had faded away quickly, and the tumult of barking dogs in the village had calmed down at last. My uncle, lounging in the corner of a small couch, smoked his long Turkish *chibouk* in silence.

"This is an extremely nice writing-table you have got for my room," I remarked.

"It is really your property," he said, keeping his eyes on me, with an interested and wistful expression, as he had done ever since I had entered the house. "Forty years ago your mother used to write at this very table. In our house in Oratow it stood in the little sitting-room which, by a tacit arrangement, was given up to the girls—I mean to your mother and her sister who died so young. It was a present to them jointly from our uncle Nicholas B. when your mother was seventeen and your aunt two years younger. She was a very dear, delightful girl, that aunt of yours, of whom I suppose you know nothing more than the name. She did not shine so much by personal beauty and a cultivated mind, in which your mother was far superior. It was her good sense, the admirable sweetness of her nature, her exceptional facility and ease in daily relations that endeared her to everybody. Her death was a terrible grief and a serious moral loss for us all. Had she lived she would have brought the greatest blessings to the house it would have been her lot to enter, as wife, mother and mistress of a household. She would have created round herself an atmosphere of peace and content which only those who can love unselfishly are able to evoke. Your mother—of far greater beauty, exceptionally distinguished in person, manner and intellect—had a less easy disposition. Being more brilliantly gifted, she also expected more from life. At that trying time, especially, we were greatly concerned about her state. Suffering in her health from the shock of her father's death (she was alone in the house with him when he died suddenly), she was torn by the inward struggle between her love for the man whom she was to marry in the end and her knowledge of her dead father's declared objection to that match. Unable to bring herself to disregard that cherished memory and that judgment she had always respected and trusted, and, on the other hand, feeling the impossibility to resist a sentiment so deep and so true, she could not have been expected to preserve her mental and moral balance. At war with herself, she could not give to others that feeling of peace which was not her own. It was only later, when united at last with the man of her choice, that she developed those uncommon gifts of mind and heart which compelled the respect and admiration even of our foes. Meeting with calm fortitude the cruel trials of a life reflecting all the national and social misfortunes of the community, she realised the highest conceptions of duty as a wife, a mother and a patriot, sharing the exile of her husband and representing nobly the ideal of Polish womanhood. Our Uncle Nicholas was not a man very accessible to feelings of affection. Apart from his worship for Napoleon the Great, he loved really, I believe, only three people in the world: his mother—your great-grandmother, whom you have seen but cannot possibly remember; his brother, our father, in whose house he lived for so many years; and of all of us, his nephews and nieces grown up around him, your mother alone. The modest, lovable qualities of the youngest sister he did not seem able to see. It was I who felt most profoundly this unexpected stroke of death falling upon the family less than a year after I had become its head. It was terribly unexpected. Driving home one wintry afternoon to keep me company in our empty house, where I had to remain permanently administering the estate and attending to the complicated affairs—the girls took it in turn week and week about—driving, as I said, from the house of the Countess Tekla Potocka, where our invalid mother was staying then to be near a doctor, they lost the road and got stuck in a snowdrift. She was alone with the coachman and old Valery, the personal servant of our late father. Impatient of delay while they were trying to dig themselves out, she jumped out of the sledge and went to look for the road herself. All this happened in '51, not ten miles from the house in which we are sitting now. The road was soon found, but snow had begun to fall thickly again, and they were four more hours getting home. Both the men took off their sheepskin-lined great-coats and used all their own rugs to wrap her up against the cold, notwithstanding her protests, positive orders and even struggles, as Valery afterwards related to me. 'How could I,' he remonstrated with her, 'go to meet the blessed soul of my late master if I let any harm come to you while there's a spark of life left in my body?' When they reached home, at last, the poor old man was stiff and speechless from exposure, and the coachman was in not much better plight, though he had the strength to drive round to the stables himself. To my reproaches for venturing out at all in such weather, she answered characteristically that she could not bear the thought of abandoning me to my cheerless solitude. It is incomprehensible how it was that she was allowed to start. I suppose it had to be! She made light of the cough which came on next day, but shortly afterwards inflammation of the lungs set in, and in three weeks she was no more! She was the first to be taken away of the young generation under my care. Behold the vanity of all hopes and fears! I was the most frail at birth of all the children. For years I remained so delicate that my parents had but little hope of bringing me up; and yet I have survived five brothers and two sisters, and many of my contemporaries; I have outlived my wife and daughter, too—and from all those who have had some knowledge at least of these old times, you alone are left. It has been my lot to lay in an early grave many honest hearts, many brilliant promises, many hopes full of life."

He got up brusquely, sighed, and left me, saying: "We will dine in half an hour." Without moving, I listened to his quick steps resounding on the waxed floor of the next room, traversing the ante-room lined with bookshelves, where he paused to put his *chibouk* in the pipe-stand before passing into the drawing-room (these were all *en suite*), where he became inaudible on the thick carpet. But I heard the door of his study-bedroom close. He was then sixty-two years old and had been for a quarter of a century the wisest, the firmest, the most indulgent of guardians, extending over me a paternal care and affection, a moral support which I seemed to feel always near me in the most distant parts of the earth.

As to Mr. Nicholas B., sub-lieutenant of 1808, lieutenant of 1813 in the French Army, and for a short time *Officier d'Ordonnance* of Marshal Marmont; afterwards Captain in the 2nd Regiment of Mounted Rifles in the Polish Army—such as it existed up to 1830 in the reduced kingdom established by the Congress of Vienna—I must say that from all that more distant past, known to me traditionally and a little *de visu,* and called out by the words of the man just gone away, he remains the most incomplete figure. It is obvious that I must have seen him in '64, for it is certain that he would not have missed the opportunity of seeing my mother for what he must have known would be the last time. From my early boyhood to this day, if I try to call up his image, a sort of mist rises before my eyes, a mist in which I perceive vaguely only a neatly brushed head of white hair (which is exceptional in the case of the B. family, where it is the rule for men to go bald in a becoming manner, before thirty) and a thin, curved, dignified nose, a feature in strict accordance with the physical tradition of the B. family. But it is not by these fragmentary remains of perishable mortality that he lives in my memory. I knew, at a very early age, that my grand-uncle Nicholas B. was a Knight of the Legion of Honour and that he had also the Polish Cross for valour, *Virtuti Militari.* The knowledge of these glorious facts inspired in me an admiring veneration; yet it is not that sentiment, strong as it was, which resumes for me the force and the significance of his personality. It is overborne by another and complex impression of awe, compassion and horror. Mr. Nicholas B. remains for me the unfortunate and miserable (but heroic) being who once upon a time had eaten a dog.

It is a good forty years since I heard the tale, and the effect has not worn off yet. I believe this is the very first, say, realistic, story I heard in my life; but all the same, I don't know why I should have been so frightfully impressed. Of course I know what our village dogs look like—but still . . . No! At this very day, recalling the horror and compassion of my childhood, I ask myself whether I am right in disclosing to a cold and fastidious world that awful episode in the family history. I ask myself—is it right?—especially as the B. family had always been honourably known in a wide country-side for the delicacy of their tastes in the matter of eating and drinking. But upon the whole, and considering that this gastronomical degradation overtaking a gallant young officer lies really at the door of the Great Napoleon, I think that to cover it up by silence would be an exaggeration of literary restraint. Let the truth stand here. The responsibility rests with the Man of St. Helena in view of his deplorable levity in the conduct of the Russian campaign. It was during the memorable retreat from Moscow that Mr. Nicholas B., in company of two brother officers—as to whose morality and natural refinement I know nothing—bagged a dog on the outskirts of a village and subsequently devoured him. As far as I can remember, the weapon used was a cavalry sabre, and the issue of the sporting episode was rather more of a matter of life and death than if it had been an encounter with a tiger. A picket of Cossacks was sleeping in that village lost in the depths of the great Lithuanian forest. The three sportsmen had observed them from a hiding-place making themselves very much at home amongst the huts just before the early winter darkness set in at four o'clock. They had observed them with disgust and perhaps with despair. Late in the night the rash counsels of hunger overcame the dictates of prudence. Crawling through the snow, they crept up to the fence of dry branches which generally encloses a village in that part of Lithuania. What they expected to get, and in what manner, and whether this expectation was worth the risk, goodness only knows. However, these Cossack parties in most cases wandering without an officer, were known to guard themselves badly and often not at all. In addition, the village lying at a great distance from the line of French retreat, they could not suspect the presence of stragglers from the Grand Army. The three officers had strayed away in a blizzard from the main column and had been lost for days in the woods, which explains sufficiently the terrible straits to which they were reduced. Their plan was to try and attract the attention of the peasants in that one of the huts which was nearest to the enclosure; but as they were preparing to venture into the very jaws of the lion, so to speak, a dog (it is mighty strange that there was but one), a creature quite as formidable under the circumstances as a lion, began to bark on the other side of the fence. . . .

At this stage of the narrative, which I heard many times (by request) from the lips of Captain Nicholas B.'s sister-in-law, my grandmother, I used to tremble with excitement.

The dog barked. And if he had done no more than bark, three officers of the Great Napoleon's army would have perished honourably on the points of Cossacks' lances, or perchance escaping the chase, would have died decently of starvation. But before they had time to think of running away, that fatal and revolting dog, being carried away by the excess of his zeal, dashed out through a gap in the fence. He dashed out and died. His head, I understand, was severed at one blow from his body. I understand also that, later on, within the gloomy solitudes of the snow-laden woods, when in a sheltering hollow, a fire had been lit by the party, the condition of the quarry was discovered to be distinctly unsatisfactory. It was not thin—on the contrary, it seemed unhealthily obese; its skin showed bare patches of an unpleasant character. However, they had not killed that dog for the sake of the pelt. He was large. . . . He was eaten. . . . The rest is silence . . . A silence in which a small boy shudders and says firmly:

"I could not have eaten that dog."

And his grandmother remarks with a smile:

"Perhaps you don't know what it is to be hungry."

I have learned something of it since. Not that I have been reduced to eat dog. I have fed on the emblematical animal, which, in the language of the volatile Gauls, is called *la vache enragée;* I have lived on ancient salt junk, I know the taste of shark, of trepang, of snake, of nondescript dishes containing things without a name—but of the Lithuanian village dog, never! I wish it to be distinctly understood that it is not I, but my grand-uncle Nicholas, of the Polish landed gentry, *Chevalier de la Légion d'Honneur*, etc. etc., who, in his young days, had eaten the Lithuanian dog.

I wish he had not. The childish horror of the deed clings absurdly to the grizzled man. I am perfectly helpless against it. Still, if he really had to, let us charitably remember that he had eaten him on active service, while bearing up bravely against the greatest military disaster of modern history, and, in a manner, for the sake of his country. He had eaten him to appease his hunger, no doubt, but also for the sake of an unappeasable and patriotic desire, in the glow of a great faith that lives still, and in the pursuit of a great illusion kindled like a false beacon by a great man to lead astray the effort of a brave nation.

Pro patria!

Looked at in that light it appears a sweet and decorous meal.

And looked at in the same light, my own diet of *la vache enragée* appears a fatuous and extravagant form of self-indulgence; for why should I, the son of a land which such men as these have turned up with their ploughshares and bedewed with their blood, undertake the pursuit of fantastic meals of salt junk and hard tack upon the wide seas? On the kindest view it seems an unanswerable question. Alas! I have the conviction that there are men of unstained rectitude who are ready to murmur scornfully the word desertion. Thus the taste of innocent adventure may be made bitter to the palate. The part of the inexplicable should be allowed for in appraising the conduct of men in a world where no explanation is final. No charge of faithlessness ought to be lightly uttered. The appearances of this perishable life are deceptive like everything that falls under the judgment of our imperfect senses. The inner voice may remain true enough in its secret counsel. The fidelity to a special tradition may last through the events of an unrelated existence, following faithfully, too, the traced way of an inexplicable impulse.

It would take too long to explain the intimate alliance of contradictions in human nature which makes love itself wear at times the desperate shape of betrayal. And perhaps there is no possible explanation. Indulgence—as somebody said—is the most intelligent of all the virtues. I venture to think that it is one of the least common, if not the most uncommon of all. I would not imply by this that men are foolish—or even most men. Far from it. The barber and the priest, backed by the whole opinion of the village, condemned justly the conduct of the ingenious hidalgo who, sallying forth from his native place, broke the head of the muleteer, put to death a flock of inoffensive sheep, and went through very doleful experiences in a certain stable. God forbid that an unworthy churl should escape merited censure by hanging on to the stirrup-leather of the sublime *caballero*. His was a very noble, a very unselfish fantasy, fit for nothing except to raise the envy of baser mortals. But there is more than one aspect to the charm of that exalted and dangerous figure. He, too, had his frailties. After reading so many romances he desired naïvely to escape with his very body from the intolerable reality of things. He wished to meet eye to eye the valorous giant Brandabarbaran, Lord of Arabia, whose armour is made of the skin of a dragon, and whose shield, strapped to his arm, is the gate of a fortified city. O amiable and natural weakness! O blessed simplicity of a gentle heart without guile! Who would not succumb to such a consoling temptation? Nevertheless it was a form of self-indulgence, and the ingenious hidalgo of La Mancha was not a good citizen. The priest and the barber were not unreasonable in their strictures. Without going so far as the old King Louis-Philippe, who used to say in his exile, "The people are never in fault"—one may admit that there must be some righteousness in the assent of a whole village. Mad! Mad! He who kept in pious meditation the ritual vigil-of-arms by the well of an inn and knelt reverently to be knighted at daybreak by the fat, sly rogue of a landlord, has come very near perfection. He rides forth, his head encircled by a halo—the patron saint of all lives spoiled or saved by the irresistible grace of imagination. But he was not a good citizen.

Perhaps that and nothing else was meant by the well-remembered exclamation of my tutor.

It was in the jolly year 1873, the very last year in which I have had a jolly holiday. There have been idle years afterwards, jolly enough in a way and not altogether without their lesson, but this year of which I speak was the year of my last schoolboy holiday. There are other reasons why I should remember that year, but they are too long to state formally in this place. Moreover they have nothing to do with that holiday. What has to do with the holiday is that before the day on which the remark was made we had seen Vienna, the Upper Danube, Munich, the Falls of the Rhine, the Lake of Constance—in fact it was a memorable holiday of travel. Of late we had been tramping slowly up the Valley of the Reuss. It was a delightful time. It was much more like a stroll than a tramp. Landing from a Lake of Lucerne steamer in Fluellen, we found ourselves at the end of the second day, with the dusk overtaking our leisurely footsteps, a little way beyond Hospenthal. This is not the day on which the remark was made: in the shadows of the deep valley and with the habitations of men left some way behind, our thoughts ran not upon the ethics of conduct but upon the simpler human problem of shelter and food. There did not seem anything of the kind in sight, and we were thinking of turning back when suddenly at a bend of the road we came upon a building, ghostly in the twilight.

At that time the work on the St. Gothard Tunnel was going on, and that magnificent enterprise of burrowing was directly responsible for the unexpected building standing all alone upon the very roots of the mountains. It was long, though not big at all; it was low; it was built of boards, without ornamentation, in barrack hut style, with the white window-frames quite flush with the yellow face of its plain front. And yet it was an hotel; it had even a name which I have forgotten. But there was no gold-laced door-keeper at its humble door. A plain but vigorous servant-girl answered our inquiries, then a man and a woman who owned the place appeared. It was clear that no travellers were expected, or perhaps even desired, in this strange hostelry, which in its severe style resembled the house which surmounts the unseaworthy-looking hulls of the toy Noah's Arks, the universal possession of European childhood. However, its roof was not hinged and it was not full to the brim of slab-sided and painted animals of wood. Even the live tourist animal was nowhere in evidence. We had something to eat in a long, narrow room at one end of a long, narrow table, which, to my tired perception and to my sleepy eyes, seemed as if it would tilt up like a see-saw plank, since there was no one at the other end to balance it against our two dusty and travel-stained figures. Then we hastened upstairs to bed in a room smelling of pine planks, and I was fast asleep before my head touched the pillow.

In the morning my tutor (he was a student of the Cracow University) woke me up early, and as we were dressing remarked: "There seems to be a lot of people staying in this hotel. I have heard noises of talking up till eleven o'clock." This statement surprised me; I had heard no noise whatever, having slept like a top.

We went downstairs into the long and narrow dining-room with its long and narrow table. There were two rows of plates on it. At one of the many uncurtained windows stood a tall, bony man with a bald head set off by a bunch of black hair above each ear and with a long black beard. He glanced up from the paper he was reading and seemed genuinely astonished at our intrusion. By and by more men came in. Not one of them looked like a tourist. Not a single woman appeared. These men seemed to know each other with some intimacy, but I cannot say they were a very talkative lot. The bald-headed man sat down gravely at the head of the table. It all had the air of a family party. By and by, from one of the vigorous servant-girls in national costume, we discovered that the place was really a boarding-house for some English engineers engaged at the works of the St. Gothard Tunnel; and I could listen my fill to the sounds of the English language as far as it is used at a breakfast-table by men who do not believe in wasting many words on the mere amenities of life.

This was my first contact with British mankind apart from the tourist kind seen in the hotels of Zurich and Lucerne—the kind which has no real existence in a workaday world. I know now that the bald-headed man spoke with a strong Scotch accent. I have met many of his kind since, both ashore and afloat. The second engineer of the steamer *Mavis*, for instance, ought to have been his twin brother. I cannot help thinking that he really was, though for some reasons of his own he assured me that he never had a twin brother. Anyway, the deliberate, bald-headed Scot with the coal-black beard appeared to my boyish eyes a very romantic and mysterious person.

We slipped out unnoticed. Our mapped-out route led over the Furca Pass towards the Rhône Glacier, with the further intention of following down the trend of the Häsli Valley. The sun was already declining when we found ourselves on the top of the pass, and the remark alluded to was presently uttered.

We sat down by the side of the road to continue the argument begun half a mile or so before. I am certain it was an argument because I remember perfectly how my tutor argued and how without the power of reply I listened with my eyes fixed obstinately on the ground. A stir on the road made me look up—and then I saw my unforgettable Englishman. There are acquaintances of later years, familiars, shipmates, whom I remember less clearly. He marched rapidly towards the east (attended by a hang-dog Swiss guide) with the mien of an ardent and fearless traveller. He was clad in a knickerbocker suit, but as at the same time he wore short socks under his laced boots, for reasons which whether hygienic or conscientious, were surely imaginative, his calves exposed to the public gaze and to the tonic air of high altitudes, dazzled the beholder by the splendour of their marble-like condition and their rich tone of young ivory. He was the leader of a small caravan. The light of a headlong, exalted satisfaction with the world of men and the scenery of mountains illumined his clean-cut, very red face, his short, silver-white whiskers, his innocently eager and triumphant eyes. In passing he cast a glance of kindly curiosity and a friendly gleam of big, sound, shiny teeth towards the man and the boy sitting like dusty tramps by the roadside, with a modest knapsack lying at their feet. His white calves twinkled sturdily, the uncouth Swiss guide with a surly mouth stalked like an unwilling bear at his elbow; a small train of three mules followed in single file the lead of this inspiring enthusiast. Two ladies rode past one behind the other, but from the way they sat I only saw their calm, uniform backs, and the long ends of blue veils hanging behind far down over their identical hat-brims. His two daughters, surely. An industrious luggage-mule, with unstarched ears and guarded by a slouching, sallow driver, brought up the rear. My tutor, after pausing for a look and a faint smile, resumed his earnest argument.

I tell you it was a memorable year! One does not meet such an Englishman twice in a lifetime. Was he in the mystic ordering of common events the ambassador of my future, sent out to turn the scale at a critical moment on the top of an Alpine pass, with the peaks of the Bernese Oberland for mute and solemn witnesses? His glance, his smile, the unextinguishable and comic ardour of his striving-forward appearance helped me to pull myself together. It must be stated that on that day and in the exhilarating atmosphere of that elevated spot I had been feeling utterly crushed. It was the year in which I had first spoken aloud of my desire to go to sea. At first, like those sounds that, ranging outside the scale to which men's ears are attuned, remain inaudible to our sense of hearing, this declaration passed unperceived. It was as if it had not been. Later on, by trying various tones, I managed to arouse here and there a surprised momentary attention—the "What was that funny noise?" sort of inquiry. Later on it was—"Did you hear what that boy said? What an extraordinary outbreak!" Presently a wave of scandalised astonishment (it could not have been greater if I had announced the intention of entering a Carthusian monastery) ebbing out of the educational and academical town of Cracow spread itself over several provinces. It spread itself shallow but far-reaching. It stirred up a mass of remonstrance, indignation, pitying wonder, bitter irony and downright chaff. I could hardly breathe under its weight, and certainly had no words for an answer. People wondered what Mr. T. B. would do now with his worrying nephew and, I dare say, hoped kindly that he would make short work of my nonsense.

What he did was to come down all the way from Ukraine to have it out with me and to judge by himself, unprejudiced, impartial and just, taking his stand on the ground of wisdom and affection. As far as is possible for a boy whose power of expression is still unformed, I opened the secret of my thoughts to him and he in return allowed me a glimpse into his mind and heart; the first glimpse of an inexhaustible and noble treasure of clear thought and warm feeling, which through life was to be mine to draw upon with a never-deceived love and confidence. Practically, after several exhaustive conversations, he concluded that he would not have me later on reproach him for having spoiled my life by an unconditional opposition. But I must take time for serious reflection. And I must not only think of myself but of others; weigh the claims of affection and conscience against my own sincerity of purpose. "Think well what it all means in the larger issues, my boy," he exhorted me finally with special friendliness. "And meantime try to get the best place you can at the yearly examinations."

The scholastic year came to an end. I took a fairly good place at the exams, which for me (for certain reasons) happened to be a more difficult task than for other boys. In that respect I could enter with a good conscience upon that holiday which was like a long visit *pour prendre congé* of the mainland of old Europe I was to see so little of for the next four-and-twenty years. Such, however, was not the avowed purpose of that tour. It was rather, I suspect, planned in order to distract and occupy my thoughts in other directions. Nothing had been said for months of my going to sea. But my attachment to my young tutor and his influence over me were so well known that he must have received a confidential mission to talk me out of my romantic folly. It was an excellently appropriate arrangement, as neither he nor I had ever had a single glimpse of the sea in our lives. That was to come by and by for both of us in Venice, from the outer shore of Lido. Meantime he had taken his mission to heart so well that I began to feel crushed before we reached Zurich. He argued in railway trains, in lake steamboats, he had argued away for me the obligatory sunrise on the Rigi, by Jove! Of his devotion to his unworthy pupil there can be no doubt. He had proved it already by two years of unremitting and arduous care. I could not hate him. But he had been crushing me slowly, and when he started to argue on the top of the Furca Pass he was perhaps nearer a success than either he or I imagined. I listened to him in despairing silence, feeling that ghostly, unrealised and desired sea of my dreams escape from the unnerved grip of my will.

The enthusiastic old Englishman had passed—and the argument went on. What reward could I expect from such a life at the end of my years, either in ambition, honour or conscience? An unanswerable question. But I felt no longer crushed. Then our eyes met and a genuine emotion was visible in his as well as in mine. The end came all at once. He picked up the knapsack suddenly and got on to his feet.

"You are an incorrigible, hopeless Don Quixote. That's what you are."

I was surprised. I was only fifteen and did not know what he meant exactly. But I felt vaguely flattered at the name of the immortal knight turning up in connection with my own folly, as some people would call it to my face. Alas! I don't think there was anything to be proud of. Mine was not the stuff the protectors of forlorn damsels, the redressers of this world's wrongs are made of; and my tutor was the man to know that best. Therein, in his indignation, he was superior to the barber and the priest when he flung at me an honoured name like a reproach.

I walked behind him for full five minutes; then without looking back he stopped. The shadows of distant peaks were lengthening over the Furca Pass. When I came up to him he turned to me and in full view of the Finster-Aarhorn, with his band of giant brothers rearing their monstrous heads against a brilliant sky, put his hand on my shoulder affectionately.

"Well! That's enough. We will have no more of it."

And indeed there was no more question of my mysterious vocation between us. There was to be no more question of it at all, nowhere or with any one. We began the descent of the Furca Pass conversing merrily. Eleven years later, month for month, I stood on Tower Hill on the steps of the St. Katherine's Dockhouse, a master in the British Merchant Service. But the man who put his hand on my shoulder at the top of the Furca Pass was no longer living.

That very year of our travels he took his degree of the Philosophical Faculty—and only then his true vocation declared itself. Obedient to the call, he entered at once upon the four-year course of the Medical Schools. A day came when, on the deck of a ship moored in Calcutta, I opened a letter telling me of the end of an enviable existence. He had made for himself a practice in some obscure little town of Austrian Galicia. And the letter went on to tell me how all the bereaved poor of the district, Christians and Jews alike, had mobbed the good doctor's coffin with sobs and lamentations at the very gate of the cemetery.

How short his years and how clear his vision! What greater reward in ambition, honour and conscience could he have hoped to win for himself when, on the top of the Furca Pass, he bade me look well to the end of my opening life.

The Heart of Darkness

This long tale was originally published in a volume with two others: "Youth" and "The End of the Tether" in 1902.

I

The *Nellie*, a cruising yawl, swung to her anchor without a flutter of the sails, and was at rest. The flood had made, the wind was nearly calm, and being bound down the river, the only thing for it was to come to and wait for the turn of the tide.

The sea-reach of the Thames stretched before us like the beginning of an interminable waterway. In the offing the sea and the sky were welded together without a joint, and in the luminous space the tanned sails of the barges drifting up with the tide seemed to stand still in red clusters of canvas sharply peaked, with gleams of varnished sprits. A haze rested on the low shores that ran out to sea in vanishing flatness. The air was dark above Gravesend, and farther back still seemed condensed into a mournful gloom, brooding motionless over the biggest, and the greatest, town on earth.

The Director of Companies was our captain and our host. We four affectionately watched his back as he stood in the bows looking to seaward. On the whole river there was nothing that looked half so nautical. He resembled a pilot, which to a seaman is trustworthiness personified. It was difficult to realise his work was not out there in the luminous estuary, but behind him, within the brooding gloom.

Between us there was, as I have already said somewhere, the bond of the sea. Besides holding our hearts together through long periods of separation, it had the effect of making us tolerant of each other's yarns—and even convictions. The Lawyer—the best of old fellows—had, because of his many years and many virtues, the only cushion on deck, and was lying on the only rug. The Accountant had brought out already a box of dominoes, and was toying architecturally with the bones. Marlow sat cross-legged right aft, leaning against the mizzen-mast. He had sunken cheeks, a yellow complexion, a straight back, an ascetic aspect, and, with his arms dropped, the palms of hands outwards, resembled an idol. The Director, satisfied the anchor had good hold, made his way aft and sat down amongst us. We exchanged a few words lazily. Afterwards there was silence on board the yacht. For some reason or other we did not begin that game of dominoes. We felt meditative, and fit for nothing but placid staring. The day was ending in a serenity of still and exquisite brilliance. The water shone pacifically; the sky, without a speck, was a benign immensity of unstained light; the very mist on the Essex marshes was like a gauzy and radiant fabric, hung from the wooded rises inland, and draping the low shores in diaphanous folds. Only the gloom to the west, brooding over the upper reaches, became more sombre every minute, as if angered by the approach of the sun.

And at last, in its curved and imperceptible fall, the sun sank low, and from glowing white changed to a dull red without rays and without heat, as if about to go out suddenly, stricken to death by the touch of that gloom brooding over a crowd of men.

Forthwith a change came over the waters, and the serenity became less brilliant but more profound. The old river in its broad reach rested unruffled at the decline of day, after ages of good service done to the race that peopled its banks, spread out in the tranquil dignity of a waterway leading to the uttermost ends of the earth. We looked at the venerable stream not in the vivid flush of a short day that comes and departs for ever, but in the august light of abiding memories. And indeed nothing is easier for a man who has, as the phrase goes, "followed the sea" with reverence and affection, than to evoke the great spirit of the past upon the lower reaches of the Thames. The tidal current runs to and fro in its unceasing service, crowded with memories of men and ships it has borne to the rest of home or to the battles of the sea. It had known and served all the men of whom the nation is proud, from Sir Francis Drake to Sir John Franklin, knights all, titled and untitled—the great knights-errant of the sea. It had borne all the ships whose names are like jewels flashing in the night of time, from the *Golden Hind* returning with her round flanks full of treasure, to be visited by the Queen's Highness and thus pass out of the gigantic tale, to the *Erebus* and *Terror*, bound on other conquests—and that never returned. It had known the ships and the men. They had sailed from Deptford, from Greenwich, from Erith—the adventurers and the settlers; kings' ships and the ships of men on 'Change; captains, admirals, the dark "interlopers" of the Eastern trade, and the commissioned "generals" of East India fleets. Hunters for gold or pursuers of fame, they all had gone out on that stream, bearing the sword, and often the torch, messengers of the might within the land, bearers of a spark from the sacred fire. What greatness had not floated on the ebb of that river into the mystery of an unknown earth! . . . The dreams of men, the seed of commonwealths, the germs of empires.

The sun set; the dusk fell on the stream, and lights began to appear along the shore. The Chapman lighthouse, a three-legged thing erect on a mud-flat, shone strongly. Lights of ships moved in the fairway—a great stir of lights going up and going down. And farther west on the upper reaches the place of the monstrous town was still marked ominously on the sky, a brooding gloom in sunshine, a lurid glare under the stars.

"And this also," said Marlow suddenly, "has been one of the dark places of the earth."

He was the only man of us who still "followed the sea." The worst that could be said of him was that he did not represent his class. He was a seaman, but he was a wanderer too, while most seamen lead, if one may so express it, a sedentary life. Their minds are of the stay-at-home order, and their home is always with them—the ship; and so is their country—the sea. One ship is very much like another, and the sea is always the same. In the immutability of their surroundings the foreign shores, the foreign faces, the changing immensity of life, glide past, veiled not by a sense of mystery but by a slightly disdainful ignorance; for there is nothing mysterious to a seaman unless it be the sea itself, which is the mistress of his existence and as inscrutable as Destiny. For the rest, after his hours of work, a casual stroll or a casual spree on shore suffices to unfold for him the secret of a whole continent, and generally he finds the secret not worth knowing. The yarns of seamen have a direct simplicity, the whole meaning of which lies within the shell of a cracked nut. But Marlow was not typical (if his propensity to spin yarns be excepted), and to him the meaning of an episode was not inside like a kernel but outside, enveloping the tale which brought it out only as a glow brings out a haze, in the likeness of one of these misty halos that sometimes are made visible by the spectral illumination of moonshine.

His remark did not seem at all surprising. It was just like Marlow. It was accepted in silence. No one took the trouble to grunt even; and presently he said, very slow:

"I was thinking of very old times, when the Romans first came here, nineteen hundred years ago—the other day. . . . Light came out of this river since—you say Knights? Yes; but it is like a running blaze on a plain, like a flash of lightning in the clouds. We live in the flicker—may it last as long as the old earth keeps rolling! But darkness was here yesterday. Imagine the feelings of a commander of a fine—what d'ye call 'em?—trireme in the Mediterranean, ordered suddenly to the north; run overland across the Gauls in a hurry; put in charge of one of these craft the legionaries—a wonderful lot of handy men they must have been too—used to build, apparently by the hundred, in a month or two, if we may believe what we read. Imagine him here—the very end of the world, a sea the colour of lead, a sky the colour of smoke, a kind of ship about as rigid as a concertina—and going up this river with stores, or orders, or what you like. Sandbanks, marshes, forests, savages—precious little to eat fit for a civilised man, nothing but Thames water to drink. No Falernian wine here, no going ashore. Here and there a military camp lost in a wilderness, like a needle in a bundle of hay—cold, fog, tempests, disease, exile, and death—death skulking in the air, in the water, in the bush. They must have been dying like flies here. Oh yes—he did it. Did it very well, too, no doubt, and without thinking much about it either, except afterwards to brag of what he had gone through in his time, perhaps. They were men enough to face the darkness. And perhaps he was cheered by keeping his eye on a chance of promotion to the fleet at Ravenna by and by, if he had good friends in Rome and survived the awful climate. Or think of a decent young citizen in a toga—perhaps too much dice, you know—coming out here in the train of some prefect, or tax-gatherer, or trader, even, to mend his fortunes. Land in a swamp, march through the woods, and in some inland post feel the savagery, the utter savagery, had closed round him—all that mysterious life of the wilderness that stirs in the forest, in the jungles, in the hearts of wild men. There's no initiation either into such mysteries. He has to live in the midst of the incomprehensible, which is also detestable. And it has a fascination, too, that goes to work upon him. The fascination of the abomination—you know. Imagine the growing regrets, the longing to escape, the powerless disgust, the surrender, the hate."

He paused.

"Mind," he began again, lifting one arm from the elbow, the palm of the hand outwards, so that, with his legs folded before him, he had the pose of a Buddha preaching in European clothes and without a lotus-flower—"Mind, none of us would feel exactly like this. What saves us is efficiency—the devotion to efficiency. But these chaps were not much account, really. They were no colonists; their administration was merely a squeeze, and nothing more, I suspect. They were conquerors, and for that you want only brute force—nothing to boast of, when you have it, since your strength is just an accident arising from the weakness of others. They grabbed what they could get for the sake of what was to be got. It was just robbery with violence, aggravated murder on a great scale, and men going at it blind—as is very proper for those who tackle a darkness. The conquest of the earth, which mostly means the taking it away from those who have a different complexion or slightly flatter noses than ourselves, is not a pretty thing when you look into it too much. What redeems it is the idea only. An idea at the back of it; not a sentimental pretence but an idea; and an unselfish belief in the idea—something you can set up, and bow down before, and offer a sacrifice to. . . ."

He broke off. Flames glided in the river, small green flames, red flames, white flames, pursuing, overtaking, joining, crossing each other—then separating slowly or hastily. The traffic of the great city went on in the deepening night upon the sleepless river. We looked on, waiting patiently—there was nothing else to do till the end of the flood; but it was only after a long silence, when he said, in a hesitating voice, "I suppose you fellows remember I did once turn fresh-water sailor for a bit," that we knew we were fated, before the ebb began to run, to hear about one of Marlow's inconclusive experiences.

"I don't want to bother you much with what happened to me

personally," he began, showing in this remark the weakness of many tellers of tales who seem so often unaware of what their audience would best like to hear; "yet to understand the effect of it on me you ought to know how I got out there, what I saw, how I went up that river to the place where I first met the poor chap. It was the farthest point of navigation and the culminating point of my experience. It seemed somehow to throw a kind of light on everything about me—and into my thoughts. It was sombre enough too—and pitiful—not extraordinary in any way—not very clear either. No, not very clear. And yet it seemed to throw a kind of light.

"I had then, as you remember, just returned to London after a lot of Indian Ocean, Pacific, China Seas—a regular dose of the East—six years or so, and I was loafiing about, hindering you fellows in your work and invading your homes, just as though I had got a heavenly mission to civilise you. It was very fine for a time, but after a bit I did get tired of resting. Then I began to look for a ship—I should think the hardest work on earth. But the ships wouldn't even look at me. And I got tired of that game too.

"Now when I was a little chap I had a passion for maps. I would look for hours at South America, or Africa, or Australia, and lose myself in all the glories of exploration. At that time there were many blank spaces on the earth, and when I saw one that looked particularly inviting on a map (but they all look that) I would put my finger on it and say, When I grow up I will go there. The North Pole was one of these places, I remember. Well, I haven't been there yet, and shall not try now. The glamour's off. Other places were scattered about the Equator, and in every sort of latitude all over the two hemispheres. I have been in some of them, and . . . well, we won't talk about that. But there was one yet—the biggest, the most blank, so to speak—that I had a hankering after.

"True, by this time it was not a blank space any more. It had got filled since my boyhood with rivers and lakes and names. It had ceased to be a blank space of delightful mystery—a white patch for a boy to dream gloriously over. It had become a place of darkness. But there was in it one river especially, a mighty big river, that you could see on the map, resembling an immense snake uncoiled, with its head in the sea, its body at rest curving afar over a vast country, and its tail lost in the depths of the land. And as I looked at the map of it in a shop-window, it fascinated me as a snake would a bird—a silly little bird. Then I remembered there was a big concern, a Company for trade on that river. Dash it all! I thought to myself, they can't trade without using some kind of craft on that lot of fresh water—steamboats! Why shouldn't I try to get charge of one? I went on along Fleet Street, but could not shake off the idea. The snake had charmed me.

"You understand it was a Continental concern, that Trading Society; but I have a lot of relations living on the Continent, because it's cheap and not so nasty as it looks, they say.

"I am sorry to own I began to worry them. This was already a fresh departure for me. I was not used to get things that way, you know. I always went my own road and on my own legs where I had a mind to go. I wouldn't have believed it of myself; but, then—you see—I felt somehow I must get there by hook or by crook. So I worried them. The men said, 'My dear fellow,' and did nothing. Then—would you believe it?—I tried the women. I, Charlie Marlow, set the women to work—to get a job. Heavens! Well, you see, the notion drove me. I had an aunt, a dear enthusiastic soul. She wrote: 'It will be delightful. I am ready to do anything, anything for you. It is a glorious idea. I know the wife of a very high personage in the Administration, and also a man who has lots of influence with,' etc. etc. She was determined to make no end of fuss to get me appointed skipper of a river steamboat, if such was my fancy.

"I got my appointment—of course; and I got it very quick. It appears the Company had received news that one of their captains had been killed in a scuffle with the natives. This was my chance, and it made me the more anxious to go. It was only months and months afterwards, when I made the attempt to recover what was left of the body, that I heard the original quarrel arose from a misunderstanding about some hens. Yes, two black hens. Fresleven—that was the fellow's name, a Dane—thought himself wronged somehow in the bargain, so he went ashore and started to hammer the chief of the village with a stick. Oh, it didn't surprise me in the least to hear this, and at the same time to be told that Fresleven was the gentlest, quietest creature that ever walked on two legs. No doubt he was; but he had been a couple of years already out there engaged in the noble cause, you know, and he probably felt the need at last of asserting his self-respect in some way. Therefore he whacked the old nigger mercilessly, while a big crowd of his people watched him, thunderstruck, till some man—I was told the chief's son—in desperation at hearing the old chap yell, made a tentative jab with a spear at the white man—and of course it went quite easy between the shoulder-blades. Then the whole population cleared into the forest, expecting all kinds of calamities to happen, while, on the other hand, the steamer Fresleven commanded left also in a bad panic, in charge of the engineer, I believe. Afterwards nobody seemed to trouble much about Fresleven's remains, till I got out and stepped into his shoes. I couldn't let it rest, though; but when an opportunity offered at last to meet my predecessor, the grass growing through his ribs was tall enough to hide his bones. They were all there. The supernatural being had not been touched after he fell. And the village was deserted, the huts gaped black, rotting, all askew within the fallen enclosures. A calamity had come to it, sure enough. The people had vanished. Mad terror had scattered them, men, women, and children, through the bush, and they had never returned. What became of the hens I don't know either. I should think the cause of progress got them, anyhow. However, through this glorious affair I got my appointment, before I had fairly begun to hope for it.

"I flew around like mad to get ready, and before forty-eight hours I was crossing the Channel to show myself to my employers, and sign the contract. In a very few hours I arrived in a city that always makes me think of a whited sepulchre. Prejudice no doubt. I had no difficulty in finding the Company's offices. It was the biggest thing in the town, and everybody I met was full of it. They were going to run an over-sea empire, and make no end of coin by trade.

"A narrow and deserted street in deep shadow, high houses, innumerable windows with venetian blinds, a dead silence, grass sprouting between the stones, imposing carriage archways right and left, immense double doors standing ponderously ajar. I slipped through one of these cracks, went up a swept and ungarnished staircase, as arid as a desert, and opened the first door I came to. Two women, one fat and the other slim, sat on straw-bottomed chairs, knitting black wool. The slim one got up and walked straight at me—still knitting with downcast eyes—and only just as I began to think of getting out of her way, as you would for a somnambulist, stood still, and looked up. Her dress was as plain as an umbrella-cover, and she turned round without a word and preceded me into a waiting-room. I gave my name, and looked about. Deal table in the middle, plain chairs all round the walls, on one end a large shining map, marked with all the colours of a rainbow. There was a vast amount of red—good to see at any time, because one knows that some real work is done in there, a deuce of a lot of blue, a little green, smears of orange, and, on the East Coast, a purple patch, to show where the jolly pioneers of progress drink the jolly lager-beer. However, I wasn't going into any of these. I was going into the yellow. Dead in the centre. And the river was there—fascinating—deadly—like a snake. Ough! A door opened, a white-haired secretarial head, but wearing a compassionate expression, appeared, and a skinny forefinger beckoned me into the sanctuary. Its light was dim, and a heavy writing-desk squatted in the middle. From behind that structure came out an impression of pale plumpness in a frock-coat. The great man himself. He was five feet six, I should judge, and had his grip on the handle-end of ever so many millions. He shook hands, I fancy, murmured vaguely, was satisfied with my French. *Bon voyage.*

"In about forty-five seconds I found myself again in the waiting-room with the compassionate secretary, who, full of desolation and sympathy, made me sign some document. I believe I undertook amongst other things not to disclose any trade secrets. Well, I am not going to.

"I began to feel slightly uneasy. You know I am not used to such ceremonies, and there was something ominous in the atmosphere. It was just as though I had been let into some conspiracy—I don't know—something not quite right; and I was glad to get out. In the outer room the two women knitted black wool feverishly. People were arriving, and the younger one was walking back and forth introducing them. The old one sat on her chair. Her flat cloth slippers were propped up on a foot-warmer, and a cat reposed on her lap. She wore a starched white affair on her head, had a wart on one cheek, and silver-rimmed spectacles hung on the tip of her nose. She glanced at me above the glasses. The swift and indifferent placidity of that look troubled me. Two youths with foolish and cheery countenances were being piloted over, and she threw at them the same quick glance of unconcerned wisdom. She seemed to know all about them and about me too. An eerie feeling came over me. She seemed uncanny and fateful. Often far away there I thought of these two, guarding the door of Darkness, knitting black wool as for a warm pall, one introducing, introducing continuously to the unknown, the other scrutinising the cheery and foolish faces with unconcerned old eyes. *Ave!* Old knitter of black wool. *Morituri te salutant.* Not many of those she looked at ever saw her again—not half, by a long way.

"There was yet a visit to the doctor. 'A simple formality,' assured me the secretary, with an air of taking an immense part in all my sorrows. Accordingly a young chap wearing his hat over the left eyebrow, some clerk I suppose—there must have been clerks in the business, though the house was as still as a house in a city of the dead—came from somewhere upstairs, and led me forth. He was shabby and careless, with ink-stains on the sleeves of his jacket, and his cravat was large and billowy, under a chin shaped like the toe of an old boot. It was a little too early for the doctor, so I proposed a drink, and thereupon he developed a vein of joviality. As we sat over our vermuths he glorified the Company's business, and by and by I expressed casually my surprise at him not going out there. He became very cool and collected all at once. 'I am not such a fool as I look, quoth Plato to his disciples,' he said sententiously, emptied his glass with great resolution, and we rose.

"The old doctor felt my pulse, evidently thinking of something else the while. 'Good, good for there,' he mumbled, and then with a certain eagerness asked me whether I would let him measure my head. Rather surprised, I said Yes, when he produced a thing like callipers and got the dimensions back and front and every way, taking notes carefully. He was an unshaven little man in a threadbare coat like a gaberdine, with his feet in slippers, and I thought him a harmless fool. 'I always ask leave, in the interests of science, to measure the crania of those going out there,' he said. 'And when they come back too?' I asked. 'Oh, I never see them,' he remarked; 'and, moreover, the changes take place inside, you know.' He smiled, as if at some quiet joke. 'So you are going out there. Famous. Interesting too.' He gave me a searching glance, and made another note. 'Ever any madness in your family?' he asked, in a matter-of-fact tone. I felt very annoyed. 'Is that question in the interests of science too?' 'It would be,' he said, without taking notice of my irritation, 'interesting for science to watch the mental changes of individuals, on the spot, but . . .' 'Are you an alienist?' I interrupted. 'Every doctor should be—a little,' answered that original imperturbably. 'I have a little theory which you Messieurs who go out there must help me to prove. This is my share in the advantages my country shall reap from the possession of such a magnificent dependency. The mere wealth I leave to others. Pardon my questions, but you are the first Englishman coming under my observation . . .' I hastened to assure him I was not in the least typical. 'If I were,' said I, 'I wouldn't be talking like this with you.' 'What you say is rather profound, and probably erroneous,' he said, with a laugh. 'Avoid irritation more than exposure to the sun. Adieu. How do you English say, eh? Good-bye. Ah! Good-bye. Adieu. In the tropics one must before everything keep calm.' . . . He lifted a warning forefinger. . . . '*Du calme, du calme. Adieu.*'

"One thing more remained to do—say good-bye to my excellent aunt. I found her triumphant. I had a cup of tea—the last decent cup of tea for many days—and in a room that most soothingly looked just as you would expect a lady's drawing-room to look, we had a long quiet chat by the fireside. In the course of these confidences it became quite plain to me I had been represented to the wife of the high dignitary, and goodness knows to how many more people besides, as an exceptional and gifted creature—a piece of good fortune for the Company—a man you don't get hold of every day. Good heavens! and I was going to take charge of a two-penny-halfpenny river-steamboat with a penny whistle attached! It appeared, however, I was also one of the Workers, with a capital—you know. Something like an emissary of light, something like a lower sort of apostle. There had been a lot of such rot let loose in print and talk just about that time, and the excellent woman, living right in the rush of all that humbug, got carried off her feet. She talked about 'weaning those ignorant millions from their horrid ways,' till, upon my word, she made me quite uncomfortable. I ventured to hint that the Company was run for profit.

" 'You forget, dear Charlie, that the labourer is worthy of his hire,' she said brightly. It's queer how out of touch with truth women are. They live in a world of their own, and there has never been anything like it, and never can be. It is too beautiful altogether, and if they were to set it up it would go to pieces before the first sunset. Some confounded fact we men have been living contentedly with ever since the day of creation would start up and knock the whole thing over.

"After this I got embraced, told to wear flannel, be sure to write often, and so on—and I left. In the street—I don't know why—a queer feeling came to me that I was an impostor. Odd thing that I, who used to clear out for any part of the world at twenty-four hours' notice, with less thought than most men give to the crossing of a street, had a moment—I won't say of hesitation, but of startled pause, before this commonplace affair. The best way I can explain it to you is by saying that, for a second or two, I felt as though, instead of going to the centre of a continent, I were about to set off for the centre of the earth.

"I left in a French steamer, and she called in every blamed port they have out there, for, as far as I could see, the sole purpose of landing soldiers and custom-house officers. I watched the coast. Watching a coast as it slips by the ship is like thinking about an enigma. There it is before you—smiling, frowning, inviting, grand, mean, insipid, or savage, and always mute with an air of whispering, Come and find out. This one was almost featureless, as if still in the making, with an aspect of monotonous grimness. The edge of a colossal jungle, so dark green as to be almost black, fringed with white surf, ran straight, like a ruled line, far, far away along a blue sea whose glitter was blurred by a creeping mist. The sun was fierce, the land seemed to glisten and drip with steam. Here and there greyish-whitish specks showed up clustered inside the white surf, with a flag flying above them perhaps—settlements some centuries old, and still no bigger than pin-heads on the untouched expanse of their background. We pounded along, stopped, landed soldiers; went on, landed custom-house clerks to levy toll in what looked like a God-forsaken wilderness, with a tin shed and a flag-pole lost in it; landed more soldiers—to take care of the custom-house clerks presumably. Some, I heard, got drowned in the surf; but whether they did or not, nobody seemed particularly to care. They were just flung out there, and on we went. Every day the coast looked the same, as though we had not moved; but we passed various places—trading places—with names like Gran' Bassam, Little Popo; names that seemed to belong to some sordid farce acted in front of a sinister back-cloth. The idleness of a passenger, my isolation amongst all these men with whom I had no point of contact, the oily and languid sea, the uniform sombreness of the coast, seemed to keep me away from the truth of things, within the toil of a mournful and senseless delusion. The voice of the surf heard now and then was a positive pleasure, like the speech of a brother. It was something natural, that had its reason, that had a meaning. Now and then a boat from the shore gave one a momentary contact with reality. It was paddled by black fellows. You could see from afar the white of their eyeballs glistening. They shouted, sang; their bodies streamed with perspiration; they had faces like grotesque masks—these chaps; but they had bone, muscle, a wild vitality, an intense energy of movement, that was as natural and true as the surf along their coast. They wanted no excuse for being there. They were a great comfort to look at. For a time I would feel I belonged still to a world of straightforward facts; but the feeling would not last long. Something would turn up to scare it away. Once, I remember, we came upon a man-of-war anchored off the coast. There wasn't even a shed there, and she was shelling the bush. It appears the French had one of their wars going on thereabouts. Her ensign dropped limp like a rag; the muzzles of the long six-inch guns stuck out all over the low hull; the greasy, slimy swell swung her up lazily and let her down, swaying her thin masts. In the empty immensity of earth, sky, and water, there she was, incomprehensible, firing into a continent. Pop, would go one of the six-inch guns; a small flame would dart and vanish, a little white smoke would disappear, a tiny projectile would give a feeble screech—and nothing happened. Nothing could happen. There was a touch of insanity in the proceeding, a sense of lugubrious drollery in the sight; and it was not dissipated by somebody on board assuring me earnestly there was a camp of natives—he called them enemies!—hidden out of sight somewhere.

"We gave her her letters (I heard the men in that lonely ship were dying of fever at the rate of three a day) and went on. We called at some more places with farcical names, where the merry dance of death and trade goes on in a still and earthy atmosphere as of an overheated catacomb; all along the formless coast bordered by dangerous surf, as if Nature herself had tried to ward off intruders; in and out of rivers, streams of death in life, whose banks were rotting into mud, whose waters, thickened into slime, invaded the contorted mangroves, that seemed to writhe at us in the extremity of an impotent despair. Nowhere did we stop long enough to get a particularised impression, but the general sense of vague and oppressive wonder grew upon me. It was like a weary pilgrimage amongst hints for nightmares.

"It was upward of thirty days before I saw the mouth of the big river. We anchored off the seat of the government. But my work would not begin till some two hundred miles farther on. So as soon as I could I made a start for a place thirty miles higher up.

"I had my passage on a little sea-going steamer. Her captain was a Swede, and knowing me for a seaman, invited me on the bridge. He was a young man, lean, fair, and morose, with lanky hair and a shuffling gait. As we left the miserable little wharf, he tossed his head contemptuously at the shore. 'Been living there?' he asked. I said, 'Yes.' 'Fine lot these government chaps—are they not?' he went on, speaking English with great precision and considerable bitterness. 'It is funny what some people will do for a few francs a month. I wonder what becomes of that kind when it goes up country?' I said to him I expected to see that soon. 'So-o-o!' he exclaimed. He shuffled athwart, keeping one eye ahead vigilantly. 'Don't be too sure,' he continued. 'The other day I took up a man who hanged himself on the road. He was a Swede, too.' 'Hanged himself! Why, in God's name?' I cried. He kept on looking out watchfully. 'Who knows? The sun too much for him, or the country perhaps.'

"At last we opened a reach. A rocky cliff appeared, mounds of turned-up earth by the shore, houses on a hill, others with iron roofs, amongst a waste of excavations, or hanging to the declivity. A continuous noise of the rapids above hovered over this scene of inhabited devastation. A lot of people, mostly black and naked, moved about like ants. A jetty projected into the river. A blinding sunlight drowned all this at times in a sudden recudescence of glare. 'There's your Company's station,' said the Swede, pointing to three wooden barrack-like structures on the rocky slope. 'I will send your things up. Four boxes did you say? So. Farewell.'

"I came upon a boiler wallowing in the grass, then found a path leading up the hill. It turned aside for the boulders, and also for an undersized railway truck lying there on its back with its wheels in the air. One was off. The thing looked as dead as the carcass of some animal. I came upon more pieces of decaying machinery, a stack of rusty nails. To the left a clump of trees made a shady spot, where dark things seemed to stir feebly. I blinked, the path was steep. A horn tooted to the right, and I saw the black people run. A heavy and dull detonation shook the ground, a puff of smoke came out of the cliff, and that was all. No change appeared on the face of the rock. They were building a railway. The cliff was not in the way or anything; but this objectless blasting was all the work going on.

"A slight clinking behind me made me turn my head. Six black men advanced in a file, toiling up the path. They walked erect and slow, balancing small baskets full of earth on their heads, and the clink kept time with their footsteps. Black rags were wound round their loins, and the short ends behind waggled to and fro like tails. I could see every rib, the joints of their limbs were like knots in a rope; each had an iron collar on his neck, and all were connected together with a chain whose bights swung between them, rhythmically clinking. Another report from the cliff made me think suddenly of that ship of war I had seen firing into a continent. It was the same kind of ominous voice; but these men could by no stretch of imagination be called enemies. They were called criminals, and the outraged law, like the bursting shells, had come to them, an insoluble mystery from the sea. All their meagre breasts panted together, the violently dilated nostrils quivered, the eyes stared stonily uphill. They passed me within six inches, without a glance, with that complete, deathlike indifference of unhappy savages. Behind this raw matter one of the reclaimed, the product of the new forces at work, strolled despondently, carrying a rifle by its middle. He had a uniform jacket with one button off, and seeing a white man on the path, hoisted his weapon to his shoulder with alacrity. This was simple prudence, white men being so much alike at a distance that he could not tell who I might be. He was speedily reassured, and with a large, white, rascally grin, and a glance at his charge, seemed to take me into partnership in his exalted trust. After all, I also was a part of the great cause of these high and just proceedings.

"Instead of going up, I turned and descended to the left. My idea was to let that chain-gang get out of sight before I climbed the hill. You know I am not particularly tender; I've had to strike and to fend off. I've had to resist and to attack sometimes—that's only one way of resisting—without counting the exact cost, according to the demands of such sort of life as I had blundered into. I've seen the devil of violence, and the devil of greed, and the devil of hot desire; but, by all the stars! these were strong, lusty, red-eyed devils, that swayed and drove men—men, I tell you. But as I stood on this hillside, I foresaw that in the blinding sunshine of that land I would become acquainted with a flabby, pretending, weak-eyed devil of a rapacious and pitiless folly. How insidious he could be, too, I was only to find out several months later and a thousand miles farther. For a moment I stood appalled, as though by a warning. Finally I descended the hill, obliquely, towards the trees I had seen.

"I avoided a vast artificial hole somebody had been digging on the slope, the purpose of which I found it impossible to divine. It wasn't a quarry or a sandpit, anyhow. It was just a hole. It might have been connected with the philanthropic desire of giving the criminals something to do. I don't know. Then I nearly fell into a very narrow ravine, almost no more than a scar in the hillside. I discovered that a lot of imported drainage-pipes for the settlement had been tumbled in there. There wasn't one that was not broken. It was a wanton smash-up. At last I got under the trees. My purpose was to stroll into the shade for a moment; but no sooner within than it seemed to me I had stepped into the gloomy circle of some Inferno. The rapids were near, and an uninterrupted, uniform, headlong, rushing noise filled the mournful stillness of the grove, where not a breath stirred, not a leaf moved, with a mysterious sound—as though the tearing pace of the launched earth had suddenly become audible.

"Black shapes crouched, lay, sat between the trees, leaning against the trunks, clinging to the earth, half coming out, half effaced within the dim light, in all the attitudes of pain, abandonment, and despair. Another mine on the cliff went off, followed by a slight shudder of the soil under my feet. The work was going on. The work! And this was the place where some of the helpers had withdrawn to die.

"They were dying slowly—it was very clear. They were not enemies, they were not criminals, they were nothing earthly now—nothing but black shadows of disease and starvation, lying confusedly in the greenish gloom. Brought from all the recesses of the coast in all the legality of time contracts, lost in uncongenial surroundings, fed on unfamiliar food, they sickened, became inefficient, and were then allowed to crawl away and rest. These moribund shapes were free as air—and nearly as thin. I began to distinguish the gleam of eyes under the trees. Then, glancing down, I saw a face near my hand. The black bones reclined at full length with one shoulder against the tree, and slowly the eyelids rose and the sunken eyes looked up at me, enormous and vacant, a kind of blind, white flicker in the depths of the orbs, which died out slowly. The man seemed young—almost a boy—but you know with them it's hard to tell. I found nothing else to do but to offer him one of my good Swede's ship's biscuits I had in my pocket. The fingers closed slowly on it and held—there was no other movement and no other glance. He had tied a bit of white worsted round his neck—Why? Where did he get it? Was it a badge—an ornament—a charm—a propitiatory act? Was there any idea at all connected with it? It looked startling round his black neck, this bit of white thread from beyond the seas.

"Near the same tree two more bundles of acute angles sat with their legs drawn up. One, with his chin propped on his knees, stared at nothing, in an intolerable and appalling manner: his brother phantom rested its forehead, as if overcome with a great weariness; and all about others were scattered in every pose of contorted collapse, as in some picture of a massacre or a pestilence. While I stood horror-struck, one of these creatures rose to his hands and knees, and went off on all-fours towards the river to drink. He lapped out of his hand, then sat up in the sunlight, crossing his shins in front of him, and after a time let his woolly head fall on his breastbone.

"I didn't want any more loitering in the shade, and I made haste towards the station. When near the buildings I met a white man, in such an unexpected elegance of get-up that in the first moment I took him for a sort of vision. I saw a high starched collar, white cuffs, a light alpaca jacket, snowy trousers, a clear necktie, and varnished boots. No hat. Hair parted, brushed, oiled, under a green-lined parasol held in a big white hand. He was amazing, and had a penholder behind his ear.

"I shook hands with this miracle, and I learned he was the Company's chief accountant, and that all the book-keeping was done at this station. He had come out for a moment, he said, 'to get a breath of fresh air.' The expression sounded wonderfully odd, with its suggestion of sedentary desk-life. I wouldn't have mentioned the fellow to you at all, only it was from his lips that I first heard the name of the man who is so indissolubly connected with the memories of that time. Moreover, I respected the fellow. Yes; I respected his collars, his vast cuffs, his brushed hair. His appearance was certainly that of a hairdresser's dummy; but in the great demoralisation of the land he kept up his appearance. That's backbone. His starched collars and got-up shirt-fronts were achievements of character. He had been out nearly three years; and, later, I could not help asking him how he managed to sport such linen. He had just the faintest blush, and said modestly, 'I've been teaching one of the native women about the station. It was difficult. She had a distaste for the work.' Thus this man had verily accomplished something. And he was devoted to his books, which were in apple-pie order.

"Everything else in the station was in a muddle,—heads, things, buildings. Strings of dusty niggers with splay feet arrived and departed; a stream of manufactured goods, rubbishy cottons, beads, and brass-wire set into the depths of darkness, and in return came a precious trickle of ivory.

"I had to wait in the station for ten days—an eternity. I lived in a hut in the yard, but to be out of the chaos I would sometimes get into the accountant's office. It was built of horizontal planks, and so badly put together that, as he bent over his high desk, he was barred from neck to heels with narrow strips of sunlight. There was no need to open the big shutter to see. It was hot there too; big flies buzzed fiendishly, and did not sting, but stabbed. I sat generally on the floor, while, of faultless appearance (and even slightly scented), perching on a high stool, he wrote, he wrote. Sometimes he stood up for exercise. When a truckle-bed with a sick man (some invalided agent from up-country) was put in there, he exhibited a gentle annoyance. 'The groans of this sick person,' he said, 'distract my attention. And without that it is extremely difficult to guard against clerical errors in this climate.'

"One day he remarked, without lifting his head, 'In the interior you will no doubt meet Mr. Kurtz.' On my asking who Mr. Kurtz was, he said he was a first-class agent; and seeing my disappointment at this information, he added slowly, laying down his pen, 'He is a very remarkable person.' Further questions elicited from him that Mr. Kurtz was at present in charge of a trading-post, a very important one, in the true ivory-country, at 'the very bottom of there. Sends in as much ivory as all the others put together . . .' He began to write again. The sick man was too ill to groan. The flies buzzed in a great peace.

"Suddenly there was a growing murmur of voices and a great tramping of feet. A caravan had come in. A violent babble of uncouth sounds burst out on the other side of the planks. All the carriers were speaking together, and in the midst of the uproar the lamentable voice of the chief agent was heard 'giving it up' tearfully for the twentieth time that day. . . . He rose slowly. 'What a frightful row,' he said. He crossed the room gently to look at the sick man, and returning, said to me, 'He does not hear.' 'What! Dead?' I asked, startled. 'No, not yet,' he answered, with great composure. Then, alluding with a toss of the head to the tumult in the station-yard, 'When one has got to make correct entries, one comes to hate those savages—hate them to the death.' He remains thoughtful for a moment. 'When you see Mr. Kurtz,' he went on, 'tell him from me that everything here'—he glanced at the desk—'is very satisfactory. I don't like to write to him—with those messengers of ours you never know who may get hold of your letter—at that Central Station.' He stared at me for a moment with his mild, bulging eyes. 'Oh, he will go far, very far,' he began again. 'He will be a somebody in the Administration before long. They, above—the Council in Europe, you know—mean him to be.'

"He turned to his work. The noise outside had ceased, and presently in going out I stopped at the door. In the steady buzz of flies the homeward-bound agent was lying flushed and insensible; the other, bent over his books, was making correct entries of perfectly correct transactions; and fifty feet below the doorstep I could see the still tree-tops of the grove of death.

"Next day I left that station at last, with a caravan of sixty men, for a two-hundred-mile tramp.

"No use telling you much about that. Paths, paths, everywhere; a stamped-in network of paths spreading over the empty land, through long grass, through burnt grass, through thickets, down and up chilly ravines, up and down stony hills ablaze with heat; and a solitude, a solitude, nobody, not a hut. The population had cleared out a long time ago. Well, if a lot of mysterious niggers armed with all kinds of fearful weapons suddenly took to travelling on the road between Deal and Gravesend, catching the yokels right and left to carry heavy loads for them, I fancy every farm and cottage thereabouts would get empty very soon. Only here the dwellings were gone too. Still, I passed through several abandoned villages. There's something pathetically childish in the ruins of grass walls. Day after day, with the stamp and shuffle of sixty pair of bare feet behind me, each pair under a 60-lb. load. Camp, cook, sleep, strike camp, march. Now and then a carrier dead in harness, at rest in the long grass near the path, with an empty water-gourd and his long staff lying by his side. A great silence around and above. Perhaps on some quiet night the tremor of far-off drums, sinking, swelling, a tremor vast, faint; a sound weird, appealing, suggestive, and wild—and perhaps with as profound a meaning as the sound of bells in a Christian country. Once a white man in an unbuttoned uniform, camping on the path with an armed escort of lank Zanzibaris, very hospitable and festive—not to say drunk. Was looking after the upkeep of the road, he declared. Can't say I saw any road or any upkeep, unless the body of a middle-aged negro, with a bullet-hole in the forehead, upon which I absolutely stumbled three miles farther on, may be considered as a permanent improvement. I had a white companion too, not a bad chap, but rather too fleshy and with the exasperating habit of fainting on the hot hillsides, miles away from the least bit of shade and water. Annoying, you know, to hold your own coat like a parasol over a man's head while he is coming-to. I couldn't help asking him once what he meant by coming there at all. 'To make money, of course. What do you think?' he said scornfully. Then he got fever, and had to be carried in a hammock slung under a pole. As he weighed sixteen stone I had no end of rows with the carriers. They jibbed, ran away, sneaked off with their loads in the night—quite a mutiny. So, one evening, I made a speech in English with gestures, not one of which was lost to the sixty pairs of eyes before me, and the next morning I started the hammock off in front all right. An hour afterwards I came upon the whole concern wrecked in a bush—man, hammock, groans, blankets, horrors. The heavy pole had skinned his poor nose. He was very anxious for me to kill somebody, but there wasn't the shadow of a carrier near. I remembered the old doctor—'It would be interesting for science to watch the mental changes of individuals, on the spot.' I felt I was becoming scientifically interesting. However, all that is to no purpose. On the fifteenth day I came in sight of the big river again, and hobbled into the Central Station. It was on a back water surrounded by scrub and forest, with a pretty border of smelly mud on one side, and on the three others enclosed by a crazy fence of rushes. A neglected gap was all the gate it had, and the first glance at the place was enough to let you see the flabby devil was running that show. White men with long staves in their hands appeared languidly from amongst the buildings, strolling up to take a look at me, and then retired out of sight somewhere. One of them, a stout, excitable chap with black moustaches, informed me with great volubility and many digressions, as soon as I told him who I was, that my steamer was at the bottom of the river. I was thunderstruck. What, how, why? Oh, it was 'all right.' The 'manager himself' was there. All quite correct. 'Everybody had behaved splendidly! splendidly!'—'You must,' he said in agitation, 'go and see the general manager at once. He is waiting!'

"I did not see the real significance of that wreck at once. I fancy I see it now, but I am not sure—not at all. Certainly the affair was too stupid—when I think of it—to be altogether natural. Still . . . But at the moment it presented itself simply as a confounded nuisance. The steamer was sunk. They had started two days before in a sudden hurry up the river with the manager on board, in charge of some volunteer skipper, and before they had been out three hours they tore the bottom out of her on stones, and she sank near the south bank. I asked myself what I was to do there, now my boat was lost. As a matter of fact, I had plenty to do in fishing my command out of the river. I had to set about in the very next day. That, and the repairs when I brought the pieces to the station, took some months.

"My first interview with the manager was curious. He did not ask me to sit down after my twenty-mile walk that morning. He was commonplace in complexion, in feature, in manners, and in voice. He was of middle size and of ordinary build. His eyes, of the usual blue, were perhaps remarkably cold, and he certainly could make his glance fall on one as trenchant and heavy as an axe. But even at these times the rest of his person seemed to disclaim the intention. Otherwise there was only an indefinable, faint expression of his lips, something stealthy—a smile—not a smile—I remember it, but I can't explain. It was unconscious, this smile was, though just after he had said something it got intensified for an instant. It came at the end of his speeches like a seal applied on the words to make the meaning of the commonest phrase appear absolutely inscrutable. He was a common trader, from his youth up employed in these parts—nothing more. He was obeyed, yet he inspired neither love nor fear, nor even respect. He inspired uneasiness. That was it! Uneasiness. Not a definite mistrust—just uneasiness—nothing more. You have no idea how effective such a . . . a . . . faculty can be. He had no genius for organising, for initiative, or for order even. That was evident in such things as the deplorable state of the station. He had no learning, and no intelligence. His position had come to him—why? Perhaps because he was never ill . . . He had served three terms of three years out there . . . Because triumphant health in the general rout of constitutions is a kind of power in itself. When he went home on leave he rioted on a large scale—pompously. Jack ashore—with a difference—in externals only. This one could gather from his casual talk. He originated nothing, he could keep the routine going—that's all. But he was great. He was great by this little thing that it was impossible to tell what could control such a man. He never gave that secret away. Perhaps there was nothing within him. Such a suspicion made one pause—for out there there were no external checks. Once when various tropical diseases had laid low almost every 'agent' in the station, he was heard to say, 'Men who come out here should have no entrails.' He sealed the utterance with that smile of his, as though it had been a door opening into a darkness he had in his keeping. You fancied you had seen things—but the seal was on. When annoyed at meal-times by the constant quarrels of the white men about precedence, he ordered an immense round table to be made, for which a special house had to be built. This was the station's mess-room. Where he sat was the first place—the rest were nowhere. One felt this to be his unalterable conviction. He was neither civil nor uncivil. He was quiet. He allowed his 'boy'—an overfed young negro from the coast—to treat the white men, under his very eyes, with provoking insolence.

"He began to speak as soon as he saw me. I had been very long on the road. He could not wait. Had to start without me. The up-river stations had to be relieved. There had been so many delays already that he did not know who was dead and who was alive, and how they got on—and so on, and so on. He paid no attention to my explanations, and, playing with a stick of sealing wax, repeated several times that the situation was 'very grave, very grave.' There were rumours that a very important station was in jeopardy, and its chief, Mr. Kurtz, was ill. Hoped it was not true. Mr. Kurtz was . . . I felt weary and irritable. Hang Kurtz, I thought. I interrupted him by saying I had heard of Mr. Kurtz on the coast. 'Ah! So they talk of him down there,' he murmured to himself. Then he began again, assuring me Mr. Kurtz was the best agent he had, an exceptional man, of the greatest importance to the Company; therefore I could understand his anxiety. He was, he said, 'very, very uneasy.' Certainly he fidgeted on his chair a good deal, exclaimed, 'Ah, Mr. Kurtz!' broke the stick of sealing-wax and seemed dumbfounded by the accident. Next thing he wanted to know 'how long it would take to' . . . I interrupted him again. Being hungry, you know, and kept on my feet too, I was getting savage. 'How can I tell?' I said. 'I haven't even seen the wreck yet—some months, no doubt.' All this talk seemed to me so futile. 'Some months,' he said. 'Well, let us say three months before we can make a start. Yes. That ought to do the affair.' I flung out of his hut (he lived all alone in a clay hut with a sort of verandah) muttering to myself my opinion of him. He was a chattering idiot. Afterwards I took it back when it was borne in upon me startlingly with what extreme nicety he had estimated the time requisite for the 'affair.'

"I went to work the next day, turning, so to speak, my back on that station. In that way only it seemed to me I could keep my hold on the redeeming facts of life. Still, one must look about sometimes; and then I saw this station, these men strolling aimlessly about in the sunshine of the yard. I asked myself sometimes what it all meant. They wandered here and there with their absurd long staves in their hands, like a lot of faithless pilgrims bewitched inside a rotten fence. The word 'ivory' rang in the air, was whispered, was sighed. You would think they were praying to it. A taint of imbecile rapacity blew through it all, like a whiff from some corpse. By Jove! I've never been anything so unreal in my life. And outside, the silent wilderness surrounding this cleared speck on the earth struck me as something great and invincible, like evil or truth, waiting patiently for the passing away of this fantastic invasion.

"Oh, these months! Well, never mind. Various things happened. One evening a grass shed full of calico, cotton prints, beads, and I don't know what else, burst into a blaze so suddenly that you would have thought the earth had opened to let an avenging fire consume all that trash. I was smoking my pipe quietly by my dismantled steamer, and saw them all cutting capers in the light, with their arms lifted high, when the stout man with moustaches came tearing down to the river, a tin pail in his hand, assured me that everybody was 'behaving splendidly, splendidly,' dipped about a quart of water and tore back again. I noticed there was a hole in the bottom of his pail.

"I strolled up. There was no hurry. You see the thing had gone off like a box of matches. It had been hopeless from the very first. The flame had leaped high, driven everybody back, lighted up everything—and collapsed. The shed was already a heap of embers glowing fiercely. A nigger was being beaten near by. They said he had caused the fire in some way; be that as it may, he was screeching most horribly. I saw him, later, for several days, sitting in a bit of shade looking very sick and trying to recover himself: afterwards he arose and went out—and the wilderness without a sound took him into its bosom again. As I approached the glow from the dark I found myself at the back of two men, talking. I heard the name of Kurtz pronounced, then the words, 'take advantage of this unfortunate accident.' One of the men was the manager. I wished him a good evening. 'Did you ever see anything like it—eh? it is incredible,' he said, and walked off. The other man remained. He was a first-class agent, young, gentlemanly, a bit reserved, with a forked little beard and a hooked nose. He was standoffish with the other agents, and they on their side said he was the manager's spy upon them. As to me, I had hardly ever spoken to him before. We got into talk, and by and by we strolled away from the hissing ruins. Then he asked me to his room, which was in the main building of the station. He struck a match, and I perceived that this young aristocrat had not only a silver-mounted dressing-case but also a whole candle all to himself. Just at that time the manager was the only man supposed to have any right to candles. Native mats covered the clay walls; a collection of spears, assegais, shields, knives, was hung up in trophies. The business entrusted to his fellow was the making of bricks—so I had been informed; but there wasn't a fragment of a brick anywhere in the station, and he had been there more than a year—waiting. It seems he could not make bricks without something, I don't know what—straw maybe. Anyway, it could not be found there, and as it was not likely to be sent from Europe, it did not appear clear to me what he was waiting for. An act of special creation perhaps. However, they were all waiting—all the sixteen or twenty pilgrims of them—for something; and upon my word it did not seem an uncongenial occupation, from the way they took it, though the only thing that ever came to them was disease—as far as I could see. They beguiled the time by backbiting and intriguing against each other in a foolish kind of way. There was an air of plotting about that station, but nothing came of it, of course. It was as unreal as everything else—as the philanthropic pretence of the whole concern, as their talk, as their government, as their show of work. The only real feeling was a desire to get appointed to a trading-post where ivory was to be had, so that they could earn percentages. They intrigued and slandered and hated each other only on that account—but as to effectually lifting a little finger—oh no. By heavens! there is something after all in the world allowing one man to steal a horse while another must not look at a halter. Steal a horse straight out. Very well. He has done it. Perhaps he can ride. But there is a way of looking at a halter that would provoke the most charitable of saints into a kick.

"I had no idea why he wanted to be sociable, but as we chatted in there it suddenly occurred to me the fellow was trying to get at something—in fact, pumping me. He alluded constantly to Europe, to the people I was supposed to know there—putting leading questions as to my acquaintances in the sepulchral city, and so on. His little eyes glittered like mica discs—with curiosity—though he tried to keep up a bit of superciliousness. At first I as astonished, but very soon I became awfully curious to see what he would find out from me. I couldn't possibly imagine what I had in me to make it worth his while. It was very pretty to see how he baffled himself, for in truth my body was full only of chills, and my head had nothing in it but that wretched steamboat business. It was evident he took me for a perfectly shameless prevaricator. At last he got angry, and, to conceal a movement of furious annoyance, he yawned. I rose. Then I noticed a small sketch in oils, on a panel, representing a woman, draped and blindfolded, carrying a lighted torch. The background was sombre—almost black. The movement of the woman was stately, and the effect of the torchlight on the face was sinister.

"It arrested me, and he stood by civilly, holding an empty half-pint champagne bottle (medical comforts) with the candle stuck in it. To my question he said Mr. Kurtz had painted this—in this very station more than a year ago—while waiting for means to go to his trading-post. 'Tell me, pray,' said I, 'who is this Mr. Kurtz?'

" 'The chief of the Inner Station,' he answered in a short tone, looking away. 'Much obliged,' I said, laughing. 'And you are the brickmaker of the Central Station. Every one knows that.' He was silent for a while. 'He is a prodigy,' he said at last. 'He is an emissary of pity, and science, and progress, and devil knows what else. We want,' he began to declaim suddenly, 'for the guidance of the cause entrusted to us by Europe, so to speak, higher intelligence, wide sympathies, a singleness of purpose.' 'Who says that?' I asked. 'Lots of them,' he replied. 'Some even write that; and so *he* comes here, a special being, as you ought to know.' 'Why ought I to know?' I interrupted, really surprised. He paid no attention. 'Yes. To-day he is chief of the best station, next year he will be assistant-manager, two years more and . . . but I daresay you know what he will be in two years' time. You are of the new gang—the gang of virtue. The same people who sent him specially also recommended you. Oh, don't say no. I've my own eyes to trust.' Light dawned upon me. My dear aunt's influential acquaintances were producing an unexpected effect upon that young man. I nearly burst into a laugh. 'Do you read the Company's confidential correspondence?' I asked. He hadn't a word to say. It was great fun. 'When Mr. Kurtz,' I continued severely, 'is General Manager, you won't have the opportunity.'

"He blew the candle out suddenly, and we went outside. The moon had risen. Black figures strolled about listlessly, pouring water on the glow, whence proceeded a sound of hissing; steam ascended in the moonlight; the beaten nigger groaned somewhere. 'What a row the brute makes!' said the indefatigable man with the moustaches, appearing near us. 'Serve him right. Transgression—punishment—bang! Pitiless, pitiless. That's the only way. This will prevent all conflagrations for the future. I was just telling the manager . . .' He noticed my companion, and became crestfallen all at once. 'Not in bed yet,' he said, with a kind of servile heartiness; 'it's so natural. Ha! Danger—agitation.' He vanished. I went on to the river-side, and the other followed me. I heard a scathing murmur at my ear, 'Heap of muffs—go to.' The pilgrims could be seen in knots gesticulating, discussing. Several had still their staves in their hands. I verily believe they took these sticks to bed with them. Beyond the fence the forest stood up spectrally in the moonlight, and through the dim stir, through the faint sounds of that lamentable courtyard, the silence of the land went home to one's very heart—its mystery, its greatness, the amazing reality of its concealed life. The hurt nigger moaned feebly somewhere near by, and then fetched a deep sigh that made me mend my pace away from there. I felt a hand introducing itself under my arm. 'My dear sir,' said the fellow, 'I don't want to be misunderstood, and especially by you, who will see Mr. Kurtz long before I can have that pleasure. I wouldn't like him to get a false idea of my disposition. . . .'

"I let him run on, this papier-mâché Mephistopheles, and it seemed to me that if I tried I could poke my forefinger through him, and would find nothing inside but a little loose dirt, maybe. He, don't you see, had been planning to be assistant-manager by and by under the present man, and I could see that the coming of that Kurtz had upset them both not a little. He talked precipitately, and I did not try to stop him. I had my shoulders against the wreck of my steamer, hauled up on the slope like a carcass of some big river animal. The smell of mud, of primeval mud, by Jove! was in my nostrils, the high stillness of primeval forest was before my eyes; there were shiny patches on the black creek. The moon had spread over everything a thin layer of silver—over the rank grass, over the mud, upon the wall of matted vegetation standing higher than the wall of a temple, over the great river I could see through a sombre gap glittering, glittering, as it flowed broadly by without a murmur. All this was great, expectant, mute, while the man jabbered about himself. I wondered whether the stillness on the face of the immensity looking at us two were meant as an appeal or as a menace. What were we who had strayed in here? Could we handle that dumb thing, or would it handle us? I felt how big, how confoundedly big, was that thing that couldn't talk and perhaps was deaf as well. What was in there? I could see a little ivory coming out from there, and I had heard Mr. Kurtz was in there. I had heard enough about it too—God knows! Yet somehow it didn't bring any image with it—no more than if I had been told an angel or a fiend was in there. I believed it in the same way one of you might believe there are inhabitants in the planet Mars. I knew once a Scotch sailmaker who was certain, dead sure, there were people in Mars. If you asked him for some idea how they looked and behaved, he would get shy and mutter something about 'walking on all-fours.' If you as much as smiled, he would—though a man of sixty—offer to fight you. I would not have gone so far as to fight for Kurtz, but I went for him near enough to a lie. You know I hate, detest, and can't bear a lie, not because I am straighter than the rest of us, but simply because it appals me. There is a taint of death, a flavour of mortality in lies—which is exactly what I hate and detest in the world—what I want to forget. It makes me miserable and sick, like biting something rotton would do. Temperament, I suppose. Well, I went near enough to it by letting the young fool there believe anything he liked to imagine as to my influence in Europe. I became in an instant as much of a pretence as the rest of the bewitched pilgrims. This simply because I had a notion it somehow would be of help to that Kurtz whom at the time I did not see—you understand. He was just a word for me. I did not see the man in the name any more than you do. Do you see him? Do you see the story? Do you see anything? It seems to me I am trying to tell you a dream—making a vain attempt, because no relation of a dream can convey the dream-sensation, that commingling of absurdity, surprise, and bewilderment in a tremor of struggling revolt, that notion of being captured by the incredible which is of the very essence of dreams. . . ."

He was silent for a while.

". . . No, it is impossible; it is impossible to convey the life-sensation of any given epoch of one's existence—that which makes its truth, its meaning—its subtle and penetrating essence. It is impossible. We live, as we dream—alone. . . ."

He paused again as if reflecting, then added:

"Of course in this you fellows see more than I could then. You see me, whom you know. . . ."

It had become so pitch dark that we listeners could hardly see one another. For a long time already he, sitting apart, had been no more to us than a voice. There was not a word from anybody. The others might have been asleep, but I was awake. I listened, I listened on the watch for the sentence, for the word, that would give me the clue to the faint uneasiness inspired by this narrative that seemed to shape itself without human lips in the heavy night-air of the river.

". . . Yes—I let him run on," Marlow began again, "and think what he pleased about the powers that were behind me. I did! And there was nothing behind me! There was nothing but that wretched, old, mangled steamboat I was leaning against, while he talked fluently about 'the necessity for every man to get on.' 'And when one comes out here, you conceive, it is not to gaze at the moon.' Mr. Kurtz was a 'universal genius,' but even a genius would find it easier to work with 'adequate tools—intelligent men.' He did not make bricks—why, there was a physical impossibility in the way—as I was well aware; and if he did secretarial work for the manager, it was because 'no sensible man rejects wantonly the confidence of his superiors.' Did I see it? I saw it. What more did I want? What I really wanted was rivets, by heaven! Rivets. To get on with the work—to stop the hole. Rivets I wanted. There were cases of them down at the coast—cases—piled up—burst—split! You kicked a loose rivet at every second step in that station yard on the hillside. Rivets had rolled into the grove of death. You could fill your pockets with rivets for the trouble of stooping down—and there wasn't one rivet to be found where it was wanted. We had plates that would do, but nothing to fasten them with. And every week the messenger, a lone negro, letter-bag on shoulder and staff in hand, left our station for the coast. And several times a week a coast caravan came in with trade goods—ghastly glazed calico that made you shudder only to look at it, glass beads value about a penny a guart, confounded spotted cotton handkerchiefs. And no rivets. Three carriers could have brought all that was wanted to set that steamboat afloat.

"He was becoming confidential now, but I fancy my unresponsive attitude must have exasperated him at last, for he judged it necessary to inform me he feared neither God nor devil, let alone any mere man. I said I could see that very well, but what I wanted was a certain quantity of rivets—and rivets were what really Mr. Kurtz wanted, if he had only known it. Now letters went to the coast every week. . . . 'My dear sir,' he cried, 'I write from dictation.' I demanded rivets. There was a way—for an intelligent man. He changed his manner; became very cold, and suddenly began to talk about a hippopotamus; wondered whether sleeping on board the steamer (I stuck to my salvage night and day) I wasn't disturbed. There was an old hippo that had the bad habit of getting out on the bank and roaming at night over the station grounds. The pilgrims used to turn out in a body and empty every rifle they could lay hands on at him. Some even had sat up o' nights for him. All this energy was wasted, though. 'That animal has a charmed life,' he said; 'but you can say this only of brutes in this country. No man—you apprehend me?—no man here bears a charmed life.' He stood there for a moment in the moonlight with his delicate hooked nose set a little askew, and his mica eyes glittering without a wink, then, with a curt Good-night, he strode off. I could see he was disturbed and considerably puzzled, which made me feel more hopeful than I had been for days. It was a great comfort to turn from that chap to my influential friend, the battered, twisted, ruined, tin-pot steamboat. I clambered on board. She rang under my feet like an empty Huntley & Palmer biscuit-tin kicked along a gutter; she was nothing so solid in make, and rather less pretty in shape, but I had expended enough hard work on her to make me love her. No influential friend would have served me better. She had given me a chance to come out a bit—to find out what I could do. No, I don't like work. I had rather laze about and think of all the fine things that can be done. I don't like work—no man does—but I like what is in the work—the chance to find yourself. Your own reality—for yourself, not for others—what no other man can ever know. They can only see the mere show, and never can tell what it really means.

"I was not surprised to see somebody sitting aft, on the deck, with his legs dangling over the mud. You see I rather chummed with the few mechanics there were in that station, whom the other pilgrims naturally despised—on account of their imperfect manners, I suppose. This was the foreman—a boiler-maker by trade—a good worker. He was a lank, bony, yellow-faced man, with hig intense eyes. His aspect was worried, and his head was as bald as the palm of my hand; but his hair in falling seemed to have stuck to his chin, and had prospered in the new locality, for his beard hung down to his waist. He was a widower with six young children (he had left them in charge of a sister of his to come out there), and the passion of his life was pigeon-flying. He was an enthusiast and a connoisseur. He would rave about pigeons. After work hours he used sometimes to come over from his hut for a talk about his children and his pigeons; at work, when he had to crawl in the mud under the bottom of the steamboat, he would tie up that beard of his in a kind of white serviette he brought for the purpose. It had loops to go over his ears. In the evening he could be seen squatted on the bank rinsing that wrapper in the creek with great care, then spreading it solemnly on a bush to dry.

"I slapped him on the back and shouted 'We shall have rivets!' He scrambled to his feet exclaiming 'No! Rivets!' as though he couldn't believe his ears. Then in a low voice, 'You . . . eh?' I don't know why we behaved like lunatics. I put my finger to the side of my nose and nodded mysteriously. 'Good for you!' he cried, snapped his fingers above his head, lifting one foot. I tried a jig. We capered on the iron deck. A frightful clatter came out of that hulk, and the virgin forest on the other bank of the creek sent it back in a thundering roll upon the sleeping station. It must have made some of the pilgrims sit up in their hovels. A dark figure obscured the lighted doorway of the manager's hut, vanished, then, a second or so after, the doorway itself vanished too. We stopped, and the silence driven away by the stamping of our feet flowed back again from the recesses of the land. The great wall of vegetation, an exuberant and entangled mass of trunks, branches, leaves, boughs, festoons, motionless in the moonlight, was like a rioting invasion of soundless life, a rolling wave of plants, piled up, crested, ready to topple over the creek, to sweep every little man of us out of his little existence. And it moved not. A deadened burst of mighty splashes and snorts reached us from afar, as though an ichthyosaurus had been taking a bath of glitter in the great river. 'After all,' said the boiler-maker in a reasonable tone, 'why shouldn't we get the rivets?' Why not, indeed! I did not know of any reason why we shouldn't. 'They'll come in three weeks,' I said confidently.

"But they didn't. Instead of rivets there came an invasion, an infliction, a visitation. It came in sections during the next three weeks, each section headed by a donkey carrying a white man in new clothes and tan shoes, bowing from that elevation right and left to the impressed pilgrims. A quarrelsome band of footsore sulky niggers trod on the heels of the donkey; a lot of tents, camp-stools, tin boxes, white cases, brown bales would be shot down in the courtyard, and the air of mystery would deepen a little over the muddle of the station. Five such instalments came, with their absurd air of disorderly flight with the loot of innumerable outfit shops and provision stores, that, one would think, they were lugging, after a raid, into the wilderness for equitable division. It was an inextricable mess of things decent in themselves but that human folly made look like the spoils of thieving.

"This devoted band called itself the Eldorado Exploring Expedition, and I believe they were sworn to secrecy. Their talk, however, was the talk of sordid buccaneers: it was reckless without hardihood, greedy without audacity, and cruel without courage; there was not an atom of foresight or of serious intention in the whole batch of them, and they did not seem aware these things are wanted for the work of the world. To tear treasure out of the bowels of the land was their desire, with no more moral purpose at the back of it than there is in burglars breaking into a safe. Who paid the expenses of the noble enterprise I don't know; but the uncle of our manager was leader of that lot.

"In exterior he resembled a butcher in a poor neighbourhood, and his eyes had a look of sleepy cunning. He carried his fat paunch with ostentation on his short legs, and during the time his gang infested the station spoke to no one but his nephew. You could see these two roaming about all day long with their heads close together in an everlasting confab.

"I had given up worrying myself about the rivets. One's capacity for that kind of folly is more limited than you would suppose. I said Hang!—and let things slide. I had plenty of time for meditation, and now and then I would give some thought to Kurtz. I wasn't very interested in him. No. Still, I was curious to see whether this man, who had come out equipped with moral ideas of some sort, would climb to the top after all, and how he would set about his work when there."

II

"One evening as I was lying flat on the deck of my steamboat, I heard voices approaching—and there were the nephew and the uncle strolling along the bank. I laid my head on my arm again, and had nearly lost myself in a doze, when somebody said in my ear, as it were: 'I am as harmless as a little child, but I don't like to be dictated to. Am I the manager—or am I not? I was ordered to send him there. It's incredible.' . . . I became aware that the two were standing on the shore alongside the forepart of the steamboat, just below my head. I did not move; it did not occur to me to move: I was sleepy. 'It *is* unpleasant,' grunted the uncle. 'He has asked the Administration to be sent there,' said the other, 'with the idea of showing what he could do; and I was instructed accordingly. Look at the influence that man must have. Is it not frightful?' They both agreed it was frightful, then made several bizarre remarks: 'Make rain and fine weather—one man—the Council—by the nose'—bits of absurd sentences that got the better of my drowsiness, so that I had pretty near the whole of my wits about me when the uncle said, 'The climate may do away with this difficulty for you. Is he alone there?' 'Yes,' answered the manager; 'he sent his assistant down the river with a note to me in these terms: "Clear this poor devil out of the country, and don't bother sending more of that sort. I had rather be alone than have the kind of men you can dispose of with me." It was more than a year ago. Can you imagine such impudence?' 'Anything since then?' asked the other hoarsely. 'Ivory,' jerked the nephew; 'lots of it—prime sort—lots—most annoying, from him.' 'And with that?' questioned the heavy rumble. 'Invoice,' was the reply fired out, so to speak. Then silence. They had been talking about Kurtz.

"I was broad awake by this time, but, lying perfectly at ease, remained still, having no inducement to change my position. 'How did that ivory come all this way?' growled the elder man, who seemed very vexed. The other explained that it had come with a fleet of canoes in charge of an English half-caste clerk Kurtz had with him; that Kurtz had apparently intended to return himself, the station being by that time bare of goods and stores, but after coming three hundred miles, had suddenly decided to go back, which he started to do alone in a small dugout with four paddlers, leaving the half-caste to continue down the river with the ivory. The two fellows there seemed astounded at anybody attempting such a thing. They were at a loss for an adequate motive. As for me, I seemed to see Kurtz for the first time. It was a distant glimpse: the dugout, four paddling savages, and the lone white man turning his back suddenly on the headquarters, on relief, on thoughts of home—perhaps; setting his face towards the depths of the wilderness, towards his empty and desolate station. I did not know the motive. Perhaps he was just simply a fine fellow who stuck to his work for its own sake. His name, you understand, had not been pronounced once. He was 'that man.' The half-caste, who, as far as I could see, had conducted a difficult trip with great prudence and pluck, was invariably alluded to as 'that scoundrel.' The 'scoundrel' had reported that the 'man' had been very ill—had recovered imperfectly. . . . The two below me moved away then a few paces, and strolled back and forth at some little distance. I heard: 'Military post—doctor—two hundred miles—quite alone now—unavoidable delays—nine months—no news—strange rumours.' They approached again, just as the manager was saying, 'No one, as far as I know, unless a species of wandering trader—a pestilential fellow, snapping ivory from the natives.' Who was it they were talking about now? I gathered in snatches that this was some man supposed to be in Kurtz's district, and of whom the manager did not approve. 'We will not be free from unfair competition till one of these fellows is hanged for an example,' he said. 'Certainly,' grunted the other; 'get him hanged! Why not? Anything—anything can be done in this country. That's what I say; nobody here, you understand, *here*, can endanger your position. And why? You stand the climate—you outlast them all. The danger is in Europe; but there before I left I took care to—' They moved off and whispered, then their voices rose again. 'The extraordinary series of delays is not my fault. I did my possible.' The fat man sighed, 'Very sad.' 'And the pestiferous absurdity of his talk,' continued the other; 'he bothered me enough when he was here. "Each station should be like a beacon on the road towards better things, a centre for trade of course, but also for humanising, improving, instructing." Conceive you—that ass! And he wants to be manager! No, it's—' Here he got choked by excessive indignation, and I lifted my head the least bit. I was surprised to see how near they were—right under me. I could have spat upon their hats. They were looking on the ground, absorbed in thought. The manager was switching his leg with a slender twig: his sagacious relative lifted his head. 'You have been well since you came out this time?' he asked. The other gave a start. 'Who? I? Oh! Like a charm—like a charm. But the rest—oh, my goodness! All sick. They die so quick, too, that I haven't the time to send them out of the country—it's incredible!' 'H'm. Just so,' grunted the uncle. 'Ah! my boy, trust to this—I say, trust to this.' I saw him extend his short flipper of an arm for a gesture that took in the forest, the creek, the mud, the river—seemed to beckon with a dishonouring flourish before the sunlit face of the land a treacherous appeal to the lurking death, to the hidden evil, to the profound darkness of its heart. It was so startling that I leaped to my feet and looked back at the edge of the forest, as though I had expected an answer of some sort to that black display of confidence. You know the foolish notions that come to one sometimes. The high stillness confronted these two figures with its ominous patience, waiting for the passing away of a fantastic invasion.

"They swore aloud together—out of sheer fright, I believe—then, pretending not to know anything of my existence, turned back to the station. The sun was low; and leaning forward side by side, they seemed to be tugging painfully uphill their two ridiculous shadows of unequal length, that trailed behind them slowly over the tall grass without bending a single blade.

"In a few days the Eldorado Expedition went into the patient wilderness, that closed upon it as the sea closes over a diver. Long afterwards the news came that all the donkeys were dead. I know nothing as to the fate of the less valuable animals. They, no doubt, like the rest of us, found what they deserved. I did not inquire. I was then rather excited at the prospect of meeting Kurtz very soon. When I say very soon I mean it comparatively. It was just two months from the day we left the creek when we came to the bank below Kurtz's station.

"Going up that river was like travelling back to the earliest beginnings of the world, when vegetation rioted on the earth and the big trees were kings. An empty stream, a great silence, an impenetrable forest. The air was warm, thick, heavy, sluggish. There was no joy in the brilliance of sunshine. The long stretches of the waterway ran on, deserted, into the gloom of overshadowed distances. On silvery sand banks hippos and alligators sunned themselves side by side. The broadening waters flowed through a mob of wooded islands; you lost your way on that river as you would in a desert, and butted all day long against shoals, trying to find the channel, till you thought yourself bewitched and cut off for ever from everything you had known once—somewhere—far away—in another existence perhaps. There were moments when one's past came back to one, as it will sometimes when you have not a moment to spare to yourself; but it came in the shape of an unrestful and noisy dream, remembered with wonder amongst the overwhelming realities of this strange world of plants, and water, and silence. And this stillness of life did not in the least resemble a peace. It was the stillness of an implacable force brooding over an inscrutable intention. It looked at you with a vengeful aspect. I got used to it afterwards; I did not see it any more; I had no time. I had to keep guessing at the channel; I had to discern, mostly by inspiration, the signs of hidden banks; I watched for sunken stones; I was learning to clap my teeth smartly before my heart flew out, when I shaved by a fluke some infernal sly old snag that would have ripped the life out of the tin-pot steamboat and drowned all the pilgrims; I had to keep a look-out for the signs of dead wood we could cut up in the night for next day's steaming. When you have to attend to things of that sort, to the mere incidents of the surface, the reality—the reality, I tell you—fades. The inner truth is hidden—luckily, luckily. But I felt it all the same; I felt often its mysterious stillness watching me at my monkey tricks, just as it watches you fellows performing on your respective tight-ropes for—what is it? half a crown a tumble—"

"Try to be civil, Marlow," growled a voice, and I knew there was at least one listener awake besides myself.

"I beg your pardon. I forgot the heartache which makes up the rest of the price. And indeed what does the price matter, if the trick be well done? You do your tricks very well. And I didn't do badly either, since I managed not to sink that steamboat on my first trip. It's a wonder to me yet. Imagine a blindfolded man set to drive a van over a bad road. I sweated and shivered over that business considerably, I can tell you. After all, for a seaman, to scrape the bottom of the thing that's supposed to float all the time under his care is the unpardonable sin. No one may know of it, but you never forget the thump—eh? A blow on the very heart. You remember it, you dream of it, you wake up at night and think of it—years after—and go hot and cold all over. I don't pretend to say that steamboat floated all the time. More than once she had to wade for a bit, with twenty cannibals splashing around and pushing. We had enlisted some of these chaps on the way for a crew. Fine fellows—cannibals—in their place. They were men one could work with, and I am grateful to them. And, after all, they did not eat each other before my face: they had brought along a provision of hippo-meat which went rotten, and made the mystery of the wilderness stink in my nostrils. Phoo! I can sniff it now. I had the manager on board and three or four pilgrims with their staves—all complete. Sometimes we came upon a station close by the bank, clinging to the skirts of the unknown, and the white men rushing out of a tumble-down hovel, with great gestures of joy and surprise and welcome, seemed very strange—had the appearance of being held there captive by a spell. The word 'ivory' would ring in the air for a while—and on we went again into the silence, along empty reaches, round the still bends, between the high walls of our winding way, reverberating in hollow claps the ponderous beat of the stern-wheel. Trees, trees, millions of trees, massive, immense, running up high; and at their foot, hugging the bank against the stream, crept the little begrimed steamboat, like a sluggish beetle crawling on the floor of a lofty portico. It made you feel very small, very lost, and yet it was not altogether depressing, that feeling. After all, if you were small, the grimy beetle crawled on—which was just what you wanted it to do. Where the pilgrims imagined it crawled to I don't know. To some place where they expected to get something, I bet! For me it crawled towards Kurtz—exclusively; but when the steam-pipes started leaking we crawled very slow. The reaches opened before us and closed behind, as if the forest had stepped leisurely across the water to bar the way for our return. We penetrated deeper and deeper into the heart of darkness. It was very quiet there. At night sometimes the roll of drums behind the curtain of trees would run up the river and remain sustained faintly, as if hovering in the air high over our heads, till the first break of day. Whether it meant war, peace, or prayer we could not tell. The dawns were heralded by the descent of a chill stillness; the woodcutters slept, their fires burned low; the snapping of a twig would make you start. We were wanderers on a prehistoric earth, on an earth that wore the aspect of an unknown planet. We could have fancied ourselves the first of men taking possession of an accursed inheritance, to be subdued at the cost of profound anguish and of excessive toil. But suddenly, as we struggled round a bend, there would be a glimpse of rush walls, of peaked grass-roofs, a burst of yells, a whirl of black limbs, a mass of hands clapping, of feet stamping, of bodies swaying, of eyes rolling, under the droop of heavy and motionless foliage. The steamer toiled along slowly on the edge of a black and incomprehensible frenzy. The prehistoric man was cursing us, praying to us, welcoming us—who could tell? We were cut off from the comprehension of our surroundings; we glided past like phantoms, wondering and secretly appalled, as sane men would be before an enthusiastic outbreak in a madhouse. We could not understand because we were too far and could not remember, because we were travelling in the night of first ages, of those ages that are gone, leaving hardly a sign—and no memories.

"The earth seemed unearthly. We are accustomed to look upon the shackled form of a conquered monster, but there—there you could look at a thing monstrous and free. It was unearthly, and the men were— No, they were not inhuman. Well, you know, that was the worst of it—this suspicion of their not being inhuman. It would come slowly to one. They howled and leaped, and spun, and made horrid faces; but what thrilled you was just the thought of their humanity—like yours—the thought of your remote kinship with this wild and passionate uproar. Ugly. Yes, it was ugly enough; but if you were man enough you would admit to yourself that there was in you just the faintest trace of a response to the terrible frankness of that noise, a dim suspicion of there being a meaning in it which you—you so remote from the night of first ages—could comprehend. And why not? The mind of man is capable of anything—because everything is in it, all the past as well as all the future. What was there after all? Joy, fear, sorrow, devotion, valour, rage—who can tell?—but truth—truth stripped of its cloak of time. Let the fool gape and shudder—the man knows, and can look on without a wink. But he must at least be as much of a man as these on the shore. He must meet that truth with his own true stuff—with his own inborn strength. Principles? Principles won't do. Acquisitions, clothes, pretty rags—rags that would fly off at the first good shake. No; you want a deliberate belief. An appeal to me in this fiendish row—is there? Very well; I hear; I admit, but I have a voice too, and for good or evil mine is the speech that cannot be silenced. Of course, a fool, what with sheer fright and fine sentiments, is always safe. Who's that grunting? You wonder I didn't go ashore for a howl and a dance? Well, no—I didn't. Fine sentiments, you say? Fine sentiments be hanged! I had no time. I had to mess about with white-lead and strips of woollen blanket helping to put bandages on those leaky steam-pipes—I tell you. I had to watch the steering, and circumvent those snags, and get the tin-pot along by hook or by crook. There was surface-truth enough in these things to save a wiser man. And between whiles I had to look after the savage who was fireman. He was an improved specimen; he could fire up a vertical boiler. He was there below me, and, upon my word, to look at him was as edifying as seeing a dog in a parody of breeches and a feather hat, walking on his hind legs. A few months of training had done for that really fine chap. He squinted at the steam-gauge and at the water-gauge with an evident effort of intrepidity—and he had filed teeth too, the poor devil, and the wool of his pate shaved into queer patterns, and three ornamental scars on each of his cheeks. He ought to have been clapping his hands and stamping his feet on the bank, instead of which he was hard at work, a thrall to strange witchcraft, full of improving knowledge. He was useful because he had been instructed; and what he knew was this—that should the water in that transparent thing disappear, the evil spirit inside the boiler would get angry through the greatness of his thirst, and take a terrible vengeance. So he sweated and fired up and watched the glass fearfully (with an impromptu charm, made of rags, tied to his arm, and a piece of polished bone, as big as a watch, stuck flatways through his lower lip), while the wooded banks slipped past us slowly, the short noise was left behind, the interminable miles of silence—and we crept on, towards Kurtz. But the snags were thick, the water was treacherous and shallow, the boiler seemed indeed to have a sulky devil in it, and thus neither that fireman nor I had any time to peer into our creepy thoughts.

"Some fifty miles below the Innner Station we came upon a hut of reeds, an inclined and melancholy pole, with the unrecognisable tatters of what had been a flag of some sort flying from it, and a neatly stacked wood-pile. This was unexpected. We came to the bank, and on the stack of firewood found a flat piece of board with some faded pencil-writing on it. When deciphered it said: 'Wood for you. Hurry up. Approach cautiously.' There was a signature, but it was illegible—not Kurtz—a much longer word. Hurry up. Where? Up the river? 'Approach cautiously.' We had not done so. But the warning could not have been meant for the place where it could be only found after approach. Something was wrong above. But what—and how much? That was the question. We commented adversely upon the imbecility of that telegraphic style. The bush around said nothing, and would not let us look very far, either. A torn curtain of red twill hung in the doorway of the hut, and flapped sadly in our faces. The dwelling was dismantled; but we could see a white man had lived there not very long ago. There remained a rude table—a plank on two posts; a heap of rubbish reposed in a dark corner, and by the door I picked up a book. It had lost its covers, and the pages had been thumbed into a state of extremely dirty softness; but the back had been lovingly stitched afresh with white cotton thread, which looked clean yet. It was an extraordinary find. Its title was, *An Inquiry into some Points of Seamanship*, by a man Towser, Towson—some such name—Master in

His Majesty's Navy. The matter looked dreary reading enough, with illustrative diagrams and repulsive tables of figures, and the copy was sixty years old. I handled this amazing antiquity with the greatest possible tenderness, lest it should dissolve in my hands. Within, Towson or Towser was inquiring earnestly into the breaking strain of ships' chains and tackle, and other such matters. Not a very enthralling book; but at the first glance you could see there a singleness of intention, an honest concern for the right way of going to work, which made these humble pages, thought out so many years ago, luminous with another than a professional light. The simple old sailor, with his talk of chains and purchases, made me forget the jungle and the pilgrims in a delicious sensation of having come upon something unmistakably real. Such a book being there was wonderful enough; but still more astounding were the notes pencilled in the margin, and plainly referring to the text. I couldn't believe my eyes! They were in cipher! Yes, it looked like cipher. Fancy a man lugging with him a book of that description into this nowhere and studying it—and making notes—in cipher at that! It was an extravagant mystery.

"I had been dimly aware for some time of a worrying noise, and when I lifted my eyes I saw the wood-pile was gone, and the manager, aided by all the pilgrims, was shouting at me from the river-side. I slipped the book into my pocket. I assure you to leave off reading was like tearing myself away from the shelter of an old and solid friendship.

"I started the lame engine ahead. 'It must be this miserable trader—this intruder,' exclaimed the manager, looking back malevolently at the place we had left. 'He must be English,' I said. 'It will not save him from getting into trouble if he is not careful,' muttered the manager darkly. I observed with assumed innocence that no man was safe from trouble in this world.

"The current was more rapid now, the steamer seemed at her last gasp, the stern-wheel flopped languidly, and I caught myself listening on tiptoe for the next beat of the float, for in sober truth I expected the wretched thing to give up every moment. It was like watching the last flickers of a life. But still we crawled. Sometimes I would pick out a tree a little way ahead to measure our progress towards Kurtz by, but I lost it invariably before we got abreast. To keep the eyes so long on one thing was too much for human patience. The manager displayed a beautiful resignation. I fretted and fumed and took to arguing with myself whether or no I would talk openly with Kurtz; but before I could come to any conclusion it occurred to me that my speech or my silence, indeed any action of mine, would be a mere futility. What did it matter what any one knew or ignored? What did it matter who was manager? One gets sometimes such a flash of insight. The essentials of this affair lay deep under the surface, beyond my reach, and beyond my power of meddling.

"Towards the evening of the second day we judged ourselves about eight miles from Kurtz's station. I wanted to push on; but the manager looked grave, and told me the navigation up there was so dangerous that it would be advisable, the sun being very low already, to wait where we were till next morning. Moreover, he pointed out that if the warning to approach cautiously were to be followed, we must aproach in daylight—not at dusk, or in the dark. This was sensible enough. Eight miles meant nearly three hours' steaming for us, and I could also see suspicious ripples at the upper end of the reach. Nevertheless, I was annoyed beyond expression at the delay, and most unreasonably too, since one night more could not matter much after so many months. As we had plenty of wood, and caution was the word, I brought up in the middle of the stream. The reach was narrow, straight, with high sides like a railway cutting. The dusk came gliding into it long before the sun had set. The current ran smooth and swift, but a dumb immobility sat on the banks. The living trees, lashed together by the creepers and every living bush of the undergrowth, might have been changed into stone, even to the slenderest twig, to the lightest leaf. It was not sleep—it seemed unnatural, like a state of trance. Not the faintest sound of any kind could be heard. You looked on amazed, and began to suspect yourself of being deaf—then the night came suddenly, and struck you blind as well. About three in the morning some large fish leaped, and the loud splash made me jump as though a gun had been fired. When the sun rose there was a white fog, very warm and clammy, and more blinding than the night. It did not shift or drive; it was just there, standing all round you like something solid. At eight or nine, perhaps, it lifted as a shutter lifts. We had a glimpse of the towering multitude of trees, of the immense matted jungle, with the blazing little ball of the sun hanging over it—all perfectly still—and then the white shutter came down again, smoothly, as if sliding in greased grooves. I ordered the chain, which we had begun to heave in, to be paid out again. Before it stopped running with a muffled rattle, a cry, a very loud cry, as of infinite desolation, soared slowly in the opaque air. It ceased. A complaining clamour, modulated in savage discords, filled our ears. The sheer unexpectedness of it made my hair stir under my cap. I don't know how it struck the others: to me it seemed as though the mist itself had screamed, so suddenly, and apparently from all sides at once, did this tumultuous and mournful uproar arise. It culminated in a hurried outbreak of almost intolerably excessive shrieking, which stopped short, leaving us stiffened in a variety of silly attitudes, and obstinately listening to the nearly as appalling and excessive silence. 'Good God! What is the meaning—?' stammered at my elbow one of the pilgrims—a little fat man, with sandy hair and red whiskers, who wore side-spring boots, and pink pyjamas tucked into his socks. Two others remained open-mouthed a whole minute, then dashed into the little cabin, to rush out incontinently and stand darting scared glances, with Winchesters at 'ready' in their hands. What we could see was just the steamer we were on, her outlines blurred as though she had been on the point of dissolving, and a misty strip of water, perhaps two feet broad, around her—and that was all. The rest of the world was nowhere, as far as our eyes and ears were concerned. Just nowhere. Gone, disappeared; swept off without leaving a whisper or a shadow behind.

"I went forward, and ordered the chain to be hauled in short, so as to be ready to trip the anchor and move the steamboat at once if necessary, 'Will they attack?' whispered an awed voice, 'We will all be butchered in this fog,' murmured another. The faces twitched with the strain, the hands trembled slightly, the eyes forgot to wink. It was very curious to see the contrast of expressions of the white men and of the black fellows of our crew, who were as much strangers to that part of the river as we, though their homes were only eight hundred miles away. The whites, of course greatly discomposed, had besides a curious look of being painfully shocked by such an outrageous row. The others had an alert, naturally interested expression; but their faces were essentially quiet, even those of the one or two who grinned as they hauled at the chain. Several exchanged short, grunting phrases, which seemed to settle the matter to their satisfaction. Their headman, a young, broad-chested black, severely draped in dark-blue fringed cloths, with fierce nostrils and his hair all done up artfully in oily ringlets, stood near me. 'Aha!' I said, just for good fellowship's sake. 'Catch 'im,' he snapped, with a bloodshot widening of his eyes and a flash of sharp teeth—'catch 'im. Give 'im to us.' 'To you, eh?' I asked; 'what would you do with them?' 'Eat 'im!' he said curtly, and, leaning his elbow on the rail, looked out into the fog in a dignified and profoundly pensive attitude. I would no doubt have been properly horrified, had it not occurred to me that he and his chaps must be very hungry: that they must have been growing increasingly hungry for at least this month past. They had been engaged for six months (I don't think a single one of them had any clear idea of time, as we at the end of countless ages have. They still belonged to the beginnings of time—had no inherited experience to teach them, as it were), and of course, as long as there was a piece of paper written over in accordance with some farcical law or other made down the river, it didn't enter anybody's head to trouble how they would live. Certainly they had brought with them some rotten hippo-meat, which couldn't have lasted very long, anyway, even if the pilgrims hadn't, in the midst of a shocking hullabaloo, thrown a considerable quantity of it overboard. It looked like a high-handed proceeding; but it was really a case of legitimate self-defence. You can't breathe dead hippo waking, sleeping, and eating, and at the same time keep your precarious grip on existence. Besides that, they had given them every week three pieces of brass wire, each about nine inches long; and the theory was they were to buy their provisions with that currency in river-side villages. You can see how *that* worked. There were either no villages, or the people were hostile, or the director, who like the rest of us fed out of tins, with an occasional old he-goat thrown in, didn't want to stop the steamer for some more or less recondite reasons. So, unless they swallowed the wire itself, or made loops of it to snare the fishes with, I don't see what good their extravagant salary could be to them. I must say it was paid with a regularity worthy of a large and honourable trading company. For the rest, the only thing to eat—though it didn't look eatable in the least—I saw in their possession was a few lumps of some stuff like half-cooked dough, of a dirty lavender colour, they kept wrapped in leaves, and now and then swallowed a piece of, but so small that it seemed done more for the look of the thing than for any serious purpose of sustenance. Why in the name of all the gnawing devils of hunger they didn't go for us—they were thirty to five—and have a good tuck-in for once, amazes me now when I think of it. They were big powerful men, with not much capacity to weigh the consequences, with courage, with strength, even yet, though their skins were no longer glossy and their muscles no longer hard. And I saw that something restraining, one of those human secrets that baffle probability, had come into play there. I looked at them with a swift quickening of interest—not because it occurred to me I might be eaten by them before very long, though I own to you that just then I perceived—in a new light, as it were—how unwholesome the pilgrims looked, and I hoped, yes, I positively hoped, that my aspect was not so—what shall I say?—so—unappetising: a touch of fantastic vanity which fitted well with the dream-sensation that pervaded all my days at that time. Perhaps I had a little fever too. One can't live with one's finger everlastingly on one's pulse. I had often 'a little fever,' or a little touch of other things—the playful paw-strokes of the wilderness, the preliminary trifling before the more serious onslaught which came in due course. Yes; I looked at them as you would on any human being, with a curiosity of their impulses, motives, capacities, weaknesses, when brought to the test of an inexorable physical necessity. Restraint! What possible restraint? Was it superstition, disgust, patience, fear—or some kind of primitive honour? No fear can stand up to hunger, no patience can wear it out, disgust simply does not exist where hunger is; and as to superstition, beliefs, and what you may call principles, they are less than chaff in a breeze. Don't you know the devilry of lingering starvation, its exasperating torment, its black thoughts, its sombre and brooding ferocity? Well, I do. It takes a man all his inborn strength to fight hunger properly. It's really easier to face bereavement, dishonour, and the perdition of one's soul—than this kind of prolonged hunger. Sad, but true. And these chaps too had no earthly reason for any kind of scruple. Restraint! I would just as soon have expected restraint from a hyena prowling amongst the corpses of a battlefield. But there was the fact facing me—the fact dazzling, to be seen, like the foam on the depths of the sea, like a ripple on an unfathomable enigma, a mystery greater—when I thought of it—than the curious, inexplicable note of desperate grief in this savage clamour that had swept by us on the river-bank, behind the blind whiteness of the fog.

"Two pilgrims were quarrelling in hurried whispers as to which bank. 'Left.' 'No, no; how can you? Right, right, of course.' 'It is very serious,' said the manager's voice behind me; 'I would be desolated if anything should happen to Mr. Kurtz before we came up.' I looked at him, and had not the slightest doubt he was sincere. He was just the kind of man who would wish to preserve appearances. That was his restraint. But when he muttered something about going on at once, I did not even take the trouble to answer him. I knew, and he knew, that it was impossible. Were we to let go our hold of the bottom, we would be absolutely in the air—in space. We wouldn't be able to tell where we were going to—whether up or down stream, or across—till we fetched against one bank or the other—and then we wouldn't know at first which it was. Of course I made no move. I had no mind for a smash-up. You couldn't imagine a more deadly place for a shipwreck. Whether drowned at once or not, we were sure to perish speedily in one way or another. 'I authorise you to take all the risks,' he said, after a short silence. 'I refuse to take any,' I said shortly; which was just the answer he expected, though its tone might have surprised him. 'Well, I must defer to your judgment. You are captain,' he said, with marked civility. I turned my shoulder to him in sign of my appreciation, and looked into the fog. How long would it last? It was the most hopeless look-out. The approach to this Kurtz grubbing for ivory in the wretched bush was beset by as many dangers as though he had been an enchanted princess sleeping in a fabulous castle. 'Will they attack, do you think?' asked the manager, in a confidential tone.

"I did not think they would attack, for several obvious reasons. The thick fog was one. If they left the bank in their canoes they would get lost in it, as we would be if we attempted to move. Still, I had also judged the jungle of both banks quite impenetrable—and yet eyes were in it, eyes that had seen us. The river-side bushes were certainly very thick; but the undergrowth behind was evidently penetrable. However, during the short lift I had seen no canoes anywhere in the reach—certainly not abreast of the steamer. But what made the idea of attack inconceivable to me was the nature of the noise—of the cries we had heard. They had not the fierce character boding of immediate hostile intention. Unexpected, wild, and violent as they had been, they had given me an irresistible impression of sorrow. The glimpse of the steamboat had for some reason filled those savages with unrestrained grief. The danger, if any, I expounded, was from our proximity to a great human passion let loose. Even extreme grief may ultimately vent itself in violence—but more generally takes the form of apathy. . . .

"You should have seen the pilgrims stare! They had no heart to grin, or even to revile me; but I believe they thought me gone mad—with fright, maybe. I delivered a regular lecture. My dear boys, it was no good bothering. Keep a look-out? Well, you may guess I watched the fog for the signs of lifting as a cat watches a mouse; but for anything else our eyes were of no more use to us than if we had been buried miles deep in a heap of cotton-wool. It felt like it too—choking, warm, stifling. Besides, all I said, though it sounded extravagant, was absolutely true to fact. What we afterwards alluded to as an attack was really an attempt at repulse. The action was very far from being aggressive—it was not even defensive, in the usual sense: it was undertaken under the stress of desperation, and in its essence was purely protective.

"It developed itself, I should say, two hours after the fog lifted, and its commencement was at a spot, roughly speaking, about a mile and a half below Kurtz's station. We had just floundered and flopped round a bend, when I saw an islet, a mere grassy hummock of bright green, in the middle of the stream. It was the only thing of the kind; but as we opened the reach more, I perceived it was the head of a long sandbank, or rather of a chain of shallow patches stretching down the middle of the river. They were discoloured, just awash, and the whole lot was seen just under the water, exactly as a man's backbone is seen running down the middle of his back under the skin. Now, as far as I did see, I could go to the right or to the left of this. I didn't know either channel, of course. The banks looked pretty well alike, the depth appeared the same; but as I had been informed the station was on the west side, I naturally headed for the western passage.

"No sooner had we fairly entered it than I became aware it was much narrower than I had supposed. To the left of us there was the long uninterrupted shoal, and to the right a high steep bank heavily overgrown with bushes. Above the bush the trees stood in serried ranks. The twigs overhung the current thickly, and from distance to distance a large limb of some tree projected rigidly over the stream. It was then well on in the afternoon, the face of the forest was gloomy, and a broad strip of shadow had already fallen on the water. In this shadow we steamed up—very slowly, as you may imagine. I sheered her well inshore—the water being deepest near the bank, as the sounding-pole informed me.

"One of my hungry and forbearing friends was sounding in the bows just below me. This steamboat was exactly like a decked scow. On the deck there were two little teak-wood houses, with doors and windows. The boiler was in the fore-end, and the machinery right astern. Over the whole there was a light roof, supported on stanchions. The funnel projected through that roof, and in front of the funnel a small cabin built of light planks served for a pilot-house. It contained a couch, two camp-stools, a loaded Martini-Henry leaning in one corner, a tiny table, and the steering-wheel. It had a wide door in front and a broad shutter at each side. All these were always thrown open, of course. I spent my days perched up there on the extreme fore-end of that roof, before the door. At night I slept, or tried to, on the couch. An athletic black belonging to some coast tribe, and educated by my poor predecessor, was the helmsman. He sported a pair of brass earrings, wore a blue cloth wrapper from the waist to the ankles, and thought all the world of himself. He was the most unstable kind of fool I had ever seen. He steered with no end of a swagger while you were by; but if he lost sight of you, he became instantly the prey of an abject funk, and would let that cripple of a steamboat get the upper hand of him in a minute.

"I was looking down at the sounding-pole, and feeling much annoyed to see at each try a little more of it stick out of that river, when I saw my poleman give up the business suddenly, and stretch himself flat on the deck, without even taking the trouble to haul his pole in. He kept hold on it though, and it trailed in the water. At the same time the fireman, whom I could also see below me, sat down abruptly before his furnace and ducked his head. I was amazed. Then I had to look at the river mighty quick, because there was a snag in the fairway. Sticks, little sticks, were flying about—thick: they were whizzing before my nose, dropping below me, striking behind me against my pilot-house. All this time the river, the shore, the woods, were very quiet—perfectly quiet. I could only hear the heavy splashing thump of the stern-wheel and the patter of these things. We cleared the snag clumsily. Arrows, by Jove! We were being shot at! I stepped in quickly to close the shutter on the land-side. That fool-helmsman, his hands on the spokes, was lifting his knees high, stamping his feet, champing his mouth, like a reined-in horse. Confound him! And we were staggering within ten feet of the bank. I had to lean right out to swing the heavy shutter, and I saw a face amongst the leaves on the level with my own, looking at me very fierce and steady; and then suddenly, as though a veil had been removed from my eyes, I made out, deep in the tangled gloom, naked breasts, arms, legs, glaring eyes—the bush was swarming with human limbs in movement, glistening, of bronze colour. The twigs shook, swayed, and rustled, the arrows flew out of them, and then the shutter came to. 'Steer her straight,' I said to the helmsman. He held his head rigid, face forward; but his eyes rolled, he kept lifting and setting down his feet gently, his mouth foamed a little. 'Keep quiet!' I said in a fury. I might just as well have ordered a tree not to sway in the wind. I darted out. Below me there was a great scuffle of feet on the iron deck; confused exclamations; a voice screamed, 'Can you turn back?' I caught sight of a V-shaped ripple on the water ahead. What? Another snag? A fusillade burst out under my feet. The pilgrims had opened with their Winchesters, and were simply squirting lead into that bush. A deuce of a lot of smoke came up and drove slowly forward. I swore at it. Now I couldn't see the ripple or the snag either. I stood in the doorway, peering, and the arrows came in swarms. They might have been poisoned, but they looked as though they wouldn't kill a cat. The bush began to howl. Our wood-cutters raised a warlike whoop; the report of a rifle just at my back deafened me. I glanced over my shoulder, and the pilot-house was yet full of noise and smoke when I made a dash at the wheel. The fool-nigger had dropped everything, to throw the shutter open and let off that Martini-Henry. He stood before the wide opening, glaring, and I yelled at him to come back, while I straightened the sudden twist out of that steamboat. There was no room to turn even if I had wanted to, the snag was somewhere very near ahead in that confounded smoke, there was no time to lose, so I just crowded her into the bank—right into the bank, where I knew the water was deep.

"We tore slowly along the overhanging bushes in a whirl of broken twigs and flying leaves. The fusillade below stopped short, as I had foreseen it would when the squirts got empty. I threw my head back to a glinting whizz that traversed the pilot-house, in at one shutter-hole and out at the other. Looking past that mad helmsman, who was shaking the empty rifle and yelling at the shore, I saw vague forms of men running bent double, leaping, gliding, distinct, incomplete, evanescent. Something big appeared in the air before the shutter, the rifle went overboard, and the man stepped back swiftly, looked at me over his shoulder in an extraordinary, profound, familiar manner, and fell upon my feet. The side of his head hit the wheel twice, and the end of what appeared a long cane clattered round and knocked over a little camp-stool. It looked as though after wrenching that thing from somebody ashore he had lost his balance in the effort. The thin smoke had blown away, we were clear of the snag, and looking ahead I could see that in another hundred yards or so I would be free to sheer off, away from the bank; but my feet felt so very warm and wet that I had to look down. The man had rolled on his back and stared straight up at me; both his hands clutched that cane. It was the shaft of a spear that, either thrown or lunged through the opening, had caught him in the side just below the ribs; the blade had gone in out of sight, after making a frightful gash; my shoes were full; a pool of blood lay very still, gleaming dark-red under the wheel; his eyes shone with an amazing lustre. The fusillade burst out again. He looked at me anxiously, gripping the spear like something precious, with an air of being afraid I would try to take it way from him. I had to make an effort to free my eyes from his gaze and attend to the steering. With one hand I felt above my head for the line of the steam whistle, and jerked out screech after screech hurriedly. The tumult of angry and warlike yells was checked instantly, and then from the depths of the woods went out such a tremulous and prolonged wail of mournful fear and utter despair as may be imagined to follow the flight of the last hope from the earth. There was a great commotion in the bush; the shower of arrows stopped, a few dropping shots rang out sharply—then silence, in which the languid beat of the stern-wheel came plainly to my ears. I put the helm hard a-starboard at the moment when the pilgrim in pink pyjamas, very hot and agitated, appeared in the doorway. 'The manager sends me—' he began in an official tone, and stopped short. 'Good God!' he said, glaring at the wounded man.

"We two whites stood over him, and his lustrous and inquiring glance enveloped us both. I declare it looked as though he would presently put to us some question in an understandable language; but he died without uttering a sound, without moving a limb, without twitching a muscle. Only in the very last moment, as though in response to some sign we could not see, to some whisper we could not hear, he frowned heavily, and that frown gave to his black death-mask an inconceivably sombre, brooding, and menacing expression. The lustre of inquiring glance faded swiftly into vacant glassiness. 'Can you steer?' I asked the agent eagerly. He looked very dubious; but I made a grab at his arm, and he understood at once I meant him to steer whether or no. To tell you the truth, I was morbidly anxious to change my shoes and socks. 'He is dead,' murmured the fellow, immensely impressed. 'No doubt about it,' said I, tugging like mad at the shoe-laces. 'And by the way, I suppose Mr. Kurtz is dead as well by this time.'

"For the moment that was the dominant thought. There was a sense of extreme disappointment, as though I had found out I had been striving after something altogether without a substance. I couldn't have been more disgusted if I had travelled all this way for the sole purpose of talking with Mr. Kurtz. Talking with . . . I flung one shoe overboard, and became aware that that was exactly what I had been looking forward to—a talk with Kurtz. I made the strange discovery that I had never imagined him as doing, you know, but as discoursing. I didn't say to myself, 'Now I will never see him,' or 'Now I will never shake him by the hand,' but, 'Now I will never hear him.' The man presented himself as a voice. Not of course that I did not connect him with some sort of action. Hadn't I been told in all the tones of jealousy and admiration that he had collected, bartered, swindled, or stolen more ivory than all the other agents together? That was not the point. The point was in his being a gifted creature, and that of all his gifts the one that stood out pre-eminently, that carried with it a sense of real presence, was his ability to talk, his words—the gift of expression, the bewildering, the illuminating, the most exalted and the most contemptible, the pulsating stream of light, or the deceitful flow from the heart of an impenetrable darkness.

"The other shoe went flying unto the devil-god of that river. I thought, By Jove! it's all over. We are too late; he has vanished—the gift has vanished, by means of some spear, arrow, or club. I will never hear that chap speak after all—and my sorrow had a startling extravagance of emotion, even such as I had noticed in the howling sorrow of these savages in the bush. I couldn't have felt more of lonely desolation somehow, had I been robbed of a belief or had missed my destiny in life. . . . Why do you sigh in this beastly way, somebody? Absurd? Well, absurd. Good Lord! mustn't a man ever— Here, give me some tobacco." . . .

There was a pause of profound stillness, then a match flared, and Marlow's lean face appeared, worn, hollow, with downward folds and dropped eyelids, with an aspect of concentrated attention; and as he took vigorous draws at his pipe, it seemed to retreat and advance out of the night in the regular flicker of the tiny flame. The match went out.

"Absurd!" he cried. "This is the worst of trying to tell . . . Here you all are, each moored with two good addresses, like a hulk with two anchors, a butcher round one corner, a policeman round another, excellent appetites, and temperature normal—you hear—normal from year's end to year's end. And you say, Absurd! Absurd be—exploded! Absurd! My dear boys, what can you expect from a man who out of sheer nervousness had just flung overboard a pair of new shoes? Now I think of it, it is amazing I did not shed tears. I am, upon the whole, proud of my fortitude. I was cut to the quick at the idea of having lost the inestimable privilege of listening to the gifted Kurtz. Of course I was wrong. The privilege was waiting for me. Oh yes, I heard more than enough. And I was right, too. A voice. He was very little more than a voice. And I heard—him—it—this voice—other voices—all of them were so little more than voices—and the memory of that time itself lingers around me, impalpable, like a dying vibration of one immense jabber, silly, atrocious, sordid, savage, or simply mean, without any kind of sense. Voices, voices—even the girl herself—now—"

He was silent for a long time.

"I laid the ghost of his gifts at last with a lie," he began suddenly. "Girl! What? Did I mention a girl? Oh, she is out of it—completely. They—the women I mean—are out of it—should be out of it. We must help them to stay in the beautiful world of their own, lest ours gets worse. Oh, she had to be out of it. You should have heard the disinterred body of Mr. Kurtz saying, 'My Intended.' You would have perceived directly then how completely she was out of it. And the lofty frontal bone of Mr. Kurtz! They say the hair goes on growing sometimes, but this—ah—specimen was impressively bald. The wilderness had patted him on the head, and, behold, it was like a ball—an ivory ball; it had caressed him, and—lo!—he had withered; it had taken him, loved him, embraced him, got into his veins, consumed his flesh, and sealed his soul to its own by the inconceivable ceremonies of some devilish initiation. He was its spoiled and pampered favourite. Ivory? I should think so. Heaps of it, stacks of it. The old mud shanty was bursting with it. You would think there was not a single tusk left either above or below the ground in the whole country. 'Mostly fossil,' the manager had remarked disparagingly. It was no more fossil than I am; but they call it fossil when it is dug up. It appears these niggers do bury the tusks sometimes—but evidently they couldn't bury this parcel deep enough to save the gifted Mr. Kurtz from his fate. We filled the steamboat with it, and had to pile a lot on the deck. Thus he could see and enjoy as long as he could see, because the appreciation of this favour had remained with him to the last. You should have heard him say, 'My ivory.' Oh yes, I heard him. 'My Intended, my ivory, my station, my river, my—' everything belonged to him. It made me hold my breath in expectation of hearing the wilderness burst into a prodigious peal of laughter that would shake the fixed stars in their places. Everything belonged to him—but that was a trifle. The thing was to know what he belonged to, how many powers of darkness claimed him for their own. That was the reflection that made you creepy all over. It was impossible—it was not good for one either—trying to imagine. He had taken a high seat amongst the devils of the land—I mean literally. You can't understand. How could you?—with solid pavement under your feet, surrounded by kind neighbours ready to cheer you or to fall on you, stepping delicately between the butcher and the policeman, in the holy terror of scandal and gallows and lunatic asylums—how can you imagine what particular region of the first ages a man's untrammelled feet may take him into by the way of solitude—utter solitude without a policeman—by the way of silence—utter silence, where no warning voice of a kind neighbour can be heard whispering of public opinion? These little things make all the great difference. When they are gone you must fall back upon your own innate strength, upon your own capacity for faithfulness. Of course you may be too much of a fool to go wrong—too dull even to know you are being assaulted by the powers of darkness. I take it, no fool ever made a bargain for his soul with the devil: the fool is too much of a fool, or the devil too much of a devil—I don't know which. Or you may be such a thunderingly exalted creature as to be altogether deaf and blind to anything but heavenly sights and sounds. Then the earth for you is only a standing place—and whether to be like this is your loss or your gain I won't pretend to say. But most of us are neither one nor the other. The earth for us is a place to live in, where we must put up with sights, with sounds, with smells, too, by Jove!—breathe dead hippo, so to speak, and not be contaminated. And there, don't you see? your strength comes in, the faith in your ability for the digging of unostentatious holes to bury the stuff in—your power of devotion, not to yourself, but to an obscure, back-breaking business.

And that's difficult enough. Mind, I am not trying to excuse or even explain—I am trying to account to myself for—for—Mr. Kurtz—for the shade of Mr. Kurtz. This initiated wraith from the back of Nowhere honoured me with its amazing confidence before it vanished altogether. This was because it could speak English to me. The original Kurtz had been educated partly in England, and—as he was good enough to say himself—his sympathies were in the right place. His mother was half-English, his father was half-French. All Europe contributed to the making of Kurtz; and by and by I learned that, most appropriately, the International Society for the Suppression of Savage Customs had entrusted him with the making of a report, for its future guidance. And he had written it too. I've seen it. I've read it. It was eloquent, vibrating with eloquence, but too high-strung, I think. Seventeen pages of close writing he had found time for! But this must have been before his—let us say—nerves went wrong, and caused him to preside at certain midnight dances ending with unspeakable rites, which—as far as I reluctantly gathered from what I heard at various times—were offered up to him—do you understand?—to Mr. Kurtz himself. But it was a beautiful piece of writing. The opening paragraph, however, in the light of later information, strikes me now as ominous. He began with the argument that we whites, from the point of development we had arrived at, 'must necessarily appear to them [savages] in the nature of supernatural beings—we approach them with the might as of a deity,' and so on, and so on. 'By the simple exercise of our will we can exert a power for good practically unbounded,' etc. etc. From that point he soared and took me with him. The peroration was magnificent, though difficult to remember, you know. It gave me the notion of an exotic Immensity ruled by an august Benevolence. It made me tingle with enthusiasm. This was the unbounded power of eloquence—of words—of burning noble words. There were no practical hints to interrupt the magic current of phrases, unless a kind of note at the foot of the last page, scrawled evidently much later, in an unsteady hand, may be regarded as the exposition of a method. It was very simple, and at the end of that moving appeal to every altruistic sentiment it blazed at you, luminous and terrifying, like a flash of lightning in a serene sky: 'Exterminate all the brutes!' The curious part was that he had apparently forgotten all about that valuable postscriptum, because, later on, when he in a sense came to himself, he repeatedly entreated me to take good care of 'my pamphlet' (he called it), as it was sure to have in the future a good influence upon his career. I had full information about all these things, and, besides, as it turned out, I was to have the care of his memory. I've done enough for it to give me the indisputable right to lay it, if I choose, for an everlasting rest in the dust-bin of progress, amongst all the sweepings and, figuratively speaking, all the dead cats of civilisation. But then, you see, I can't choose. He won't be forgotten. Whatever he was, he was not common. He had the power to charm or frighten rudimentary souls into an aggravated witch-dance in his honour; he could also fill the small souls of the pilgrims with bitter misgivings: he had one devoted friend at least, and he had conquered one soul in the world that was neither rudimentary nor tainted with self-seeking. No; I can't forget him, though I am not prepared to affirm the fellow was exactly worth the life we lost in getting to him. I missed my late helmsman awfully—I missed him even while his body was still lying in the pilot-house. Perhaps you will think it passing strange this regret for a savage who was no more account than a grain of sand in a black Sahara. Well, don't you see, he had done something, he had steered; for months I had him at my back—a help—an instrument. It was a kind of partnership. He steered for me—I had to look after him, I worried about his deficiencies, and thus a subtle bond had been created, of which I only became aware when it was suddenly broken. And the intimate profundity of that look he gave me when he received his hurt remains to this day in my memory—like a claim of distant kinship affirmed in a supreme moment.

"Poor fool! If he had only left that shutter alone. He had no restraint, no restraint—just like Kurtz—a tree swayed by the wind. As soon as I had put on a dry pair of slippers, I dragged him out, after first jerking the spear out of his side, which operation I confess I performed with my eyes shut tight. His heels leaped together over the little doorstep; his shoulders were pressed to my breast; I hugged him from behind desperately. Oh! he was heavy, heavy; heavier than any man on earth, I should imagine. Then without more ado I tipped him overboard. The current snatched him as though he had been a wisp of grass, and I saw the body roll over twice before I lost sight of it for ever. All the pilgrims and the manager were then congregated on the awning-deck about the pilot-house, chattering at each other like a flock of excited magpies, and there was a scandalised murmur at my heartless promptitude. What they wanted to keep that body hanging about for I can't guess. Embalm it, maybe. But I had also heard another, and a very ominous, murmur on the deck below. My friends the wood-cutters were likewise scandalised, and with a better show of reason—though I admit that the reason itself was quite inadmissible. Oh, quite! I had made up my mind that if my late helmsman was to be eaten, the fishes alone should have him. He had been a very second-rate helmsman while alive, but now he was dead he might have become a first-class temptation, and possibly cause some startling trouble. Besides, I was anxious to take the wheel, the man in pink pyjamas showing himself a hopeless duffer at the business.

"This I did directly the simple funeral was over. We were going half-speed, keeping right in the middle of the stream, and I listened to the talk about me. They had given up Kurtz, they had given up the station; Kurtz was dead, and the station had been burnt—and so on—and so on. The red-haired pilgrim was beside himself with the thought that at least this poor Kurtz had been properly revenged. 'Say! We must have made a glorious slaughter of them in the bush. Eh? What do you think? Say?' He positively danced, the bloodthirsty little gingery beggar. And he had nearly fainted when he saw the wounded man! I could not help saying. 'You made a glorious lot of smoke, anyhow.' I had seen, from the way the tops of the bushes rustled and flew, that almost all the shots had gone too high. You can't hit anything unless you take aim and fire from the shoulder; but these chaps fired from the hip with their eyes shut. The retreat, I maintained—and I was right—was caused by the screeching of the steam-whistle. Upon this they forgot Kurtz, and began to howl at me with indignant protests.

"The manager stood by the wheel murmuring confidentially about the necessity of getting well away down the river before dark at all events, when I saw in the distance a clearing on the river-side and the outlines of some sort of building. 'What's this?' I asked. He clapped his hands in wonder. 'The station!' he cried. I edged in at once, still going half-speed.

"Through my glasses I saw the slope of a hill interspersed with rare trees and perfectly free from undergrowth. A long decaying building on the summit was half buried in the high grass; the large holes in the peaked roof gaped black from afar; the jungle and the woods made a background. There was no enclosure or fence of any kind; but there had been one apparently, for near the house half a dozen slim posts remained in a row, roughly trimmed, and with their upper ends ornamented with round carved balls. The rails, or whatever there had been between, had disappeared. Of course the forest surrounded all that. The river-bank was clear, and on the water side I saw a white man under a hat like a cart-wheel beckoning persistently with his whole arm. Examining the edge of the forest above and below, I was almost certain I could see movements—human forms gliding here and there. I steamed past prudently, then stopped the engines and let her drift down. The man on the shore began to shout, urging us to land. 'We have been attacked,' screamed the manager. 'I know—I know. It's all right,' yelled back the other, as cheerful as you please. 'Come along. It's all right. I am glad.'

"His aspect reminded me of something I had seen—something funny I had seen somewhere. As I manœuvred to get alongside, I was asking myself, 'What does this fellow look like?' Suddenly I got it. He looked like a harlequin. His clothes had been made of some stuff that was brown holland probably, but it was covered with patches all over, with bright patches, blue, red, and yellow—patches on the back, patches on the front, patches on elbows, on knees; coloured binding round his jacket, scarlet edging at the bottom of his trousers; and the sunshine made him look extremely gay and wonderfully neat withal, because you could see how beautifully all this patching had been done. A beardless, boyish face, very fair, no features to speak of, nose peeling, little blue eyes, smiles and frowns chasing each other over that open countenance like sunshine and shadow on a wind-swept plain. 'Look out, captain!' he cried, 'there's a snag lodged in here last night.' What! Another snag? I confess I swore shamefully. I had nearly holed my cripple, to finish off that charming trip. The harlequin on the bank turned his little pug nose up to me. 'You English?' he asked, all smiles. 'Are you?' I shouted from the wheel. The smile vanished, and he shook his head as if sorry for my disappointment. Then he brightened up. 'Never mind!' he cried encouragingly. 'Are we in time?' I asked. 'He is up there,' he replied, with a toss of the head up the hill, and becoming gloomy all of a sudden. His face was like the autumn sky, overcast one moment and bright the next.

"When the manager, escorted by the pilgrims, all of them armed to the teeth, had gone to the house, this chap came on board. 'I say, I don't like this. These natives are in the bush,' I said. He assured me earnestly it was all right. 'They are simple people,' he added; 'well, I am glad you came. It took me all my time to keep them off.' 'But you said it was all right,' I cried. 'Oh, they meant no harm,' he said; and as I stared he corrected himself, 'Not exactly.' Then vivaciously, 'My faith, your pilot-house wants a clean up!' In the next breath he advised me to keep enough steam on the boiler to blow the whistle in case of any trouble. 'One good screech will do more for you than all your rifles. They are simple people,' he repeated. He rattled away at such a rate he quite overwhelmed me. He seemed to be trying to make up for lots of silence, and actually hinted, laughing, that such was the case. 'Don't you talk with Mr. Kurtz?' I said. 'You don't talk with that man—you listen to him,' he exclaimed with severe exaltation. 'But now—' He waved his arm, and in the twinkling of an eye was in the uttermost depths of despondency. In a moment he came up again with a jump, possessed himself of both my hands, shook them continuously, while he gabbled: 'Brother sailor . . . honour . . . pleasure . . . delight . . . introduce myself . . . Russian . . . son of an arch-priest . . . Government of Tambov . . . What? Tobacco! English tobocco; the excellent English tobacco! Now, that's brotherly. Smoke? Where's a sailor that does not smoke?'

"The pipe soothed him, and gradually I made out he had run away from school, had gone to sea in a Russian ship; ran away again; served some time in English ships; was now reconciled with the arch-priest. He made a point of that. 'But when one is young one must see things, gather experience, ideas; enlarge the mind.' 'Here!' I interrupted. 'You can never tell! Here I met Mr. Kurtz,' he said, youthfully solemn and reproachful. I held my tongue after that. It appears he had persuaded a Dutch trading-house on the coast to fit him out with stores and goods, and had started for the interior with a light heart, and no more idea of what would happen to him than a baby. He had been wandering about that river for nearly two years alone, cut off from everybody and everything. 'I am not so young as I look. I am twenty-five,' he said. 'At first old Van Shuyten would tell me to go to the devil,' he narrated with keen enjoyment; 'but I stuck to him, and talked and talked, till at last he got afraid I would talk the hind-leg off his favourite dog, so he gave me some cheap things and a few guns, and told me he hoped he would never see my face again. Good old Dutchman, Van Shuyten. I sent him one small lot of ivory a year ago, so that he can't call me a little thief when I get back. I hope he got it. And for the rest I don't care. I had some wood stacked for you. That was my old house. Did you see?'

"I gave him Towson's book. He made as though he would kiss me, but restrained himself. 'The only book I had left, and I thought I had lost it,' he said, looking at it ecstatically. 'So many accidents happen to a man going about alone, you know. Canoes get upset sometimes—and sometimes you've got to clear out so quick when the people get angry.' He thumbed the pages. 'You made notes in Russian?' I asked. He nodded. 'I thought they were written in cipher,' I said. He laughed, then became serious. 'I had lots of trouble to keep these people off,' he said. 'Did they want to kill you?' I asked. 'Oh no!' he cried, and checked himself. 'Why did they attack us?' I pursued. He hesitated, then said shamefacedly, 'They don't want him to go.' 'Don't they?' I said curiously. He noded a nod full of mystery and wisdom. 'I tell you,' he cried, 'this man has enlarged my mind.' He opened his arms wide, staring at me with his little blue eyes that were perfectly round."

III

"I looked at him, lost in astonishment. There he was before me, in motley, as though he had absconded from a troupe of mimes, enthusiastic, fabulous. His very existence was improbable, inexplicable, and altogether bewildering. He was an insoluble problem. It was inconceivable how he had existed, how he had succeeded in getting so far, how he had managed to remain—why he did not instantly disappear. 'I went a little farther,' he said, 'then still a little farther—till I had gone so far that I don't know how I'll ever get back. Never mind. Plenty time. I can manage. You take Kurtz away quick—quick—I tell you.' The glamour of youth enveloped his particoloured rags, his destitution, his loneliness, the essential desolation of his futile wanderings. For months—for years—his life hadn't been worth a day's purchase; and there he was gallantly, thoughtlessly alive, to all appearance indestructible solely by the virtue of his few years and of his unreflecting audacity. I was seduced into something like admiration—like envy. Glamour urged him on, glamour kept him unscathed. He surely wanted nothing from the wilderness but space to breathe in and to push on through. His need was to exist, and to move onwards at the greatest possible risk, and with a maximum of privation. If the absolutely pure, uncalculating, unpractical spirit of adventure had ever ruled a human being, it ruled this be-patched youth. I almost envied him the possession of this modest and clear flame. It seemed to have consumed all thought of self so completely, that, even while he was talking to you, you forgot that it was he—the man before your eyes—who had gone through these things. I did not envy him his devotion to Kurtz, though. He had not meditated over it. It came to him, and he accepted it with a sort of eager fatalism. I must say that to me it appeared about the most dangerous thing in every way he had come upon so far.

"They had come together unavoidably, like two ships becalmed near each other, and lay rubbing sides at last. I suppose Kurtz wanted an audience, because on a certain occasion, when encamped in the forest, they had talked all night, or more probably Kurtz had talked. 'We talked of everything,' he said, quite transported at the recollection. 'I forgot there was such a thing as sleep. The night did not seem to last an hour. Everything! Everything! . . . Of love too.' 'Ah, he talked to you of love!' I said, much amused. 'It isn't what you think,' he cried, almost passionately. 'It was in general. He made me see things—things.'

"He threw his arms up. We were on deck at the time, and the head-man of my wood-cutters, lounging near by, turned upon him his heavy and glittering eyes. I looked around, and I don't know why, but I assure you that never, never before, did this land, this river, this jungle, the very arch of this blazing sky, appear to me so hopeless and so dark, so impenetrable to human thought, so pitiless to human weakness. 'And, ever since, you have been with him, of course?' I said.

"On the contrary. It appears their intercourse had been very much broken by various causes. He had, as he informed me proudly, managed to nurse Kurtz through two illnesses (he alluded to it as you would to some risky feat), but as a rule Kurtz wandered alone, far in the depths of the forest. 'Very often coming to this station, I had to wait days and days before he would turn up,' he said. 'Ah, it was worth waiting for!—sometimes.' 'What was he doing? exploring or what?' I asked. 'Oh yes, of course'; he had discovered lots of villages, a lake too—he did not know exactly in what direction; it was dangerous to inquire too much—but mostly his expeditions had been for ivory. 'But he had no goods to trade with by that time,' I objected. 'There's a good lot of cartridges left even yet,' he answered, looking away. 'To speak plainly, he raided the country,' I said. He nodded. 'Not alone, surely!' He muttered something about the villages round that lake.

'Kurtz got the tribe to follow him, did he?' I suggested. He fidgeted a little. 'They adored him,' he said. The tone of these words was so extraordinary that I looked at him searchingly. It was curious to see his mingled eagerness and reluctance to speak of Kurtz. The man filled his life, occupied his thoughts, swayed his emotions. 'What can you expect?' he burst out; 'he came to them with thunder and lightning, you know—and they had never seen anything like it—and very terrible. He could be very terrible. You can't judge Mr. Kurtz as you would an ordinary man. No, no, no! Now—just to give you an idea—I don't mind telling you, he wanted to shoot me too one day—but I don't judge him.' 'Shoot you!' I cried. 'What for?' 'Well, I had a small lot of ivory the chief of that village near my house gave me. You see I used to shoot game for them. Well, he wanted it, and wouldn't hear reason. He declared he would shoot me unless I gave him the ivory and then cleared out of the country, because he could do so, and had a fancy for it, and there was nothing on earth to prevent him killing whom he jolly well pleased. And it was true too. I gave him the ivory. What did I care! But I didn't clear out. No, no. I couldn't leave him. I had to be careful, of course, till we got friendly again for a time. He had his second illness then. Afterwards I had to keep out of the way; but I didn't mind. He was living for the most part in those villages on the lake. When he came down to the river, sometimes he would take to me, and sometimes it was better for me to be careful. This man suffered too much. He hated all this, and somehow he couldn't get away. When I had a chance I begged him to try and leave while there was time; I offered to go back with him. And he would say yes, and then he would remain; go off on another ivory hunt; disappear for weeks; forget himself amongst these people—forget himself—you know.' 'Why! he's mad,' I said. He protested indignantly. Mr. Kurtz couldn't be mad. If I had heard him talk, only two days ago, I wouldn't dare hint at such a thing. . . . I had taken up my binoculars while we talked, and was looking at the shore, sweeping the limit of the forest at each side and at the back of the house. The consciousness of there being people in that bush, so silent, so quiet—as silent and quiet as the ruined house on the hill—made me uneasy. There was no sign on the face of nature of this amazing tale that was not so much told as suggested to me in desolate exclamations, completed by shrugs, in interrupted phrases, in hints ending in deep sighs. The woods were unmoved, like a mask—heavy, like the closed door of a prison—they looked with their air of hidden knowledge, of patient expectation, of unapproachable silence. The Russian was explaining to me that it was only lately that Mr. Kurtz had come down to the river, bringing along with him all the fighting men of that lake tribe. He had been absent for several months—getting himself adored, I suppose—and had come down unexpectedly, with the intention to all appearance of making a raid either across the river or down stream. Evidently the appetite for more ivory had got the better of the—what shall I say?—less material aspirations. However, he had got much worse suddenly. 'I heard he was lying helpless, and so I came up—took my chance,' said the Russian. 'Oh, he is bad, very bad.' I directed my glass to the house. There were no signs of life, but there was the ruined roof, the long mud wall peeping above the grass, with three little square window-holes, no two of the same size; all this brought within reach of my hand, as it were. And then I made a brusque movement, and one of the remaining posts of that vanished fence leaped up in the field of my glass. You remember I told you I had been struck at the distance by certain attempts at ornamentation, rather remarkable in the ruinous aspect of the place. Now I had suddenly a nearer view, and its first result was to make me throw my head back as if before a blow. Then I went carefully from post to post with my glass, and I saw my mistake. These round knobs were not ornamental but symbolic; they were expressive and puzzling, striking and disturbing—food for thought and also for the vultures if there had been any looking down from the sky; but at all events for such ants as were industrious enough to ascend the pole. They would have been even more impressive, those heads on the stakes, if their faces had not been turned to the house. Only one, the first I had made out, was facing my way. I was not so shocked as you may think. The start back I had given was really nothing but a movement of surprise. I had expected to see a knob of wood there, you know. I returned deliberately to the first I had seen—and there it was, black, dried, sunken, with closed eyelids—a head that seemed to sleep at the top of that pole, and, with the shrunken dry lips showing a narrow white line of the teeth, was smiling too, smiling continuously at some endless and jocose dream of that eternal slumber.

"I am not disclosing any trade secrets. In fact the manager said afterwards that Mr. Kurtz's methods had ruined the district. I have no opinion on that point, but I want you clearly to understand that there was nothing exactly profitable in these heads being there. They only showed that Mr. Kurtz lacked restraint in the gratification of his various lusts, that there was something wanting in him—some small matter which, when the pressing need arose, could not be found under his magnificent eloquence. Whether he knew of this deficiency himself I can't say. I think the knowledge came to him at last—only at the very last. But the wilderness had found him out early, and had taken on him a terrible vengeance for the fantastic invasion. I think it had whispered to him things about himself which he did not know, things of which he had no conception till he took counsel with this great solitude—and the whisper had proved irresistibly fascinating. It echoed loudly within him because he was hollow at the core. . . . I put down the glass, and the head that had appeared near enough to be spoken to seemed at once to have leaped away from me into inaccessible distance.

"The admirer of Mr. Kurtz was a bit crestfallen. In a hurried, indistinct voice he began to assure me he had not dared to take these—say, symbols—down. He was not afraid of the natives; they would not stir till Mr. Kurtz gave the word. His ascendancy was extraordinary. The camps of these people surrounded the place, and the chiefs came every day to see him. They would crawl . . . 'I don't want to know anything of the ceremonies used when approaching Mr. Kurtz,' I shouted. Curious, this feeling that came over me that such details would be more intolerable than those heads drying on the stakes under Mr. Kurtz's windows. After all, that was only a savage sight, while I seemed at one bound to have been transported into some lightless region of subtle horrors, where pure, uncomplicated savagery was a positive relief, being something that had a right to exist—obviously—in the sunshine. The young man looked at me with surprise. I suppose it did not occur to him that Mr. Kurtz was no idol of mine. He forgot I hadn't heard any of these splendid monologues on, what was it? on love, justice, conduct of life—or what not. If it had come to crawling before Mr Kurtz, he crawled as much as the veriest savage of them all. I had no idea of the conditions, he said: these heads were the heads of rebels. I shocked him excessively by laughing. Rebels! What would be the next definition I was to hear? There had been enemies, criminals, workers—and these were rebels. Those rebellious heads looked very subdued to me on their sticks. 'You don't know how such a life tries a man like Kurtz,' cried Kurtz's last disciple. 'Well, and you?' I said. 'I! I! I am a simple man. I have no great thoughts. I want nothing from anybody. How can you compare me to . . . ?' His feelings were too much for speech, and suddenly he broke down. 'I don't understand,' he groaned. 'I've been doing my best to keep him alive, and that's enough. I had no hand in all this. I have no abilities. There hasn't been a drop of medicine or a mouthful of invalid food for months here. He was shamefully abandoned. A man like this, with such ideas. Shamefully! Shamefully! I—I—haven't slept for the last ten nights. . . .'

"His voice lost itself in the calm of the evening. The long shadows of the forest had slipped down hill while we talked, had gone far beyond the ruined hovel, beyond the symbolic row of stakes. All this was in the gloom, while we down there were yet in the sunshine, and the stretch of the river abreast of the clearing glittered in a still and dazzling splendour, with a murky and overshadowed bend above and blow. Not a living soul was seen on the shore. The bushes did not rustle.

"Suddenly round the corner of the house a group of men appeared, as though they had come up from the ground. They waded waist-deep in the grass, in a compact body, bearing an improvised stretcher in their midst. Instantly, in the emptiness of the landscape, a cry arose whose shrillness pierced the still air like a sharp arrow flying straight to the very heart of the land; and, as if by enchantment, streams of human beings—of naked human beings—with spears in their hands, with bows, with shields, with wild glances and savage movements, were poured into the clearing by the dark-faced and pensive forest. The bushes shook, the grass swayed for a time, and then everything stood still in attentive immobility.

" 'Now, if he does not say the right thing to them we are all done for,' said the Russian at my elbow. The knot of men with the stretcher had stopped too, half-way to the steamer, as if petrified. I saw the man on the stretcher sit up, lank and with an uplifted arm, above the shoulders of the bearers. 'Let us hope that the man who can talk so well of love in general will find some particular reason to spare us this time,' I said. I resented bitterly the absurd danger of our situation, as if to be at the mercy of that atrocious phantom had been a dishonouring necessity. I could not hear a sound, but through my glasses I saw the thin arm extended commandingly, the lower jaw moving, the eyes of that apparition shining darkly far in its bony head that nodded with grotesque jerks. Kurtz—Kurtz—that means 'short' in German—don't it? Well, the name was as true as everything else in his life—and death. He looked at least seven feet long. His covering had fallen off, and his body emerged from it pitiful and appalling as from a winding-sheet. I could see the cage of his ribs all astir, the bones of his arm waving. It was as though an animated image of death carved out of old ivory had been shaking its hand with menaces at a motionless crowd of men made of dark and glittering bronze. I saw him open his mouth wide—it gave him a weirdly voracious aspect, as though he had wanted to swallow all the air, all the earth, all the men before him. A deep voice reached me faintly. He must have been shouting. He fell back suddenly. The stretcher shook as the bearers staggered forward again, and almost at the same time I noticed that the crowd of savages was vanishing without any perceptible movement of retreat, as if the forest that had ejected these beings so suddenly had drawn them in again as the breath is drawn in a long aspiration.

"Some of the pilgrims behind the stretcher carried his arms—two shot-guns, a heavy rifle, and a light revolver-carbine—the thunderbolts of that pitiful Jupiter. The manager bent over him murmuring as he walked beside his head. They laid him down in one of the little cabins—just a room for a bedplace and a camp-stool or two, you know. We had brought his belated correspondence, and a lot of torn envelopes and open letters littered his bed. His hand roamed feebly amongst these papers. I was struck by the fire of his eyes and the composed languor of his expression. It was not so much the exhaustion of disease. He did not seem in pain. This shadow looked satiated and calm, as though for the moment it had had its fill of all the emotions.

"He rustled one of the letters, and looking straight in my face said, 'I am glad.' Somebody had been writing to him about me. These special recommendations were turning up again. The volume of tone he emitted without effort, almost without the trouble of moving his lips, amazed me. A voice! A voice! It was grave, profound, vibrating, while the man did not seem capable of a whisper. However, he had enough strength in him—factitious no doubt—to very nearly make an end of us, as you shall hear directly.

"The manager appeared silently in the doorway; I stepped out at once and he drew the curtain after me. The Russian, eyed curiously by the pilgrims, was staring at the shore. I followed the direction of his glance.

"Dark human shapes could be made out in the distance, flitting indistinctly again the gloomy border of the forest, and near the river two bronze figures, leaning on tall spears, stood in the sunlight under fantastic head-dresses of spotted skins, warlike and still in statuesque repose. And from right to left along the lighted shore moved a wild and gorgeous apparition of a woman.

"She walked with measured steps, draped in striped and fringed cloths, treading the earth proudly, with a slight jingle and flash of barbarous ornaments. She carried her head high; her hair was done in the shape of a helmet; she had brass leggings to the knee, brass wire gauntlets to the elbow, a crimson spot on her tawny cheek, innumerable necklaces of glass beads on her neck; bizarre things, charms, gifts of witch-men, that hung about her, glittered and trembled at every step. She must have had the value of several elephant tusks upon her. She was savage and superb, wild-eyed and magnificent; there was something ominous and stately in her deliberate progress. And in the hush that had fallen suddenly upon the whole sorrowful land, the immense wilderness, the colossal body of the fecund and mysterious life seemed to look at her, pensive, as though it had been looking at the image of its own tenebrous and passionate soul.

"She came abreast of the steamer, stood still, and faced us. Her long shadow fell to the water's edge. Her face had a tragic and fierce aspect of wild sorrow and of dumb pain mingled with the fear of some struggling, half-shaped resolve. She stood looking at us without a stir, and like the wilderness itself, with an air of brooding over an inscrutable purpose. A whole minute passed, and then she made a step forward. There was a low jingle, a glint of yellow metal, a sway of fringed draperies, and she stopped as if her heart had failed her. The young fellow by my side growled. The pilgrims murmured at my back. She looked at us all as if her life had depended upon the unswerving steadiness of her glance. Suddenly she opened her bared arms and threw them up rigid above her head, as though in an uncontrollable desire to touch the sky, and at the same time the swift shadows darted out on the earth, swept around on the river, gathering the steamer into a shadowy embrace. A formidable silence hung over the scene.

"She turned away slowly, walked on, following the bank, and passed into the bushes to the left. Once only her eyes gleamed back at us in the dusk of the thickets before she disappeared.

" 'If she had offered to come aboard I really think I would have tried to shoot her,' said the man of patches nervously. 'I had been risking my life every day for the last fortnight to keep her out of the house. She got in one day and kicked up a row about those miserable rags I picked up in the storeroom to mend my clothes with. I wasn't decent. At least it must have been that, for she talked like a fury to Kurtz for an hour, pointing at me now and then. I don't understand the dialect of this tribe. Luckily for me, I fancy Kurtz felt too ill that day to care, or there would have been mischief. I don't understand. . . . No—it's too much for me. Ah, well, it's all over now.'

"At this moment I heard Kurtz's deep voice behind the curtain: 'Save me!—save the ivory, you mean. Don't tell me. Save *me!* Why, I've had to save you. You are interrupting my plans now. Sick! Sick! Not so sick as you would like to believe. Never mind. I'll carry my ideas out yet—I will return. I'll show you what can be done. You with your little peddling notions—you are interfering with me. I will return. I . . .'

"The manager came out. He did me the honour to take me under the arm and lead me aside. 'He is very low, very low,' he said. He considered it necessary to sigh, but neglected to be consistently sorrowful. 'We have done all we could for him—haven't we? But there is no disguising the fact, Mr. Kurtz has done more harm than good to the Company. He did not see the time was not ripe for vigorous action. Cautiously, cautiously—that's my principle. We must be cautious yet. The district is closed to us for a time. Deplorable! Upon the whole, the trader will suffer. I don't deny there is a remarkable quantity of ivory—mostly fossil. We must save it, at all events—but look how precarious the position is—and why? Because the method is unsound.' 'Do you,' said I, looking at the shore, 'call it "unsound method"?' 'Without doubt,' he exclaimed hotly. 'Don't you?' . . . 'No method at all,' I murmured after a while. 'Exactly,' he exulted. 'I anticipated this. Shows a complete want of judgment. It is my duty to point it out in the proper quarter.' 'Oh,' said I, 'that fellow—what's his name?—the brickmaker, will make a readable report for you.' He appeared confounded for a moment. It seemed to me I had never breathed an atmosphere so vile, and I turned mentally to Kurtz for relief—positively for relief. 'Nevertheless, I think Mr. Kurtz is a remarkable man,' I said with emphasis. He started, dropped on me a cold heavy glance, said very quietly, 'He *was,*' and turned his back on me. My hour of favour was over; I found myself lumped along with Kurtz as a partisan of methods for which the time was not ripe: I was unsound! Ah! but it was something to have at least a choice of nightmares.

"I had turned to the wilderness really, not to Mr. Kurtz, who, I was ready to admit, was as good as buried. And for a moment it seemed to me as if I also were buried in a vast grave full of unspeakable secrets. I felt an intolerable weight oppressing my breast, the smell of the damp earth, the unseen presence of victorious corruption, the darkness of an impenetrable night. . . . The Russian tapped me on the shoulder. I heard him mumbling and stammering something about 'brother seaman—couldn't conceal—knowledge of matters that would affect Mr. Kurtz's reputation.' I waited. For him evidently Mr. Kurtz was not in his grave; I suspect that for him Mr. Kurtz was one of the immortals. 'Well!' said I at last, 'speak out. As it happens, I am Mr. Kurtz's friend—in a way.'

"He stated with a good deal of formality that had we not been 'of the same profession,' he would have kept the matter to himself without regard to consequences. He suspected 'there was an active ill-will towards him on the part of these white men that—' 'You are right,' I said, remembering a certain conversation I had overheard. 'The manager thinks you ought to be hanged.' He showed a concern at this intelligence which amused me at first. 'I had better get out of the way quietly,' he said earnestly. 'I can do no more for Kurtz now, and they would soon find some excuse. What's to stop them? There's a military post three hundred miles from here.' 'Well, upon my word,' said I, 'perhaps you had better go if you have any friends amongst the savages near by.' 'Plenty,' he said. 'They are simple people—and I want nothing, you know.' He stood biting his lip, then: 'I don't want any harm to happen to these whites here, but of course I was thinking of Mr. Kurtz's reputation—but you are a brother seaman and—' 'All right,' said I, after a time. 'Mr. Kurtz's reputation is safe with me.' I did not know how truly I spoke.

"He informed me, lowering his voice, that it was Kurtz who had ordered the attack to be made on the steamer. 'He hated sometimes the idea of being taken away—and then again . . . But I don't understand these matters. I am a simple man. He thought it would scare you away—that you would give it up, thinking him dead. I could not stop him. Oh, I had an awful time of it this last month.' 'Very well,' I said. 'He is all right now.' 'Ye-e-es,' he muttered, not very convinced apparently. 'Thanks,' said I; 'I shall keep my eyes open.' 'But quiet—eh?' he urged anxiously. 'It would be awful for his reputation if anybody here—' I promised a complete discretion with great gravity. 'I have a canoe and three black fellows waiting not very far. I am off.

Could you give me a few Martini-Henry cartridges?' I could, and did, with proper secrecy. He helped himself, with a wink at me, to a handful of my tobacco. 'Between sailors—you know—good English tobacco.' At the door of the pilot-house he turned round—'I say, haven't you a pair of shoes you could spare?' He raised one leg. 'Look.' The soles were tied with knotted strings sandal-wise under his bare feet. I rooted out an old pair, at which he looked with admiration before tucking it under his left arm. One of his pockets (bright red) was bulging with cartridges, from the other (dark blue) peeped 'Towson's Inquiry,' etc. etc. He seemed to think himself excellently well equipped for a renewed encounter with the wilderness. 'Ah! I'll never, never meet such a man again. You ought to have heard him recite poetry—his own too it was, he told me. Poetry!' He rolled his eyes at the recollection of these delights. 'Oh, he enlarged my mind!' 'Good-bye,' said I. He shook hands and vanished in the night. Sometimes I ask myself whether I had ever really seen him—whether it was possible to meet such a phenomenon! . . .

"When I woke up shortly after midnight his warning came to my mind with its hint of danger that seemed, in the starred darkness, real enough to make me get up for the purpose of having a look around. On the hill a big fire burned, illuminating fitfully a crooked corner of the station-house. One of the agents with a picket of a few of our blacks, armed for the pupose, was keeping guard over the ivory; but deep within the forest, red gleams that wavered, that seemed to sink and rise from the ground amongst confused columnar shapes of intense blackness, showed the exact position of the camp where Mr. Kurtz's adorers were keeping their uneasy vigil. The monotonous beating of a big drum filled the air with muffled shocks and a lingering vibration. A steady droning sound of many men chanting each to himself some weird incantation came out from the black, flat wall of the woods as the humming of bees comes out of a hive, and had a strange narcotic effect upon my half-awake senses. I believe I dozed off leaning over the rail, till an abrupt burst of yells, an overwhelming outbreak of a pent-up and mysterious frenzy, woke me up in a bewildered wonder. It was cut short all at once, and the low droning went on with an effect of audible and soothing silence. I glanced casually into the little cabin. A light was burning within, but Mr. Kurtz was not there.

"I think I would have raised an outcry if I had believed my eyes. But I didn't believe them at first—the thing seemed so impossible. The fact is I was completely unnerved by a sheer blank fright, pure abstract terror, unconnected with any distinct shape of physical danger. What made this emotion so overpowering was—how shall I define it?—the moral shock I received, as if something altogether monstrous, intolerable to thought and odious to the soul, had been thrust upon me unexpectedly. This lasted of course the merest fraction of a second, and then the usual sense of commonplace, deadly danger, the possibility of a sudden onslaught and massacre, or something of the kind, which I saw impending, was positively welcome and composing. It pacified me, in fact, so much, that I did not raise an alarm.

"There was an agent buttoned up inside an ulster and sleeping on a chair on deck within three feet of me. The yells had not awakened him; he snored very slightly; I left him to his slumbers and leaped ashore. I did not betray Mr. Kurtz—it was ordered I should never betray him—it was written I should be loyal to the nightmare of my choice. I was anxious to deal with this shadow by myself alone—and to this day I don't know why I was so jealous of sharing with any one the peculiar blackness of that experience.

"As soon as I got on the bank I saw a trail—a broad trail through the grass. I remember the exultation with which I said to myself, 'He can't walk—he is crawling on all-fours—I've got him.' The grass was wet with dew. I strode rapidly with clenched fists. I fancy I had some vague notion of falling upon him and giving him a drubbing. I don't know. I had some imbecile thoughts. The knitting old woman with the cat obtruded herself upon my memory as a most improper person to be sitting at the other end of such an affair. I saw a row of pilgrims squirting lead in the air out of Winchesters held to the hip. I thought I would never get back to the steamer, and imagined myself living alone and unarmed in the woods to an advanced age. Such silly things—you know. And I remember I confounded the beat of the drum with the beating of my heart, and was pleased at its calm regularity.

"I kept to the track though—then stopped to listen. The night was very clear; a dark blue space, sparkling with dew and starlight, in which black things stood very still. I thought I could see a kind of motion ahead of me. I was strangely cocksure of everything that night. I actually left the track and ran in a wide semicircle (I verily believe chuckling to myself) so as to get in front of that stir, of that motion I had seen—if indeed I had seen anything. I was circumventing Kurtz as though it had been a boyish game.

"I came upon him, and, if he had not heard me coming, I would have fallen over him too, but he got up in time. He rose, unsteady, long, pale, indistinct, like a vapour exhaled by the earth, and swayed slightly, misty and silent before me; while at my back the fires loomed between the trees, and the murmur of many voices issued from the forest. I had cut him off cleverly; but when actually confronting him I seemed to come to my senses, I saw the danger in its right proportion. It was by no means over yet. Suppose he began to shout? Though he could hardly stand, there was still plenty of vigour in his voice. 'Go away—hide yourself,' he said, in that profound tone. It was very awful. I glanced back. We were within thirty yards of the nearest fire. A black figure stood up, strode on long black legs, waving long black arms, across the glow. It had horns—antelope horns, I think—on its head. Some sorcerer, some witch-man no doubt: it looked fiend-like enough. 'Do you know what you are doing?' I whispered. 'Perfectly,' he answered, raising his voice for that single word: it sounded to me far off and yet loud, like a hail through a speaking-trumpet. If he makes a row we are lost, I thought to myself. This clearly was not a case for fisticuffs, even apart from the very natural aversion I had to beat that Shadow—this wandering and tormented thing. 'You will be lost,' I said—'utterly lost.' One gets sometimes such a flash of inspiration, you know. I did say the right thing, though indeed he could not have been more irretrievably lost than he was at this very moment, when the foundations of our intimacy were being laid—to endure—to endure—even to the end—even beyond.

" 'I had immense plans,' he muttered irresolutely. 'Yes,' said I; 'but if you try to shout I'll smash your head with—' There was not a stick or a stone near. 'I will throttle you for good,' I corrected myself. 'I was on the threshold of great things,' he pleaded, in a voice of longing, with a wistfulness of tone that made my blood run cold. 'And now for this stupid scoundrel—' 'Your success in Europe is assured in any case,' I affirmed steadily. I did not want to have the throttling of him, you understand—and indeed it would have been very little use for any practical purpose. I tried to break the spell—the heavy, mute spell of the wilderness—that seemed to draw him to its pitiless breast by the awakening of forgotten and brutal instincts, by the memory of gratified and monstrous passions. This alone, I was convinced, had driven him out of the edge of the forest, to the bush, towards the gleam of fires, the throb of drums, the drone of weird incantations; this alone had beguiled his unlawful soul beyond the bounds of permitted aspirations. And, don't you see, the terror of the position was not in being knocked on the head—though I had a very lively sense of that danger too—but in this, that I had to deal with a being to whom I could not appeal in the name of anything high or low. I had, even like the niggers, to invoke him—himself—his own exalted and incredible degradation. There was nothing either above or below him, and I knew it. He had kicked himself loose of the earth. Confound the man! he had kicked the very earth to pieces. He was alone, and I before him did not know whether I stood on the ground or floated in the air. I've been telling you what we said—repeating the phrases we pronounced—but what's the good? They were common everyday words—the familiar, vague sounds exchanged on every waking day of life. But what of that? They had behind them, to my mind, the terrific suggestiveness of words heard in dreams, of phrases spoken in nightmares. Soul! If anybody had ever struggled with a soul, I am the man. And I wasn't arguing with a lunatic either. Believe me or not, his intelligence was perfectly clear—concentrated, it is true, upon himself with horrible intensity, yet clear; and therein was my only chance—barring, of course, the killing him there and then, which wasn't so good, on account of unavoidable noise. But his soul was mad. Being alone in the wilderness, it had looked within itself, and, by heavens! I tell you, it had gone mad. I had—for my sins, I suppose, to go through the ordeal of looking into it myself. No eloquence could have been so withering to one's belief in mankind as his final burst of sincerity. He struggled with himself too. I saw it—I heard it. I saw the inconceivable mystery of a soul that knew no restraint, no faith, and no fear, yet struggling blindly with itself. I kept my head pretty well; but when I had him at last stretched on the couch, I wiped my forehead, while my legs shook under me as though I had carried half a ton on my back down that hill. And yet I had only supported him, his bony arm clasped round my neck—and he was not much heavier than a child.

"When next day we left at noon, the crowd, of whose presence behind the curtain of trees I had been acutely conscious all the time, flowed out of the woods again, filled the clearing, covered the slope with a mass of naked, breathing, quivering, bronze bodies. I steamed up a bit, then swung down-stream, and two thousand eyes followed the evolutions of the splashing, thumping, fierce river-demon beating the water with its terrible tail and breathing black smoke into the air. In front of the first rank, along the river, three men, plastered with bright red earth from head to foot, strutted to and fro restlessly. When we came abreast again, they faced the river, stamped their feet, nodded their horned heads, swayed their scarlet bodies; they shook towards the fierce river-demon a bunch of black feathers, a mangy skin with a pendent tail—something that looked like a dried gourd; they shouted periodically together strings of amazing words that resembled no sounds of human language; and the deep murmurs of the crowd, interrupted suddenly, were like the responses of some satanic litany.

"We had carried Kurtz into the pilot-house: there was more air there. Lying on the couch, he stared through the open shutter. There was an eddy in the mass of human bodies, and the woman with helmeted head and tawny cheeks rushed out to the very brink of the stream. She put out her hands, shouted something, and all that wild mob took up the shout in a roaring chorus of articulated, rapid, breathless utterance.

" 'Do you understand this?' I asked.

"He kept on looking out past me with fiery, longing eyes, with a mingled expression of wistfulness and hate. He made no answer, but I saw a smile, a smile of indefinable meaning, appear on his colourless lips that a moment after twitched convulsively. 'Do I not?' he said slowly, grasping, as if the words had been torn out of him by a supernatural power.

"I pulled the string of the whistle, and I did this because I saw the pilgrims on deck getting out their rifles with an air of anticipating a jolly lark. At the sudden screech there was a movement of abject terror through that wedged mass of bodies. 'Don't! don't you frighten them away,' cried some one on deck disconsolately. I pulled the string time after time. They broke and ran, they leaped, they crouched, they swerved, they dodged the flying terror of the sound. The three red chaps had fallen flat, face down on the shore, as though they had been shot dead. Only the barbarous and superb woman did not so much as flinch, and stretched tragically her bare arms after us over the sombre and glittering river.

"And then that imbecile crowd down on the deck started their little fun, and I could see nothing more for smoke.

"The brown current ran swiftly out of the heart of darkness, bearing us down towards the sea with twice the speed of our upward progress; and Kurtz's life was running swiftly too, ebbing, ebbing out of his heart into the sea of inexorable time. The manager was very placid, he had no vital anxieties now, he took us both in with a comprehensive and satisfied glance: the 'affair' had come off as well as could be wished. I saw the time approaching when I would be left alone of the party of 'unsound method.' The pilgrims looked upon me with disfavour. I was, so to speak, numbered with the dead. It is strange how I accepted this unforeseen partnership, this choice of nightmares forced upon me in the tenebrous land invaded by these mean and greedy phantoms.

"Kurtz discoursed. A voice! a voice! It rang deep to the very last. It survived his strength to hide in the magnificent folds of eloquence the barren darkness of his heart. Oh, he struggled! he struggled! The wastes of his weary brain were haunted by shadowy images now—images of wealth and fame revolving obsequiously round his unextinguishable gift of noble and lofty expression. My Intended, my station, my career, my ideas—these were the subjects for the occasional utterances of elevated sentiments. The shade of the original Kurtz frequented the bedside of the hollow sham, whose fate it was to be buried presently in the mould of primeval earth. But both the diabolic love and the unearthly hate of the mysteries it had penetrated fought for the possession of that soul satiated with primitive emotions, avid of lying fame, of sham distinction, of all the appearances of success and power.

"Sometimes he was contemptibly childish. He desired to have kings meet him at railway stations on his return from some ghastly Nowhere, where he intended to accomplish great things. 'You show them you have in you something that is really profitable, and then there will be no limits to the recognition of your ability,' he would say. 'Of course you must take care of the motives—right motives—always.' The long reaches that were like one and the same reach, monotonous bends that were exactly alike, slipped past the steamer with their multitude of secular trees looking patiently after this grimy fragment of another world, the forerunner of change, of conquest, of trade, of massacres, of blessings. I looked ahead—piloting. 'Close the shutter,' said Kurtz suddenly one day; 'I can't bear to look at this.' I did so. There was a silence. 'Oh, but I will wring your heart yet!' he cried at the invisible wilderness.

"We broke down—as I had expected—and had to lie up for repairs at the head of an island. This delay was the first thing that shook Kurtz's confidence. One morning he gave me a packet of papers and a photograph—the lot tied together with a shoe-string. 'Keep this for me,' he said. 'This noxious fool' (meaning the manager) 'is capable of prying into my boxes when I am not looking.' In the afternoon I saw him. He was lying on his back with closed eyes, and I withdrew quietly, but I heard him mutter, 'Live rightly, die, die . . .' I listened. There was nothing more. Was he rehearsing some speech in his sleep, or was it a fragment of a phrase from some newspaper article? He had been writing for the papers and meant to do so again, 'for the furthering of my ideas. It's a duty.'

"His was an impenetrable darkness. I looked at him as you peer down at a man who is lying at the bottom of a precipice where the sun never shines. But I had not much time to give him, because I was helping the engine-driver to take to pieces the leaky cylinders, to straighten a bent connecting-rod, and in other such matters. I lived in an infernal mess of rust, filings, nuts, bolts, spanners, hammers, ratchet-drills—things I abominate, because I don't get on with them. I tended the little forge we fortunately had aboard; I toiled wearily in a wretched scrap-heap—unless I had the shakes too bad to stand.

"One evening coming in with a candle I was startled to hear him say a little tremulously, "I am lying here in the dark waiting for death.' The light was within a foot of his eyes. I forced myself to murmur, 'Oh, nonsense!' and stood over him as if transfixed.

"Anything approaching the change that came over his features I have never seen before, and hope never to see again. Oh, I wasn't touched. I was fascinated. It was as though a veil had been rent. I saw on that ivory face the expression of sombre pride, of ruthless power, of craven terror—of an intense and hopeless despair. Did he live his life again in every detail of desire, temptation, and surrender during that supreme moment of complete knowledge? He cried in a whisper at some image, at some vision—he cried out twice, a cry that was no more than a breath:

" 'The horror! The horror!'

"I blew the candle out and left the cabin. The pilgrims were dining in the mess-room, and I took my place opposite the manager, who lifted his eyes to give me a questioning glance, which I successfully ignored. He leaned back, serene, with that peculiar smile of his sealing the unexpressed depths of his meanness. A continuous shower of small flies streamed upon the lamp, upon the cloth, upon our hands and faces. Suddenly the manager's boy put his insolent black head in the doorway, and said in a tone of scathing contempt:

" 'Mistah Kurtz—he dead.'

"All the pilgrims rushed out to see. I remained, and went on with my dinner. I believe I was considered brutally callous. However, I did not eat much. There was a lamp in there—light, don't you know—and outside it was so beastly, beastly dark. I went no more near the remarkable man who had pronounced a judgment upon the adventures of his soul on this earth. The voice was gone. What else had been there? But I am of course aware that next day the pilgrims buried something in a muddy hole.

"And then they very nearly buried me.

"However, as you see, I did not go to join Kurtz there and then. I did not. I remained to dream the nightmare out to the end, and to show my loyalty to Kurtz once more. Destiny. My destiny! Droll thing life is—that mysterious arrangement of merciless logic for a futile purpose. The most you can hope from it is some knowledge of yourself—that comes too late—a crop of unextinguishable regrets. I have wrestled with death. It is the most unexciting contest you can imagine. It takes place in an impalpable greyness, with nothing underfoot, with nothing around, without spectators, without clamour, without glory, without the great desire of victory, without the great fear of defeat, in a sickly atmosphere of tepid scepticism, without much belief in your own right, and still less in that of your adversary. If such is the form of ultimate wisdom, then life is a greater riddle than some of us think it to be. I was within a hair's-breadth of the last opportunity for pronouncement, and I found with humiliation that probably I would have nothing to say. This is the reason why I affirm that Kurtz was a remarkable man. He had something to say. He said it. Since I had peeped over the edge myself, I understand better the meaning of his stare, that could not see the flame of the candle, but was wide enough to embrace the whole universe, piercing enough to penetrate all the hearts that beat in the darkness. He had summed up—he had judged. 'The horror!' He was a remarkable man. After all, this was the expression of some sort of belief; it had candour, it had conviction, it had a vibrating note of revolt in its whisper, it had the appalling face of a glimpsed truth—the strange commingling of desire and hate. And it is not my own extremity I remember best—a vision of greyness without form filled with physical pain, and a careless contempt for the evanescence of all things—even of this pain itself. No! It is his extremity that I seem to have lived through. True, he had made that last stride, he had stepped over the edge, while I had been permitted to draw back my hesitating foot. And perhaps in this is the whole difference; perhaps all the wisdom, and all truth, and all sincerity, are just compressed into that inappreciable moment of time in which we step over the threshold of the invisible. Perhaps! I like to think my summing-up would not have been a word of careless contempt. Better his cry—much better. It was an affirmation, a moral victory paid for by innumerable defeats, by abominable terrors, by abominable satisfactions. But it was a victory! That is why I have remained loyal to Kurtz to the last, and even beyond, when a long time after I heard once more, not his own voice, but the echo of his magnificent eloquence thrown to me from a soul as translucently pure as a cliff of crystal.

"No, they did not bury me, though there is a period of time which I remember mistily, with a shuddering wonder, like a passage through some inconceivable world that had no hope in it and no desire. I found myself back in the sepulchral city resenting the sight of people hurrying through the streets to filch a little money from each other, to devour their infamous cookery, to gulp their unwholesome beer, to dream their insignificant and silly dreams. They trespassed upon my thoughts. They were intruders whose knowledge of life was to me an irritating pretence, because I felt so sure they could not possibly know the things I knew. Their bearing, which was simply the bearing of commonplace individuals going about their business in the assurance of perfect safety, was offensive to me like the outrageous flauntings of folly in the face of a danger it is unable to comprehend. I had no particular desire to enlighten them, but I had some difficulty in restraining myself from laughing in their faces, so full of stupid importance. I daresay I was not very well at that time. I tottered about the streets—there were various affairs to settle—grinning bitterly at perfectly respectable persons. I admit my behaviour was inexcusable, but then my temperature was seldom normal in these days. My dear aunt's endeavours to 'nurse up my strength' seemed altogether beside the mark. It was not my strength that wanted nursing, it was my imagination that wanted soothing. I kept the bundle of papers given me by Kurtz, not knowing exactly what to do with it. His mother had died lately, watched over, as I was told, by his Intended. A clean-shaved man, with an official manner and wearing gold-rimmed spectacles, called on me one day and made inquiries, at first circuitous, afterwards suavely pressing, about what he was pleased to denominate certain 'documents.' I was not surprised, because I had had two rows with the manager on the subject out there. I had refused to give up the smallest scrap out of that package, and I took the same attitude with the spectacled man. He became darkly menacing at last, and with much heat argued that the Company had the right to every bit of information about its 'territories.' And, said he, 'Mr. Kurtz's knowledge of unexplored regions must have been necessarily extensive and peculiar—owing to his great abilities and to the deplorable circumstances in which he had been placed: therefore—' I assured him Mr. Kurtz's knowledge, however extensive, did not bear upon the problems of commerce or administration. He invoked then the name of science. 'It would be an incalculable loss if,' etc. etc. I offered him the report on the 'Suppression of Savage Customs,' with the postscriptum torn off. He took it up eagerly, but ended by sniffing at it with an air of contempt. 'This is not what we had a right to expect,' he remarked. 'Expect nothing else,' I said. 'There are only private letters.' He withdrew upon some threat of legal proceedings, and I saw him no more; but another fellow, calling himself Kurtz's cousin, appeared two days later, and was anxious to hear all the details about his dear relative's last moments. Incidentally he gave me to understand that Kurtz had been essentially a great musician. 'There was the making of an immense success,' said the man, who was an organist, I believe, with lank grey hair flowing over a greasy coat-collar. I had no reason to doubt his statement; and to this day I am unable to say what was Kurtz's profession, whether he ever had any—which was the greatest of his talents. I had taken him for a painter who wrote for the papers, or else for a journalist who could paint—but even the cousin (who took snuff during the interview) could not tell me what he had been—exactly. He was a universal genius—on that point I agreed with the old chap, who thereupon blew his nose noisily into a large cotton handkerchief and withdrew in senile agitation, bearing off some family letters and memoranda without importance. Ultimately a journalist anxious to know something of the fate of his 'dear colleague' turned up. This visitor informed me Kurtz's proper sphere ought to have been politics 'on the popular side.' He had furry straight eyebrows, bristly hair cropped short, an eyeglass on a broad ribbon, and, becoming expansive, confessed his opinion that Kurtz really couldn't write a bit—'but heavens! how that man could talk! He electrified large meetings. He had faith—don't you see?—he had the faith. He could get himself to believe anything—anything. He would have been a splendid leader of an extreme party.' 'What party?' I asked. 'Any party,' answered the other. 'He was an—an—extremist.' Did I not think so? I assented. Did I know, he asked, with a sudden flash of curiosity, 'what it was that had induced him to go out there?' 'Yes,' said I, and forthwith handed him the famous Report for publication, if he thought fit. He glanced through it hurriedly, mumbling all the time, judged 'it would do,' and took himself off with this plunder.

"Thus I was left at last with a slim packet of letters and the girl's portrait. She struck me as beautiful—I mean she had a beautiful expression. I know that the sunlight can be made to lie too, yet one felt that no manipulation of light and pose could have conveyed the delicate shade of truthfulness upon those features. She seemed ready to listen without mental reservation, without suspicion, without a thought for herself. I concluded I would go and give her back her portrait and those letters myself. Curiosity? Yes; and also some other feeling perhaps. All that had been Kurtz's had passed out of my hands: his soul, his body, his station, his plans, his ivory, his career. There remained only his memory and his Intended—and I wanted to give that up too to the past, in a way—to surrender personally all that remained of him with me to that oblivion which is the last word of our common fate. I don't defend myself. I had no clear perception of what it was I really wanted. Perhaps it was an impulse of unconscious loyalty, or the fulfilment of one of those ironic necessities that lurk in the facts of human existence. I don't know. I can't tell. But I went.

"I thought his memory was like the other memories of the dead that accumulate in every man's life—a vague impress on the brain of shadows that had fallen on it in their swift and final passage; but before the high and ponderous door, between the tall houses of a street as still and decorous as a well-kept alley in a cemetery, I had a vision of him on the stretcher, opening his mouth voraciously, as if to devour all the earth with all its mankind. He lived then before me; he lived as much as he had ever lived—a shadow insatiable of splendid appearances, of frightful realities; a shadow darker than the shadow of the night, and draped nobly in the folds of a gorgeous eloquence. The vision seemed to enter the house with me—the stretcher, the phantom-bearers, the wild crowd of obedient worshippers, the gloom of the forests, the glitter of the reach between the murky bends, the beat of the drum, regular and muffled like the beating of a heart—the heart of a conquering darkness. It was a moment of triumph for the wilderness, an invading and vengeful rush which, it seemed to me, I would have to keep back alone for the salvation of another soul. And the memory of what I had heard him say afar there, with the horned shapes stirring at my back, in the glow of fires, within the patient woods, those broken phrases came back to me, were heard again in their ominous and terrifying simplicity. I remembered his abject pleading, his abject threats, the colossal scale of his vile desires, the meanness, the torment, the tempestuous anguish of his soul. And later on I seemed to see his collected languid manner, when he said one day. 'This lot of ivory now is really mine. The Company did not pay for it. I collected it myself at a very great personal risk. I am afraid they will try to claim it as theirs though. H'm. It is a difficult case. What do you think I ought to do—resist? Eh? I want no more than justice.' . . . He wanted no more than justice—no more than justice. I rang the bell before a mahogany door on the first floor, and while I waited he seemed to stare at me out of the glassy panel—stare with that wide and immense stare embracing, condemning, loathing all the universe. I seemed to hear the whispered cry, 'The horror! The horror!'

"The dusk was falling. I had to wait in a lofty drawing-room with three long windows from floor to ceiling that were like three luminous and bedraped columns. The bent gilt legs and backs of the furniture shone in indistinct curves. The tall marble fireplace had a cold and monumental whiteness. A grand piano stood massively in a corner; with dark gleams on the flat surfaces like a sombre and polished sarcophagus. A high door opened—closed. I rose.

"She came forward, all in black, with a pale head, floating towards me in the dusk. She was in mourning. It was more than a year since his death, more than a year since the news came; she seemed as though she would remember and mourn for ever. She took both my hands in hers and murmured, 'I had heard you were coming.' I noticed she was not very young—I mean not girlish. She had a mature capacity for fidelity, for belief, for suffering. The room seemed to have grown darker, as if all the sad light of the cloudy evening had taken refuge on her forehead. This fair hair, this pale visage, this pure brow, seemed surrounded by an ashy halo from which the dark eyes looked out at me. Their glance was guileless, profound, confident, and trustful. She carried her sorrowful head as though she were proud of that sorrow, as though she would say, I—I alone know how to mourn for him as he deserves. But while we were still shaking hands, such a look of awful desolation came upon her face that I perceived she was one of those creatures that are not the playthings of Time. For her he had died only yesterday. And, by Jove! the impression was so powerful that for me too he seemed to have died only yesterday—nay, this very minute. I saw her and him in the same instant of time—his death and her sorrow—I saw her sorrow in the very moment of his death. Do you understand? I saw them together—I heard them together. She had said, with a deep catch of the breath, 'I have survived'; while my strained ears seemed to hear distinctly, mingled with her tone of despairing regret, the summing-up whisper of his eternal condemnation. I asked myself what I was doing there, with a sensation of panic in my heart as though I had blundered into a place of cruel and absurd mysteries not fit for a human being to behold. She motioned me to a chair. We sat down. I laid the packet gently on the little table, and she put her hand over it. . . . 'You knew him well,' she murmured, after a moment of mourning silence.

" 'Intimacy grows quickly out there,' I said. 'I knew him as well as it is possible for one man to know another.'

" 'And you admired him,' she said. 'It was impossible to know him and not to admire him. Was it?'

" 'He was a remarkable man,' I said unsteadily. Then before the appealing fixity of her gaze, that seemed to watch for more words on my lips, I went on, 'It was impossible not to—'

" 'Love him,' she finished eagerly, silencing me into an appalled dumbness. 'How true! how true! But when you think that no one knew him so well as I! I had all his noble confidence. I knew him best.'

" 'You knew him best,' I repeated. And perhaps she did. But with every word spoken the room was growing darker, and only her forehead, smooth and white, remained illumined by the unextinguishable light of belief and love.

" 'You were his friend,' she went on. 'His friend,' she repeated, a little louder. 'You must have been, if he had given you this, and sent you to me. I feel I can speak to you—and oh! I must speak. I want you—you who have heard his last words—to know I have been worthy of him. . . . It is not pride. . . . Yes! I am proud to know I understood him better than any one on earth—he told me so himself. And since his mother died I have had no one—no one—to—to—'

"I listened. The darkness deepened. I was not even sure whether he had given me the right bundle. I rather suspect he wanted me to take care of another batch of his papers which, after his death, I saw the manager examining under the lamp. And the girl talked, easing her pain in the certitude of my sympathy; she talked as thirsty men drink. I had heard that her engagement with Kurtz had been disapproved by her people. He wasn't rich enough or something. And indeed I don't know whether he had not been a pauper all his life. He had given me some reason to infer that it was his impatience of comparative poverty that drove him out there.

" '. . . Who was not his friend who had heard him speak once?' she was saying. 'He drew men towards him by what was best in them.' She looked at me with intensity. 'It is the gift of the great,' she went on, and the sound of her low voice seemed to have the accompaniment of all the other sounds, full of mystery, desolation, and sorrow, I had ever heard—the ripple of the river, the soughing of the trees swayed by the wind, the murmurs of the crowds, the faint ring of incomprehensible words cried from afar, the whisper of a voice speaking from beyond the threshold of an eternal darkness. 'But you have heard him! You know!' she cried.

" 'Yes, I know,' I said with something like despair in my heart, but bowing my head before the faith that was in her, before that great and saving illusion that shone with an unearthly glow in the darkness, in the triumphant darkness from which I could not have defended her—from which I could not even defend myself.

" 'What a loss to me—to us!'—she corrected herself with beautiful generosity; then added in a murmur, 'To the world.' By the last gleams of twilight I could see the glitter of her eyes, full of tears—of tears that would not fall.

" 'I have been very happy—very fortunate—very proud,' she went on. 'Too fortunate. Too happy for a little while. And now I am unhappy for—for life.'

"She stood up; her fair hair seemed to catch all the remaining light in a glimmer of gold. I rose too.

" 'And of all this,' she went on mournfully, 'of all his promise, and of all his greatness, of his generous mind, of his noble heart, nothing remains—nothing but a memory. You and I—'

" 'We shall always remember him,' I said hastily.

" 'No!' she cried. 'It is impossible that all this should be lost—that such a life should be sacrificed to leave nothing—but sorrow. You know what vast plans he had. I knew of them too—I could not perhaps understand—but others knew of them. Something must remain. His words, at least, have not died.'

" 'His words will remain,' I said.

" 'And his example,' she whispered to herself. 'Men looked up to him—his goodness shone in every act. His example—'

" 'True,' I said; 'his example too. Yes, his example. I forgot that.'

" 'But I do not. I cannot—I cannot believe—not yet. I cannot believe that I shall never see him again, that nobody will see him again, never, never, never.'

"She put out her arms as if after a retreating figure, stretching them black and with clasped pale hands across the fading and narrow sheen of the window. Never see him! I saw him clearly enough then. I shall see this eloquent phantom as long as I live, and I shall see her too, a tragic and familiar Shade, resembling in this gesture another one, tragic also, and bedecked with powerless charms, stretching bare brown arms over the glitter of the infernal stream, the stream of darkness. She said suddenly very low, 'He died as he lived.'

" 'His end,' said I, with dull anger stirring in me, 'Was in every way worthy of his life.'

" 'And I was not with him,' she murmured. My anger subsided before a feeling of infinite pity.

" 'Everything that could be done—' I mumbled.

" 'Ah, but I believed in him more than any one on earth—more than his own mother, more than—himself. He needed me! Me! I would have treasured every sigh, every word, every sign, every glance.'

"I felt like a chill grip on my chest. 'Don't,' I said, in a muffled voice.

" 'Forgive me. I—I—have mourned so long in silence—in silence. . . . You were with him—to the last? I think of his loneliness. Nobody near to understand him as I would have understood. Perhaps no one to hear. . . .'

" 'To the very end,' I said shakily. 'I heard his very last words. . . .' I stopped in a fright.

" 'Repeat them,' she murmured in a heart-broken tone. 'I want—I want—something—something—to—to live with.'

"I was on the point of crying at her, 'Don't you hear them?' The dusk was repeating them in a persistent whisper all around us, in a whisper that seemed to swell menacingly like the first whisper of a rising wind. 'The horror! The horror!'

" 'His last word—to live with,' she insisted. 'Don't you understand I loved him—I loved him—I loved him!'

"I pulled myself together and spoke slowly.

" 'The last word he pronounced was—your name.'

"I heard a light sigh and then my heart stood still, stopped dead short by an exulting and terrible cry, by the cry of inconceivable triumph and of unspeakable pain. 'I knew it—I was sure!' . . . She knew. She was sure. I heard her weeping; she had hidden her face in her hands. It seemed to me that the house would collapse before I could escape, that the heavens would fall upon my head. But nothing happened. The heavens do not fall for such a trifle. Would they have fallen, I wonder, if I had rendered Kurtz that justice which was his due? Hadn't he said he wanted only justice? But I couldn't. I could not tell her. It would have been too dark—too dark altogether. . . ."

Marlow ceased, and sat apart, indistinct and silent, in the pose of a meditating Buddha. Nobody moved for a time. "We have lost the first of the ebb," said the Director suddenly. I raised my head. The offing was barred by a black bank of clouds, and the tranquil waterway leading to the uttermost ends of the earth flowed sombre under an overcast sky—seemed to lead into the heart of an immense darkness.

ISAK DINESEN

Karen Christentze Dinesen was born in Denmark in 1885. Her family were Danish landed gentry, whose social position was very similar to that of Conrad's family in Poland. Her father was a military officer who at one time spent two years as a hunter among the Pawnee and Chippewa Indians of Nebraska and Wisconsin. He committed suicide when she was ten years old. As a girl she was educated at home by governesses. In 1904 she went to England to study English at Oxford. Later she studied painting at the Danish Academy of Art and in Paris.

In 1914 she married a cousin, the Swedish Baron Bror von Blixen-Finecke, and went to live with him on their new coffee plantation in Kenya, British East Africa. Seven years later the couple were divorced, but Karen Blixen remained to manage the plantation alone until its failure in 1931. In Kenya, English was the language of daily use. There she began to write fiction in English as well as in her native Danish. After the failure of the farm, which took all her money, she returned to Denmark at the age of forty-six to begin a career as a professional writer.

Continuing to write in English, she perfected her first collection of fiction, Seven Gothic Tales, *in two years. After rejection by a number of publishers in England and America, her manuscript was finally accepted and published in 1934. For the publication of this book she adopted the masculine first name Isak, which has remained part of her writing name. Her volume of African reminiscences,* Out of Africa, *appeared in 1937, and* Winter's Tales *in 1942. She produced other volumes more slowly, working through years of illness and pain until her death in 1962.*

All of Isak Dinesen's volumes of tales contain works of note, but the two mentioned above have remained the best known and most read. Students interested in pursuing her African reminiscences beyond Out of Africa *itself should read* Shadows on the Grass *(1961). For further biographical information and an extraordinarily useful critical commentary on the work of Isak Dinesen, the reader should consult Robert Langbaum's* The Gayety of Vision *(Random House, 1964).*

African Reminiscences

The selections grouped here under the title "African Reminiscences" are taken from two sections of that part of Out of Africa *entitled "From an Immigrant's Notebook."*

I · THE WILD CAME TO THE AID OF THE WILD

My manager during the war had been buying up oxen for the army. He told me that he had then, down in the Masai Reserve, bought from the Masai a number of young oxen, which were offspring of Masai cattle and Buffalo. It is a much debated question whether it is possible to cross domestic animals with the game; many people have tried to create a type of small horse fitted to the country, by breeding from Zebra and horses, though I myself have never seen such cross-breeds. But my Manager assured me that these oxen were really half-Buffalo. They had been, the Masai told him, a much longer time growing up than the ordinary cattle, and the Masai, who were proud of them, were by this time pleased to get rid of them, as they were very wild.

It was found to be hard work to train these oxen for the waggon or plough. One strong young animal amongst them gave my Manager and his Native ox-drivers endless trouble. He stormed against the men, he broke their yokes, he foamed and bellowed; when tied up he shovelled up earth in thick black clouds, he turned up the bloodshot white of his eyes, and blood, the men said, was running from his nose. The man, like the beast, towards the end of their struggle, was dead beat, the sweat streaming down his aching body.

"To break the heart of this ox," my Manager narrated, "I had him thrown in the bullocks' paddock, with his four legs tied hard together, and a rein round his muzzle, and even then, as he was lying dumb on the ground, long scalding jets of steam stood out from his nose and terrible snorts and sighs came from his throat. I was looking forward to seeing him under the yoke for many years to come. I went to bed in my tent and I kept on dreaming of this black ox. I was woken up by a big row, the dogs barking and the Natives shouting and yelling down by the paddock. Two herdboys came into my tent all trembling and told me that they believed a lion had got in amongst the oxen. We ran down to the place and took lamps with us, and I myself brought my rifle. As we came near to the paddock the noise died down a little. In the light of the lamps I saw a speckled thing making off. A leopard had been at the tied-up ox, and had eaten the right hind-leg off him. We would never come to see him in the yoke now.

"Then," said my Manager, "I took my rifle and shot the ox."

The Fireflies

Here in the highlands, when the long rains are over, and in the first week of June nights begin to be cold, we get the fireflies in the woods.

On an evening you will see two or three of them, adventurous lonely stars floating in the clear air, rising and lowering, as if upon waves, or as if curtseying. To that rhythm of their flight they lighten and put out their diminutive lamps. You may catch the insect and make it shine upon the palm of your hand, giving out a strange light, a mysterious message, it turns the flesh pale green in a small circle round it. The next night there are hundreds and hundreds in the woods.

For some reason they keep within a certain height, four or five feet, above the ground. It is impossible then not to imagine that a whole crowd of children of six or seven years, are running through the dark forest carrying candles, little sticks dipped in a magic fire, joyously jumping up and down, and gambolling as they run, and swinging their small pale torches merrily. The woods are filled with a wild frolicsome life, and it is all perfectly silent.

The Roads of Life

When I was a child I was shown a picture,—a kind of moving picture inasmuch as it was created before your eyes and while the artist was telling the story of it. This story was told, every time, in the same words.

In a little round house with a round window and a little triangular garden in front there lived a man.

Not far from the house there was a pond with a lot of fish in it.

One night the man was woken up by a terrible noise, and set out in the dark to find the cause of it. He took the road to the pond.

Here the story-teller began to draw, as upon a map of the movements of an army, a plan of the roads taken by the man.

He first ran to the South. Here he stumbled over a big stone in the middle of the road, and a little farther he fell into a ditch, got up, fell into a ditch, got up, fell into a third ditch, and got out of that.

Then he saw that he had been mistaken, and ran back to the North. But here again the noise seemed to him to come from the South, and he again ran back there. He first stumbled over a big stone in the middle of the road, then a little later he fell into a ditch, got up, fell into another ditch, got up, fell into a third ditch, and got out of that.

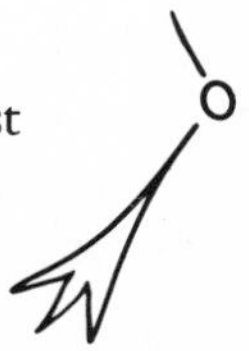

He now distinctly heard that the noise came from the end of the pond. He rushed to the place, and saw that a big leakage had been made in the dam, and the water was running out with all the fishes in it. He set to work and stopped the hole, and only when this had been done did he go back to bed.

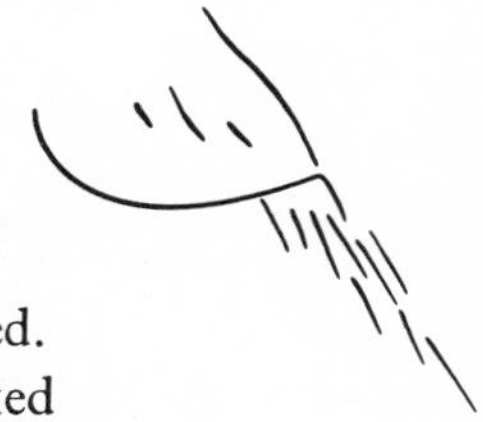

When now the next morning the man looked out of his little round window,—thus the tale was finished, as dramatically as possible, —what did he see?—

A stork!

I am glad that I have been told this story and I will remember it in the hour of need. The man in the story was cruelly deceived, and had obstacles put in his way. He must have thought: "What ups and downs! What a run of bad luck!" He must have wondered what was the idea of all his trials, he could not know that it was a stork. But through them all he kept his purpose in view, nothing made him turn round and go home, he finished his course, he kept his faith. That man had his reward. In the morning he saw the stork. He must have laughed out loud then.

The tight place, the dark pit in which I am now lying, of what bird is it the talon? When the design of my life is completed, shall I, shall other people see a stork?

Infandum, Regina, jubes renovare delorem. Troy in flames, seven years of exile, thirteen good ships lost. What is to come out of it? "Unsurpassed elegance, majestic stateliness, and sweet tenderness."

You are bewildered when you read the second article of faith of the Christian Church: That He was crucified, dead and buried, that He went down into Hell, and also did rise again the third day, that He ascended into Heaven, and from thence shall come again.

What ups and downs, as terrible as those of the man in the story. What is to come of all this?—The second article of the Creed of half the world.

Esa's Story

At the time of the war I had a Cook named Esa, an old man of much sense and a gentle disposition. One day when I was in Mackinnon's grocery shop in Nairobi, buying tea and spices, a small lady with a sharp face came up to me and remarked that she knew Esa was in my service; I said that it was so. "But he has been with me before," said the lady, "and I want him back." I said that I was sorry about that, as she would not get him. "Oh, I do not know about that," she said. "My husband is a Government Official. Will you please tell Esa when you go home, that I want him back, and that if he does not come he will be taken for the Carrier Corps? I understand," she added, "that you have got enough servants without Esa."

I did not tell Esa of these happenings straight away, only the next evening did I remember about them, and told him that I had met his old mistress, and of what she had said to me. To my surprise Esa was immediately beside himself with fear and despair. "Oh, why did you not tell me at once, Memsahib!" said he, "the lady will do what she has told you, and I must leave you to-night." "That is all nonsense," I said. "I do not think that they can take you like that." "God help me," said Esa, "I am afraid it may be too late already." "But what am I to do for a Cook, Esa?" I asked him. "Well," said Esa, "you will not have me for a Cook either when I am with the Carrier Corps, nor when I am lying dead, as I shall surely then be very soon."

So deep was the fear of the Carrier Corps in the people in those days that Esa would not listen to anything I had to say. He asked me for the loan of a hurricane-lamp, and set off in the night to Nairobi, with what belongings he had in the world tied up in a cloth.

Esa was away from the farm for nearly a year. During that time I saw him a couple of times in Nairobi and once I passed him on the Nairobi road. He was growing old and thin, and drawn in the face, in the course of this year, his dark round head was going grey on the top. In the town he would not stop to speak to me, but when we met on the flat road and I pulled up my car, he put down the chicken-coop which he was carrying on his head, and settled down to a talk.

He had, as before, a gentle manner, but all the same he was changed, and it was now difficult to get into contact with him; he remained, all through our conversation, absent-minded, as if at a distance. He had been ill-used by fate, and deadly frightened, and had had to draw upon resources unknown to me, and through these experiences he had become chastened or clarified. It was like talking with an old acquaintance who has entered upon his novitiate in a monastery.

He asked me about things on the farm, taking it, as Native servants usually do, that his fellow-servants in his absence were behaving as badly as possible to the white master.

When will the war be over?" he asked me. I said that I had been told that now it would not last much longer. "If it lasts ten years longer," he said, "you must know that I shall have forgotten to make the dishes you have taught me."

The mind of the little old Kikuyu, upon the road across the plains, was running upon the same line as that of Brillat Savarin, who said that if the Revolution had lasted five years longer, the art of making a chicken-ragout would have been lost.

It was obvious that Esa's regrets were mainly on my behalf, and to put an end to his commiserations I asked him how he was himself. He thought my question over for a minute, there were thoughts which had to be collected from far away before he could answer. "Do you remember, Memsahib?" he said in the end, "that you said it was hard on the oxen of the Indian firewood-contractors to be inspanned every day, and never to have a whole day's rest, as the farm oxen have got? Now, with the lady, I am like an Indian firewood-contractor's ox." Esa looked away when he had spoken, apologetically,—Natives have in themselves very little feeling for animals; my saying about the Indian's oxen probably had struck him as very far-fetched. That now he should, on his own, come back to it for himself, was to him an unaccountable thing.

During the war it was to me a cause of much annoyance that all letters, which I wrote or received, were opened by a little sleepy Swedish Censor in Nairobi. He can never have found anything the least suspicious in them, but he came, I believe, within a monotonous life, to take an interest in the people on whom they turned, and to read my letters as you read a serial in a magazine. I used to add in my own letters a few threats against our Censor, to be carried out after the end of the war, for him to read. When the end of the war came he may have remembered these threats, or he may on his own have woken up and repented; in any case he sent a runner to the farm with news of the Armistice. I was alone in the house when the runner arrived; I walked out in the woods. It was very silent there, and it was strange to think that it was silent on the fronts of France and Flanders as well,—all the guns had been stilled. In this stillness Europe and Africa seemed near to one another, as if you could have walked by the forest-path on to Vimy Ridge. When I came back to the house I saw a figure standing outside. It was Esa with his bundle. He at once told me that he had come back and that he had brought me a present.

Esa's present was a picture, framed and under glass, of a tree, very carefully penned down in ink, every one of its hundred leaves painted a clear green. Upon each leaf, in diminutive Arabic letters, a word was written in red ink. I take it that the writings came out of the Koran, but Esa was incapable of explaining what they meant, he kept on wiping off the glass with his sleeve and assuring me that it was a very good present. He told me that he had had the picture made, during his year of trial, by the old Mohammedan priest of Nairobi, it must have taken the old man hours and hours to print it down.

Esa now stayed with me till he died.

The Iguana

In the Reserve I have sometimes come upon the Iguana, the big lizards, as they were sunning themselves upon a flat stone in a river-bed. They are not pretty in shape, but nothing can be imagined more beautiful than their colouring. They shine like a heap of precious stones or like a pane cut out of an old church window. When, as you approach, they swish away, there is a flash of azure, green and purple over the stones, the colour seems to be standing behind them in the air, like a comet's luminous tail.

Once I shot an Iguana. I thought that I should be able to make some pretty things from his skin. A strange thing happened then, that I have never afterwards forgotten. As I went up to him, where he was lying dead upon his stone, and actually while I was walking the few steps, he faded and grew pale, all colour died out of him as in one long sigh, and by the time that I touched him he was grey and dull like a lump of concrete. It was the live impetuous blood pulsating within the animal, which had radiated out all that glow and splendour. Now that the flame was put out, and the soul had flown, the Iguana was as dead as a sandbag.

Often since I have, in some sort, shot an Iguana, and I have remembered the one of the Reserve. Up at Meru I saw a young Native girl with a bracelet on, a leather strap two inches wide, and embroidered all over with very small turquoise-coloured beads which varied a little in colour and played in green, light blue and ultramarine. It was an extraordinarily live thing; it seemed to draw breath on her arm, so that I wanted it for myself, and made Farah buy it from her. No sooner had it come upon my own arm than it gave up the ghost. It was nothing now, a small, cheap, purchased article of finery. It had been the play of colours, the duet between the turquoise and the "nègre",—that quick, sweet, brownish black, like peat and black pottery, of the Native's skin,—that had created the life of the bracelet.

In the Zoological Museum of Pietermaritzburg, I have seen, in a stuffed deep-water fish in a showcase, the same combination of colouring, which there had survived death; it made me wonder what life can well be like, on the bottom of the sea, to send up something so live and airy. I stood in Meru and looked at my pale hand and at the dead bracelet, it was as if an injustice had been done to a noble thing, as if truth had been suppressed. So sad did it seem that I remembered the saying of the hero in a book that I had read as a child: "I have conquered them all, but I am standing amongst graves."

In a foreign country and with foreign species of life one should take measures to find out whether things will be keeping their value when dead. To the settlers of East Africa I give the advice: "For the sake of your own eyes and heart, shoot not the Iguana."

Farah and the Merchant of Venice

Once a friend at home wrote out to me and described a new staging of "The Merchant of Venice." In the evening as I was reading the letter over again, the play became vivid to me, and seemed to fill the house, so much, that I called in Farah to talk with him about it, and explained the plot of the comedy to him.

Farah, like all people of African blood, liked to hear a story told, but only when he was sure that he and I were alone in the house, did he consent to listen to one. It was therefore when the houseboys were back in their own huts, and any passer-by from the farm, looking in through the windows, would have believed him and me to be discussing household matters, that I narrated, and he listened, standing up immovable at the end of the table, his serious eyes on my face.

Farah gave his full attention to the affairs of Antonio, Bassanio and Shylock. Here was a big, complicated business deal, somewhat on the verge of the law, the real thing to the heart of a Somali. He asked me a question or two as to the clause of the pound of flesh: it obviously seemed to him an eccentric, but not impossible agreement; men might go in for that sort of thing. And here the story began to smell of blood,—his interest in it rose. When Portia came upon the stage, he pricked his ears; I imagined that he saw her as a woman of his own tribe, Fathima with all sails set, crafty and insinuating, out to outman man. Coloured people do not take sides in a tale, the interest to them lies in the ingeniousness of the plot itself; and the Somali, who in real life have a stong sense of values, and a gift for moral indignation, give these a rest in their fiction. Still, here Farah's sympathy was with Shylock, who had come down with the cash; he repugned his defeat.

"What?" said he. "Did the Jew give up his claim? He should not have done that. The flesh was due to him, it was little enough for him to get for all that money."

"But what else could he do," I asked, "when he must not take one drop of blood?"

"Memsahib," said Farah, "he could have used a red-hot knife. That brings out no blood."

"But," I said, "he was not allowed to take either more or less than one pound of flesh."

"And who," said Farah, "would have been frightened by that, exactly a Jew? He might have taken little bits at a time, with a small scale at hand to weight it on, till he had got just one pound. Had the Jew no friends to give him advice?"

All Somalis have in their countenance something exceedingly dramatic. Farah, with the slightest change of mien and carriage, now took on a dangerous aspect, as if he were really in the Court of Venice, putting heart into his friend or partner Shylock, in the face of the crowd of Antonio's friends, and of the Doge of Venice himself. His eyes flickered up and down the figure of the Merchant before him, with the breast bared to the knife.

"Look, Memsahib," he said, "he could have taken small bits, very small. He could have done that man a lot of harm, even a long time before he had got that one pound of his flesh."

I said: "But in the story the Jew gave it up."

"Yes, that was a great pity, Memsahib," said Farah.

The Élite of Bournemouth

I had as neighbor a settler who had been a doctor at home. Once, when the wife of one of my houseboys was about to die in childbirth, and I could not get into Nairobi, because the long rains had ruined the roads, I wrote to my neighbour and asked him to do me the great service to come over and help her. He very kindly came, in the midst of a terrible thunderstorm and torrents of tropical rain, and, at the last moment, by his skill, he saved the life of the woman and the child.

Afterwards he wrote me a letter to say, that although he had for once, on my appeal, treated a Native, I must understand that he could not let that sort of thing occur again. I myself would fully realize the fact, he felt convinced, when he informed me that he had before now practised to the Élite of Bournemouth.

Of Pride

The neighbourhood of the Game Reserve and the presence, outside our boundary, of the big game, gave a particular character to the farm, as if we had been the neighbours of a great king. Very proud things were about, and made their nearness felt.

The barbarian loves his own pride, and hates, or disbelieves in, the pride of others. I will be a civilized being, I will love the pride of my adversaries, of my servants, and my lover; and my house shall be, in all humility, in the wilderness a civilized place.

Pride is faith in the idea that God had, when he made us. A proud man is conscious of the idea, and aspires to realize it. He does not strive towards a happiness, or comfort, which may be irrelevant to God's idea of him. His success is the idea of God, successfully carried through, and he is in love with his destiny. As the good citizen finds his happiness in the fulfilment of his duty to the community, so does the proud man find his happiness in the fulfilment of his fate.

People who have no pride are not aware of any idea of God in the making of them, and sometimes they make you doubt that there has ever been much of an idea, or else it has been lost, and who shall find it again? They have got to accept as success what others warrant to be so, and to take their happiness, and even their own selves, at the quotation of the day. They tremble, with reason, before their fate.

Love the pride of God beyond all things, and the pride of your neighbour as your own. The pride of lions: do not shut them up in Zoos. The pride of your dogs: let them not grow fat. Love the pride of your fellow-partisans, and allow them no self-pity.

Love the pride of the conquered nations, and leave them to honour their father and their mother.

The Oxen

Saturday afternoon was a blessed time on the farm. First of all, there would now be no mail in till Monday afternoon, so that no distressing business letters could reach us till then, and this fact in itself seemed to close the whole place in, as within an enceinte. Secondly, everybody was looking forward to the day of Sunday, when they would rest or play all the day, and the Squatters could work on their own land. The thought of the oxen on Saturday pleased me more than all other things. I used to walk down to their paddock at six o'clock, when they were coming in after the day's work and a few hours' grazing. To-morrow, I thought, they would do nothing but graze all day.

We had one hundred and thirty-two oxen on the farm, which meant eight working teams and a few spare oxen. Now in the golden dust of the sunset they came wandering home across the plain in a long row, walking sedately, as they did all things; while I sat sedately on the fence of the paddock, smoking a cigarette of peace, and watching them. Here came Nyose, Ngufu and Faru, with Msungu,—which means a white man. The drivers also often give to their teams the proper names of white men, and Delamere is a common name in an ox. Here came old Malinda, the big yellow ox that I liked best of the lot; his skin was strangely marked with shadowy figures, like starfishes, from which pattern perhaps he had his name, for Malinda means a skirt.

As in civilized countries all people have a chronic bad conscience towards the slums, and feel uncomfortable when they think of them, so in Africa you have got a bad conscience, and feel a pang, when you think of the oxen. But towards the oxen on the farm, I felt as, I suppose, a king will be feeling towards his slums: "You are I, and I am you."

The oxen in Africa have carried the heavy load of the advance of European civilization. Wherever new land has been broken they have broken it, panting and pulling knee-deep in the soil before the ploughs, the long whips in the air over them. Where a road has been made they have made it; and they have trudged the iron and tools through the land, to the yelling and shouting of the drivers, by tracks in the dust and the long grass of the plains, before there ever were any roads. They have been inspanned before daybreak, and have sweated up and down the long hills, and across dungas and river-beds, through the burning hours of the day. The whips have marked their sides, and you will often see oxen that have had an eye, or both of them, taken away by the long cutting whip-lashes. The waggon-oxen of many Indian and white contractors worked every day, all their lives through, and did not know of the Sabbath.

It is a strange thing that we have done to the oxen. The bull is in a constant stage of fury, rolling his eyes, shovelling up the earth, upset by everything that gets within his range of vision,—still he has got a life of his own, fire comes from his nostrils, and new life from his loins; his days are filled with his vital cravings and satisfactions. All of that we have taken away from the oxen, and in reward we have claimed their existence for ourselves. The oxen walk along within our own daily life, pulling hard all the time, creatures without a life, things made for our use. They have moist, limpid, violet eyes, soft muzzles, silky ears, they are patient and dull in all their ways; sometimes they look as if they were thinking about things.

There was in my time a law against bringing a waggon or cart on the roads without a brake, and the waggon-drivers were supposed to put on the brakes down all the long hills of the country. But the law was not kept; half the waggons and carts on the roads had no brakes to them, and on the others the brakes were but rarely put on. This made downhill work terribly hard on the oxen. They had to hold the loaded waggons up with their bodies, they laid their heads back under the labour until their horns touched the hump on their backs; their sides went like a pair of bellows. I have many times seen the carts of the firewood merchants which came along the Ngong Road, going into Nairobi the one after the other, like a long caterpillar, gain speed down the hill in the Forest Reserve, the oxen violently zig-zagging down in front of them. I have also seen the oxen stumble and fall under the weight of the cart, at the bottom of the hill.

The oxen thought: "Such is life, and the conditions of the world. They are hard, hard. It has all to be borne,—there is nothing for it. It is a terribly difficult thing to get the carts down the hill, it is a matter of life and death. It cannot be helped."

If the fat Indians of Nairobi, who owned the carts, could have brought themselves to pay two Rupees and have the brakes put in order, or if the slow young Native driver on the top of the loaded cart, had had it in him to get off and put on the brake, if it was there, then it could have been helped, and the oxen could have walked quietly down the hill. But the oxen did not know, and went on, day after day, in their heroic and desperate struggle, with the conditions of life.

Of the Two Races

The relation between the white and the black race in Africa in many ways resembles the relation between the two sexes.

If the one of the two sexes were told that they did not play any greater part in the life of the other sex, than this other sex plays within their own existence, they would be shocked and hurt. If the lover or the husband were told that he did not play any greater part in the life of his wife or his mistress, than she played in his own existence, he would be puzzled and indignant. If a wife or a mistress were told that she did not play any greater part in the life of her husband or her lover, than he played in her life, she would be exasperated.

The real old-time mens' story that was never meant to get to the ears of women, goes to prove this theory; and the talk of the women, when they sit amongst themselves and know that no man can hear them, goes to prove it.

The tales that white people tell you of their Native servants are conceived in the same spirit. If they had been told that they played no more important part in the lives of the Natives than the Natives played in their own lives, they would have been highly indignant and ill at ease.

If you had told the Natives that they played no greater part in the life of the white people than the white people played in their lives, they would never have believed you, but would have laughed at you. Probably in Native circles, stories are passing about, and being repeated, which prove the all-absorbing interest of the white people in the Kikuyu or Kavirondo, and their complete dependence upon them.

II · KITOSCH'S STORY

Kitosch's story has been in the papers. A case rose from it, and a jury was set to go through it from beginning to end, searching for enlightenment; some of the enlightenment will still be found in the old documents.

Kitosch was a young Native in the service of a young white settler of Molo. One Wednesday in June, the settler lent his brown mare to a friend, to ride to the station on. He sent Kitosch there to bring back the mare, and told him not to ride her, but to lead her. But Kitosch jumped on to the mare, and rode her back, and on Saturday the settler, his master, was told of the offence by a man who had seen it. In punishment the settler, on Sunday afternoon, had Kitosch flogged, and afterwards tied up in his store, and here late on Sunday night Kitosch died.

Upon the matter the High Court was set in Nakuru, in the Railway Institute, on the 1st of August.

The Natives who gathered and sat round the Railway Institute, will have been wondering what it was all about. To their mind the case was plain, for Kitosch had died, of that there was no doubt, and, according to Native ideas, a compensation for his death should now be made to his people.

But the idea of justice of Europe varies from that of Africa, and, to the jury of white men, the problem of guilt and innocence at once presented itself. The verdict in the case might be one of murder, of manslaughter, or of grievous hurt. The Judge reminded the jury that the degree of an offence rests upon the intentions of the persons concerned, and not upon the results. What, then, had been the intentions, and the attitude of mind, of the persons concerned in the Kitosch case?

To decide upon the intention and attitude of mind of the settler, the court had him cross-examined for many hours a day. They were trying to make up a picture of what had happened, and brought in all the details that they could lay hands on. It is in this way written down that when the settler called Kitosch, he came, and stood three yards away. This insignificant detail in the report is of great effect. Here they are at the opening of the drama, the white and the black man, at three yards' distance.

But from now on, as the story advances, the balance of the picture is broken, and the figure of the settler is blurred and grows smaller. It cannot be helped. It becomes only an accessory figure in a great landscape, a pale puny face, it loses its weight, and looks like a figure cut out in paper, and it is blown about, as by a draught, by the unknown freedom to do what it likes.

The settler stated that he began by asking Kitosch who had given him permission to ride the brown mare, and that he repeated this question forty to fifty times; he admitted at the same time that nobody could possibly have given Kitosch any such permission. Here his perdition begins. In England he would not have been able to ask a question forty to fifty times, he would have been stopped, in one way or the other, long before the fortieth time. Here in Africa were people to whom he could shriek the same question fifty times over. In the end Kitosch answered that he was not a thief, and the settler stated that it was as a result of the insolence of the answer that he had the boy flogged.

At this point the report has got a second irrelevant, and effective, detail. It says that during the flogging, two Europeans, who are designated as friends of the settler, came over to see him. They looked on for ten minutes, or a quarter of an hour, and walked away.

After the flogging the settler could not let Kitosch go.

Late in the evening, he tied Kitosch with a rein, and locked him into his store. When the jury asked him why he did so, he gave an answer that he had no sense, he said that he wanted to keep such a boy from running about on the farm. After supper, he went back to the store, and found Kitosch lying unconscious a little way from where he had tied him up, with the reins loosened. He called in his Baganda cook, and with his assistance tied up the boy tighter than before, with his hands fastened to a post at his back, and with his right leg tied to a post in front. He left the store, locking the door, but half an hour later went back there, got hold of his cook and the kitchen-Toto, and let them into the store. Then he went to bed, and the next thing he remembered, he said, was that the Toto came from the store, and told him that Kitosch had died.

The jury kept in mind the words that the degree of an offence rests upon the intention, and looked for an intention. They went into a number of detailed questions about the flogging of Kitosch, and about what happened after, and as you read the papers you seem to see them shake their heads.

But what now had been the intention and the attitude of mind of Kitosch? This, when gone into, was found to be a different thing. Kitosch had had an intention, and in the end it came to weigh in the scales of the case. It can be said that by his intention, and his attitude of mind, the African, in his grave, saved the European.

Kitosch had not much opportunity for expressing his intention. He was locked up in the store, his message, therefore, comes very simply, and in a single gesture. The night-watch states that he cried all night. But it was not so, for at one o'clock he talked with the Toto, who was in the store with him. He indicated to the child that he must shout to him, because the flogging had made him deaf. But at one o'clock he asked the Toto to loosen his feet, and explained that in any case he could not run away. When the Toto had done as he asked him, Kitosch said to him that he wanted to die. At four, the child said, he again said that he wanted to die. A little while after, he rocked himself from side to side, cried: "I am dead!" and died.

Three doctors gave evidence in the case.

The District Surgeon, who had done the post mortem examination, pronounced death to be due to the injuries and wounds that he had found on the body. He did not believe that any immediate medical attention could have saved Kitosch's life.

The two doctors from Nairobi, called in for the defence, were however, of a different mind.

The flogging in itself, they held, was not sufficient to have caused death. An important factor came into the matter, not to be ignored: that was the will to die. On this point, the first doctor stated, he could speak with authority, for he had been in the country twenty-five years, and knew the Native mind. Many medical men could support him that the wish to die, in a Native, had actually caused death. In the present case the matter was particularly clear for Kitosch had himself said that he wanted to die. The second doctor bore him up in this point of view.

It was very likely, the doctor now went on, that if Kitosch had not taken this attitude, he would not have died. If, for instance, he had eaten something, he might not have lost courage, for starvation is known to reduce courage. He added that the wound on the lip might not be due to a kick, but might be just a bite by the boy himself, in severe pain.

The doctor, furthermore, did not believe that Kitosch would have made up his mind to die till after nine o'clock, as by that time he seemed to have tried to escape. Neither had he died till after nine o'clock. When he had been caught in the attempt to escape, and had been tied up again, the fact of being a prisoner, the doctor said, might have weighed on his mind.

The two doctors from Nairobi summed up their view of the case. The death of Kitosch, they held, was due to the flogging, to starvation, and to the wish to die, the latter being the subject of special emphasis. The wish to die might, they considered, have been caused by the effects of the flogging.

After the doctors' evidence, the case turned upon what was called in Court "The wish-to-die theory." The District Surgeon, who was the only one who had seen Kitosch's body, rejected the theory, and gave examples of cancer patients of his practice who had wished to die, but all the same had not died. These people, however, were found to have been Europeans.

The Jury in the end gave a verdict of: Guilty of grievous hurt. The same verdict was applied to the Natives accused, but it was considered that as they had acted under the orders of their master, a European, it would be an injustice to imprison them. The Judge imposed a sentence of two years R.I. on the settler, and of one day on each of the Natives.

It seems to you, as you read the case through, a strange, a humiliating fact that the Europeans should not, in Africa, have power to throw the African out of existence. The country is his Native land, and whatever you do to him, when he goes he goes by his own free will, and because he does not want to stay. Who is to take the responsibility for what happens in a house? The man who owns it, who has inherited it.

By this strong sense in him of what is right and decorous, the figure of Kitosch, with his firm will to die, although now removed from us by many years, stands out with a beauty of its own. In it is embodied the fugitiveness of the wild things who are, in the hour of need, conscious of a refuge somewhere in existence; who go when they like; of whom we can never get hold.

Sorrow Acre

This story appeared first in Winter's Tales.

The low, undulating Danish landscape was silent and serene, mysteriously wide-awake in the hour before sunrise. There was not a cloud in the pale sky, not a shadow along the dim, pearly fields, hills and woods. The mist was lifting from the valleys and hollows, the air was cool, the grass and the foliage dripping wet with morning-dew. Unwatched by the eyes of man, and undisturbed by his activity, the country breathed a timeless life, to which language was inadequate.

All the same, a human race had lived on this land for a thousand years, had been formed by its soil and weather, and had marked it with its thoughts, so that now no one could tell where the existence of the one ceased and the other began. The thin grey line of a road, winding across the plain and up and down hills, was the fixed materialisation of human longing, and of the human notion that it is better to be in one place than another.

A child of the country would read this open landscape like a book. The irregular mosaic of meadows and cornlands was a picture, in timid green and yellow, of the people's struggle for its daily bread; the centuries had taught it to plough and sow in this way. On a distant hill the immovable wings of a windmill, in a small blue cross against the sky, delineated a later stage in the career of bread. The blurred outline of thatched roofs—a low, brown growth of the earth—where the huts of the village thronged together, told the history, from his cradle to his grave, of the peasant, the creature nearest to the soil and dependent on it, prospering in a fertile year and dying in years of drought and pests.

A little higher up, with the faint horizontal line of the white cemetery-wall round it, and the vertical contour of tall poplars by its side, the red-tiled church bore witness, as far as the eye reached, that this was a Christian country. The child of the land knew it as a strange house, inhabited only for a few hours every seventh day, but with a strong, clear voice in it to give out the joys and sorrows of the land: a plain, square embodiment of the nation's trust in the justice and mercy of heaven. But where, amongst cupular woods and groves, the lordly, pyramidal silhouette of the cut lime avenues rose in the air, there a big country house lay.

The child of the land would read much within these elegant, geometrical ciphers on the hazy blue. They spoke of power, the lime trees paraded round a stronghold. Up here was decided the destiny of the surrounding land and of the men and beasts upon it, and the peasant lifted his eyes to the green pyramids with awe. They spoke of dignity, decorum and taste. Danish soil grew no finer flower than the mansion to which the long avenue led. In its lofty rooms life and death bore themselves with stately grace. The country house did not gaze upward, like the church, nor down to the ground like the huts; it had a wider earthly horizon than they, and was related to much noble architecture all over Europe. Foreign artisans had been called in to panel and stucco it, and its own inhabitants travelled and brought back ideas, fashions and things of beauty. Paintings, tapestries, silver and glass from distant countries had been made to feel at home here and now formed part of Danish country life.

The big house stood as firmly rooted in the soil of Denmark as the peasants' huts, and was as faithfully allied to her four winds and her changing seasons, to her animal life, trees and flowers. Only its interests lay in a higher plane. Within the domain of the lime trees it was no longer cows, goats and pigs on which the minds and the talk ran, but horses and dogs. The wild fauna, the game of the land, that the peasant shook his fist at, when he saw it on his young green rye or in his ripening wheat field, to the residents of the country houses were the main pursuit and the joy of existence.

The writing in the sky solemnly proclaimed continuance, a worldly immortality. The great country houses had held their ground through many generations. The families who lived in them revered the past as they honoured themselves, for the history of Denmark was their own history.

A Rosenkrantz had sat at Rosenholm, a Juel at Hverringe, a Skeel at Gammel-Estrup as long as people remembered. They had seen kings and schools of style succeed one another and, proudly and humbly, had made over their personal existence to that of their land, so that amongst their equals and with the peasants they passed by its name: Rosenholm, Hverringe, Gammel-Estrup. To the King and the country, to his family and to the individual lord of the manor himself it was a matter of minor consequence which particular Rosenkrantz, Juel or Skeel, out of a long row of fathers and sons, at the moment in his person incarnated the fields and woods, the peasants, cattle and game of the estate. Many duties rested on the shoulders of the big landowners—towards God in heaven, towards the King, his neighbour and himself—and they were all harmoniously consolidated into the idea of his duties towards his land. Highest amongst these ranked his obligation to uphold the sacred continuance, and to produce a new Rosenkrantz, Juel or Skeel for the service of Rosenholm, Hverringe and Gammel-Estrup.

Female grace was prized in the manors. Together with good hunting and fine wine it was the flower and emblem of the higher existence led there, and in many ways the families prided themselves more on their daughters than on their sons.

The ladies who promenaded in the lime avenues, or drove through them in heavy coaches with four horses, carried the future of the name in their laps and were, like dignified and debonair caryatides, holding up the houses. They were themselves conscious of their value, kept up their price, and moved in a sphere of pretty worship and self-worship. They might even be thought to add to it, on their own, a graceful, arch, paradoxical haughtiness. For how free were they, how powerful! Their lords might rule the country, and allow themselves many liberties, but when it came to that supreme matter of legitimacy which was the vital principle of their world, the centre of gravity lay with them.

The lime trees were in bloom. But in the early morning only a faint fragrance drifted through the garden, an airy message, an aromatic echo of the dreams during the short summer night.

In a long avenue that led from the house all the way to the end of the garden, where, from a small white pavilion in the classic style, there was a great view over the fields, a young man walked. He was plainly dressed in brown, with pretty linen and lace, bareheaded, with his hair tied by a ribbon. He was dark, a strong and sturdy figure with fine eyes and hands; he limped a little on one leg.

The big house at the top of the avenue, the garden and the fields had been his childhood's paradise. But he had travelled and lived out of Denmark, in Rome and Paris, and he was at present appointed to the Danish Legation to the Court of King George, the brother of the late, unfortunate young Danish Queen. He had not seen his ancestral home for nine years. It made him laugh to find, now, everything so much smaller than he remembered it, and at the same time he was strangely moved by meeting it again. Dead people came towards him and smiled at him; a small boy in a ruff ran past him with his hoop and kite, in passing gave him a clear glance and laughingly asked: "Do you mean to tell me that you are I?" He tried to catch him in the flight, and to answer him: "Yes, I assure you that I am you," but the light figure did not wait for a reply.

The young man, whose name was Adam, stood in a particular relation to the house and the land. For six months he had been heir to it all; nominally he was so even at this moment. It was this circumstance which had brought him from England, and on which his mind was dwelling, as he walked along slowly.

The old lord up at the manor, his father's brother, had had much misfortune in his domestic life. His wife had died young, and two of his children in infancy. The one son then left to him, his cousin's playmate, was a sickly and morose boy. For ten years the father travelled with him from one watering place to another, in Germany and Italy, hardly ever in other company than that of his silent, dying child, sheltering the faint flame of life with both hands, until such time as it could be passed over to a new bearer of the name. At the same time another misfortune had struck him: he fell into disfavour at Court, where till now he had held a fine position. He was about to rehabilitate his family's prestige through the marriage which he had arranged for his son, when before it could take place the bridegroom died, not yet twenty years old.

Adam learned of his cousin's death, and his own changed fortune, in England, through his ambitious and triumphant mother. He sat with her letter in his hand and did not know what to think about it.

If this, he reflected, had happened to him while he was still a boy, in Denmark, it would have meant all the world to him. It would be so now with his friends and schoolfellows, if they were in his place, and they would, at this moment, be congratulating or envying him. But he was neither covetous nor vain by nature; he had faith in his own talents and had been content to know that his success in life depended on his personal ability. His slight infirmity had always set him a little apart from other boys; it had, perhaps, given him a keener sensibility of many things in life, and he did not, now, deem it quite right that the head of the family should limp on one leg. He did not even see his prospects in the same light as his people at home. In England he had met with greater wealth and magnificence than they dreamed of; he had been in love with, and made happy by, an English lady of such rank and fortune that to her, he felt, the finest estate of Denmark would look but like a child's toy farm.

And in England, too, he had come in touch with the great new ideas of the age: of nature, of the right and freedom of man, of justice and beauty. The universe, through them, had become infinitely wider to him; he wanted to find out still more about it and was planning to travel to America, to the new world. For a moment he felt trapped and imprisoned, as if the dead people of his name, from the family vault at home, were stretching out their parched arms for him.

But at the same time he began to dream at night of the old house and garden. He had walked in these avenues in dream, and had smelled the scent of the flowering limes. When at Ranelagh an old gypsy woman looked at his hand and told him that a son of his was to sit in the seat of his fathers, he felt a sudden, deep satisfaction, queer in a young man who till now had never given his sons a thought.

Then, six months later, his mother again wrote to tell him that his uncle had himself married the girl intended for his dead son. The head of the family was still in his best age, not over sixty, and although Adam remembered him as a small, slight man, he was a vigorous person; it was likely that his young wife would bear him sons.

Adam's mother in her disappointment lay the blame on him. If he had returned to Denmark, she told him, his uncle might have come to look upon him as a son, and would not have married; nay, he might have handed the bride over to him. Adam knew better. The family estate, differing from the neighbouring properties, had gone down from father to son ever since a man of their name first sat there. The tradition of direct succession was the pride of the clan and a sacred dogma to his uncle; he would surely call for a son of his own flesh and bone.

But at the news the young man was seized by a strange, deep, aching remorse towards his old home in Denmark. It was as if he had been making light of a friendly and generous gesture, and disloyal to someone unfailingly loyal to him. It would be but just, he thought, if from now the place should disown and forget him. Nostalgia, which before he had never known, caught hold of him; for the first time he walked in the streets and parks of London as a stranger.

He wrote to his uncle and asked if he might come and stay with him, begged leave from the Legation and took ship for Denmark. He had come to the house to make his peace with it; he had slept little in the night, and was up so early and walking in the garden, to explain himself, and to be forgiven.

While he walked, the still garden slowly took up its day's work. A big snail, of the kind that his grandfather had brought back from France, and which he remembered eating in the house as a child, was already, with dignity, dragging a silver train down the avenue. The birds began to sing; in an old tree under which he stopped a number of them were worrying an owl; the rule of the night was over.

He stood at the end of the avenue and saw the sky lightening. An ecstatic clarity filled the world; in half an hour the sun would rise. A rye field here ran along the garden; two roe-deer were moving in it and looked roseate in the dawn. He gazed out over the fields, where as a small boy he had ridden his pony, and towards the wood where he had killed his first stag. He remembered the old servants who had taught him; some of them were now in their graves.

The ties which bound him to this place, he reflected, were of a mystic nature. He might never again come back to it, and it would make no difference. As long as a man of his own blood and name should sit in the house, hunt in the fields and be obeyed by the people in the huts, wherever he travelled on earth, in England or amongst the red Indians of America, he himself would still be safe, would still have a home, and would carry weight in the world.

His eyes rested on the church. In old days, before the time of

Martin Luther, younger sons of great families, he knew, had entered the Church of Rome, and had given up individual wealth and happiness to serve the greater ideals. They, too, had bestowed honour upon their homes and were remembered in its registers. In the solitude of the morning half in jest he let his mind run as it listed; it seemed to him that he might speak to the land as to a person, as to the mother of his race. "Is it only my body that you want," he asked her, "while you reject my imagination, energy and emotions? If the world might be brought to acknowledge that the virtue of our name does not belong to the past only, will it give you no satisfaction?" The landscape was so still that he could not tell whether it answered him yes or no.

After a while he walked on, and came to the new French rose garden laid out for the young mistress of the house. In England he had acquired a freer taste in gardening, and he wondered if he could liberate these blushing captives, and make them thrive outside their cut hedges. Perhaps, he meditated, the elegantly conventional garden would be a floral portrait of his young aunt from Court, whom he had not yet seen.

As once more he came to the pavilion at the end of the avenue his eyes were caught by a bouquet of delicate colours which could not possibly belong to the Danish summer morning. It was in fact his uncle himself, powdered and silk-stockinged, but still in a brocade dressing-gown, and obviously sunk in deep thought. "And what business, or what meditations," Adam asked himself, "drags a connoisseur of the beautiful, but three months married to a wife of seventeen, from his bed into his garden before sunrise?" He walked up to the small, slim, straight figure.

His uncle on his side showed no surprise at seeing him, but then he rarely seemed surprised at anything. He greeted him, with a compliment on his matunality, as kindly as he had done on his arrival last evening. After a moment he looked to the sky, and solemnly proclaimed: "It will be a hot day." Adam, as a child, had often been impressed by the grand, ceremonial manner in which the old lord would state the common happenings of existence; it looked as if nothing had changed here, but all was what it used to be.

The uncle offered the nephew a pinch of snuff. "No, thank you, Uncle," said Adam, "it would ruin my nose to the scent of your garden, which is as fresh as the Garden of Eden, newly created."

"From every tree of which," said his uncle, smiling, "thou, my Adam, mayest freely eat." They slowly walked up the avenue together.

The hidden sun was now already gilding the top of the tallest trees. Adam talked of the beauties of nature, and of the greatness of Nordic scenery, less marked by the hand of man than that of Italy. His uncle took the praise of the landscape as a personal compliment, and congratulated him because he had not, in likeness to many young travellers in foreign countries, learned to despise his native land. No, said Adam, he had lately in England longed for the fields and woods of his Danish home. And he had there become acquainted with a new piece of Danish poetry which had enchanted him more than any English or French work. He named the author, Johannes Ewald, and quoted a few of the mighty, turbulent verses.

"And I have wondered, while I read," he went on after a pause, still moved by the lines he himself had declaimed, "that we have not till now undrstood how much our Nordic mythology in moral greatness surpasses that of Greece and Rome. If it had not been for the physical beauty of the ancient gods, which has come down to us in marble, no modern mind could hold them worthy of worship. They were mean, capricious and treacherous. The gods of our Danish forefathers are as much more divine than they as the Druid is nobler than the Augur. For the fair gods of Asgaard did possess the sublime human virtues; they were righteous, trustworthy, benevolent and even, within a barbaric age, chivalrous." His uncle here for the first time appeared to take any real interest in the conversation. He stopped, his majestic nose a little in the air. "Ah, it was easier to them," he said.

"What do you mean, Uncle?" Adam asked. "It was a great deal easier," said his uncle, "to the northern gods than to those of Greece to be, as you will have it; righteous and benevolent. To my mind it even reveals a weakness in the souls of our ancient Danes that they should consent to adore such divinities." "My dear uncle," said Adam, smiling, "I have always felt that you would be familiar with the modes of Olympus. Now please let me share your insight, and tell me why virtue should come easier to our Danish gods than to those of milder climates." "They were not as powerful," said his uncle.

"And does power," Adam again asked, "stand in the way of virtue?" "Nay," said his uncle gravely. "Nay, power is in itself the supreme virtue. But the gods of which you speak were never all-powerful. They had, at all times, by their side those darker powers which they named the Jotuns, and who worked the suffering, the disasters, the ruin of our world. They might safely give themselves up to temperance and kindness. The omnipotent gods," he went on, "have no such facilitation. With their omnipotence they take over the woe of the universe."

They had walked up the avenue till they were in view of the house. The old lord stopped and ran his eyes over it. The stately building was the same as ever; behind the two tall front windows, Adam knew, was now his young aunt's room. His uncle turned and walked back.

"Chivalry," he said, "chivalry, of which you were speaking, is not a virtue of the omnipotent. It must needs imply mighty rival powers for the knight to defy. With a dragon inferior to him in strength, what figure will St. George cut? The knight who finds no superior forces ready to hand must invent them, and combat wind-mills; his knighthood itself stipulates dangers, vileness, darkness on all sides of him. Nay, believe me, my nephew, in spite of his moral worth, your chivalrous Odin of Asgaard as a Regent must take rank below that of Jove who avowed his sovereignty, and accepted the world which he ruled. But you are young," he added, "and the experience of the aged to you will sound pedantic."

He stood immovable for a moment and then with deep gravity proclaimed: "The sun is up."

The sun did indeed rise above the horizon. The wide landscape was suddenly animated by its splendour, and the dewy grass shone in a thousand gleams.

"I have listened to you, Uncle," said Adam, "with great interest. But while we have talked you yourself have seemed to me preoccupied; your eyes have rested on the field outside the garden, as if something of great moment, a matter of life and death, was going on there. Now that the sun is up, I see the mowers in the rye and hear them whetting their sickles. It is, I remember you telling me, the first day of the harvest. That is a great day to a landowner and enough to take his mind away from the gods. It is very fine weather, and I wish you a full barn."

The elder man stood still, his hands on his walking-stick. "There is indeed," he said at last, "something going on in that field, a matter of life and death. Come, let us sit down here, and I will tell you the whole story." They sat down on the seat that ran all along the pavilion, and while he spoke the old lord of the land did not take his eyes off the rye field.

"A week ago, on Thursday night," he said, "someone set fire to my barn at Rødmosegaard—you know the place, close to the moor—and burned it all down. For two or three days we could not lay hands on the offender. Then on Monday morning the keeper at Rødmose, with the wheelwright over there, came up to the house; they dragged with them a boy, Goske Piil, a widow's son, and they made their Bible oath that he had done it; they had themselves seen him sneaking round the barn by nightfall on Thursday. Goske had no good name on the farm; the keeper bore him a grudge upon an old matter of poaching, and the wheelwright did not like him either, for he did, I believe, suspect him with his young wife. The boy, when I talked to him, swore to his innocence, but he could not hold his own against the two old men. So I had him locked up, and meant to send him in to our judge of the district, with a letter.

"The judge is a fool, and would naturally do nothing but what he thought I wished him to do. He might have the boy sent to the convict prison for arson, or put amongst the soldiers as a bad character and a poacher. Or again, if he thought that that was what I wanted, he could let him off.

"I was out riding in the fields, looking at the corn that was soon ripe to be mowed, when a woman, the widow, Goske's mother, was brought up before me, and begged to speak to me. Anne-Marie is her name. You will remember her; she lives in the small house east of the village. She has not got a good name in the place either. They tell as a girl she had a child and did away with it.

"From five days' weeping her voice was so cracked that it was difficult for me to understand what she said. Her son, she told me at last, had indeed been over at Rødmose on Thursday, but for no ill purpose; he had gone to see someone. He was her only son, she called the Lord God to witness on his innocence, and she wrung her hands to me that I should save the boy for her.

"We were in the rye field that you and I are looking at now. That gave me an idea. I said to the widow: 'If in one day, between sunrise and sunset, with your own hands you can mow this field, and it be well done, I will let the case drop and you shall keep your son. But if you cannot do it, he must go, and it is not likely that you will then ever see him again.'

"She stood up then and gazed over the field. She kissed my riding boot in gratitude for the favour shown to her."

The old lord here made a pause, and Adam said: "Her son meant much to her?" "He is her only child," said his uncle. "He means to her her daily bread and support in old age. It may be said that she holds him as dear as her own life. As," he added, "within a higher order of life, a son to his father means the name and the race, and he holds him as dear as life everlasting. Yes, her son means much to her. For the mowing of that field is a day's work to three men, or three days' work to one man. Today, as the sun rose, she set to her task. And down there, by the end of the field, you will see her now, in a blue head-cloth, with the man I have set to follow her and to ascertain that she does the work unassisted, and with two or three friends by her, who are comforting her."

Adam looked down, and did indeed see a woman in a blue head-cloth, and a few other figures in the corn.

They sat for a while in silence. "Do you yourself," Adam then said, "believe the boy to be innocent?" "I cannot tell," said his uncle. "There is no proof. The word of the keeper and the wheelwright stand against the boy's word. If indeed I did believe the one thing or the other, it would be merely a matter of chance, or maybe of sympathy. The boy," he said after a moment, "was my son's playmate, the only other child that I ever knew him to like or to get on with." "Do you," Adam again asked, "hold it possible to her to fulfill your condition?" "Nay, I cannot tell," said the old lord. "To an ordinary person it would not be possible. No ordinary person would ever have taken it on at all. I chose it so. We are not quibbling with the law, Anne-Marie and I."

Adam for a few minutes followed the movement of the small group in the rye. "Will you walk back?" he asked. "No," said his uncle, "I think that I shall stay here till I have seen the end of the thing." "Until sunset?" Adam asked with surprise. "Yes," said the old lord. Adam said: "It will be a long day." "Yes," said his uncle, "a long day. But," he added, as Adam rose to walk away, "if, as you said, you have got that tragedy of which you spoke in your pocket, be as kind as to leave it here, to keep me company." Adam handed him the book.

In the avenue he met two footmen who carried the old lord's morning chocolate down to the pavilion on large silver trays.

As now the sun rose in the sky, and the day grew hot, the lime trees gave forth their exuberance of scent, and the garden was filled with unsurpassed, unbelievable sweetness. Towards the still hour of midday the long avenue reverberated like a soundboard with a low, incessant murmur: the humming of a million bees that clung to the pendulous, thronging clusters of blossoms and were drunk with bliss.

In all the short lifetime of Danish summer there is no richer or more luscious moment than that week wherein the lime trees flower. The heavenly scent goes to the head and to the heart; it seems to unite the fields of Denmark with those of Elysium; it contains both hay, honey and holy incense, and is half fairy-land and half apothecary's locker. The avenue was changed into a mystic edifice, a dryad's cathedral, outward from summit to base lavishly adorned, set with multitudinous ornaments, and golden in the sun. But behind the walls the vaults were benignly cool and sombre, like ambrosial sanctuaries in a dazzling and burning world, and in here the ground was still moist.

Up in the house, behind the silk curtains of the two front windows, the young mistress of the estate from the wide bed stuck her feet into two little high-heeled slippers. Her lace-trimmed nightgown had slid up above her knee and down from the shoulder; her hair, done up in curling-pins for the night, was still frosty with the powder of yesterday, her round face flushed with sleep. She stepped out to the middle of the floor and stood there, looking extremely grave and thoughtful, yet she did not think at all. But through her head a long procession of pictures marched, and she was unconsciously endeavouring to put them in order, as the pictures of her existence had used to be.

She had grown up at Court; it was her world, and there was probably not in the whole country a small creature more exquisitely and innocently drilled to the stately measure of a palace. By favour of the old Dowager Queen she bore her name and that of the King's sister, the Queen of Sweden: Sophie Magdalena. It was with a view to these things that her husband, when he wished to restore his status in high places, had chosen her as a bride, first for his son and then for himself. But her own father, who held an office in the Royal Household and belonged to the new Court aristocracy, in his day had done the same thing the other way round, and had married a country lady, to get a foothold within the old nobility of Denmark. The little girl had her mother's blood in her veins. The country to her had been an immense surprise and delight.

To get into her castle-court she must drive through the farm yard, through the heavy stone gateway in the barn itself, wherein the rolling of her coach for a few seconds re-echoed like thunder. She must drive past the stables and the timber-mare, from which sometimes a miscreant would follow her with sad eyes, and might here startle a long string of squalling geese, or pass the heavy, scowling bull, led on by a ring in his nose and kneading the earth in dumb fury. At first this had been to her, every time, a slight shock and a jest. But after a while all these creatures and things, which belonged to her, seemed to become part of herself. Her mothers, the old Danish country ladies, were robust persons, undismayed by any kind of weather; now she herself had walked in the rain and had laughed and glowed in it like a green tree.

She had taken her great new home in possession at a time when all the world was unfolding, mating and propagating. Flowers, which she had known only in bouquets and festoons, sprung from the earth round her; birds sang in all the trees. The new-born lambs seemed to her daintier than her dolls had been. From her husband's Hanoverian stud, foals were brought to her to give names; she stood and watched as they poked their soft noses into their mothers' bellies to drink. Of this strange process she had till now only vaguely heard. She had happened to witness, from a path in the park, the rearing and screeching stallion on the mare. All this luxuriance, lust and fecundity was displayed before her eyes, as for her pleasure.

And for her own part, in the midst of it, she was given an old husband who treated her with punctilious respect because she was to bear him a son. Such was the compact; she had known of it from the beginning. Her husband, she found, was doing his best to fulfill his part of it, and she herself was loyal by nature and strictly brought up. She would not shirk her obligation. Only she was vaguely aware of a discord or an incompatibility within her majestic existence, which prevented her from being as happy as she had expected to be.

After a time her chagrin took a strange form: as the consciousness of an absence. Someone ought to have been with her who was not. She had no experience in analysing her feelings; there had not been time for that at Court. Now, as she was more often left to herself, she vaguely probed her own mind. She tried to set her father in that void place, her sisters, her music master, an Italian singer whom she had admired; but none of them would fill it for her. At times she felt lighter at heart, and believed the misfortune to have left her. And then again it would happen, if she were alone, or in her husband's company, and even within his embrace, that everything round her would cry out: Where? Where? so that she let her wild eyes run about the room in search for the being who should have been there, and who had not come.

When, six months ago, she was informed that her first young bridegroom had died and that she was to marry his father in his place, she had not been sorry. Her youthful suitor, the one time she had seen him, had appeared to her infantile and insipid; the father would make a statelier consort. Now she had sometimes thought of the dead boy, and wondered whether with him life would have been more joyful. But she soon again dismissed the picture, and that was the sad youth's last recall to the stage of this world.

Upon one wall of her room there hung a long mirror. As she gazed into it new images came along. The day before, driving with her husband, she had seen, at a distance, a party of village girls bathe in the river, and the sun shining on them. All her life she had moved amongst naked marble deities, but it had till now never occurred to her that the people she knew should themselves be naked under their bodices and trains, waistcoats and satin breeches, that indeed she herself felt naked within her clothes. Now, in front of the looking-glass, she tardily untied the ribbons of her nightgown, and let it drop to the floor.

The room was dim behind the drawn curtains. In the mirror her body was silvery like a white rose; only her cheeks and mouth, and the tips of her fingers and breasts had a faint carmine. Her slender torso was formed by the whalebones that had clasped it tightly from her childhood; above the slim, dimpled knee a gentle narrowness marked the place of the garter. Her limbs were rounded as if, at whatever place they might be cut through with a sharp knife, a perfectly circular transverse incision would be obtained. The side and belly were so smooth that her own gaze slipped and glided, and grasped for a hold. She was not altogether like a statue, she found, and lifted her arms above her head. She turned to get a view of her back, the curves below the waistline were still blushing from the pressure of the bed. She called to mind a few tales about nymphs and goddesses, but they all seemed a long way off, so her mind returned to the peasant girls in the river. They were, for a few minutes, idealized into playmates, or sisters even, since they belonged to her as did the meadow and the blue river itself. And within the next moment the sense of forlornness once more came upon her, a *horror vaccui* like a physical pain. Surely, surely someone should have been with her now, her other self, like the image in the glass, but nearer, stronger, alive. There was no one, the universe was empty round her.

A sudden, keen itching under her knee took her out of her reveries, and awoke in her the hunting instincts of her breed. She wetted a finger on her tongue, slowly brought it down and quickly slapped it to the spot. She felt the diminutive, sharp body of the insect against the silky skin, pressed the thumb to it, and triumphantly lifted up the small prisoner between her fingertips. She stood quite still, as if meditating upon the fact that a flea was the only creature risking its life for her smoothness and sweet blood.

Her maid opened the door and came in, loaded with the attire of the day—shift, stays, hoop and petticoats. She remembered that she had a guest in the house, the new nephew arrived from England. Her husband had instructed her to be kind to their young kinsman, disinherited, so to say, by her presence in the house. They would ride out on the land together.

In the afternoon the sky was no longer blue as in the morning. Large clouds slowly towered up on it, and the great vault itself was colourless, as if diffused into vapours round the white-hot sun in zenith. A low thunder ran along the western horizon; once or twice the dust of the roads rose in tall spirals. But the fields, the hills and the woods were as still as a painted landscape.

Adam walked down the avenue to the pavilion, and found his uncle there, fully dressed, his hands upon his walking-stick and his eyes on the rye field. The book that Adam had given him lay by his side. The field now seemed alive with people. Small groups stood here and there in it, and a long row of men and women were slowly advancing towards the garden in the line of the swath.

The old lord nodded to his nephew, but did not speak or change his position. Adam stood by him as still as himself.

The day to him had been strangely disquieting. At the meeting again with old places the sweet melodies of the past had filled his senses and his mind, and had mingled with new, bewitching tunes of the present. He was back in Denmark, no longer a child but a youth, with a keener sense of the beautiful, with tales of other countries to tell, and still a true son of his own land and enchanted by its loveliness as he had never been before.

But through all these harmonies the tragic and cruel tale which the old lord had told him in the morning, and the sad contest which he knew to be going on so near by, in the corn field, had re-echoed, like the recurrent, hollow throbbing of a muffled drum, a redoubtable sound. It came back time after time, so that he had felt himself to change colour and to answer absently. It brought with it a deeper sense of pity with all that lived than he had ever known. When he had been riding with his young aunt, and their road ran along the scene of the drama, he had taken care to ride between her and the field, so that she should not see what was going on there, or question him about it. He had chosen the way home through the deep, green wood for the same reason.

More dominantly even than the figure of the woman struggling with her sickle for her son's life, the old man's figure, as he had seen it at sunrise, kept him company through the day. He came to ponder on the part which that lonely, determinate form had played in his own life. From the time when his father died, it had impersonated to the boy law and order, wisdom of life and kind guardianship. What was he to do, he thought, if after eighteen years these filial feelings must change, and his second father's figure take on to him a horrible aspect, as a symbol of the tyranny and oppression of the world? What was he to do if ever the two should come to stand in opposition to each other as adversaries?

At the same time an unaccountable, a sinister alarm and dread on behalf of the old man himself took hold of him. For surely here the Goddess Nemesis could not be far away. This man had ruled the world round him for a longer period than Adam's own lifetime and had never been gainsaid by anyone. During the years when he had wandered through Europe with a sick boy of his own blood as his sole companion he had learned to set himself apart from his surroundings, and to close himself up to all outer life, and he had become insusceptible to the ideas and feelings of other human beings. Strange fancies might there have run in his mind, so that in the end he had seen himself as the only person really existing, and the world as a poor and vain shadow-play, which had no substance to it.

Now, in senile wilfullness, he would take in his hand the life of those simpler and weaker than himself, of a woman, using it to his own ends, and he feared of no retributive justice. Did he not know, the young man thought, that there were powers in the world, different from and more formidable than the short-lived might of a despot?

With the sultry heat of the day this foreboding of impending disaster grew upon him, until he felt ruin threatening not the old lord only, but the house, the name and himself with him. It seemed to him that he must cry out a warning to the man he had loved, before it was too late.

But as now he was once more in his uncle's company, the green calm of the garden was so deep that he did not find his voice to cry out. Instead a little French air which his aunt had sung to him up in the house kept running in his mind.—"*C'est un trop doux effort . . .*" He had good knowledge of music; he had heard the air before, in Paris, but not so sweetly sung.

After a time he asked: "Will the woman fulfill her bargain?" His uncle unfolded his hands. "It is an extraordinary thing," he said animatedly, "that it looks as if she might fulfill it. If you count the hours from sunrise till now, and from now till sunset, you will find the time left her to be half of that already gone. And see! She has now mowed two-thirds of the field. But then we will naturally have to reckon with her strength declining as she works on. All in all, it is an idle pursuit in you or me to bet on the issue of the matter; we must wait and see. Sit down, and keep me company in my watch." In two minds Adam sat down.

"And here," said his uncle, and took up the book from the seat, "is your book, which has passed the time finely. It is great poetry, ambrosia to the ear and the heart. And it has, with our discourse on divinity this morning, given me stuff for thought. I have been reflecting upon the law of retributive justice." He took a pinch of snuff, and went on. "A new age," he said, "has made to itself a god in its own image, an emotional god. And now you are already writing a tragedy on your god."

Adam had no wish to begin a debate on poetry with his uncle, but he also somehow dreaded a silence, and said: "It may be, then, that we hold tragedy to be, in the scheme of life, a noble, a divine phenomenon."

"Aye," said his uncle solemnly, "a noble phenomenon, the noblest on earth. But of the earth only, and never divine. Tragedy is the privilege of man, his highest privilege. The God of the Christian Church Himself, when He wished to experience tragedy, had to assume human form. And even at that," he added thoughtfully, "the tragedy was not wholly valid, as it would have become had the hero of it been, in very truth, a man. The divinity of Christ conveyed to it a divine note, the moment of comedy. The real tragic part, by the nature of things, fell to the executors, not to the victim. Nay, my nephew, we should not adulterate the pure elements of the cosmos. Tragedy should remain the right of human beings, subject, in their conditions or in their own nature, to the dire law of necessity. To them it is salvation and beatification. But the gods, whom we must believe to be unacquainted with and incomprehensive of necessity, can have no knowledge of the tragic. When they are brought face to face with it they will, according to my experience, have the good taste and decorum to keep still, and not interfere.

"No," he said after a pause, "the true art of the gods is the comic. The comic is a condescension of the divine to the world of man; it is the sublime vision, which cannot be studied, but must ever be celestially granted. In the comic the gods see their own being reflected as in a mirror, and while the tragic poet is bound by strict laws, they will allow the comic artist a freedom as unlimited as their own. They do not even withhold their own existence from his sports. Jove may favour Lucianos of Samosata. As long as your mockery is in true godly taste you may mock at the gods and still remain a sound devotee. But in pitying, or condoling with your god, you deny and annihilate him, and such is the most horrible of atheisms.

"And here on earth, too," he went on, "we, who stand in lieu of the gods and have emancipated ourselves from the tyranny of necessity, should leave to our vassals their monopoly of tragedy, and for ourselves accept the comic with grace. Only a boorish and cruel master—a parvenu, in fact—will make a jest of his servants' necessity, or force the comic upon them. Only a timid and pedantic ruler, a *petit-maître*, will fear the ludicrous on his own behalf. Indeed," he finished his long speech, "the very same fatality, which, in striking the burgher or peasant, will become tragedy, with the aristocrat is exalted to the comic. By the grace and wit of our acceptance hereof our aristocracy is known."

Adam could not help smiling a little as he heard the apotheosis of the comic on the lips of the erect, ceremonious prophet. In this ironic smile he was, for the first time, estranging himself from the head of his house.

A shadow fell across the landscape. A cloud had crept over the sun; the country changed colour beneath it, faded and bleached, and even all sounds for a minute seemed to die out of it.

"Ah, now," said the old lord, "if it is going to rain, and the rye gets wet, Anne-Marie will not be able to finish in time. And who comes there?" he added, and turned his head a little.

Preceded by a lackey a man in riding boots and a striped waistcoat with silver buttons, and with his hat in his hand, came down the avenue. He bowed deeply, first to the old lord and then to Adam.

"My bailiff," said the old lord. "Good afternoon, Bailiff. What news have you to bring?" The bailiff made a sad gesture. "Poor news only, my lord," he said. "And how poor news?" asked his master. "There is," said the bailiff with weight, "not a soul at work on the land, and not a sickle going except that of Anne-Marie in this rye field. The mowing has stopped; they are all at her heels. It is a poor day for a first day of the harvest." "Yes, I see," said the old lord. The bailiff went on. "I have spoken kindly to them," he said, "and I have sworn at them; it is all one. They might as well all be deaf."

"Good bailiff," said the old lord, "leave them in peace; let them do as they like. This day may, all the same, do them more good than many others. Where is Goske, the boy, Anne-Marie's son?" "We have set him in the small room by the barn," said the bailiff. "Nay, let him be brought down," said the old lord; "let him see his mother at work. But what do you say—will she get the field mowed in time?" "If you ask me, my lord," said the bailiff, "I believe that she will. Who would have thought so? She is only a small woman. It is as hot a day today as, well, as I do ever remember. I myself, you yourself, my lord, could not have done what Anne-Marie has done today." "Nay, nay, we could not, Bailiff," said the old lord.

The bailiff pulled out a red handkerchief and wiped his brow, somewhat calmed by venting his wrath. "If," he remarked with bitterness, "they would all work as the widow works now, we would make a profit on the land." "Yes," said the old lord, and fell into thought, as if calculating the profit it might make. "Still," he said, "as to the question of profit and loss, that is more intricate than it looks. I will tell you something that you may not know: The most famous tissue ever woven was ravelled out again every night. But come," he added, "she is close by now. We will go and have a look at her work ourselves." With these words he rose and set his hat on.

The cloud had drawn away again; the rays of the sun once more burned the wide landscape, and as the small party walked out from under the shade of the trees the dead-still heat was heavy as lead; the sweat sprang out on their faces and their eyelids smarted. On the narrow path they had to go one by one, the old lord stepping along first, all black, and the footman, in his bright livery, bringing up the rear.

The field was indeed filled with people like a market-place; there were probably a hundred or more men and women in it. To Adam the scene recalled pictures from his Bible: the meeting between Esau and Jacob in Edom, or Boas' reapers in his barley field near Bethlehem. Some were standing by the side of the field, others pressed in small groups close to the mowing woman, and a few followed in her wake, binding up sheaves where she had cut the corn, as if thereby they thought to help her, or as if by all means they meant to have part in her work. A younger woman with a pail on her head kept close to her side, and with her a number of half-grown children. One of these first caught sight of the lord of the estate and his suite, and pointed to him. The binders let their sheaves drop, and as the old man stood still many of the onlookers drew close round him.

The woman on whom till now the eyes of the whole field had rested—a small figure on the large stage—was advancing slowly and unevenly, bent double as if she were walking on her knees, and stumbling as she walked. Her blue head-cloth had slipped back from her head; the grey hair was plastered to the skull with sweat, dusty and stuck with straw. She was obviously totally unaware of the multitude round her; neither did she now once turn her head or her gaze towards the new arrivals.

Absorbed in her work she again and again stretched out her left hand to grasp a handful of corn, and her right hand with the sickle in it to cut it off close to the soil, in wavering, groping pulls, like a tired swimmer's strokes. Her course took her so close to the feet of the old lord that his shadow fell on her. Just then she staggered and swayed sideways, and the woman who followed her lifted the pail from her head and held it to her lips. Anne-Marie drank without leaving her hold on her sickle, and the water ran from the corners of her mouth. A boy, close to her, quickly bent one knee, seized her hands in his own and, steadying and guiding them, cut off a gripe of rye.

"No, no," said the old lord, "you must not do that, boy. Leave Anne-Marie in peace to her work." At the sound of his voice the woman, faltering, lifted her face in his direction.

The bony and tanned face was streaked with sweat and dust; the eyes were dimmed. But there was not in its expression the slightest trace of fear or pain. Indeed amongst all the grave and concerned faces of the field hers was the only one perfecaly calm, peaceful and mild. The mouth was drawn together in a thin line, a prim, keen, patient little smile, such as will be seen in the face of an old woman at her spinning-wheel or her knitting, eager on her work, and happy in it. And as the younger woman lifted back the pail, she immediately again fell to her mowing, with an ardent, tender craving, like that of a mother who lays a baby to the nipple. Like an insect that bustles along in high grass, or like a small vessel in a heavy sea, she butted her way on, her quiet face once more bent upon her task.

The whole throng of onlookers, and with them the small group from the pavilion, advanced as she advanced, slowly and as if drawn by a string. The bailiff, who felt the intense silence of the field heavy on him, said to the old lord: "The rye will yield better this year than last," and got no reply. He repeated his remark to Adam, and at last to the footman, who felt himself above a discussion on agriculture, and only cleared his throat in answer. In a while the bailiff again broke the silence. "There is the boy," he said and pointed with his thumb. "They have brought him down." At that moment the woman fell forward on her face and was lifted up by those nearest to her.

Adam suddenly stopped on the path, and covered his eyes with his hand. The old lord without turning asked him if he felt incommoded by the heat. "No," said Adam, "but stay. Let me speak to you." His uncle stopped, with his hand on the stick and looking ahead, as if regretful of being held back.

"In the name of God," cried the young man in French, "force not this woman to continue." There was a short pause. "But I force her not, my friend," said his uncle in the same language. "She is free to finish at any moment." "At the cost of her child only," again cried Adam. "Do you not see that she is dying? You know not what you are doing, or what it may bring upon you."

The old lord, perplexed by this unexpected animadversion, after a second turned all round, and his pale, clear eyes sought his nephew's face with stately surprise. His long, waxen face, with two symmetrical curls at the sides, had something of the mien of an idealized and ennobled old sheep or ram. He made sign to the bailiff to go on. The footman also withdrew a little, and the uncle and nephew were, so to say, alone on the path. For a minute neither of them spoke.

"In this very place where we now stand," said the old lord, then, with hauteur, "I gave Anne-Marie my word."

"My uncle!" said Adam. "A life is a greater thing even than a word. Recall that word, I beseech you, which was given in caprice, as a whim. I am praying you more for your sake than for my own, yet I shall be grateful to you all my life if you will grant me my prayer."

"You will have learned in school," said his uncle, "that in the beginning was the word. It may have been pronounced in caprice, as a whim, the Scripture tells us nothing about it. It is still the principle of our world, its law of gravitation. My own humble word has been the principle of the land on which we stand, for an age of man. My father's word was the same, before my day."

"You are mistaken," cried Adam. "The word is creative—it is imagination, daring and passion. By it the world was made. How much greater are these powers which bring into being than any restricting or controlling law! You wish the land on which we look to produce and propagate; you should not banish from it the forces which cause, and which keep up life, nor turn it into a desert by dominance of law. And when you look at the people, simpler than we and nearer to the heart of nature, who do not analyse their feelings, whose life is one with the life of the earth, do they not inspire in you tenderness, respect, reverence even? This woman is ready to die for her son; will it ever happen to you or me that a woman willingly gives up her life for us? And if it did indeed come to pass, should we make so light of it as not to give up a dogma in return?"

"You are young," said the old lord. "A new age will undoubtedly applaud you. I am old-fashioned, I have been quoting to you texts a thousand years old. We do not, perhaps, quite understand one another. But with my own people I am, I believe, in good understanding. Anne-Marie might well feel that I am making light of her exploit, if now, at the eleventh hour, I did nullify it by a second word. I myself should feel so in her place. Yes, my nephew, it is possible, did I grant you your prayer and pronounce such an amnesty, that I should find it void against her faithfulness, and that we would still see her at her work, unable to give it up, as a shuttle in the rye field, until she had it all mowed. But she would then be a shocking, a horrible sight, a figure of unseemly fun, like a small planet running wild in the sky, when the law of gravitation had been done away with."

"And if she dies at her task," Adam exclaimed, "her death, and its consequences will come upon your head."

The old lord took off his hat and gently ran his hand over his powdered head. "Upon my head?" he said. "I have kept up my head in many weathers. Even," he added proudly, "against the cold wind from high places. In what shape will it come upon my head, my nephew?" "I cannot tell," cried Adam in despair. "I have spoken to warn you. God only knows." "Amen," said the old lord with a little delicate smile. "Come, we will walk on." Adam drew in his breath deeply.

"No," he said in Danish. "I cannot come with you. This field is yours; things will happen here as you decide. But I myself must go away. I beg you to let me have, this evening, a coach as far as town. For I could not sleep another night under your roof, which I have honoured beyond any on earth." So many conflicting feelings at his own speech thronged in his breast that it would have been impossible for him to give them words.

The old lord, who had already begun to walk on, stood still, and with him the lackey. He did not speak for a minute, as if to give Adam time to collect his mind. But the young man's mind was in uproar and would not be collected.

"Must we," the old man asked, in Danish, "take leave here, in the rye field? I have held you dear, next to my own son. I have followed your career in life from year to year, and have been proud of you. I was happy when you wrote to say that you were coming back. If now you will go away, I wish you well." He shifted his walking-stick from the right hand to the left and gravely looked his nephew in the face.

Adam did not meet his eyes. He was gazing out over the landscape. In the late mellow afternoon it was resuming its colours, like a painting brought into proper light; in the meadows the little black stacks of peat stood gravely distinct upon the green sward. On this same morning he had greeted it all, like a child running laughingly to its mother's bosom; now already he must tear himself from it, in discordance, and forever. And at the moment of parting it seemed infinitely dearer than any time before, so much beautified and solemnized by the coming separation that it looked like the place in a dream, a landscape out of paradise, and he wondered if it was really the same. But, yes—there before him was, once more, the hunting-ground of long ago. And there was the road on which he had ridden today.

"But tell me where you mean to go from here," said the old lord slowly. "I myself have travelled a good deal in my days. I know the word of leaving, the wish to go away. But I have learned by experience that, in reality, the word has a meaning only to the place and the people which one leaves. When you have left my house—although it will see you go with sadness—as far as it is concerned the matter is finished and done with. But to the person who goes away it is a different thing, and not so simple. At the moment that he leaves one place he will be already, by the laws of life, on his way to another, upon this earth. Let me know, then, for the sake of our old acquaintance, to which place you are going when you leave here. To England?"

"No," said Adam. He felt in his heart that he could never again go back to England or to his easy and carefree life there. It was not far enough away; deeper waters than the North Sea must now be laid between him and Denmark. "No, not to England," he said. "I shall go to America, to the new world." For a moment he shut his eyes, trying to form to himself a picture of existence in America, with the grey Atlantic Ocean between him and these fields and woods.

"To America?" said his uncle and drew up his eyebrows. "Yes, I have heard of America. They have got freedom there, a big waterfall, savage red men. They shoot turkeys, I have read, as we shoot partridges. Well, if it be your wish, go to America, Adam, and be happy in the new world."

He stood for some time, sunk in thought, as if he had already sent off the young man to America, and had done with him. When at last he spoke, his words had the character of a monologue, enunciated by the person who watches things come and go, and himself stays on.

"Take service, there," he said, "with the power which will give you an easier bargain than this: That with your own life you may buy the life of your son."

Adam had not listened to his uncle's remarks about America, but the conclusive, solemn words caught his ear. He looked up. As if for the first time in his life, he saw the old man's figure as a whole, and conceived how small it was, so much smaller than himself, pale, a thin black anchorite upon his own land. A thought ran through his head: "How terrible to be old!" The abhorrence of the tyrant, and the sinister dread on his behalf, which had followed him all day, seemed to die out of him, and his pity with all creation to extend even to the sombre form before him.

His whole being had cried out for harmony. Now, with the possibility of forgiving, of a reconciliation, a sense of relief went through him; confusedly he bethought himself of Anne-Marie drinking the water held to her lips. He took off his hat, as his uncle had done a moment ago, so that to a beholder at a distance it would seem that the two dark-clad gentlemen on the path were repeatedly and respectfully saluting one another, and brushed the hair from his forehead. Once more the tune of the garden-room rang in his mind:

"*Mourir pour ce qu'on aime*
C'est un trop doux effort . . ."

He stood for a long time immobile and dumb. He broke off a few ears of rye, kept them in his hand and looked at them.

He saw the ways of life, he thought, as a twined and tangled design, complicated and mazy; it was not given him or any mortal to command or control it. Life and death, happiness and woe, the past and the present, were interlaced within the pattern. Yet to the initiated it might be read as easily as our ciphers—which to the savage must seem confused and incomprehensible—will be read by the schoolboy. And out of the contrasting elements concord rose. All that lived must suffer; the old man, whom he had judged hardly, had suffered, as he had watched his son die, and had dreaded the obliteration of his being. He himself would come to know ache, tears and remorse, and, even through these, the fullness of life. So might now, to the woman in the rye field, her ordeal be a triumphant procession. For to die for the one you loved was an effort too sweet for words.

As now he thought of it, he knew that all his life he had sought the unity of things, the secret which connects the phenomena of existence. It was this strife, this dim presage, which had sometimes made him stand still and inert in the midst of the games of his playfellows, or which had, at other moments—on moonlight nights, or in his little boat on the sea—lifted the boy to ecstatic happiness. Where other young people, in their pleasures or their amours, had searched for contrast and variety, he himself had yearned only to comprehend in full the oneness of the world. If things had come differently to him, if his young cousin had not died, and the events that followed his death had not brought him to Denmark, his search for understanding and harmony might have taken him to America, and he might have found them there, in the virgin forests of a new world. Now they have been disclosed to him today, in the place where he had played as a child. As the song is one with the voice that sings it, as the road is one with the goal, as lovers are made one in their embrace, so is man one with his destiny, and he shall love it as himself.

He looked up again, towards the horizon. If he wished to, he felt, he might find out what it was that had brought to him, here, the sudden conception of the unity of the universe. When this same morning he had philosophized, lightly and for his own sake, on his feeling of belonging to this land and soil, it had been the beginning of it. But since then it had grown; it had become a mightier thing, a revelation to his soul. Some time he would look into it, for the law of cause and effect was a wonderful and fascinating study. But not now. This hour was consecrated to greater emotions, to a surrender to fate and to the will of life.

"No," he said at last. "If you wish it I shall not go. I shall stay here."

At that moment a long, loud roll of thunder broke the stillness of the afternoon. It re-echoed for a while amongst the low hills, and it reverberated within the young man's breast as powerfully as if he had been seized and shaken by hands. The landscape had spoken. He remembered that twelve hours ago he had put a question to it, half in jest, and not knowing what he did. Here it gave him its answer.

What it contained he did not know; neither did he inquire. In his promise to his uncle he had given himself over to the mightier powers of the world. Now what must come must come.

"I thank you," said the old lord, and made a little stiff gesture with his hand. "I am happy to hear you say so. We should not let the difference in our ages, or of our views, separate us. In our family we have been wont to keep peace and faith with one another. You have made my heart lighter."

Something within his uncle's speech faintly recalled to Adam the misgivings of the afternoon. He rejected them; he would not let them trouble the new, sweet felicity which his resolution to stay had brought him.

"I shall go on now," said the old lord. "But there is no need for you to follow me. I will tell you tomorrow how the matter has ended." "No," said Adam, "I shall come back by sunset, to see the end of it myself."

All the same he did not come back. He kept the hour in his mind, and all through the evening the consciousness of the drama, and the profound concern and compassion with which, in his thoughts, he followed it, gave to his speech, glance and movements a grave and pathetic substance. But he felt that he was, in the rooms of the manor, and even by the harpsichord on which he accompanied his aunt to her air from *Alceste,* as much in the centre of things as if he had stood in the rye field itself, and as near to those human beings whose fate was now decided there. Anne-Marie and he were both in the hands of destiny, and destiny would, by different ways, bring each to the designated end.

Later on he remembered what he had thought that evening.

But the old lord stayed on. Late in the afternoon he even had an idea; he called down his valet to the pavilion and made him shift his clothes on him and dress him up in a brocaded suit that he had worn at Court. He let a lace-trimmed shirt be drawn over his head and stuck out his slim legs to have them put into thin silk stockings and buckled shoes. In this majestic attire he dined alone, of a frugal meal, but took a bottle of Rhenish wine with it, to keep up his strength. He sat on for a while, a little sunk in his seat; then, as the sun neared the earth, he straightened himself, and took the way down to the field.

The shadows were now lengthening, azure blue along all the eastern slopes. The lonely trees in the corn marked their site by narrow blue pools running out from their feet, and as the old man walked a thin, immensely elongated reflection stirred behind him on the path. Once he stood still; he thought he heard a lark singing over his head, a spring-like sound; his tired head held no clear perception of the season; he seemed to be walking, and standing, in a kind of eternity.

The people in the field were no longer silent, as they had been in the afternoon. Many of them talked loudly among themselves, and a little farther away a woman was weeping.

When the bailiff saw his master, he came up to him. He told him, in great agitation, that the widow would, in all likelihood, finish the mowing of the field within a quarter of an hour.

"Are the keeper and the wheelwright here?" the old lord asked him. "They have been here," said the bailiff, "and have gone away, five times. Each time they have said that they would not come back. But they have come back again, all the same, and they are here now." "And where is the boy?" the old lord asked again. "He is with her," said the bailiff. "I have given him leave to follow her. He has walked close to his mother all the afternoon, and you will see him now by her side, down there."

Anne-Marie was now working her way up towards them more evenly than before, but with extreme slowness, as if at any moment she might come to a standstill. This excessive tardiness, the old lord reflected, if it had been purposely performed, would have been an inimitable, dignified exhibition of skilled art; one might fancy the Emperor of China advancing in like manner on a divine procession or rite. He shaded his eyes with his hand, for the sun was now just beyond the horizon, and its last rays made light, wild, many-coloured specks dance before his sight. With such splendour did the sunset emblazon the earth and the air that the landscape was turned into a melting-pot of glorious metals. The meadows and the grasslands became pure gold; the barley field near by, with its long ears, was a live lake of shining silver.

There was only a small patch of straw standing in the rye field, when the woman, alarmed by the change in the light, turned her head a little to get a look at the sun. The while she did not stop her work, but grasped one handful of corn and cut it off, then another, and another. A great stir, and a sound like a manifold, deep sigh, ran through the crowd. The field was now mowed from one end to the other. Only the mower herself did not realize the fact; she stretched out her hand anew, and when she found nothing in it, she seemed puzzled or disappointed. Then she let her arms drop, and slowly sank to her knees.

Many of the women burst out weeping, and the swarm drew close round her, leaving only a small open space at the side where the old lord stood. Their sudden nearness frightened Anne-Marie; she made a slight, uneasy movement, as if terrified that they should put their hands on her.

The boy, who had kept by her all day, now fell on his knees beside her. Even he dared not touch her, but held one arm low behind her back and the other before her, level with her collar-bone, to catch hold of her if she should fall, and all the time he cried aloud. At that moment the sun went down.

The old lord stepped forward and solemnly took off his hat. The crowd became silent, waiting for him to speak. But for a minute or two he said nothing. Then he addressed her, very slowly.

"Your son is free, Anne-Marie," he said. He again waited a little, and added: "You have done a good day's work, which will long be remembered."

Anne-Marie raised her gaze only as high as his knees, and he understood that she had not heard what he said. He turned to the boy. "You tell your mother, Goske," he said, gently, "what I have told her."

The boy had been sobbing wildly, in raucous, broken moans. It took him some time to collect and control himself. But when at last he spoke, straight into his mother's face, his voice was low, a little impatient, as if he were conveying an everyday message to her. "I am free, Mother," he said. "You have done a good day's work that will long be remembered."

At the sound of his voice she lifted her face to him. A faint, bland shadow of surprise ran over it, but still she gave no sign of having heard what he said, so that the people round them began to wonder if the exhaustion had turned her deaf. But after a moment she slowly and waveringly raised her hand, fumbling in the air as she aimed at his face, and with her fingers touched his cheek. The cheek was wet with tears, so that at the contact her fingertips lightly stuck to it, and she seemed unable to overcome the infinitely slight resistance, or to withdraw her hand. For a minute the two looked each other in the face. Then, softly and lingeringly, like a sheaf of corn that falls to the ground, she sank forward onto the boy's shoulder, and he closed his arms round her.

He held her thus, pressed against him, his own face buried in her hair and head-cloth, for such a long time that those nearest to them, frightened because her body looked so small in his embrace, drew closer, bent down and loosened his grip. The boy let them do so without a word or a movement. But the woman who held Anne-Marie, in her arms to lift her up, turned her face to the old lord. "She is dead," she said.

The people who had followed Anne-Marie all through the day kept standing and stirring in the field for many hours, as long as the evening light lasted, and longer. Long after some of them had made a stretcher from branches of the trees and had carried away the dead woman, others wandered on, up and down the stubble, imitating and measuring her course from one end of the rye field to the other, and binding up the last sheaves, where she had finished her mowing.

The old lord stayed with them for a long time, stepping along a little, and again standing still.

In the place where the woman had died the old lord later on had a stone set up, with a sickle engraved in it. The peasants on the land then named the rye field "Sorrow-Acre." By this name it was known a long time after the story of the woman and her son had itself been forgotten.

D. H. LAWRENCE

David Herbert Richards Lawrence was born in 1885 at Eastwood, a coal-mining village in the English Midlands. His father was a miner, his mother a woman from the middle class who never accepted her husband's way of life. Lawrence was torn between them: close to his mother during her life, appreciating his father only after his death. The story of this family struggle is told in one of Lawrence's finest works, his novel Sons and Lovers *(1913).*

In 1901 Lawrence nearly died of pneumonia. After this his lungs were never entirely sound, and his health was delicate until his death of tuberculosis at the age of forty-five. In 1904 he took the King's Scholarship examination and came out first in all England and Wales. He seems to have been good at all academic subjects from mathematics to botany, painting, and writing. He began a career as a teacher, but trouble with his health and his early success as a writer took him away from teaching.

In 1912 he ran off with the wife of a former professor of his at Nottingham University, and in 1914, when her divorce became final, he married her. From then on the Lawrences traveled, staying in England at times, but also living in Germany, Italy, Ceylon, Australia, the

United States, and Mexico. After Lawrence died in southern France, his body was cremated and the ashes were brought to the United States and buried on a hill near Taos, New Mexico.

Lawrence's personality has drawn almost as much attention as his books. He spoke and wrote informally with the same vitality that animates all his literary work. And some of the informality of talk and personal correspondence can be found in his poetry and fiction. For a time censorship of his works and controversy over the supposed immorality of his views on sex obscured the seriousness and beauty of his work for many readers. But now his books are in print and his place in English letters is secure.

The best biography of Lawrence is the late Edward Nehls's three-volume D. H. Lawrence: A Composite Biography *(U. of Wisconsin Press, 1957–59). Harry T. Moore's* The Intelligent Heart *is handier and available in a convenient edition (Grove Press, 1962). Lawrence himself should be read variously and extensively. Most of his work, including three volumes of his short fiction, can be found in inexpensive Viking Compass paperbacks. Viking also has in print a two-volume edition of Lawrence's letters, and another of his poetry. In addition to the short stories, the student of Lawrence's fiction will want especially to read his novels* The Rainbow *(1915),* Women in Love *(1920), and* Lady Chatterly's Lover *(1928); and the last three works in a Viking Compass Edition called* 4 Short Novels of D. H. Lawrence. *Finally, no one interested in Lawrence should neglect his extraordinary travel books, such as* Twilight in Italy *(1916) and* Mornings in Mexico *(1927).*

Three Essays on Art and Literature

These essays were collected in the posthumous volume of Lawrence's miscellaneous prose, Phoenix.

I · SURGERY FOR THE NOVEL —OR A BOMB

You talk about the future of the baby, little cherub, when he's in the cradle cooing; and it's a romantic, glamorous subject. You also talk, with the parson, about the future of the wicked old grandfather who is at last lying on his death-bed. And there again you have a subject for much vague emotion, chiefly of fear this time.

How do we feel about the novel? Do we bounce with joy thinking of the wonderful novelistic days ahead? Or do we grimly shake our heads and hope the wicked creature will be spared a little longer? Is the novel on his death-bed, old sinner? Or is he just toddling round his cradle, sweet little thing? Let us have another look at him before we decide this rather serious case.

There he is, the monster with many faces, many branches to him, like a tree: the modern novel. And he is almost dual, like Siamese twins. On the one hand, the pale-faced, high-browed, earnest novel, which you have to take seriously; on the other, that smirking, rather plausible hussy, the popular novel.

Let us just for the moment feel the pulses of *Ulysses* and of Miss Dorothy Richardson and M. Marcel Proust, on the earnest side of Briareus; on the other, the throb of *The Sheik* and Mr. Zane Grey, and, if you will, Mr. Robert Chambers and the rest. Is *Ulysses* in his cradle? Oh, dear! What a grey face! And *Pointed Roofs*, are they a gay little toy for nice little girls? And M. Proust? Alas! You can hear the death-rattle in their throats. They can hear it themselves. They are listening to it with acute interest, trying to discover whether the intervals are minor thirds or major fourths. Which is rather infantile, really.

So there you have the "serious" novel, dying in a very long-drawn-out fourteen-volume death-agony, and absorbedly, childishly interested in the phenomenon. "Did I feel a twinge in my little toe, or didn't I?" asks every character of Mr. Joyce or of Miss Richardson or M. Proust. Is my aura a blend of frankincense and orange pekoe and boot-blacking, or is it myrrh and bacon-fat and Shetland tweed? The audience round the death-bed gapes for the answer. And when, in a sepulchral tone, the answer comes at length, after hundreds of pages: "It is none of these, it is abysmal chloro-coryambasis," the audience quivers all over, and murmurs: "That's just how I feel myself."

Which is the dismal, long-drawn-out comedy of the death-bed of the serious novel. It is self-consciousness picked into such fine bits that the bits are most of them invisible, and you have to go by smell. Through thousands and thousands of pages Mr. Joyce and Miss Richardson tear themselves to pieces, strip their smallest emotions to the finest threads, till you feel you are sewed inside a wool mattress that is being slowly shaken up, and you are turning to wool along with the rest of the woolliness.

It's awful. And it's childish. It really is childish, after a certain age, to be absorbedly self-conscious. One has to be self-conscious at seventeen: still a little self-conscious at twenty-seven; but if we are going it strong at thirty-seven, then it is a sign of arrested development, nothing else. And if it is still continuing at forty-seven, it is obvious senile precocity.

And there's the serious novel: senile-precocious. Absorbedly, childishly concerned with *what I am*. "I am this, I am that, I am the other. My reactions are such, and such, and such. And, oh, Lord, if I liked to watch myself closely enough, if I liked to analyse my feelings minutely, as I unbutton my gloves, instead of saying crudely I unbuttoned them, then I could go on to a million pages instead of a thousand. In fact, the more I come to think of it, it is gross, it is uncivilized bluntly to say: I unbuttoned my gloves. After all, the absorbing adventure of it! Which button did I begin with?" etc.

The people in the serious novels are so absorbedly concerned with themselves and what they feel and don't feel, and how they react to every mortal button; and their audience as frenziedly absorbed in the application of the author's discoveries to their own reactions: "That's me! That's exactly it! I'm just finding myself in this book!" Why, this is more than death-bed, it is almost post-mortem behaviour.

Some convulsion or cataclysm will have to get this serious novel out of its self-consciousness. The last great war made it worse. What's to be done? Because, poor thing, it's really young yet. The novel has never become fully adult. It has never quite grown to years of discretion. It has always youthfully hoped for the best, and felt rather sorry for itself on the last page. Which is just childish. The childishness has become very long-drawn-out. So very many adolescents who drag their adolescence on into their forties and their fifties and their sixties! There needs some sort of surgical operation, somewhere.

Then the popular novels—the *Sheiks* and *Babbitts* and Zane Grey novels. They are just as self-conscious, only they do have more illusions about themselves. The heroines do think they are lovelier, and more fascinating, and purer. The heroes do see themselves more heroic, braver, more chivalrous, more fetching. The mass of the populace "find themselves" in the popular novels. But nowadays it's a funny sort of self they find. A Sheik with a whip up his sleeve, and a heroine with weals on her back, but adored in the end, adored, the whip out of sight, but the weals still faintly visible.

It's a funny sort of self they discover in the popular novels. And the essential moral of *If Winter Comes,* for example, is so shaky. "The gooder you are, the worse it is for you, poor you, oh, poor you. Don't you be so blimey good, it's not good enough." Or *Babbitt:* "Go on, you make your pile, and then pretend you're too good for it. Put it over the rest of the grabbers that way. They're only pleased with themselves when they've made their pile. You go one better."

Always the same sort of baking-powder gas to make you rise: the soda counteracting the cream of tartar, and the tartar counteracted by the soda. Sheik heroines, duly whipped, wildly adored. Babbitts with solid fortunes, weeping from self-pity. Winter-Comes heroes as good as pie, hauled off to jail. *Moral:* Don't be too good, because you'll go to jail for it. *Moral:* Don't feel sorry for yourself till you've made your pile and don't need to feel sorry for yourself. *Moral:* Don't let him adore you till he's whipped you into it. Then you'll be partners in mild crime as well as in holy matrimony.

Which again is childish. Adolescence which *can't* grow up. Got into the self-conscious rut and going crazy, quite crazy in it. Carrying on their adolescence into middle age and old age, like the looney Cleopatra in *Dombey and Son,* murmuring "Rose-coloured curtains" with her dying breath.

The future of the novel? Poor old novel, it's in a rather dirty, messy tight corner. And it's either got to get over the wall or knock a hole through it. In other words, it's got to grow up. Put away childish things like: "Do I love the girl, or don't I?"—"Am I pure and sweet, or am I not?"—"Do I unbutton my right glove first, or my left?"—"Did my mother ruin my life by refusing to drink the cocoa which my bride had boiled for her?" These questions and their answers don't really interest me any more, though the world still goes sawing them over. I simply don't care for any of these things now, though I used to. The purely emotional and self-analytical stunts are played out in me. I'm finished. I'm deaf to the whole band. But I'm neither *blasé* nor cynical, for all that. I'm just interested in something else.

Supposing a bomb were put under the whole scheme of things, what would we be after? What feelings do we want to carry through into the next epoch? What feelings will carry us through? What is the underlying impulse in us that will provide the motive power for a new state of things, when this democratic-industrial-lovey-dovey-darling-take-me-to-mamma state of things is bust?

What next? That's what interests me. "What now?" is no fun any more.

If you wish to look into the past for what-next books, you can go back to the Greek philosophers. Plato's Dialogues are queer little novels. It seems to me it was the greatest pity in the world, when philosophy and fiction got split. They used to be one, right from the days of myth. Then they went and parted, like a nagging married couple, with Aristotle and Thomas Aquinas and that beastly Kant. So the novel went sloppy, and philosophy went abstract-dry. The two should come together again—in the novel.

You've got to find a new impulse for new things in mankind, and it's really fatal to find it through abstraction. No, no; philosophy and religion, they've both gone too far on the algebraical tack: Let X stand for sheep and Y for goats: then X minus Y equals Heaven, and X plus Y equals Earth, and Y minus X equals Hell. Thank you! But what coloured shirt does X have on?

The novel has a future. It's got to have the courage to tackle new propositions without using abstractions; it's got to present us with new, really new feelings, a whole line of new emotion, which will get us out of the emotional rut. Instead of snivelling about what is and has been, or inventing new sensations in the old line, it's got to break a way through, like a hole in the wall. And the public will scream and say it is sacrilege: because, of course, when you've been jammed for a long time in a tight corner, and you get really used to its stuffiness and its tightness, till you find it suffocatingly cozy; then, of course, you're horrified when you see a new glaring hole in what was your cozy wall. You're horrified. You back away from the cold stream of fresh air as if it were killing you. But gradually, first one and then another of the sheep filters through the gap, and finds a new world outside.

II · ART AND MORALITY

It is a part of the common claptrap that "art is immoral." Behold, everywhere, artists running to put on jazz underwear, to demoralize themselves; or, at least, to *débourgeoiser* themselves.

For the bourgeois is supposed to be the fount of morality. Myself, I have found artists far more morally finicky.

Anyhow, what has a water-pitcher and six insecure apples on a crumpled tablecloth got to do with bourgeois moralty? Yet I notice that most people, who have not learnt the trick of being arty, feel a real moral repugnance of a Cézanne still-life. They think it is not *right*.

For them, it isn't.

Yet how can they feel, as they do, that it is subtly *immoral?*

The very same design, if it was humanized, and the tablecloth was a draped nude and the water-pitcher a nude semi-draped, weeping over the draped one, would instantly become highly moral. Why?

Perhaps from painting better than from any other art we can realize the subtlety of the distinction between what is dumbly *felt* to be moral, and what is felt to be immoral. The moral instinct in the man in the street.

But instinct is largely habit. The moral instinct of the man in the street is largely an emotional defence of an old habit.

Yet what can there be in a Cézanne still-life to rouse the aggressive moral instinct of the man in the street? What ancient habit in man do these six apples and a water-pitcher succeed in hindering?

A water-pitcher that isn't so very much like a water-pitcher, apples that aren't very appley, and a tablecloth that's not particularly much of a tablecloth. I could do better myself!

Probably! But then, why not dismiss the picture as a poor attempt? Whence this anger, this hostility? The derisive resentment?

Six apples, a pitcher, and a tablecloth can't suggest improper *behaviour.* They don't—not even to a Freudian. If they did, the man in the street would feel much more at home with them.

Where, then, does the immorality come in? Because come in it does.

Because of a very curious habit that civilized man has been forming down the whole course of civilization, and in which he is now hard-boiled. The slowly formed habit of seeing just as the photographic camera sees.

You may say, the object reflected on the retina is *always* photographic. It may be. I doubt it. But whatever the image on the retina may be, it is rarely, even now, the photographic image of the object which is actually *taken in* by the man who sees the object. He does not, even now, see for himself. He sees what the Kodak has taught him to see. And man, try as he may, is not a Kodak.

When a child sees a man, what does the child *take in,* as an impression? Two eyes, a nose, a mouth of teeth, two straight legs, two straight arms: a sort of hieroglyph which the human child has used through all the ages to represent man. At least, the old hieroglyph was still in use when I was a child.

Is this what the child actually *sees?*

If you mean by seeing, consciously registering, then this is what the child actually sees. The photographic image may be there all right, upon the retina. But there the child leaves it: outside the door, as it were.

Through many ages, mankind has been striving to register the image on the retina *as it is:* no more glyphs and hieroglyphs. We'll have the real objective reality.

And we have succeeded. As soon as we succeed, the Kodak is invented, to prove our success. Could lies come out of a black box, into which nothing but light had entered? Impossible! It takes life to tell a lie.

Colour also, which primitive man cannot really *see,* is now seen by us, and fitted to the spectrum.

Eureka! We have seen it, with our own eyes.

When we see a red cow, we see a red cow. We are quite sure of it, because the unimpeachable Kodak sees exactly the same.

But supposing we had all of us been born blind, and had to get our image of a red cow by touching her, and smelling her, hearing her moo, and "feeling" her? Whatever should we think of her? Whatever sort of image should we have of her, in our dark minds? Something very different, surely!

As vision developed towards the Kodak, man's idea of himself developed towards the snapshot. Primitive man simply didn't know *what* he was: he was always half in the dark. But we have learned to see, and each of us has a complete Kodak idea of himself.

You take a snap of your sweetheart, in the field among the buttercups, smiling tenderly at the red cow with a calf, and dauntlessly offering a cabbage-leaf.

Awfully nice, and absolutely "real." There is your sweetheart, complete in herself, enjoying a sort of absolute objective reality: complete, perfect, all her surroundings contributing to her, incontestable. She is really a "picture."

This is the habit we have formed: of visualizing *everything.* Each man to himself is a picture. That is, he is a complete little objective reality, complete in himself, existing by himself, absolutely, in the middle of the picture. All the rest is just setting, background. To every man, to every woman, the universe is just a setting to the absolute little picture of himself, herself.

This has been the development of the conscious ego in man, through several thousand years: since Greece first broke the spell of "darkness." Man has learnt to *see* himself. So now, he *is* what he sees. He makes himself in his own image.

Previously, even in Egypt, men had not learnt to *see straight.* They fumbled in the dark, and didn't quite know where they were, or what they were. Like men in a dark room, they only *felt* their own existence surging in the darkness of other creatures.

We, however, have learned to see ourselves for what we are, as the sun sees us. The Kodak bears witness. We see as the All-Seeing Eye sees, with the universal vision. And we *are* what is seen: each man to himself an identity, an isolated absolute, corresponding with a universe of isolated absolutes. A picture! A Kodak snap, in a universal film of snaps.

We have achieved universal vision. Even god could not see *differently* from what we see: only more extensively, like a telescope, or more intensively, like a microscope. But the same vision. A vision of images which are real, and each one limited to itself.

We behave as if we had got to the bottom of the sack, and seen the Platonic Idea with our own eyes, in all its photographically developed perfection, lying in the bottom of the sack of the universe. Our own ego!

The identifying of ourselves with the visual image of ourselves has become an instinct; the habit is already old. The picture of me, the me that is *seen,* is me.

As soon as we are supremely satisfied about it, somebody starts to upset us. Comes Cézanne with his pitcher and his apples, which not only are not life-like, but are a living lie. The Kodak will prove it,

The Kodak will take all sorts of snaps, misty, atmospheric, sundazed, dancing—all quite different. Yet the image is *the* image. There is only more or less sun, more or less vapour, more or less light and shade.

The All-Seeing Eye sees with every degree of intensity and in every possible kind of mood: Giotto, Titian, El Greco, Turner, all so different, yet all the true image in the All-Seeing Eye.

This Cézanne still-life, however, is *contrary* to the All-Seeing Eye. Apples, to the eye of God, could not look like that, nor could a tablecloth, nor could a pitcher. So, it is *wrong.*

Because man, since he grew out of a personal God, has taken over to himself all the attributes of the Personal Godhead. It is the all-seeing human eye which is now the Eternal Eye.

And if apples don't *look* like that, in any light or circumstance, or under any mood, then they shouldn't be painted like that.

Oh, *là-là-là!* The apples *are* just like that, to me! cries Cézanne. They *are* like that, no matter what they look like.

Apples are always apples! says Vox Populi, Vox Dei.

Sometimes they're a sin, sometimes they're a knock on the head, sometimes they're a bellyache, sometimes they're part of a pie, sometimes they're sauce for the goose.

And you can't see a bellyache, neither can you see a sin, neither can you see a knock on the head. So paint the apple in these aspects, and you get—probably, or approximately—a Cézanne still-life.

What an apple looks like to an urchin, to a thrush, to a browsing cow, to Sir Isaac Newton, to a caterpillar, to a hornet, to a mackerel who finds one bobbing on the sea, I leave you to conjecture. But the All-Seeing must have mackerel's eyes, as well as man's.

And this is the immorality in Cézanne: he begins to see more than the All-Seeing Eye of humanity can possibly see, Kodak-wise. If you can see in the apple a bellyache and a knock on the head, and paint these in the image, among the prettiness, then it is the death of the Kodak and the movies, and must be immoral.

It's all very well talking about decoration and illustration, significant form, or tactile values, or plastique, or movement, or space-composition, or colour-mass relations, afterwards. You might as well force your guests to eat the menu card, at the end of the dinner.

What art has got to do, and will go on doing, is to reveal things in their different relationships. That is to say, you've got to see in the apple the bellyache, Sir Isaac's knock on the cranium, the vast, moist wall through which the insect bores to lay her eggs in the middle, and the untasted, unknown quality which Eve saw hanging on a tree. Add to this the glaucous glimpse that the mackerel gets as he comes to the surface, and Fantin-Latour's apples are no more to you than enamelled rissoles.

The true artist doesn't substitute immorality for morality. On the contrary, he *always* substitutes a finer morality for a grosser. And as soon as you see a finer morality, the grosser becomes relatively immoral.

The universe is like Father Ocean, a stream of all things slowly moving. We move, and the rock of ages moves. And since we move and move for ever, in no discernible direction, there is no centre to the movement, to us. To us, the centre shifts at every moment. Even the pole-star ceases to sit on the pole. *Allons!* there is no road before us!

There is nothing to do but to maintain a true relationship to the things we move with and amongst and against. The apple, like the moon, has still an unseen side. The movement of Ocean will turn it round to us, or us to it.

There is nothing man can do but maintain himself in true relationship to his contiguous universe. An ancient Rameses can sit in stone absolute, absolved from visual contact, deep in the silent ocean of sensual contact. Michelangelo's Adam can open his eyes for the first time, and see the old man in the skies, objectively. Turner can tumble into the open mouth of the objective universe of light, till we see nothing but his disappearing heels. As the stream carries him, each in his own relatedness, each one differently, so a man must go through life.

Each thing, living or unliving, streams in its own odd, intertwining flux, and nothing, not even man nor the God of man, nor anything that man has thought or felt or known, is fixed or abiding. All moves. And nothing is true, or good, or right, except in its own living relatedness to its own circumambient universe; to the things that are in the stream with it.

Design, in art, is a recognition of the relation between various things, various elements in the creative flux. You can't *invent* a design. You recognize it, in the fourth dimension. That is, with your blood and your bones, as well as with your eyes.

Egypt had a wonderful relation to a vast living universe, only dimly visual in its reality. The dim eye-vision and the powerful blood-feeling of the Negro African, even today, gives us strange images, which our eyes can hardly see, but which we know are surpassing. The big silent statue of Rameses is like a drop of water, hanging through the centuries in dark suspense, and never static. The African fetish-statues have no movement, visually represented. Yet one little motionless wooden figure stirs more than all the Parthenon frieze. It sits in the place where no Kodak can snap it.

As for us, we have our Kodak-vision, all in bits that group or jig. Like the movies, that jerk but never move. An endless shifting and rattling together of isolated images, "snaps," miles of them, all of them jigging, but each one utterly incapable of movement or change, in itself. A kaleidoscope of inert images, mechanically shaken.

And this is our vaunted "consciousness," made up, really, of inert visual images and little else: like the cinematograph.

Let Cézanne's apples go rolling off the table for ever. They live by their own laws, in their own *ambiente*, and not by the laws of the Kodak—or of man. They are casually related to man. But to those apples, man is by no means the absolute.

A new relationship between ourselves and the universe means a new morality. Taste the unsteady apples of Cézanne, and the nailed-down apples of Fantin-Latour are apples of Sodom. If the *status quo* were paradise, it would indeed be a sin to taste the new apples; but since the *status quo* is much more prison than paradise, we can go ahead.

III · WHY THE NOVEL MATTERS

We have curious ideas of ourselves. We think of ourselves as a body with a spirit in it, or a body with a soul in it, or a body with a mind in it. *Mens sana in corpore sano*. The years drink up the wine, and at last throw the bottle away, the body, of course, being the bottle.

It is a funny sort of superstition. Why should I look at my hand, as it so cleverly writes these words, and decide that it is a mere nothing compared to the mind that directs it? Is there really any huge difference between my hand and my brain? Or my mind? My hand is alive, it flickers with a life of its own. It meets all the strange universe in touch, and learns a vast number of things, and knows a vast number of things. My hand, as it writes these words, slips gaily along, jumps like a grasshopper to dot an *i*, feels the table rather cold, gets a little bored if I write too long, has its own rudiments of thought, and is just as much *me* as is my brain, my mind, or my soul. Why should I imagine that there is a *me* which is more *me* than my hand is? Since my hand is absolutely alive, me alive.

Whereas, of course, as far as I am concerned, my pen isn't alive at all. My pen *isn't me* alive. Me alive ends at my finger-tips.

Whatever is me alive is me. Every tiny bit of my hands is alive, every little freckle and hair and fold of skin. And whatever is me alive is me. Only my finger-nails, those ten little weapons between me and an inanimate universe, they cross the mysterious Rubicon between me alive and things like my pen, which are not alive, in my own sense.

So, seeing my hand is all alive, and me alive, wherein is it just a bottle, or a jug, or a tin can, or a vessel of clay, or any of the rest of that nonsense? True, if I cut it it will bleed, like a can of cherries. But then the skin that is cut, and the veins that bleed, and the bones that should never be seen, they are all just as alive as the blood that flows. So the tin can business, or vessel of clay, is just bunk.

And that's what you learn, when you're a novelist. And that's what you are very liable *not* to know, if you're a parson, or a philosopher, or a scientist, or a stupid person. If you're a parson, you talk about souls in heaven. If you're a novelist, you know that paradise is in the palm of your hand, and on the end of your nose, because both are alive; and alive, and man alive, which is more than you can say, for certain, of paradise. Paradise is after life, and I for one am not keen on anything that is *after* life. If you are a philosopher, you talk about infinity, and the pure spirit which knows all things. But if you pick up a novel, you realize immediately that infinity is just a handle to this self-same jug of a body of mine; while as for knowing, if I find my finger in the fire, I know that fire burns, with a knowledge so emphatic and vital, it leaves Nirvana merely a conjecture. Oh, yes, my body, me alive, *knows,* and knows intensely. And as for the sum of all knowledge, it can't be anything more than an accumulation of all the things I know in the body, and you, dear reader, know in the body.

These damned philosophers, they talk as if they suddenly went off in steam, and were then much more important than they are when they're in their shirts. It is nonsense. Every man, philosopher included, ends in his own finger-tips. That's the end of his man alive. As for the words and thoughts and sighs and aspirations that fly from him, they are so many tremulations in the ether, and not alive at all. But if the tremulations reach another man alive, he may receive them into his life, and his life may take on a new colour, like a chameleon creeping from a brown rock on to a green leaf. All very well and good.

It still doesn't alter the fact that the so-called spirit, the message or teaching of the philosopher or the saint, isn't alive at all, but just a tremulation upon the ether, like a radio message. All this spirit stuff is just tremulations upon the ether. If you, as man alive, quiver from the tremulation of the ether into new life, that is because you are man alive, and you take sustenance and stimulation into your alive man in a myriad ways. But to say that the message, or the spirit which is communicated to you, is more important than your living body, is nonsense. You might as well say that the potato at dinner was more important.

Nothing is important but life. And for myself, I can absolutely see life nowhere but in the living. Life with a capital L is only man alive. Even a cabbage in the rain is cabbage alive. All things that are alive are amazing. And all things that are dead are subsidiary to the living. Better a live dog than a dead lion. But better a live lion than a live dog. *C'est la vie!*

It seems impossible to get a saint, or a philosopher, or a scientist, to stick to this simple truth. They are all, in a sense, renegades. The saint wishes to offer himself up as spiritual food for the multitude. Even Francis of Assisi turns himself into a sort of angel-cake, of which anyone may take a slice. But an angel-cake is rather less than man alive. And poor St. Francis might well apologize to his body, when he is dying: "Oh, pardon me, my body, the wrong I did you through the years!" It was no wafer, for others to eat.

The philosopher, on the other hand, because he can think, decides that nothing but thoughts matter. It is as if a rabbit, because he can make little pills, should decide that nothing but little pills matter. As for the scientist, he has absolutely no use for me so long as I am man alive. To the scientist, I am dead. He puts under the microscope a bit of dead me, and calls it me. He takes me to pieces, and says first one piece, and then another piece, is me. My heart, my liver, my stomach have all been scientifically me, according to the scientist; and nowadays I am either a brain, or nerves, or glands, or something more up-to-date in the tissue line.

Now I absolutely flatly deny that I am a soul, or a body, or a mind, or an intelligence, or a brain, or a nervous system, or a bunch of glands, or any of the rest of these bits of me. The whole is greater than the part. And therefore, I, who am man alive, am greater than my soul, or spirit, or body, or mind, or consciousness, or anything else that is merely a part of me. I am a man, and alive. I am man alive, and as long as I can, I intend to go on being man alive.

For this reason I am a novelist. And being a novelist, I consider myself superior to the saint, the scientist, the philosopher, and the poet, who are all great masters of different bits of man alive, but never get the whole hog.

The novel is the one bright book of life. Books are not life. They are only tremulations on the ether. But the novel as a tremulation can make the whole man alive tremble. Which is more than poetry, philosophy, science, or any other book-tremulation can do.

The novel is the book of life. In this sense, the Bible is a great confused novel. You may say, it is about God. But it is really about man alive. Adam, Eve, Sarai, Abraham, Isaac, Jacob, Samuel, David, Bath-Sheba, Ruth, Esther, Solomon, Job, Isaiah, Jesus, Mark, Judas, Paul, Peter: what is it but man alive, from start to finish? Man alive, not mere bits. Even the Lord is another man alive, in a burning bush, throwing the tablets of stone at Moses's head.

I do hope you begin to get my idea, why the novel is supremely important, as a tremulation on the ether. Plato makes the perfect ideal being tremble in me. But that's only a bit of me. Perfection is only a bit, in the strange make-up of man alive. The Sermon on the Mount makes the selfless spirit of me quiver. But that, too, is only a bit of me. The Ten Commandments set the old Adam shivering in me, warning me that I am a thief and a murderer, unless I watch it. But even the old Adam is only a bit of me.

I very much like all these bits of me to be set trembling with life and the wisdom of life. But I do ask that the whole of me shall tremble in its wholeness, some time or other.

And this, of course, must happen in me, living.

But as far as it can happen from a communication, it can only happen when a whole novel communicates itself to me. The Bible—but *all* the Bible—and Homer, and Shakespeare: these are the supreme old novels. These are all things to all men. Which means that in their wholeness they affect the whole man alive, which is the man himself, beyond any part of him. They set the whole tree trembling with a new access of life, they do not just stimulate growth in one direction.

I don't want to grow in any one direction any more. And, if I can help it, I don't want to stimulate anybody else into some particular direction. A particular direction ends in a *cul-de-sac*. We're in a *cul-de-sac* at present.

I don't believe in any dazzling revelation, or in any supreme Word. "The grass withereth, the flower fadeth, but the Word of the Lord shall stand for ever." That's the kind of stuff we've drugged ourselves with. As a matter of fact, the grass withereth, but comes up all the greener for that reason, after the rains. The flower fadeth, and therefore the bud opens. But the Word of the Lord, being man-uttered and a mere vibration on the ether, becomes staler and staler, more and more boring, till at last we turn a deaf ear and it ceases to exist, far more finally than any withered grass. It is grass that renews its youth like the eagle, not any Word.

We should ask for no absolutes, or absolute. Once and for all and for ever, let us have done with the ugly imperialism of any absolute. There is no absolute good, there is nothing absolutely right. All things flow and change, and even change is not absolute. The whole is a strange assembly of apparently incongruous parts, slipping past one another.

Me, man alive, I am a very curious assembly of incongruous parts. My yea! of today is oddly different from my yea! of yesterday. My tears of tomorrow will have nothing to do with my tears of a year ago. If the one I love remains unchanged and unchanging, I shall cease to love her. It is only because she changes and startles me into change and defies my inertia, and is herself staggered in her inertia by my changing, that I can continue to love her. If she stayed put, I might as well love the pepper-pot.

In all this change, I maintain a certain integrity. But woe betide me if I try to put my finger on it. If I say of myself, I am this, I am that!—then, if I stick to it, I turn into a stupid fixed thing like a lamp-post. I shall never know wherein lies my integrity, my individuality, my me. I *can* never know it. It is useless to talk about my ego. That only means that I have made up an *idea* of myself, and that I am trying to cut myself out to pattern. Which is no good. You can cut your cloth to fit your coat, but you can't clip bits off your living body, to trim it down to your idea. True, you can put yourself into ideal corsets. But even in ideal corsets, fashions change.

Let us learn from the novel. In the novel, the characters can do nothing but *live*. If they keep on being good, according to pattern, or bad, according to pattern, or even volatile, according to pattern, they cease to live, and the novel falls dead. A character in a novel has got to live, or it is nothing.

We, likewise, in life have got to live, or we are nothing.

What we mean by living is, of course, just as indescribable as what we mean by *being*. Men get ideas into their heads, of what they mean by Life, and they proceed to cut life out to pattern. Sometimes they go into the desert to seek God, sometimes they go into the desert to seek cash, sometimes it is wine, woman, and song, and again it is water, political reform, and votes. You never know what it will be next: from killing your neighbour with hideous bombs and gas that tears the lungs, to supporting a Foundlings Home and preaching infinite Love, and being co-respondent in a divorce.

In all this wild welter, we need some sort of guide. It's no good inventing Thou Shalt Nots!

What then? Turn truly, honourably to the novel, and see wherein you are man alive, and wherein you are dead man in life. You may love a woman as man alive, and you may be making love to a woman as sheer dead man in life. You may eat your dinner as man alive, or as a mere masticating corpse. As man alive you may have a shot at your enemy. But as a ghastly simulacrum of life you may be firing bombs into men who are neither your enemies nor your friends, but just things you are dead to. Which is criminal, when the things happen to be alive.

To be alive, to be man alive, to be whole man alive: that is the point. And at its best, the novel, and the novel supremely, can help you. It can help you not to be dead man in life. So much of a man walks about dead and a carcass in the street and house, today: so much of women is merely dead. Like a pianoforte with half the notes mute.

But in the novel you can see, plainly, when the man goes dead, the woman goes inert. You can develop an instinct for life, if you will, instead of a theory of right and wrong, good and bad.

In life, there is right and wrong, good and bad, all the time. But what is right in one case is wrong in another. And in the novel you see one man becoming a corpse, because of his so-called goodness, another going dead because of his so-called wickedness. Right and wrong is an instinct: but an instinct of the whole consciousness in a man, bodily, mental, spiritual at once. And only in the novel are *all* things given full play, or at least, they may be given full play, when we realize that life itself, and not inert safety, is the reason for living. For out of the full play of all things emerges the only thing that is anything, the wholeness of a man, the wholeness of a woman, man alive, and live woman.

Reflections on the Death of a Porcupine

This essay became the title essay of a volume published in 1925.

There are many bare places on the little pine trees, towards the top, where the porcupines have gnawed the bark away and left the white flesh showing. And some trees are dying from the top.

Everyone says porcupines should be killed; the Indians, Mexicans, Americans all say the same.

At full moon a month ago, when I went down the long clearing in the brilliant moonlight, through the poor dry herbage a big porcupine began to waddle away from me, towards the trees and the darkness. The animal had raised all its hairs and bristles, so that by the light of the moon it seemed to have a tall, swaying, moonlit aureole arching its back as it went. That seemed curiously fearsome, as if the animal were emitting itself demon-like on the air.

It waddled very slowly, with its white spike spoon-tail steering flat, behind the round bear-like mound of its back. It had a lumbering, beetle's, squalid motion, unpleasant. I followed it into the darkness of the timber, and there, squat like a great tick, it began scrapily to creep up a pine-trunk. It was very like a great aureoled tick, a bug, struggling up.

I stood near and watched, disliking the presence of the creature. It is a duty to kill the things. But the dislike of killing him was greater than the dislike of him. So I watched him climb.

And he watched me. When he had got nearly the height of a man, all his long hairs swaying with a bristling gleam like an aureole, he hesitated, and slithered down. Evidently he had decided, either that I was harmless, or else that it was risky to go up any further, when I could knock him off so easily with a pole. So he slithered podgily down again, and waddled away with the same bestial, stupid motion of that white-spiky repulsive spoon-tail. He was as big as a middle-sized pig: or more like a bear.

I let him go. He was repugnant. He made a certain squalor in the moonlight of the Rocky Mountains. As all savagery has a touch of squalor, that makes one a little sick at the stomach. And anyhow, it seemed almost more squalid to pick up a pine-bough and push him over, hit him and kill him.

A few days later, on a hot, motionless morning when the pine-trees put out their bristles in stealthy, hard assertion; and I was not in a good temper, because Black-eyed Susan, the cow, had disappeared into the timber, and I had had to ride hunting her, so it was nearly nine o'clock before she was milked: Madame came in suddenly out of the sunlight, saying: "I got such a shock! There are two strange dogs, and one of them has got the most awful beard, all round his nose."

She was frightened, like a child, at something unnatural.

"Beard! Porcupine quills, probably! He's been after a porcupine."

"Ah!" she cried in relief. "Very likely! Very likely!"—then with a change of tone; "Poor thing, will they hurt him?"

"They will. I wonder when he came."

"I heard dogs bark in the night."

"Did you? Why didn't you say so? I should have known Susan was hiding—"

The ranch is lonely, there is no sound in the night, save the innumerable noises of the night, that you can't put your finger on; cosmic noises in the far deeps of the sky, and of the earth.

I went out. And in the full blaze of sunlight in the field, stood two dogs, a black-and-white, and a big, bushy, rather handsome sandy-red dog, of the collie type. And sure enough, this latter did look queer and a bit horrifying, his whole muzzle set round with white spines, like some ghastly growth; like an unnatural beard.

The black-and-white dog made off as I went through the fence. But the red dog whimpered and hesitated, and moved on hot bricks. He was fat and in good condition. I thought he might belong to some shepherds herding sheep in the forest ranges, among the mountains.

He waited while I went up to him, wagging his tail and whimpering, and ducking his head, and dancing. He daren't rub his nose with his paws any more: it hurt too much. I patted his head and looked at his nose, and he whimpered loudly.

He must have had thirty quills, or more, sticking out of his nose, all the way round: the white, ugly ends of the quills protruding an inch, sometimes more, sometimes less, from his already swollen, blood-puffed muzzle.

The porcupines here have quills only two or three inches long. But they are devilish; and a dog will die if he does not get them pulled out. Because they work further and further in, and will sometimes emerge through the skin away in some unexpected place.

Then the fun began. I got him in the yard: and he drank up the whole halk-gallon of the chickens' sour milk. Then I started pulling out the quills. He was a big, bushy, handsome dog, but his nerve was gone, and every time I got a quill out, he gave a yelp. Some long quills were fairly easy. But the shorter ones, near his lips, were deep in, and hard to get hold of, and hard to pull out when you did get hold of them. And with every one that came out, came a little spurt of blood and another yelp and writhe.

The dog wanted the quills out: but his nerve was gone. Every time he saw my hand coming to his nose, he jerked his head away. I quieted him, and stealthily managed to jerk out another quill, with the blood all over my fingers. But with every one that came out, he grew more tiresome. I tried and tried and tried to get hold of another quill, and he jerked and jerked, and writhed and whimpered, and ran under the porch floor.

It was a curiously unpleasant, nerve-trying job. The day was blazing hot. The dog came out and I struggled with him again for an hour or more. Then we blindfolded him. But either he smelled my hand approaching his nose, or some weird instinct told him. He jerked his head, this way, that way, up, down, sideways, roundwise, as one's fingers came slowly, slowly, to seize a quill.

The quills on his lips and chin were deep in, only about a quarter of an inch of white stub protruding from the swollen, blood-oozed, festering black skin. It was very difficult to jerk them out.

We let him lie for an interval, hidden in the quiet cool place under the porch floor. After half an hour, he crept out again. We got a rope round his nose, behind the bristles, and one held while the other got the stubs with the pliers. But it was too trying. If a quill came out, the dog's yelp startled every nerve. And he was frightened of the pain, it was impossible to hold his head still any longer.

After struggling for two hours, and extracting some twenty quills, I gave up. It was impossible to quiet the creature, and I had had enough. His nose on the top was clear: a punctured, puffy, blood-darkened mess; and his lips were clear. But just on his round little chin, where the few white hairs are, was still a bunch of white quills, eight or nine, deep in.

We let him go, and he dived under the porch, and there he lay invisible: save for the end of his bushy, foxy tail, which moved when we came near. Towards noon he emerged, ate up the chicken-food, and stood with that doggish look of dejection, and fear, and friendliness, and greediness, wagging his tail.

But I had had enough.

"Go home!" I said. "Go home! Go home to your master, and let him finish for you."

He would not go. So I led him across the blazing hot clearing, in the way I thought he should go. He followed a hundred yards, then stood motionless in the blazing sun. He was not going to leave the place.

And I! I simply did not want him.

So I picked up a stone. He dropped his tail, and swerved towards the house. I knew what he was going to do. He was going to dive under the porch, and there stick, haunting the place.

I dropped my stone, and found a good stick under the cedar tree. Already in the heat was that sting-like biting of electricity, the thunder gathering in the sheer sunshine, without a cloud, and making one's whole body feel dislocated.

I could not bear to have that dog around any more. Going quietly to him, I suddenly gave him one hard hit with the stick, crying: "Go home!" He turned quickly, and the end of the stick caught him on his sore nose. With a fierce yelp, he went off like a wolf, downhill, like a flash, gone. And I stood in the field full of pangs of regret, at having hit him, unintentionally, on his sore nose.

But he was gone.

And then the present moon came, and again the night was clear. But in the interval there had been heavy thunder-rains, the ditch was running with bright water across the field, and the night, so fair, had not the terrific, mirror-like brilliancy, touched with terror, so startling bright, of the moon in the last days of June.

We were alone on the ranch. Madame went out into the clear night, just before retiring. The stream ran in a cord of silver across the field, in the straight line where I had taken the irrigation ditch. The pine tree in front of the house threw a black shadow. The mountain slope came down to the fence, wild and alert.

"Come!" said she excitedly. "There is a big porcupine drinking at the ditch. I thought at first it was a bear."

When I got out he had gone. But among the grasses and the coming wild sunflowers, under the moon, I saw his greyish halo, like a pallid living bush, moving over the field, in the distance, in the moonlit *clair-obscur*.

We got through the fence, and following, soon caught him up. There he lumbered, with his white spoon-tail spiked with bristles, steering behind almost as if he were moving backwards, and this was his head. His long, long hairs above the quills quivering with a dim grey gleam, like a bush.

And again I disliked him.

"Should one kill him?"

She hesitated. Then with a sort of disgust:

"Yes!"

I went back to the house, and got the little twenty-two rifle. Now never in my life had I shot at any live thing: I never wanted to. I always felt guns very repugnant: sinister, mean. With difficulty I had fired once or twice at a target: but resented doing even so much. Other people could shoot if they wanted to. Myself, individually, it was repugnant to me even to try.

But something slowly hardens in a man's soul. And I knew now it had hardened in mine. I found the gun, and with rather trembling hands got it loaded. Then I pulled back the trigger and followed the porcupine. It was still lumbering through the grass. Coming near, I aimed.

The trigger stuck. I pressed the little catch with a safety-pin I found in my pocket, and released the trigger. Then we followed the porcupine. He was still lumbering towards the trees. I went sideways on, stood quite near to him, and fired, in the clear-dark of the moonlight.

And as usual I aimed too high. He turned, went scuttling back whence he had come.

I got another shell in place, and followed. This time I fired full into the mound of his round back, below the glistening grey halo. He seemed to stumble on to his hidden nose, and struggled a few strides, ducking his head under like a hedgehog.

"He's not dead yet! Oh, fire again!" cried Madame.

I fired, but the gun was empty.

So I ran quickly, for a cedar pole. The porcupine was lying still, with subsiding halo. He stirred faintly. So I turned him and hit him hard over the nose; or where, in the dark, his nose should have been. And it was done. He was dead.

And in the moonlight, I looked down on the first creature I had ever shot.

"Does it seem mean?" I asked aloud, doubtful.

Again Madame hesitated. Then: "No!" she said resentfully.

And I felt she was right. Things like the porcupine, one must be able to shoot them, if they get in one's way.

One must be able to shoot. I, myself, must be able to shoot, and to kill.

For me, this is a *volta face*. I have always preferred to walk round my porcupine, rather than kill it.

Now, I know it's no good walking round. One must kill.

I buried him in the adobe hole. But some animal dug down and ate him; for two days later there lay the spines and bones spread out, with the long skeletons of the porcupine-hands.

The only nice thing about him—or her, for I believe it was a female, by the dugs on her belly—were the feet. They were like longish, alert black hands, paw-hands. That is why a porcupine's tracks in the snow look almost as if a child had gone by, leaving naked little human footprints, like a little boy.

So, he is gone: or she is gone. But there is another one, bigger and blacker-looking, among the west timber. That too is to be shot. It is part of the business of ranching: even when it's only a little half-abandoned ranch like this one.

Wherever man establishes himself, upon the earth, he has to fight for his place against the lower orders of life. Food, the basis of existence, has to be fought for even by the most idyllic of farmers. You plant, and you protect your growing crop with a gun. Food, food, how strangely it relates man with the animal and vegetable world! How important it is! And how fierce is the fight that goes on around it.

The same when one skins a rabbit, and takes out the inside, one realizes what an enormous part of the animal, comparatively, is intestinal, what a big part of him is just for food-apparatus; for *living on* other organisms.

And when one watches the horses in the big field, their noses to the ground, bite-bite-biting at the grass, and stepping absorbedly on, and bite-bite-biting without ever lifting their noses, cropping off the grass, the young shoots of alfalfa, the dandelions, with a blind, relentless, unwearied persistence, one's whole life pauses. One suddenly realizes again how all creatures devour, and *must* devour the lower forms of life.

So Susan, swinging across the field, snatches off the tops of the little wild sunflowers as if she were mowing. And down they go, down her black throat. And when she stands in her cowy oblivion chewing her cud, with her lower jaw swinging peacefully, and I am milking her, suddenly the camomiley smell of her breath, as she glances round with glaring, smoke-blue eyes, makes me realize it is the sunflowers that are her ball of cud. Sunflowers! And they will go to making her glistening black hide, and the thick cream on her milk.

And the chickens, when they see a great black beetle, that the Mexicans call a *toro,* floating past, they are after it in a rush. And if it settles, instantly the brown hen stabs it with her beak. It is a great beetle two or three inches long: but in a second it is in the crop of the chicken. Gone!

And Timsy, the cat, as she spies on the chipmunks, crouches in another sort of oblivion, soft, and still. The chipmunks come to drink the milk from the chickens' bowl. Two of them met at the bowl. They were little squirrely things with stripes down their backs. They sat up in front of one another, lifting their inquisitive little noses and humping their backs. Then each put its two little hands on the other's shoulders, they reared up, gazing into each other's faces; and finally they put their two little noses together, in a sort of kiss.

But Miss Timsy can't stand this. In a soft, white-and-yellow leap she is after them. They skip, with the darting jerks of chipmunks, to the wood-heap, and with one soft, high-leaping sideways bound Timsy goes through the air. Her snow-flake of a paw comes down on one of the chipmunks. She looks at it for a second. It squirms. Swiftly and triumphantly she puts her two flowery little white paws on it, legs straight out in front of her, back arched, gazing concentratedly yet whimsically. Chipmunk does not stir. She takes it softly in her mouth, where it dangles softly, like a lady's tippet. And with a proud, prancing motion the Timsy sets off towards the house, her white little feet hardly touching the ground.

But she gets shooed away. We refuse to loan her the sitting-room any more, for her gladiatorial displays. If the chippy must be "butchered to make a Timsy holiday," it shall be outside. Disappointed, but still high-stepping, the Timsy sets off towards the clay over by the shed.

There she lays the chippy gently down, and soft as a little white cloud lays one small paw on its striped back. Chippy does not move. Soft as thistle-down she raises her paw a tiny, tiny bit, to release him.

And all of a sudden, with an elastic jerk, he darts from under the white release of her paw. And instantly, she is up in the air and down she comes on him, with the forward thrusting bolts of her white paws. Both creatures are motionless.

Then she takes him softly in her mouth again, and looks round, to see if she can slip into the house. She cannot. So she trots towards the wood-pile.

It is a game, and it is pretty. Chippy escapes into the wood-pile, and she softly, softly reconnoitres among the faggots.

Of all the animals, there is no denying it, the Timsy is the most pretty, the most fine. It is not her mere *corpus* that is beautiful; it is her bloom of aliveness. Her "infinite variety"; the soft, snow-flakey lightness of her, and at the same time her lean, heavy ferocity. I had never realized the latter, till I was lying in bed one day moving my toe, unconsciously, under the bedclothes. Suddenly a terrific blow struck my foot. The Timsy had sprung out of nowhere, with a hurling, steely force, thud upon the bedclothes where the toe was moving. It was as if someone had aimed a sudden blow, vindictive and unerring.

"Timsy!"

She looked at me with the vacant, feline glare of her hunting eyes. It is not even ferocity. It is the dilation of the strange, vacant arrogance of power. The power is in her.

And so it is. Life moves in circles of power and of vividness, and each circle of life only maintains its orbit upon the subjection of some lower circle. If the lower cycles of life are not *mastered*, there can be no higher cycle.

In nature, one creature devours another, and this is an essential part of all existence and of all being. It is not something to lament over, nor something to try to reform. The Buddhist who refuses to take life is really ridiculous, since if he eats only two grains of rice per day, it is two grains of life. We did not make creation, *we* are not the authors of the universe. And if we see that the whole of creation is established upon the fact that one life devours another life, one cycle of existence can only come into existence through the subjugating of another cycle of existence, then what is the good of trying to pretend that it is not so? The only thing to do is to realize what is higher, and what is lower, in the cycles of existence.

It is nonsense to declare that there *is* no higher and lower. We know full well that the dandelion belongs to a higher cycle of existence than the hartstongue fern, that the ant's is a higher form of existence than the dandelion's, that the thrush is higher than the ant, that Timsy the cat is higher than the thrush, and that I, a man, am higher than Timsy.

What do we mean by higher? Strictly, we mean more alive. More vividly alive. The ant is more vividly alive than the pine-tree. We know it, there is no trying to refute it. It is all very well saying that they are both alive in two different ways, and therefore they are incomparable, incommensurable. This is also true.

But one truth does not displace another. Even apparently contradictory truths do not displace one another. Logic is far too coarse to make the subtle distinctions life demands.

Truly, it is futile to compare an ant with a great pine-tree, in the absolute. Yet as far as *existence* is concerned, they are not only placed in comparison to one another, they are occasionally pitted against one another. And if it comes to a contest, the little ant will devour the life of the huge tree. If it comes to a contest.

And, in the cycles of *existence*, this is the test. From the lowest form of existence to the highest, the test question is: *Can thy neighbour finally overcome thee?*

If he can, then he belongs to a higher cycle of existence.

This is the truth behind the survival of the fittest. Every cycle of existence is established upon the overcoming of the lower cycles of existence. The real question is, wherein does *fitness* lie? Fitness for what? Fit merely to survive? That which is only fit to survive will survive only to supply food or contribute in some way to the existence of a higher form of life, which is able to do more than survive, which can really *vive*, live.

Life is more vivid in the dandelion than in the green fern, or than in a palm tree.

Life is more vivid in a snake than in a butterfly.

Life is more vivid in a wren than in an alligator.

Life is more vivid in a cat than in an ostrich.

Life is more vivid in the Mexican who drives the wagon than in the two horses in the wagon.

Life is more vivid in me than in the Mexican who drives the wagon for me.

We are speaking in terms of *existence:* that is, in terms of species, race, or type.

The dandelion can take hold of the land, the palm tree is driven into a corner, with the fern.

The snake can devour the fiercest insect.

The fierce bird can destroy the greatest reptile.

The great cat can destroy the greatest bird.

The man can destroy the horse, or any animal.

One race of man can subjugate and rule another race.

All this in terms of *existence*. As far as existence goes, that life-species is the highest which can devour, or destroy, or subjugate every other life-species against which it is pitted in contest.

This is a law. There is no escaping this law. Anyone, or any race, trying to escape it will fall a victim: will fall into subjugation.

But let us insist and insist again, we are talking now of existence, of species, of types, of races, of nations, not of single individuals, nor of *beings*. The dandelion in full flower, a little sun bristling with sun-rays on the green earth, is a nonpareil, a nonsuch. Foolish, foolish, foolish to compare it to anything else on earth. It is itself incomparable and unique.

But that is the fourth dimension, of *being*. It is in the fourth dimension, nowhere else.

Because, in the time-space dimension, any man may tread on the yellow sun-mirror, and it is gone. Any cow may swallow it. Any bunch of ants may annihilate it.

This brings us to the inexorable law of life.

1. Any creature that attains to its own fullness of being, its own *living* self, becomes unique, a nonpareil. It has its place in the fourth dimension, the heaven of existence, and there it is perfect, it is beyond comparison.

2. At the same time, every creature exists in time and space. And in time and space it exists relatively to all other existence, and can never

be absolved. Its existence impinges on other existences, and is itself impinged upon. And in the struggle for existence, if an effort on the part of any one type or species or order of life can finally destroy the other species, then the destroyer is of a more vital cycle of existence than the one destroyed. (When speaking of existence we always speak in types, species, not individuals. Species exist. But even an individual dandelion has *being*.)

3. The force which we call *vitality*, and which is the determining factor in the struggle for existence, is, however, derived also from the fourth dimension. That is to say, the ultimate source of all vitality is in that other dimension, or region, where the dandelion blooms, and which men have called heaven, and which now they call the fourth dimension: which is only a way of saying that it is not to be reckoned in terms of space and time.

4. The primary way, in our existence, to get vitality, is to absorb it from living creatures lower than ourselves. It is thus transformed into a new and higher creation. (There are many ways of absorbing: devouring food is one way, love is often another. The best way is a pure relationship, which includes the *being* on each side, and which allows the transfer to take place in a living flow, enhancing the life in both beings.)

5. No creature is fully itself till it is, like the dandelion, opened in the bloom of pure relationship to the sun, the entire living cosmos.

So we still find ourselves in the tangle of existence and being, a tangle which man has never been able to get out of, except by sacrificing the one to the other.

Sacrifice is useless.

The clue to all existence is being. But you can't have being without existence, any more than you can have the dandelion flower without the leaves and the long tap root.

Being is *not* ideal, as Plato would have it: nor spiritual. It is a transcendent form of existence, and as much material as existence is. Only the matter suddenly enters the fourth dimension.

All existence is dual, and surging towards a consummation into being. In the seed of the dandelion, as it floats with its little umbrella of hairs, sits the Holy Ghost in tiny compass. The Holy Ghost is that which holds the light and the dark, the day and the night, the wet and the sunny, united in one little clue. There it sits, in the seed of the dandelion.

The seed falls to earth. The Holy Ghost rouses, saying: "*Come!*" And out of the sky come the rays of the sun, and out of earth come dampness and dark and the death-stuff. They are called in, like those bidden to a feast. The sun sits down at the hearth, inside the seed; and the dark, damp death-returner sits on the opposite side, with the host between. And the host says to them: "*Come! Be merry together!*" So the sun looks with desirous curiosity on the dark face of the earth, and the dark damp one looks with wonder on the bright face of the other, who comes from the sun. And the host says: "*Here you are at home! Lift me up, between you, that I may cease to be a Ghost. For it longs me to look out, it longs me to dance with the dancers.*"

So the sun in the seed, and the earthy one in the seed take hands, and laugh, and begin to dance. And their dancing is like a fire kindled, a bonfire with leaping flame. And the treading of their feet is like the running of little streams, down into the earth. So from the dance of the sun-in-the-seed with the earthy death-returner, green little flames of leaves shoot up, and hard little trickles of roots strike down. And the host laughs, and says: "*I am being lifted up! Dance harder! Oh wrestle, you two, like wonderful wrestlers, neither of which can win.*" So sun-in-the-seed and the death-returner, who is earthy, dance faster and faster and the leaves rising greener begin to dance in a ring above-ground, fiercely overwhelming any outsider, in a whirl of swords and lions' teeth. And the earthy one wrestles, wrestles with the sun-in-the-seed, so the long roots reach down like arms of a fighter gripping the power of earth, and strangles all intruders, strangling any intruder mercilessly. Till the two fall in one strange embrace, and from the centre the long flower-stem lifts like a phallus, budded with a bud. And out of the bud the voice of the Holy Ghost is heard crying: "*I am lifted up! Lo! I am lifted up! I am here!*" So the bud opens, and there is the flower poised in the very middle of the universe, with a ring of green swords below, to guard it, and the octopus, arms deep in earth, drinking and threatening. So the Holy Ghost, being a dandelion flower, looks round, and says: "*Lo! I am yellow! I believe the sun has lent me his body! Lo! I am sappy with golden, bitter blood! I believe death out of the damp black earth has lent me his blood! I am incarnate! I like my incarnation! But this is not all. I will keep this incarnation. It is good! But oh! if I can win to another incarnation, who knows how wonderful it will be! This one will have to give place. This one can help to create the next.*"

So the Holy Ghost leaves the clue to himself behind, in the seed, and wanders forth in the comparative chaos of our universe, seeking another incarnation.

And this will go on for ever. Man, as yet, is less than half grown. Even his flower-stem has not appeared yet. He is all leaves and roots, without any clue put forth. No sign of bud anywhere.

Either he will have to start budding, or he will be forsaken of the Holy Ghost: abandoned as a failure in creation, as the ichthyosaurus was abandoned. Being abandoned means losing his vitality. The sun and the earth-dark will cease rushing together in him. Already it is ceasing. To men, the sun is becoming stale, and the earth sterile. But the sun itself will never become stale, nor the earth barren. It is only that the *clue* is missing inside men. They are like flowerless, seedless fat cabbages, nothing inside.

Vitality depends upon the clue of the Holy Ghost inside a creature, a man, a nation, a race. When the clue goes, the vitality goes. And the Holy Ghost seeks for ever a new incarnation, and subordinates the old to the new. You will know that any creature or race is still alive with the Holy Ghost, when it can subordinate the lower creatures or races, and assimilate them into a new incarnation.

No man, or creature, or race can have vivid vitality unless it be moving towards a blossoming: and the most powerful is that which moves towards the as-yet-unknown blossom.

Blossoming means the establishing of a pure, *new* relationship with all the cosmos. This is the state of heaven. And it is the state of a flower, a cobra, a jenny-wren in spring, a man when he knows himself royal and crowned with the sun, with his feet gripping the core of the earth.

This too is the fourth dimension: this state, this mysterious other reality of things in a perfected relationship. It is into this perfected relationship that every straight line curves, as if to some core, passing out of the time-space dimension.

But any man, creature, or race moving towards blossoming will have to draw immense supplies of vitality from men, or creatures below, passionate strength. And he will have to accomplish a perfected relation with all things.

There will be conquest, always. But the aim of conquest is a perfect relation of conquerors with conquered, for a new blossoming. Freedom is illusory. Sacrifice is illusory. Almightiness is illusory. Freedom, sacrifice, almightiness, these are all human side-tracks, cul-desacs, bunk. All that is real is the overwhelmingness of a new inspirational command, a new relationship with all things.

Heaven is always there. No achieved consummation is lost. Procreation goes on for ever, to support the achieved revelation. But the torch of revelation itself is handed on. And this is all important.

Everything living wants to procreate more living things.

But more important than this is the fact that every revelation is a torch held out, to kindle new revelations. As the dandelion holds out the sun to me, saying: "*Can you take it!*"

Every gleam of heaven that is shown—like a dandelion flower, or a green beetle—quivers with strange passion to kindle a new gleam, never yet beheld. This is not self-sacrifice: it is self-contribution: in which the highest happiness lies.

The torch of existence is handed on, in the womb of procreation.

And the torch of revelation is handed on, by every living thing, from the protococcus to a brave man or a beautiful woman, handed to whomsoever can take it. He who can take it has power beyond all the rest.

The cycle of procreation exists purely for the keeping alight of the torch of perfection, in any species: the torch being the dandelion in blossom, the tree in full leaf, the peacock in all his plumage, the cobra in all his colour, the frog at full leap, woman in all the mystery of her fathomless desirableness, man in the fulness of his power: every creature become its pure self.

One cycle of perfection urges to kindle another cycle, as yet unknown.

And with the kindling from the torch of revelation comes the inrush of vitality, and the need to consume and *consummate* the lower cycles of existence, into a new thing. This consuming and this consummating means conquest, and fearless mastery. Freedom lies in the honourable yielding towards the new flame, and the honourable mastery of that which shall be new, over that which must yield. As I must master my horses, which are in a lower cycle of existence. And they, they are relieved and *happy* to serve. If I turn them loose into the mountain ranges, to run wild till they die, the thrill of real happiness is gone out of their lives.

Every lower order seeks in some measure to serve a higher order: and rebels against being conquered.

It is always conquest, and it always will be conquest. If the conquered be an old, declining race, they will have handed on their torch to the conqueror: who will burn his fingers badly, if he is too flippant. And if the conquered be a barbaric race, they will consume the fire of the conqueror, and leave him flameless, unless he watches it. But it is always conquest, conquered and conqueror, for ever. The Kingdom of heaven is the Kingdom of conquerors, who can serve the conquest for ever, after their own conquest is made.

In heaven, in the perfected relation, is peace: in the fourth dimension. But there is getting there. And that, for ever, is the process of conquest.

When the rose blossomed, then the great Conquest was made by the Vegetable Kingdom. But even this conqueror of conquerors, the rose, had to lend himself towards the caterpillar and the butterfly of a later conquest. A conqueror, but tributary to the later conquest.

There is no such thing as equality. In the kingdom of heaven, in the fourth dimension, each soul that achieves a perfect relationship with the cosmos, from its own centre, is perfect, and incomparable. It has no superior. It is a conqueror, and incomparable.

But every man, in the struggle of conquest towards his own consummation, must master the inferior cycles of life, and never relinquish his mastery. Also, if there be men beyond him, moving on to a newer consummation than his own, he must yield to their greater demand, and serve their greater mystery, and so be faithful to the kingdom of heaven which is within him, which is gained by conquest and by loyal service.

Any man who achieves his own being will, like the dandelion or the butterfly, pass into that other dimension which we call the fourth, and the old people called heaven. It is the state of perfected relationship. And here a man will have his peace for ever: whether he serve or command, in the process of living.

But even this entails his faithful allegiance to the kingdom of heaven, which must be for ever and for ever extended, as creation conquers chaos. So that my perfection will but serve a perfection which still lies ahead, unrevealed and unconceived, and beyond my own.

We have tried to build walls round the kingdom of heaven: but it's no good. It's only the cabbage rotting inside.

Our last wall is the golden wall of money. This is a fatal wall. It cuts us off from life, from vitality, from the alive sun and the alive earth, as *nothing* can. Nothing, not even the most fanatical dogmas of an iron-bound religion, can insulate us from the inrush of life and inspiration, as money can.

We are losing vitality: losing it rapidly. Unless we seize the torch of inspiration, and drop our moneybags, the moneyless will be kindled by the flame of flames, and they will consume us like old rags.

We are losing vitality, owing to money and money-standards. The torch in the hands of the moneyless will set our house on fire, and burn us to death, like sheep in a flaming corral.

The Woman Who Rode Away

This was the title story in a volume of fiction published in 1928.

She had thought that this marriage, of all marriages, would be an adventure. Not that the man himself was exactly magical to her. A little, wiry, twisted fellow, twenty years older than herself, with brown eyes and greying hair, who had come to America a scrap of a wastrel, from Holland, years ago, as a tiny boy, and from the gold-mines of the west had been kicked south into Mexico, and now was more or less rich, owning silver-mines in the wilds of the Sierra Madre: it was obvious that the adventure lay in his circumstances, rather than his person. But he was still a little dynamo of energy, in spite of accidents survived, and what he had accomplished he had accomplished alone. One of those human oddments there is no accounting for.

When she actually *saw* what he had accomplished, her heart quailed. Great green-covered, unbroken mountain-hills, and in the midst of the lifeless isolation, the sharp pinkish mounds of the dried mud from the silver-works. Under the nakedness of the works, the walled-in, one-storey adobe house, with its garden inside, and its deep inner verandah with tropical climbers on the sides. And when you looked up from this shut-in flowered patio, you saw the huge pink cone of the silver-mud refuse, and the machinery of the extracting plant against heaven above. No more.

To be sure, the great wooden doors were often open. And then she could stand outside, in the vast open world. And see great, void, tree-clad hills piling behind one another, from nowhere into nowhere. They were green in autumn time. For the rest, pinkish, stark dry, and abstract.

And in his battered Ford car her husband would take her into the dead, thrice-dead little Spanish town forgotten among the mountains. The great, sun-dried dead church, the dead portales, the hopeless covered market-place, where, the first time she went, she saw a dead dog lying between the meat stalls and the vegetable array, stretched out as if for ever, nobody troubling to throw it away. Deadness within deadness.

Everybody feebly talking silver, and showing bits of ore. But silver was at a standstill. The great war came and went. Silver was a dead market. Her husband's mines were closed down. But she and he lived on in the adobe house under the works, among the flowers that were never very flowery to her.

She had two children, a boy and a girl. And her eldest, the boy, was nearly ten years old before she aroused from her stupor of subjected amazement. She was now thirty-three, a large, blue-eyed, dazed woman, beginning to grow stout. Her little, wiry, tough, twisted, brown-eyed husband was fifty-three, a man as tough as wire, tenacious as wire, still full of energy, but dimmed by the lapse of silver from the market, and by some curious inaccessibility on his wife's part.

He was a man of principles, and a good husband. In a way, he doted on her. He never quite got over his dazzled admiration of her. But essentially, he was still a bachelor. He had been thrown out on the world, a little bachelor, at the age of ten. When he married he was over forty, and had enough money to marry on. But his capital was all a bachelor's. He was boss of his own works, and marriage was the last and most intimate bit of his own works.

He admired his wife to extinction, he admired her body, all her points. And she was to him always the rather dazzling Californian girl from Berkeley, whom he had first known. Like any sheik, he kept her guarded among those mountains of Chihuahua. He was jealous of her as he was of his silver-mine: and that is saying a lot.

At thirty-three she really was still the girl from Berkeley, in all but physique. Her conscious development had stopped mysteriously with her marriage, completely arrested. Her husband had never become real to her, neither mentally nor physically. In spite of his late sort of passion for her, he never meant anything to her, physically. Only morally he swayed her, downed her, kept her in an invincible slavery.

So the years went by, in the adobe house strung round the sunny patio, with the silver-works overhead. Her husband was never still. When the silver went dead, he ran a ranch lower down, some twenty miles away, and raised pure-bred hogs, splendid creatures. At the same time, he hated pigs. He was a squeamish waif of an idealist, and really hated the physical side of life. He loved work, work, work, and making things. His marriage, his children, were something he was making, part of his business, but with a sentimental income this time.

Gradually her nerves began to go wrong: she must get out. She must get out. So he took her to El Paso for three months. And at least it was the United States.

But he kept his spell over her. The three months ended: back she was, just the same, in her adobe house among those eternal green or pinky-brown hills, void as only the undiscovered is void. She taught her children, she supervised the Mexican boys who were her servants. And sometimes her husband brought visitors, Spaniards or Mexicans or occasionally white men.

He really loved to have white men staying on the place. Yet he had not a moment's peace when they were there. It was as if his wife were some peculiar secret vein of ore in his mines, which no one must be aware of except himself. And she was fascinated by the young gentlemen, mining engineers, who were his guests at times. He, too, was fascinated by a real gentleman. But he was an old-timer miner with a wife, and if a gentleman looked at his wife, he felt as if his mine were being looted, the secrets of it pryed out.

It was one of these young gentlemen who put the idea into her mind. They were all standing outside the great wooden doors of the patio, looking at the outer world. The eternal, motionless hills were all green, it was September, after the rains. There was no sign of anything, save the deserted mine, the deserted works, and a bunch of half-deserted miner's dwellings.

"I wonder," said the young man, "what there is behind those great blank hills."

"More hills," said Lederman. "If you go that way, Sonora and the coast. This way is the desert—you came from there.—And the other way, hills and mountains."

"Yes, but what *lives* in the hills and the mountains? *Surely* there is something wonderful? It looks *so* like nowhere on earth: like being on the moon."

"There's plenty of game, if you want to shoot. And Indians, if you call *them* wonderful."

"Wild ones?"

"Wild enough."

"But friendly?"

"It depends. Some of them are quite wild, and they don't let anybody near. They kill a missionary at sight. And where a missionary can't get, nobody can."

"But what does the government say?"

"They're so far from everywhere, the government leaves 'em alone. And they're wily; if they think there'll be trouble, they send a delegation to Chihuahua and make a formal submission. The government is glad to leave it at that."

"And do they live quite wild, with their own savage customs and religion?"

"Oh, yes. They use nothing but bows and arrows. I've seen them in town, in the Plaza, with funny sorts of hats with flowers round them, and a bow in one hand, quite naked except for a sort of shirt, even in cold weather—striding round with their savage's bare legs."

"But don't you suppose it's wonderful, up there in their secret villages?"

"No. What would there be wonderful about it? Savages are savages, and all savages behave more or less alike: rather low-down and dirty, insanitary, with a few cunning tricks, and struggling to get enough to eat."

"But surely they have old, old religions and mysteries—it *must* be wonderful, surely it must."

"I don't know about mysteries—howling and heathen practices, more or less indecent. No, I see nothing wonderful in that kind of stuff. And I wonder that you should, when you have lived in London or Paris or New York—"

"Ah, *everybody* lives in London or Paris or New York"—said the young man, as if this were an argument.

And his peculiar vague enthusiasm for unknown Indians found a full echo in the woman's heart. She was overcome by a foolish romanticism more unreal than a girl's. She felt it was her destiny to wander into the secret haunts of these timeless, mysterious, marvellous Indians of the mountains.

She kept her secret. The young man was departing, her husband was going with him down to Torreon, on business:—would be away for some days. But before the departure, she made her husband talk about the Indians: about the wandering tribes, resembling the Navajo, who were still wandering free; and the Yaquis of Sonora: and the different groups in the different valleys of Chihuahua State.

There was supposed to be one tribe, the Chilchuis, living in a high valley to the south, who were the sacred tribe of all the Indians. The descendants of Montezuma and of the old Aztec or Totonac kings still lived among them, and the old priests still kept up the ancient religion, and offered human sacrifices—so it was said. Some scientists had been to the Chilchui country, and had come back gaunt and exhausted with hunger and bitter privation, bringing various curious, barbaric objects of worship, but having seen nothing extraordinary in the hungry, stark village of savages.

Though Lederman talked in this off-hand way, it was obvious he felt some of the vulgar excitement at the idea of ancient and mysterious savages.

"How far away are they?" she asked.

"Oh—three days on horseback—past Cuchitee and a little lake there is up there."

Her husband and the young man departed. The woman made her crazy plans. Of late, to break the monotony of her life, she had harassed her husband into letting her go riding with him, occasionally, on horseback. She was never allowed to go out alone. The country truly was not safe, lawless and crude.

But she had her own horse, and she dreamed of being free as she had been as a girl, among the hills of California.

Her daughter, nine years old, was now in a tiny convent in the little half-deserted Spanish mining-town five miles away.

"Manuel," said the woman to her house-servant, "I'm going to ride to the convent to see Margarita, and take her a few things. Perhaps I shall stay the night in the convent. You look after Freddy and see everything is all right till I come back."

"Shall I ride with you on the master's horse, or shall Juan?" asked the servant.

"Neither of you. I shall go alone."

The young man looked her in the eyes, in protest. Absolutely impossible that the woman should ride alone!

"I shall go alone," repeated the large, placid-seeming, fair-complexioned woman, with peculiar overbearing emphasis. And the man silently, unhappily yielded.

"Why are you going alone, mother?" asked her son, as she made up parcels of food.

"Am I *never* to be let alone? Not one moment of my life?" she cried, with sudden explosion of energy. And the child, like the servant, shrank into silence.

She set off without a qualm, riding astride on her strong roan horse, and wearing a riding suit of coarse linen, a riding skirt over her linen breeches, a scarlet neck-tie over her white blouse, and a black felt hat on her head. She had food in her saddle-bags, an army canteen with water, and a large, native blanket tied on behind the saddle. Peering into the distance, she set off from her home. Manuel and the little boy stood in the gateway to watch her go. She did not even turn to wave them farewell.

But when she had ridden about a mile, she left the wild road and took a small trail to the right, that led into another valley, over steep places and past great trees, and through another deserted mining-settlement. It was September, the water was running freely in the little stream that had fed the now-abandoned mine. She got down to drink, and let the horse drink too.

She saw natives coming through the trees, away up the slope. They had seen her, and were watching her closely. She watched in turn. The three people, two women and a youth, were making a wide detour, so as not to come too close to her. She did not care. Mounting, she trotted ahead up the silent valley, beyond the silver-works, beyond any trace of mining. There was still a rough trail, that led over rocks and loose stones into the valley beyond. This trail she had already ridden, with her husband. Beyond that she knew she must go south.

Curiously she was not afraid, although it was a frightening country, the silent, fatal-seeming mountain-slopes, the occasional distant, suspicious, elusive natives among the trees, the great carrion birds occasionally hovering, like great flies, in the distance, over some carrion or some ranch house or some group of huts.

As she climbed, the trees shrank and the trail ran through a thorny scrub, that was trailed over with blue convolvulus and an occasional pink creeper. Then these flowers lapsed. She was nearing the pine-trees.

She was over the crest, and before her another silent, void, green-clad valley. It was past midday. Her horse turned to a little runlet of water, so she got down to eat her midday meal. She sat in silence looking at the motionless unliving valley, and at the sharp-peaked hills, rising higher to rock and pine-trees, southwards. She rested two hours in the heat of the day, while the horse cropped around her.

Curious that she was neither afraid nor lonely. Indeed, the loneliness was like a drink of cold water to one who is very thirsty. And a strange elation sustained her from within.

She travelled on, and camped at night in a valley beside a stream, deep among the bushes. She had seen cattle and had crossed several trails. There must be a ranch not far off. She heard the strange wailing shriek of a mountain-lion, and the answer of dogs. But she sat by her small camp fire in a secret hollow place and was not really afraid. She was buoyed up always by the curious, bubbling elation within her.

It was very cold before dawn. She lay wrapped in her blanket looking at the stars, listening to her horse shivering, and feeling like a woman who has died and passed beyond. She was not sure that she had not heard, during the night, a great crash at the centre of herself, which was the crash of her own death. Or else it was a crash at the centre of the earth, and meant something big and mysterious.

With the first peep of light she got up, numb with cold, and made a fire. She ate hastily, gave her horse some pieces of oil-seed cake, and set off again. She avoided any meeting—and since she met nobody, it was evident that she in turn was avoided. She came at last in sight of the village of Cuchitee, with its black houses with their reddish roofs, a sombre, dreary little cluster below another silent, long-abandoned mine. And beyond, a long, great mountain-side, rising up green and light to the darker, shaggier green of pine trees. And beyond the pine trees stretches of naked rock against the sky, rock slashed already and brindled with white stripes of snow. High up, the new snow had already begun to fall.

And now, as she neared, more or less, her destination, she began to go vague and disheartened. She had passed the little lake among yellowing aspen trees whose white trunks were round and suave like the white round arms of some woman. What a lovely place! In California she would have raved about it. But here she looked and saw that it was lovely, but she didn't care. She was weary and spent with her two nights in the open, and afraid of the coming night. She didn't know where she was going, or what she was going for. Her horse plodded dejectedly on, towards that immense and forbidding mountain-slope, following a stony little trail. And if she had had any will of her own left, she would have turned back, to the village, to be protected and sent home to her husband.

But she had no will of her own. Her horse splashed through a brook, and turned up a valley, under immense yellowing cotton-wood trees. She must have been near nine thousand feet above-sea-level, and her head was light with the altitude and with weariness. Beyond the cotton-wood trees she could see, on each side, the steep sides of mountain-slopes hemming her in, sharp-plumaged with overlapping aspen, and, higher up, with sprouting, pointed spruce and pine tree. Her horse went on automatically. In this tight valley, on this slight trail, there was nowhere to go but ahead, climbing.

Suddenly her horse jumped, and three men in dark blankets were on the trail before her.

"*Adiós!*" came the greeting, in the full, restrained Indian voice.

"*Adiós!*" she replied, in her assured, American woman's voice.

"Where are you going?" came the quiet question, in Spanish.

The men in the dark sarapes had come closer, and were looking up at her.

"On ahead," she replied coolly, in her hard, Saxon Spanish.

These were just natives to her: dark-faced, strongly-built men in dark sarapes and straw hats. They would have been the same as the men who worked for her husband, except, strangely, for the long black hair that fell over their shoulders. She noted this long black hair with a certain distaste. These must be the wild Indians she had come to see.

"Where do you come from?" the same man asked. It was always the one man who spoke. He was young, with quick, large, bright black eyes that glanced sideways at her. He had a soft black moustache on his dark face, and a sparse tuft of beard, loose hairs on his chin. His long black hair, full of life, hung unrestrained on his shoulders. Dark as he was, he did not look as if he had washed lately.

His two companions were the same, but older men, powerful and silent. One had a thin black line of moustache, but was beardless. The other had the smooth cheeks and the sparse dark hairs marking the lines of his chin with the beard characteristic of the Indians.

"I come from far away," she replied, with half-jocular evasion.

This was received in silence.

"But where do you live?" asked the young man, with that same quiet insistence.

"In the north," she replied airily.

Again there was a moment's silence. The young man conversed quietly, in Indian, with his two companions.

"Where do you want to go, up this way?" he asked suddenly, with challenge and authority, pointing briefly up the trail.

"To the Chilchui Indians," answered the woman laconically.

The young man looked at her. His eyes were quick and black, and inhuman. He saw, in the full evening light, the faint sub-smile of assurance on her rather large, calm, fresh-complexioned face; the weary, bluish lines under her large blue eyes; and in her eyes, as she looked down at him, a half-childish, half-arrogant confidence in her own female power. But in her eyes also, a curious look of trance.

"*Usted es Señora?* You are a lady?" the Indian asked her.

"Yes, I am a lady," she replied complacently.

"With a family?"

"With a husband and two children, boy and girl," she said.

The Indian turned to his companions and translated, in the low, gurgling speech, like hidden water running. They were evidently at a loss.

"Where is your husband?" asked the young man.

"Who knows?" she replied airily. "He has gone away on business for a week."

The black eyes watched her shrewdly. She, for all her weariness, smiled faintly in the pride of her own adventure and the assurance of her own womanhood, and the spell of the madness that was on her.

"And what do *you* want to do?" the Indian asked her.

"I want to visit the Chilchui Indians—to see their houses and to know their gods," she replied.

The young man turned and translated quickly, and there was a silence almost of consternation. The grave elder men were glancing at her sideways, with strange looks, from under their decorated hats. And they said something to the young man, in deep chest voices.

The latter still hesitated. Then he turned to the woman.

"Good!" he said. "Let us go. But we cannot arrive until to-morrow. We shall have to make a camp to-night."

"Good!" she said. "I can make a camp."

Without more ado, they set off at a good speed up the stony trail. The young Indian ran alongside her horse's head, the other two ran behind. One of them had taken a thick stick, and occasionally he struck her horse a resounding blow on the haunch, to urge him forward. This made the horse jump, and threw her back in the saddle, which, tired as she was, made her angry.

"Don't do that!" she cried, looking round angrily at the fellow. She met his black, large, bright eyes, and for the first time her spirit really quailed. The man's eyes were not human to her, and they did not see her as a beautiful white woman. He looked at her with a black, bright inhuman look, and saw no woman in her at all. As if she were some strange, unaccountable *thing,* incomprehensible to him, but inimical. She sat in her saddle in wonder, feeling once more as if she had died. And again he struck her horse, and jerked her badly in the saddle.

All the passionate anger of the spoilt white woman rose in her. She pulled her horse to a standstill, and turned with blazing eyes to the man at her bridle.

"Tell that fellow not to touch my horse again," she cried.

She met the eyes of the young man, and in their bright black inscrutability she saw a fine spark, as in a snake's eye, of derision. He spoke to his companion in the rear, in the low tones of the Indian. The man with the stick listened without looking. Then, giving a strange low cry to the horse, he struck it again on the rear, so that it leaped forward spasmodically up the stony trail, scattering the stones, pitching the weary woman in her seat.

The anger flew like a madness into her eyes, she went white at the gills. Fiercely she reined in her horse. But before she could turn, the young Indian had caught the reins under the horse's throat, jerked them forward, and was trotting ahead rapidly, leading the horse.

The woman was powerless. And along with her supreme anger there came a slight thrill of exultation. She knew she was dead.

The sun was setting, a great yellow light flooded the last of the aspens, flared on the trunks of the pine-trees, the pine-needles bristled and stood out with dark lustre, the rocks glowed with unearthly glamour. And through this effulgence the Indian at her horse's head trotted unweariedly on, his dark blanket swinging, his bare legs glowing with a strange transfigured ruddiness in the powerful light, and his straw hat with its half-absurd decorations of flowers and feathers shining showily above his river of long black hair. At times he would utter a low call to the horse, and then the other Indian, behind, would fetch the beast a whack with the stick.

The wonder-light faded off the mountains, the world began to grow dark, a cold air breathed down. In the sky, half a moon was struggling against the glow in the west. Huge shadows came down from steep rocky slopes. Water was rushing. The woman was conscious only of her fatigue, her unspeakable fatigue, and the cold wind from the heights. She was not aware how moonlight replaced daylight. It happened while she travelled unconscious with weariness.

For some hours they travelled by moonlight. Then suddenly they came to a standstill. The men conversed in low tones for a moment.

"We camp here," said the young man.

She waited for him to help her down. He merely stood holding the horse's bridle. She almost fell from the saddle, so fatigued.

They had chosen a place at the foot of rocks that still gave off a little warmth of the sun. One man cut pine-boughs, another erected little screens of pine-boughs against the rock for shelter, and put boughs of balsam pine for beds. The third made a small fire, to heat tortillas. They worked in silence.

The woman drank water. She did not want to eat—only to lie down.

"Where do I sleep?" she asked.

The young man pointed to one of the shelters. She crept in and lay inert. She did not care what happened to her, she was so weary, and so beyond everything. Through the twigs of spruce she could see the three men squatting round the fire on their hams, chewing the tortillas they picked from the ashes with their dark fingers, and drinking water from a gourd. They talked in low, muttering tones, with long intervals of silence. Her saddle and saddle-bags lay not far from the fire, unopened, untouched. The men were not interested in her or her belongings. There they squatted with their hats on their heads, eating, eating mechanically, like animals, the dark sarape with its fringe falling to the ground before and behind, the powerful dark legs naked and squatting like an animal's, showing the dirty white shirt and the sort of loin-cloth which was the only other garment, underneath. And they showed no more sign of interest in her than if she had been a piece of venison they were bringing home from the hunt, and had hung inside a shelter.

After a while they carefully extinguished the fire, and went inside their own shelter. Watching through the screen of boughs, she had a moment's thrill of fear and anxiety, seeing the dark forms cross and pass silently in the moonlight. Would they attack her now?

But, no! They were as if oblivious of her. Her horse was hobbled; she could hear it hopping wearily. All was silent, mountain-silent, cold, deathly. She slept and woke and slept in a semi-conscious numbness of cold and fatigue. A long, long night, icy and eternal, and she aware that she had died.

II

Yet when there was a stirring, and a clink of flint and steel, and the form of a man crouching like a dog over a bone, at a red splutter of fire, and she knew it was morning coming, it seemed to her the night has passed too soon.

When the fire was going, she came out of her shelter with one real desire left: for coffee. The men were warming more tortillas.

"Can we make coffee?" she asked.

The young man looked at her, and she imagined the same faint spark of derision in his eyes. He shook his head.

"We don't take it," he said. "There is no time."

And the elder men, squatting on their haunches, looked up at her in the terrible paling down, and there was not even derision in their eyes. Only that intense, yet remote, inhuman glitter which was terrible to her. They were inaccessible. They could not see her as a woman at all. As if she *were* not a woman. As if, perhaps, her whiteness took away all her womanhood, and left her as some giant, female white ant. That was all they could see in her.

Before the sun was up, she was in the saddle again, and they were climbing steeply, in the icy air. The sun came, and soon she was very hot, exposed to the glare in the bare places. It seemed to her they were climbing to the roof of the world. Beyond against heaven were slashes of snow.

During the course of the morning, they came to a place where the horse could not go farther. They rested for a time with a great slant of living rock in front of them, like the glossy breast of some earth-beast. Across this rock, along a wavering crack, they had to go. It seemed to her that for hours she went in torment, on her hands and knees, from crack to crevice, along the slanting face of this pure rock-mountain. An Indian in front and an Indian behind walked slowly erect, shod with sandals of braided leather. But she in her riding-boots dared not stand erect.

Yet what she wondered, all the time, was why she persisted in clinging and crawling along these mile-long sheets of rock. Why she did not hurl herself down, and have done? The world was below her.

When they emerged at last on a stony slope, she looked back, and saw the third Indian coming carrying her saddle and saddle-bags on his back, the whole hung from a band across his forehead. And he had his hat in his hand, as he stepped slowly, with the slow, soft, heavy tread of the Indian, unwavering in the chinks of rock, as if along a scratch in the mountain's iron shield.

The stony slope led downwards. The Indians seemed to grow excited. One ran ahead at a slow trot, disappearing round the curve of stones. And the track curved round and down, till at last in the full blaze of the mid-morning sun, they could see a valley below them, between walls of rock, as in a great wide chasm let in the mountains. A green valley, with a river, and trees, and clusters of low flat sparkling houses. It was all tiny and perfect, three thousand feet below. Even the flat bridge over the stream, and the square with the houses around it, the bigger buildings piled up at opposite ends of the square, the tall cotton-wood trees, the pastures and stretches of yellow-sere maize, the patches of brown sheep or goats in the distance, on the slopes, the railed enclosures by the stream-side. There it was, all small and perfect, looking magical, as any place will look magical, seen from the mountains above. The unusual thing was that the low houses glittered white, whitewashed, looking like crystals of salt, or silver. This frightened her.

They began the long, winding descent at the head of the barranca, following the stream that rushed and fell. At first it was all rocks: then the pine-trees began, and soon, the silver-limbed aspens. The flowers of autumn, big pink daisy-like flowers, and white ones, and many yellow flowers, were in profusion. But she had to sit down and rest, she was so weary. And she saw the bright flowers shadowily, as pale shadows hovering, as one who is dead must see them.

At length came grass and pasture-slopes between mingled aspen and pine-trees. A shepherd, naked in the sun save for his hat and his cotton loin-cloth, was driving his brown sheep away. In a grove of trees they sat and waited, she and the young Indian. The one with the saddle had also gone forward.

They heard a sound of someone coming. It was three men, in fine sarapes of red and orange and yellow and black, and with brilliant feather head-dresses. The oldest had his grey hair braided with fur, and his red and orange-yellow sarape was covered with curious black markings, like a leopard-skin. The other two were not grey-haired, but they were elders too. Their blankets were in stripes, and their head-dresses not so elaborate.

The young Indian addressed the elders in a few quiet words. They listened without answering or looking at him or at the woman, keeping their faces averted and their eyes turned to the ground, only listening. And at length they turned and looked at the woman.

The old chief, or medicine-man, whatever he was, had a deeply wrinkled and lined face of dark bronze, with a few sparse grey hairs round the mouth. Two long braids of grey hair, braided with fur and coloured feathers, hung on his shoulders. And yet, it was only his eyes that mattered. They were black and of extraordinary piercing strength, without a qualm of misgiving in their demonish, dauntless power. He looked into the eyes of the white woman with a long, piercing look, seeking she knew not what. She summoned all her strength to meet his eyes and keep up her guard. But it was no good. He was not looking at her as one human being looks at another. He never even perceived her resistance or her challenge, but looked past them both, into she knew not what.

She could see it was hopeless to expect any human communication with this old being.

He turned and said a few words to the young Indian.

"He asks what do you seek here?" said the young man in Spanish.

"I? Nothing! I only came to see what it was like."

This was again translated, and the old man turned his eyes on her once more. Then he spoke again, in his low muttering tone, to the young Indian.

"He says, why does she leave her house with the white men? Does she want to bring the white man's God to the Chilchui?"

"No," she replied, foolhardy. "I came away from the white man's God myself. I came to look for the God of the Chilchui."

Profound silence followed, when this was translated. Then the old man spoke again, in a small voice almost of weariness.

"Does the white woman seek the gods of the Chilchui because she is weary of her own God?" came the question.

"Yes, she does. She is tired of the white man's God," she replied, thinking that was what they wanted her to say. She would like to serve the gods of the Chilchui.

She was aware of an extraordinary thrill of triumph and exultance passing through the Indians, in the tense silence that followed when this was translated. Then they all looked at her with piercing black eyes, in which a steely covetous intent glittered incomprehensible. She was the more puzzled, as there was nothing sensual or sexual in the look. It had a terrible glittering purity that was beyond her. She was afraid, she would have been paralysed with fear, had not something died within her, leaving her with a cold, watchful wonder only.

The elders talked a little while, then the two went away, leaving her with the young man and the oldest chief. The old man now looked at her with a certain solicitude.

"He says are you tired?" asked the young man.

"Very tired," she said.

"The men will bring you a carriage," said the young Indian.

The carriage, when it came, proved to be a litter consisting of a sort of hammock of dark woollen frieze, slung on to a pole which was borne on the shoulders of two long-haired Indians. The woollen hammock was spread on the ground, she sat down on it, and the two men raised the pole to their shoulders. Swinging rather as if she were in a sack, she was carried out of the grove of trees, following the old chief, whose leopard-spotted blanket moved curiously in the sunlight.

They had emerged in the valley-head. Just in front were the maize fields, with ripe ears of maize. The corn was not very tall, in this high altitude. The well-worn path went between it, and all she could see was the erect form of the old chief, in the flame and black sarape, stepping soft and heavy and swift, his head forward, looking neither to right nor to left. Her bearers followed, stepping rhythmically, the long blue-black hair glistening like a river down the naked shoulders of the man in front.

They passed the maize, and came to a big wall or earthwork made of earth and adobe bricks. The wooden doors were open. Passing on, they were in a network of small gardens, full of flowers and herbs and fruit trees, each garden watered by a tiny ditch of running water. Among each cluster of trees and flowers was a small, glittering white house, windowless, and with closed door. The place was a network of little paths, small streams, and little bridges among square, flowering gardens.

Following the broadest path—a soft narrow track between leaves and grass, a path worn smooth by centuries of human feet, no hoof of horse nor any wheel to disfigure it—they came to the little river of swift bright water, and crossed on a log bridge. Everything was silent—there was no human being anywhere. The road went on under magnificent cotton-wood trees. It emerged suddenly outside the central plaza or square of the village.

This was a long oblong of low white houses with flat roofs, and two bigger buildings, having as it were little square huts piled on top of bigger long huts, stood at either end of the oblong, facing each other rather askew. Every little house was a dazzling white, save for the great round beam-ends which projected under the flat eaves, and for the flat roofs. Round each of the bigger buildings, on the outside of the square, was a stockyard fence, inside which was garden with trees and flowers, and various small houses.

Not a soul was in sight. They passed silently between the houses into the central square. This was quite bare and arid, the earth trodden smooth by endless generations of passing feet, passing across from door to door. All the doors of the windowless houses gave on to this blank square, but all the doors were closed. The firewood lay near the threshold, a clay oven was still smoking, but there was no sign of moving life.

The old man walked straight across the square to the big house at the end, where the two upper storeys, as in a house of toy bricks, stood each one smaller than the lower one. A stone staircase, outside, led up to the roof of the first storey.

At the foot of this staircase the litter-bearers stood still, and lowered the woman to the ground.

"You will come up," said the young Indian who spoke Spanish.

She mounted the stone stairs to the earthen roof of the first house, which formed a platform round the wall of the second storey. She followed around this platform to the back of the big house. There they descended again, into the garden at the rear.

So far they had seen no one. But now two men appeared, bareheaded, with long braided hair, and wearing a sort of white shirt gathered into a loin-cloth. These went along with the three newcomers, across the garden where red flowers and yellow flowers were blooming, to a long, low white house. There they entered without knocking.

It was dark inside. There was a low murmur of men's voices. Several men were present, their white shirts showing in the gloom, their dark faces invisible. They were sitting on a great log of smooth old wood, that lay along the far wall. And save for this log, the room seemed empty. But no, in the dark at one end was a couch, a sort of bed, and someone lying there, covered with furs.

The old Indian in the spotted sarape, who had accompanied the woman, now took off his hat and his blanket and his sandals. Laying them aside, he approached the couch, and spoke in a low voice. For some moments there was no answer. Then an old man, with the snow-white hair hanging round his darkly-visible face, roused himself like a vision, and leaned on one elbow, looking vaguely at the company, in tense silence.

The grey-haired Indian spoke again, and then the young Indian, taking the woman's hand, led her forward. In her linen riding habit, and black boots and hat, and her pathetic bit of a red tie, she stood there beside the fur-covered bed of the old, old man, who sat reared up, leaning on one elbow, remote as a ghost, his white hair streaming in disorder, his face almost black, yet with a far-off intentness, not of this world, leaning forward to look at her.

His face was so old, it was like dark glass, and the few curling hairs that sprang white from his lips and chin were quite incredible. The long white locks fell unbraided and disorderly on either side of the glassy dark face. And under a faint powder of white eyebrows, the black eyes of the old chief looked at her as if from the far, far dead, seeing something that was never to be seen.

At last he spoke a few deep, hollow words, as if to the dark air.

"He says, do you bring your heart to the god of the Chilchui?" translated the young Indian.

"Tell him yes," she said, automatically.

There was a pause. The old Indian spoke again, as if to the air. One of the men present went out. There was a silence as if of eternity, in the dim room that was lighted only through the open door.

The woman looked round. Four old men with grey hair sat on the log by the wall facing the door. Two other men, powerful and impassive, stood near the door. They all had long hair, and wore white shirts gathered into a loin-cloth. Their powerful legs were naked and dark. There was a silence like eternity.

At length the man returned, with white and dark clothing on his arm. The young Indian took them, and holding them in front of the woman, said:

"You must take off your clothes, and put these on."

"If all you men will go out," she said.

"No one will hurt you," he said quietly.

"Not while you men are here," she said.

He looked at the two men by the door. They came quickly forward, and suddenly gripped her arms as she stood, without hurting her, but with great power. Then two of the old men came, and with curious skill slit her boots down with keen knives, and drew them off, and slit her clothing so that it came away from her. In a few moments she stood there white and uncovered. The old man on the bed spoke, and they turned her round for him to see. He spoke again, and the young Indian deftly took the pins and comb from her fair hair, so that it fell over her shoulders in a bunchy tangle.

Then the old man spoke again. The Indian led her to the bedside. The white-haired, glassy-dark old man moistened his finger-tips at his mouth, and most delicately touched her on the breasts and on the body, then on the back. And she winced strangely each time, as the finger-tips drew along her skin, as if Death itself were touching her.

And she wondered, almost sadly, why she did not feel shamed in her nakedness. She only felt sad and lost. Because nobody felt ashamed. The elder men were all dark and tense with some other deep, gloomy, incomprehensible emotion, which suspended all her agitation, while the young Indian had a strange look of ecstasy on his face. And she, she was only utterly strange and beyond herself, as if her body were not her own.

They gave her the new clothing: a long white cotton shift, that came to her knees: then a tunic of thick blue woollen stuff, embroidered with scarlet and green flowers. It was fastened over one shoulder only, and belted with a braid sash of scarlet and black wool.

When she was thus dressed, they took her away, barefoot, to a little house in the stockaded garden. The young Indian told her she might have what she wanted. She asked for water to wash herself. He brought it in a jar, together with a long wooden bowl. Then he fastened the gate-door of her house, and left her a prisoner. She could see through the bars of the gate-door of her house, the red flowers of the garden, and a humming bird. Then from the roof of the big house she heard the long, heavy sound of a drum, unearthly to her in its summons, and an uplifting voice calling from the house-top in a strange language, with a far-away emotionless intonation, delivering some speech or message. And she listened as if from the dead.

But she was very tired. She lay down on a couch of skins, pulling over her the blanket of dark wool, and she slept, giving up everything.

When she woke it was later afternoon, and the young Indian was entering with a basket-tray containing food, tortillas and corn-mush with bits of meat, probably mutton, and a drink made of honey, and some fresh plums. He brought her also a long garland of red and yellow flowers with knots of blue buds at the end. He sprinkled the garland with water from a jar, then offered it to her, with a smile. He seemed very gentle and thoughtful, and on his face and in his dark eyes was a curious look of triumph and ecstasy, that frightened her a little. The glitter had gone from the black eyes, with their curving dark lashes, and he would look at her with this strange soft glow of ecstasy that was not quite human, and terribly impersonal, and which made her uneasy.

"Is there anything you want?" he said, in his low, slow, melodious voice, that always seemed withheld, as if he were speaking aside to somebody else, or as if he did not want to let the sound come out to her.

"Am I going to be kept a prisoner here?" she asked.

"No, you can walk in the garden to-morrow," he said softly. Always this curious solicitude.

"Do you like that drink?" he said, offering her a little earthenware cup. "It is very refreshing."

She sipped the liquor curiously. It was made with herbs and sweetened with honey, and had a strange, lingering flavour. The young man watched her with gratification.

"It has a peculiar taste," she said.

"It is very refreshing," he replied, his black eyes resting on her always with that look of gratified ecstasy. Then he went away. And presently she began to be sick, and to vomit violently, as if she had no control over herself.

Afterwards she felt a great soothing languor steal over her, her limbs felt strong and loose and full of languor, and she lay on her couch listening to the sounds of the village, watching the yellowing sky, smelling the scent of burning cedar-wood, or pine-wood. So distinctly she heard the yapping of tiny dogs, the shuffle of far-off feet, the murmur of voices, so keenly she detected the smell of smoke, and flowers, and evening falling, so vividly she saw the one bright star infinitely remote, stirring above the sunset, that she felt as if all her senses were diffused on the air, that she could distinguish the sound of evening flowers unfolding, and the actual crystal sound of the heavens, as the vast belts of the world-atmosphere slid past one another, and as if the moisture ascending and the moisture descending in the air resounded like some harp in the cosmos.

She was a prisoner in her house and in the stockaded garden, but she scarcely minded. And it was days before she realized that she never saw another woman. Only the men, the elderly men of the big house, that she imagined must be some sort of temple, and the men priests of some sort. For they always had the same colours, red, orange, yellow, and black, and the same grave, abstracted demeanour.

Sometimes an old man would come and sit in her room with her, in absolute silence. None spoke any language but Indian, save the one younger man. The older men would smile at her, and sit with her for an hour at a time, sometimes smiling at her when she spoke in Spanish, but never answering save with this slow, benevolent-seeming smile. And they gave off a feeling of almost fatherly solicitude. Yet their dark eyes, brooding over her, had something away in their depths that was awesomely ferocious and relentless. They would cover it with a smile, at once, if they felt her looking. But she had seen it.

Always they treated her with this curious impersonal solicitude, this utterly impersonal gentleness, as an old man treats a child. But underneath it she felt there was something else, something terrible. When her old visitor had gone away, in his silent, insidious, fatherly fashion, a shock of fear would come over her; though of what she knew not.

The young Indian would sit and talk with her freely, as if with great candour. But with him, too, she felt that everything real was unsaid. Perhaps it was unspeakable. His big dark eyes would rest on her almost cherishingly, touched with ecstasy, and his beautiful, slow, languorous voice would trail out its simple, ungrammatical Spanish. He told her he was the grandson of the old, old man, son of the man in the spotted sarape: and they were caciques, kings from the old, old days, before even the Spaniards came. But he himself had been in Mexico City, and also in the United States. He had worked as a labourer, building the roads in Los Angeles. He had travelled as far as Chicago.

"Don't you speak English, then?" she asked.

His eyes rested on her with a curious look of duplicity and conflict, and he mutely shook his head.

"What did you do with your long hair, when you were in the United States?" she asked. "Did you cut it off?"

Again, with the look of torment in his eyes, he shook his head.

"No," he said, in a low, subdued voice, "I wore a hat, and a handkerchief tied round my head."

And he relapsed into silence, as if of tormented memories.

"Are you the only man of your people who has been to the United States?" she asked him.

"Yes. I am the only one who has been away from here for a long time. The others come back soon, in one week. They don't stay away. The old men don't let them."

"And why did you go?"

"The old men want me to go—because I shall be the Cacique——"

He talked always with the same naïveté, an almost childish candour. But she felt that this was perhaps just the effect of his Spanish. Or perhaps speech altogether was unreal to him. Anyhow, she felt that all the real things were kept back.

He came and sat with her a good deal—sometimes more than she wished—as if he wanted to be near her. She asked him if he was married. He said he was—with two children.

"I should like to see your children," she said.

But he answered only with that smile, a sweet, almost ecstatic smile, above which the dark eyes hardly changed from their enigmatic abstraction.

It was curious, he would sit with her by the hour, without ever making her self-conscious, or sex-conscious. He seemed to have no sex, as he sat there so still and gentle and apparently submissive, with his head bent a little forward, and the river of glistening black hair streaming maidenly over his shoulders.

Yet when she looked again, she saw his shoulders broad and powerful, his eyebrows black and level, the short, curved, obstinate black lashes over his lowered eyes, the small, fur-like line of moustache above his blackish, heavy lips, and the strong chin, and she knew that in some other mysterious way he was darkly and powerfully male. And he, feeling her watching him, would glance up at her swiftly with a dark, lurking look in his eyes, which immediately he veiled with that half-sad smile.

The days and the weeks went by, in a vague kind of contentment. She was uneasy sometimes, feeling she had lost the power over herself. She was not in her own power, she was under the spell of some other control. And at times she had moments of terror and horror. But then these Indians would come and sit with her, casting their insidious spell over her by their very silent presence, their silent, sexless, powerful physical presence. As they sat they seemed to take her will away, leaving her will-less and victim to her own indifference. And the young man would bring her sweetened drink, often the same emetic drink, but sometimes other kinds. And after drinking, the languor filled her heavy limbs, her senses seemed to float in the air, listening, hearing. They had brought her a little female dog, which she called Flora. And once, in the trance of her senses, she felt she *heard* the little dog conceive, in her tiny womb, and begin to be complex, with young. And another day she could hear the vast sound of the earth going round, like some immense arrow-string booming.

But as the days grew shorter and colder, when she was cold, she would get a sudden revival of her will, and a desire to go out, to go away. And she insisted to the young man, she wanted to go out.

So one day, they let her climb to the topmost roof of the big house where she was, and look down the square. It was the day of the big dance, but not everybody was dancing. Women with babies in their arms stood in their doorways, watching. Opposite, at the other end of the square, there was a throng before the other big house, and a small, brilliant group on the terrace-roof of the first storey, in front of wide-open doors of the upper storey. Through these wide-open doors she could see fire glinting in darkness and priests in headdresses of black and yellow and scarlet feathers, wearing robe-like blankets of black and red and yellow, with long green fringe, were moving about. A big drum was beating slowly and regularly, in the dense, Indian silence. The crowd below waited——

Then a drum started on a high beat, and there came the deep, powerful burst of men singing a heavy, savage music, like a wind roaring in some timeless forest, many mature men singing in one breath, like the wind; and long lines of dancers walked out from under the big house. Men with naked, golden-bronze bodies and streaming black hair, tufts of red and yellow feathers on their arms, and kilts of white frieze with a bar of heavy red and black and green embroidery round their waists, bending slightly forward and stamping the earth in their absorbed, monotonous stamp of the dance, a fox-fur, hung by the nose from their belt behind, swaying with the sumptuous swaying of a beautiful fox-fur, the tip of the tail writhing above the dancer's heels. And after each man, a woman with a strange elaborate headdress of feathers and seashells, and wearing a short black tunic, moving erect, holding up tufts of feathers in each hand, swaying her wrists rhythmically and subtly beating the earth with her bare feet.

So, the long line of the dance unfurling from the big house opposite. And from the big house beneath her, strange scent of incense, strange tense silence, then the answering burst of inhuman male singing, and the long line of the dance unfurling.

It went on all day, the insistence of the drum, the cavernous, roaring, storm-like sound of male singing, the incessant swinging of the fox-skins behind the powerful, gold-bronze, stamping legs of the men, the autumn sun from a perfect blue heaven pouring on the rivers of black hair, men's and women's, the valley all still, the walls of rock beyond, the awful huge bulking of the mountain against the pure sky, its snow seething with sheer whiteness.

For hours and hours she watched, spell-bound, and as if drugged. And in all the terrible persistence of the drumming and the primeval, rushing deep singing, and the endless stamping of the dance of fox-tailed men, the tread of heavy, bird-erect women in their black tunics, she seemed at last to feel her own death; her own obliteration. As if she were to be obliterated from the field of life again. In the strange towering symbols on the heads of the changeless, absorbed women she seemed to read once more the *Mene Mene Tekel Upharsin.* Her kind of womanhood, intensely personal and individual, was to be obliterated again, and the great primeval symbols were to tower once more over the fallen individual independence of woman. The sharpness and the quivering nervous consciousness of the highly-bred white woman was to be destroyed again, womanhood was to be cast once more into the great stream of impersonal sex and impersonal passion. Strangely, as if clairvoyant, she saw the immense sacrifice prepared. And she went back to her little house in a trance of agony.

After this, there was always a certain agony when she heard the drums at evening, and the strange uplifted savage sound of men singing round the drum, like wild creatures howling to the invisible gods of the moon and the vanished sun. Something of the chuckling, sobbing cry of the coyote, something of the exultant bark of the fox, the far-off wild melancholy exultance of the howling wolf, the torment of the puma's scream, and the insistence of the ancient fierce human male, with his lapses of tenderness and his abiding ferocity.

Sometimes she would climb the high roof after nightfall, and listen to the dim cluster of young men round the drum on the bridge just beyond the square, singing by the hour. Sometimes there would be a fire, and in the fire-glow, men in their white shirts or naked save for a loin-cloth, would be dancing and stamping like spectres, hour after hour in the dark cold air, within the fire-glow, for ever dancing and stamping like turkeys, or dropping squatting by the fire to rest, throwing their blankets round them.

"Why do you all have the same colours?" she asked the young Indian. "Why do you all have red and yellow and black, over your white shirts? And the women have black tunics?"

He looked into her eyes, curiously, and the faint, evasive smile came on to his face. Behind the smile lay a soft, strange malignancy.

"Because our men are the fire and the daytime, and our women are the spaces between the stars at night," he said.

"Aren't the women even stars?" she said.

"No. We say they are the spaces between the stars, that keep the stars apart."

He looked at her oddly, and again the touch of derision came into his eyes.

"White people," he said, "they know nothing. They are like children, always with toys. We know the sun, and we know the moon. And we say, when a white woman sacrifice herself to our gods, then our gods will begin to make the world again, and the white man's gods will fall to pieces."

"How sacrifice herself?" she asked quickly.

And he, as quickly covered, covered himself with a subtle smile.

"She sacrifice her own gods and come to our gods, I mean that," he said, soothingly.

But she was not reassured. An icy pang of fear and certainty was at her heart.

"The sun he is alive at one end of the sky," he continued, "and the moon lives at the other end. And the man all the time have to keep the sun happy in his side of the sky, and the woman have to keep the moon quiet at her side of the sky. All the time she have to work at this. And the sun can't ever go into the house of the moon, and the moon can't ever go into the house of the sun, in the sky. So the woman, she asks the moon to come into her cave, inside her. And the man, he draws the sun down till he has the power of the sun. All the time he do this. Then when the man gets a woman, the sun goes into the cave of the moon, and that is how everything in the world starts."

She listened, watching him closely, as one enemy watches another who is speaking with double meaning.

"Then," she said, "why aren't you Indians masters of the white men?"

"Because," he said, "the Indian got weak, and lost his power with the sun, so the white men stole the sun. But they can't keep him—they don't know how. They got him, but they don't know what to do with him, like a boy who catch a big grizzly bear, and can't kill him, and can't run away from him. The grizzly bear eats the boy that catch him, when he want to run away from him. White men don't know what they are doing with the sun, and white women don't know what they do with the moon. The moon she got angry with white women, like a puma when someone kills her little ones. The moon, she bites white women—here inside," and he pressed his side. "The moon, she is angry in a white woman's cave. The Indian can see it—and soon," he added, "the Indian women get the moon back and keep her quiet in their house. And the Indian men get the sun, and the power over all the world. White men don't know what the sun is. They never know."

He subsided into a curious exultant silence.

"But," she faltered, "why do you hate us so? Why do you hate me?"

He looked up suddenly with a light on his face, and a startling flame of a smile.

"No, we don't hate," he said softly, looking with a curious glitter into her face.

"You do," she said, forlon and hopeless.

And after a moment's silence, he rose and went away.

III

Winter had now come, in the high valley, with snow that melted in the day's sun, and nights that were bitter cold. She lived on, in a kind of daze, feeling her power ebbing more and more away from her, as if her will were leaving her. She felt always in the same relaxed, confused, victimized state, unless the sweetened herb drink would numb her mind altogether, and release her senses into a sort of heightened, mystic acuteness and a feeling as if she were diffusing out deliciously into the harmony of things. This at length became the only state of consciousness she really recognized: this exquisite sense of bleeding out into the higher beauty and harmony of things. Then she could actually hear the great stars in heaven, which she saw through her door, speaking from their motion and brightness, saying things perfectly to the cosmos, as they trod in perfect ripples, like bells on the floor of heaven, passing one another and grouping in the timeless dance, with the spaces of dark between. And she could hear the snow on a cold, cloudy day twittering and faintly whistling in the sky, like birds that flock and fly away in autumn, suddenly calling farewell to the invisible moon, and slipping out of the plains of the air, releasing peaceful warmth. She herself would call to the arrested snow to fall from the upper air. She would call to the unseen moon to cease to be angry, to make peace again with the unseen sun like a woman who ceases to be angry in her house. And she would smell the sweetness of the moon relaxing to the sun in the wintry heaven, when the snow fell in a faint, cold-perfumed relaxation, as the peace of the sun mingled again in a sort of unison with the peace of the moon.

She was aware, too, of the sort of shadow that was on the Indians of the valley, a deep, stoical disconsolation, almost religious in its depth.

"We have lost our power over the sun, and we are trying to get him back. But he is wild with us, and shy like a horse that has got away. We have to go through a lot." So the young Indian said to her, looking into her eyes with a strained meaning. And she, as if bewitched, replied:

"I hope you will get him back."

The smile of triumph flew over his face.

"Do you hope it?" he said.

"I do," she answered fatally.

"Then all right," he said. "We shall get him."

And he went away in exultance.

She felt she was drifting on some consummation, which she had no will to avoid, yet which seemed heavy and finally terrible to her.

It must have been almost December, for the days were short, when she was taken again before the aged man, and stripped of her clothing, and touched with the old finger tips.

The aged cacique looked her in the eyes, with his eyes of lonely, far-off, black intentness, and murmured something to her.

"He wants you to make the sign of peace," the young man translated, showing her the gesture. "Peace and farewell to him."

She was fascinated by the black, glass-like, intent eyes of the old cacique, that watched her without blinking, like a basilisk's, overpowering her. In their depths also she saw a certain fatherly compassion, and pleading. She put her hand before her face, in the required manner, making the sign of peace and farewell. He made the sign of peace back again to her, then sank among his furs. She thought he was going to die, and that he knew it.

There followed a day of ceremonial, when she was brought out before all the people, in a blue blanket with white fringe, and holding blue feathers in her hands. Before an altar of one house, she was perfumed with incense and sprinkled with ash. Below the altar of the opposite house she was fumigated again with incense by the gorgeous, terrifying priests in yellow and scarlet and black, their faces painted with scarlet paint. And then they threw water on her. Meanwhile she was faintly aware of the fire on the altar, the heavy, heavy sound of a drum, the heavy sound of men beginning powerfully, deeply, savagely to sing, the swaying of the crowd of faces in the plaza below, and the formation for a sacred dance.

But at this time her commonplace consciousness was numb, she was aware of her immediate surroundings as shadows, almost immaterial. With refined and heightened senses she could hear the sound of the earth winging on its journey, like a shot arrow, the ripple-rustling of the air, and the boom of the great arrow-string. And it seemed to her there were two great influences in the upper air, one golden towards the sun, and one invisible silver; the first travelling like rain ascending to the gold presence sunwards, the second like rain silverily descending the ladders of space towards the hovering, lurking clouds over the snowy mountain-top. Then between them, another presence, waiting to shake himself free of moisture, of heavy white snow that had mysteriously collected about him. And in summer, like a scorched eagle, he would wait to shake himself clear of the weight of heavy sunbeams. And he was coloured like fire. And he was always shaking himself clear, of snow or of heavy heat, like an eagle rustling.

Then there was a still stranger presence, standing watching from the blue distance, always watching. Sometimes running in upon the wind, or shimmering in the heat-waves. The blue wind itself, rushing as it were out of the holes in the earth into the sky, rushing out of the sky down upon the earth. The blue wind, the go-between, the invisible ghost that belonged to two worlds, that played upon the ascending and the descending chords of the rains.

More and more her ordinary personal consciousness had left her, she had gone into that other state of passional cosmic consciousness, like one who is drugged. The Indians, with their heavily religious natures, had made her succumb to their vision.

Only one personal question she asked the young Indian:

"Why am I the only one that wears blue?"

"It is the colour of the wind. It is the colour of what goes away and is never coming back, but which is always here, waiting like death among us. It is the colour of the dead. And it is the colour that stands away off, looking at us from the distance, that cannot come near to us. When we go near, it goes farther. It can't be near. We are all brown and yellow and black hair, and white teeth and red blood. We are the ones that are here. You with blue eyes, you are the messengers from the far-away, you cannot stay, and now it is time for you to go back."

"Where to?" she asked.

"To the way-off things like the sun and the blue mother of rain, and tell them that we are the people on the world again, and we can bring the sun to the moon again, like a red horse to a blue mare; we are the people. The white women have driven back the moon in the sky, won't let her come to the sun. So the sun is angry. And the Indian must give the moon to the sun."

"How?" she said.

"The white woman got to die and go like a wind to the sun, tell him the Indians will open the gate to him. And the Indian women will open the gate to the moon. The white women don't let the moon come down out of the blue corral. The moon used to come down among the Indian women, like a white goat among the flowers. And the sun want to come down to the Indian men, like an eagle to the pine-trees. The sun, he is shut out behind the white man, and the moon she is shut out behind the white woman, and they can't get away. They are angry, everything in the world gets angrier. The Indian says, he will give the white woman to the sun, so the sun will leap over the white man and come to the Indian again. And the moon will be surprised, she will see the gate open, and she not know which way to go. But the Indian woman will call to the moon, *Come! Come! Come back into my grass-lands. The wicked white woman can't harm you any more.* Then the sun will look over the heads of the white men, and see the moon in the pastures of our women, with the Red Men standing around like pine trees. Then he will leap over the heads of the white men, and come running past to the Indians through the spruce trees. And we, who are red and black and yellow, we who stay, we shall have the sun on our right hand and the moon on our left. So we can bring the rain down out of the blue meadows, and up out of the black; and we can call the wind that tells the corn to grow, when we ask him, and we shall make the clouds to break, and the sheep to have twin lambs. And we shall be full of power, like a spring day. But the white people will be a hard winter, without snow——"

"But," said the white woman, "I don't shut out the moon—how can I?"

"Yes," he said, "you shut the gate, and then laugh, think you have it all your own way."

She could never quite understand the way he looked at her. He was always so curiously gentle, and his smile was so soft. Yet there was such a glitter in his eyes, and an unrelenting sort of hate came out of his words, a strange, profound, impersonal hate. Personally he liked her, she was sure. He was gentle with her, attracted by her in some strange, soft, passionless way. But impersonally he hated her with a mystic hatred. He would smile at her, winningly. Yet if, the next moment, she glanced round at him unawares, she would catch that gleam of pure after-hate in his eyes.

"Have I got to die and be given to the sun?" she asked.

"Sometime," he said, laughing evasively. "Sometime we all die."

They were gentle with her, and very considerate with her. Strange men, the old priests and the young cacique alike, they watched over her and cared for her like women. In their soft, insidious understanding, there was something womanly. Yet their eyes, with that strange glitter, and their dark, shut mouths that would open to the broad jaw, the small, strong, white teeth, had something very primitively male and cruel.

One wintry day, when snow was falling, they took her to a great dark chamber in the big house. The fire was burning in a corner on a high raised dais under a sort of hood or canopy of adobe-work. She saw in the fire-glow, the glowing bodies of the almost naked priests, and strange symbols of the roof and walls of the chamber. There was no door or window in the chamber, they had descended by a ladder from the roof. And the fire of pinewood danced continually, showing walls painted with strange devices, which she could not understand, and a ceiling of poles making a curious pattern of black and red and yellow, and alcoves or niches in which were curious objects she could not discern.

The older priests were going through some ceremony near the fire, in silence, intense Indian silence. She was seated on a low projection of the wall, opposite the fire, two men seated beside her. Presently they gave her a drink from a cup, which she took gladly, because of the semi-trance it would induce.

In the darkness and in the silence she was accurately aware of everything that happened to her: how they took off her clothes, and, standing her before a great, weird device on the wall, coloured blue and white and black, washed her all over with water and amole infusion; washed even her hair, softly, carefully, and dried it on white cloths, till it was soft and glistening. Then they laid her on a couch under another great indecipherable image of red and black and yellow, and now rubbed all her body with sweet-scented oil, and massaged all her limbs, and her back, and her sides, with a long, strange, hypnotic massage. Their dark hands were incredibly powerful, yet soft with a watery softness she could not understand. And the dark faces, leaning near her white body, she saw were darkened with red pigment, with lines of yellow round the cheeks. And the dark eyes glittered absorbed, as the hands worked upon the soft white body of the woman.

They were so impersonal, absorbed in something that was beyond her. They never saw her as a personal woman: she could tell that. She was some mystic object to them, some vehicle of passions too remote for her to grasp. Herself in a state of trance, she watched their faces bending over her, dark, strangely glistening with the transparent red paint, and lined with bars of yellow. And in this weird, luminous-dark mask of living face, the eyes were fixed with an unchanging steadfast gleam, and the purplish-pigmented lips were closed in a full, sinister, sad grimness. The immense fundamental sadness, the grimness of ultimate decision, the fixity of revenge, and the nascent exultance of those that are going to triumph—these things she could read in their faces, as she lay and was rubbed into a misty glow, by their uncanny dark hands. Her limbs, her flesh, her very bones at last seemed to be diffusing into a roseate sort of mist, in which her consciousness hovered like some sun-gleam in a flushed cloud.

She knew the gleam would fade, the cloud would go grey. But at present she did not believe it. She knew she was a victim; that all this elaborate work upon her was the work of victimizing her. But she did not mind. She wanted it.

Later, they put a short blue tunic on her and took her to the upper terrace, and presented her to the people. She saw the plaza below her full of dark faces and of glittering eyes. There was no pity: only the curious hard exultance. The people gave a subdued cry when they saw her, and she shuddered. But she hardly cared.

Next day was the last. She slept in a chamber of the big house. At dawn they put on her a big blue blanket with a fringe, and led her out into the plaza, among the throng of silent, dark-blanketed people. There was pure white snow on the ground, and the dark people in their dark-brown blankets looked like inhabitants of another world.

A large drum was slowly pounding, and an old priest was declaiming from a housetop. But it was not till noon that a litter came forth, and the people gave that low, animal cry which was so moving. In the sack-like litter sat the old, old cacique, his white hair braided with black braid and large turquoise stones. His face was like a piece of obsidian. He lifted his hand in token, and the litter stopped in front of her. Fixing her with his old eyes, he spoke to her for a few moments, in his hollow voice. No one translated.

Another litter came, and she was placed in it. Four priests moved ahead, in their scarlet and yellow and black, with plumed headdresses. Then came the litter of the old cacique. Then the light drums began, and two groups of singers burst simultaneously into song, male and wild. And the golden-red, almost naked men, adorned with ceremonial feathers and kilts, the rivers of black hair down their backs, formed into two files and began to tread the dance. So they threaded out of the snowy plaza, in two long, sumptuous lines of dark red-gold and black and fur, swaying with a faint tinkle of bits of shell and flint, winding over the snow between the two bee-clusters of men who sang around the drum.

Slowly they moved out, and her litter, with its attendance of feathered, lurid, dancing priests, moved after. Everybody danced the tread of the dance-step, even, subtly, the litter-bearers. And out of the plaza they went, past smoking ovens, on the trail to the great cotton-wood trees, that stood like grey-silver lace against the blue sky, bare and exquisite above the snow. The river, diminished, rushed among fangs of ice. The chequer-squares of gardens within fences were all snowy, and the white houses now looked yellowish.

The whole valley glittered intolerably with pure snow, away to the walls of the standing rock. And across the flat cradle of snow-bed wound the long thread of the dance, shaking slowly and sumptuously in its orange and black motion. The high drums thudded quickly, and on the crystalline frozen air the swell and roar of the chant of savages was like an obsession.

She sat looking out of her litter with big, transfixed blue eyes, under which were the wan markings of her drugged weariness. She knew she was going to die, among the glisten of this snow, at the hands of this savage, sumptuous people. And as she stared at the blaze of blue sky above the slashed and ponderous mountain, she thought: "I am dead already. What difference does it make, the transition from the dead I am to the dead I shall be, very soon!" Yet her soul sickened and felt wan.

The strange procession trailed on, in perpetual dance, slowly across the plain of snow, and then entered the slopes between the pine-trees. She saw the copper-dark men dancing the dance-treat, onwards, be-tween the copper-pale tree trunks. And at last she, too, in her swaying litter, entered the pine trees.

They were travelling on and on, upwards, across the snow under the trees, past the superb shafts of pale, flaked copper, the rustle and shake and tread of the threading dance, penetrating into the forest, into the mountain. They were following a stream-bed: but the stream was dry, like summer, dried up by the frozenness of the head-waters.

There were dark, red-bronze willow bushes with wattles like wild hair, and pallid aspen trees looking like cold flesh against the snow. Then jutting dark rocks.

At last she could tell that the dancers were moving forward no more. Nearer and nearer she came upon the drums, as to a lair of mysterious animals. Then through the bushes she emerged into a strange amphitheatre. Facing was a great wall of hollow rock, down the front of which hung a great, dripping, fang-like spoke of ice. The ice came pouring over the rock from the precipice above, and then stood arrested, dripping out of high heaven, almost down to the hollow stones where the stream-pool should be below. But the pool was dry.

On either side the dry pool, the lines of dancers had formed, and the dance was continuing without intermission, against a background of bushes.

But what she felt was that fanged inverted pinnacle of ice, hanging from the lip of the dark precipice above. And behind the great rope of ice, she saw the leopard-like figures of priests climbing the hollow cliff face, to the cave that like a dark socket bored a cavity, an orifice, half-way up the crag.

Before she could realize, her litter-bearers were staggering in the footholds, climbing the rock. She, too, was behind the ice. There it hung, like a curtain that is not spread, but hangs like a great fang. And near above her was the orifice of the cave sinking dark into the rock. She watched it as she swayed upwards.

On the platform of the cave stood the priests, waiting in all their gorgeousness of feathers and fringed robes, watching her ascent. Two of them stooped to help her litter-bearers. And at length she was on the platform of the cave, far in behind the shaft of ice, above the hollow amphitheatre among the bushes below, where men were dancing, and the whole populace of the village was clustered in silence.

The sun was sloping down the afternoon sky, on the left. She knew that this was the shortest day of the year, and the last day of her life. They stood her facing the iridescent column of ice, which fell down marvellously arrested, away in front of her.

Some signal was given, and the dance below stopped. There was now absolute silence. She was given a little to drink, then two priests took off her mantle and her tunic, and in her strange pallor she stood there, between the lurid robes of the priests, beyond the pillar of ice, beyond and above the dark-faced people. The throng below gave the low, wild cry. Then the priests turned her round, so she stood with her back to the open world, her long blonde hair to the people below. And they cried again.

She was facing the cave, inwards. A fire was burning and flickering in the depths. Four priests had taken off their robes, and were almost as naked as she was. They were powerful men in the prime of life, and they kept their dark, painted faces lowered.

From the fire came the old, old priest, with an incense-pan. He was naked and in a state of barbaric ecstasy. He fumigated his victim, reciting at the same time in a hollow voice. Behind him came another robeless priest, with two flint knives.

When she was fumigated, they laid her on a large flat stone, the four powerful men holding her by the outstretched arms and legs. Behind stood the aged man, like a skeleton covered with dark glass, holding a knife and transfixedly watching the sun; and behind him again was another naked priest, with a knife.

She felt little sensation, though she knew all that was happening. Turning to the sky, she looked at the yellow sun. It was sinking. The shaft of ice was like a shadow between her and it. And she realized that the yellow rays were filling half the cave, though they had not reached the altar where the fire was, at the far end of the funnel-shaped cavity.

Yes, the rays were creeping round slowly. As they grew ruddier, they penetrated farther. When the red sun was about to sink, he would shine full through the shaft of ice deep into the hollow of the cave, to the innermost.

She understood now that this was what the men were waiting for. Even those that held her down were bent and twisted round, their black eyes watching the sun with a glittering eagerness, and awe, and craving. The black eyes of the aged cacique were fixed like black mirrors on the sun, as if sightless, yet containing some terrible answers to the reddening winter planet. And all the eyes of the priests were fixed and glittering on the sinking orb, in the reddening, icy silence of the winter afternoon.

They were anxious, terribly anxious, and fierce. Their ferocity wanted something, and they were waiting the moment. And their ferocity was ready to leap out into a mystic exultance, of triumph. But still they were anxious.

Only the eyes of that oldest man were not anxious. Black, and fixed, and as if sightless, they watched the sun, seeing beyond the sun. And in their black, empty concentration there was power, power intensely abstract and remote, but deep, deep to the heart of the earth, and the heart of the sun. In absolute motionlessness he watched till the red sun should send his ray through the column of ice. Then the old man would strike, and strike home, accomplish the sacrifice and achieve the power.

The mastery that man must hold, and that passes from race to race.

GEORGE ORWELL

Eric Arthur Blair was born at Motihari in Bengal, India, in 1903. His father, a minor official in the Indian Customs Service, retired when his son was still very young. At considerable expense, his family sent him to a fashionable preparatory school in England, where he suffered by being a relatively poor boy in a rich man's school. There he won a scholarship to one of England's great public schools, Eton. After four years of indifferent study there, instead of continuing to Oxford or Cambridge, he took a teacher's advice and accepted a post in the Indian Imperial Police. As a result of this decision he spent the next five years in Burma, where he was—as he has written—"hated by large numbers of people."

When his five-year tour of duty was up he returned from the Far East and began a career as a writer. Out of money, he sank into the lower depths of society, but willingly, almost gratefully, recording the details of this unfamiliar world with loving precision. His first book, Down and Out in Paris and London, *tells the story of those days. It was published in 1933, with the author's name given as George Orwell, the name he used for the rest of his writing life. Gradually working himself into a socialist position, Orwell continued to write. His in-*

vestigation of working-class life in an industrial slum led to The Road to Wigan Pier, *which was published in 1937. When the Spanish Civil War broke out Orwell, who went to observe, remained to fight and be wounded defending the lost cause of the socialist republic against the fascists.*

Orwell's report on this experience, Homage to Catalonia *(1938), tells of the betrayal of the socialist Left by the Communists. The book was not a success, selling fewer than 900 copies by the time of Orwell's death. In recent years it has been recognized as a masterpiece of journalism. Suffering in health, Orwell returned to England where he lived through World War II, writing his brilliant satire on Stalinist totalitarianism,* Animal Farm, *which was refused by four publishers before its appearance in 1945. Although seriously ill with tuberculosis, he managed to produce his terrifying vision of the future,* 1984, *which was published in 1949. In January 1950, not yet forty-seven years old, he died in a London hispital.*

Though Orwell wrote some novels of contemporary life, they have never attracted much attention. Thus, the reader who wishes to extend his knowledge of Orwell will probably do best to read first the journalistic and satirical works mentioned in the previous two paragraphs, along with the full Collected Essays, Journalism and Letters of George Orwell *in four volumes (edited by Sonia Orwell and Ian Angus, and published by Harcourt, Brace & World in 1968). In addition to the full collection there are two good selections of Orwell's work available in paperback:* A Collection of Essays by George Orwell *(Doubleday Anchor Book), and* The Orwell Reader *(Harvest Books), which includes excerpts from the novels as well as the other writings. George Woodcock's* The Crystal Spirit *(Little, Brown, 1966) is a critical study with a useful chapter on Orwell's life.*

Politics and the English Language

This essay was written in 1946.

Most people who bother with the matter at all would admit that the English language is in a bad way, but it is generally assumed that we cannot by conscious action do anything about it. Our civilization is decadent and our language—so the argument runs—must inevitably share in the general collapse. It follows that any struggle against the abuse of language is a sentimental archaism, like preferring candles to electric light or hansom cabs to aeroplanes. Underneath this lies the half-conscious belief that language is a natural growth and not an instrument which we shape for our own purposes.

Now, it is clear that the decline of a language must ultimately have political and economic causes: it is not due simply to the bad influence of this or that individual writer. But an effect can become a cause, reinforcing the original cause and producing the same effect in an intensified form, and so on indefinitely. A man may take to drink because he feels himself to be a failure, and then fail all the more completely because he drinks. It is rather the same thing that is happening to the English language. It becomes ugly and inaccurate because our thoughts are foolish, but the slovenliness of our language makes it easier for us to have foolish thoughts. The point is that the process is reversible. Modern English, especially written English, is full of bad habits which spread by imitation and which can be avoided if one is willing to take the necessary trouble. If one gets rid of these habits one can think more clearly, and to think clearly is a necessary first step towards political regeneration: so that the fight against bad English is not frivolous and is not the exclusive concern of professional writers. I will come back to this presently, and I hope that by that time the meaning of what I have said here will have become clearer. Meanwhile, here are five specimens of the English language as it is now habitually written.

These five passages have not been picked out because they are especially bad—I could have quoted far worse if I had chosen—but because they illustrate various of the mental vices from which we now suffer. They are a little below the average, but are fairly representative samples. I number them so that I can refer back to them when necessary:

(*1*) *I am not, indeed, sure whether it is not true to say that the Milton who once seemed not unlike a seventeenth-century Shelley had not become, out of an experience ever more bitter in each year, more alien* [sic] *to the founder of that Jesuit sect which nothing could induce him to tolerate.*

Professor Harold Laski
(*Essay in* Freedom of Expression).

(2) *Above all, we cannot play ducks and drakes with a native battery of idioms which prescribes such egregious collocations of vocables as the Basic* put up with *for* tolerate *or* put at a loss *for* bewilder.

Professor Lancelot Hogben (Interglossa).

(*3*) *On the one side we have the free personality: by definition it is not neurotic, for it has neither conflict nor dream. Its desires, such as they are, are transparent, for they are just what institutional approval keeps in the forefront of consciousness; another institutional pattern would alter their number and intensity; there is little in them that is natural, irreducible, or culturally dangerous. But* on the other side, *the social bond itself is nothing but the mutual reflection of these self-secure integrities. Recall the definition of love. Is not this the very picture of a small academic? Where is there a place in this hall of mirrors for either personality or fraternity?*

Essay on psychology in Politics (*New York*).

(*4*) *All the "best people" from the gentlemen's clubs, and all the frantic fascist captains, united in common hatred of Socialism and bestial horror of the rising tide of the mass revolutionary movement, have turned to acts of provocation, to foul incendiarism, to medieval legends of poisoned wells, to legalize their own destruction of proletarian organizations, and rouse the agitated petty-bourgeoisie to chauvinistic fervor on behalf of the fight against the revolutionary way out of the crisis.*

Communist pamphlet.

(*5*) *If a new spirit is to be infused into this old country, there is one thorny and contentious reform which must be tackled, and that is the humanization and galvanization of the B.B.C. Timidity here will bespeak canker and atrophy of the soul. The heart of Britain may be sound and of strong beat, for instance, but the British lion's roar at present is like that of Bottom in Shakespeare's* Midsummer Night's Dream—*as gentle as any sucking dove. A virile new Britain cannot continue indefinitely to be traduced in the eyes, or rather ears, of the world by the effete languors of Langham Place, blazenly masquerading as "standard English." When the Voice of Britain is heard at nine o'clock, better far and infinitely less ludicrous to hear aitches honestly dropped than the present priggish, inflated, inhibited, school-ma'amish arch braying of blameless bashful mewing maidens!*

Letter in Tribune

Each of these passages has faults of its own, but, quite apart from avoidable ugliness, two qualities are common to all of them. The first is staleness of imagery; the other is lack of precision. The writer either has a meaning and cannot express it, or he inadvertently says something else, or he is almost indifferent as to whether his words mean anything or not. This mixture of vagueness and sheer incompetence is the most marked characteristic of modern English prose, and especially of any kind of political writing. As soon as certain topics are raised, the concrete melts into the abstract and no one seems able to think of turns of speech that are not hackneyed: prose consists less and less of *words* chosen for the sake of their meaning, and more and more of *phrases* tacked together like the sections of a prefabricated hen-house. I list below, with notes and examples, various of the tricks by means of which the work of prose-construction is habitually dodged:

Dying metaphors. A newly invented metaphor assists thought by evoking a visual image, while on the other hand a metaphor which is technically "dead" (e.g. *iron resolution*) has in effect reverted to being an ordinary word and can generally be used without loss of vividness. But in between these two classes there is a huge dump of worn-out metaphors which have lost all evocative power and are merely used because they save people the trouble of inventing phrases for themselves. Examples are: *Ring the changes on, take up the cudgels for, toe the line, ride roughshod over, stand shoulder to shoulder with, play into the hands of, no axe to grind, grist to the mill, fishing in troubled waters, on the order of the day, Achilles' heel, swam song, hotbed.* Many of these are used without knowledge of their meaning (what is a "rift," for instance?), and incompatible metaphors are frequently mixed, a sure sign that the writer is not interested in what he is saying. Some metaphors now current have been twisted out of their original meaning without those who use them even being aware of the fact. For example, *toe the line* is sometimes written *tow the line.* Another example is *the hammer and the anvil,* now always used with the implication that the anvil gets the worst of it. In real life it is always the anvil that breaks the hammer, never the other way about: a writer who stopped to think what he was saying would be aware of this, and would avoid perverting the original phrase.

Operators or *verbal false limbs.* These save the trouble of picking out appropriate verbs and nouns, and at the same time pad each sentence with extra syllables which give it an appearance of symmetry. Characteristic phrases are *render inoperative, militate against, make contact with, be subjected to, give rise to, give grounds for, have the effect of, play a leading part (role) in, make itself felt, take effect, exhibit a tendency to, serve the purpose of, etc., etc.* The keynote is the elimination of simple verbs. Instead of being a single word, such as *break, stop, spoil, mend, kill,* a verb becomes a *phrase,* made up of a noun or adjective tacked on to some general-purposes verb such as *prove, serve, form, play, render.* In addition, the passive voice is wherever possible used in preference to the active, and noun constructions are used instead of gerunds (*by examination of* instead of *by examining*). The range of verbs is further cut down by means of the *-ize* and *de-* formations, and the banal statements are given an appearance of profundity by means of the *not un-* formation. Simple conjunctions and prepositions are replaced by such phrases as *with respect to, having regard to, the fact that, by dint of, in view of, in the interests of, on the hypothesis that;* and the ends of sentences are saved by anticlimax by such resounding common-places as *greatly to be desired, cannot be left out of account, a development to be expected in the near future, deserving of serious consideration, brought to a satisfactory conclusion,* and so on and so forth.

Pretentious diction. Words like *phenomenon, element, individual* (as noun), *objective, categorical, effective, virtual, basic, primary, promote, constitute, exhibit, exploit, utilize, eliminate, liquidate,* are used to dress up simple statement and give an air of scientific impartiality to biased judgments. Adjectives like *epoch-making, epic, historic, unforgettable, triumphant, age-old, inevitable, inexorable, veritable,* are used to dignify the sordid processes of international politics, while writing that aims at glorifying war usually takes on an archaic color, its characteristic words being: *realm, throne, chariot, mailed fist, trident, sword, shield, buckler, banner, jackboot, clarion.* Foreign words and expressions such as *cul de sac, ancien régime, deus ex machina, mutatis mutandis, status quo, gleichschaltung, weltanschauung,* are used to give an air of culture and elegance. Except for the useful abbreviations *i.e., e.g.,* and *etc.,* there is no real need for any of the hundreds of foreign phrases now current in English. Bad writers, and especially scientific, political and sociological writers, are nearly always haunted by the notion that Latin or Greek words are grander than Saxon ones, and unnecessary words like *expedite, ameliorate, predict, extraneous, deracinated, clandestine, subaqueous* and hundreds of others constantly gain ground from their Anglo-Saxon opposite numbers.[1] The jargon peculiar to Marxist writing (*hyena, hangman, cannibal, petty bourgeois, these gentry, lacquey, flunkey, mad dog, White Guard,* etc.)

[1] An interesting illustration of this is the way in which the English flower names which were in use till very recently are being ousted by Greek ones, *snapdragon* becoming *antirrhinum, forget-me-not* becoming *myosotis,* etc. It is hard to see any practical reason for this change of fashion: it is probably due to an instinctive turning-away from the more homely word and a vague feeling that the Greek word is scientific.

consists largely of words and phrases translated from Russian, German or French; but the normal way of coining a new word is to use a Latin or Greek root with the appropriate affix and, where necessary, the size formation. It is often easier to make up words of this kind (*de-regionalize*, *impermissible*, *extramarital*, *non-fragmentary* and so forth) than to think up the English words that will cover one's meaning. The result, in general, is an increase in slovenliness and vagueness.

Meaningless words. In certain kinds of writing, particularly in art criticism and literary criticism, it is normal to come across long passages which are almost completely lacking in meaning.[2] Words like *romantic*, *plastic*, *values*, *human*, *dead*, *sentimental*, *natural*, *vitality*, as used in art criticism, are strictly meaningless, in the sense that they not only do not point to any discoverable object, but are hardly ever expected to do so by the reader. When one critic writes, "The outstanding feature of Mr. X's work is its living quality," while another writes, "The immediately striking thing about Mr. X's work is its peculiar deadness," the reader accepts this as a simple difference of opinion. If words like *black* and *white* were involved, instead of the jargon words *dead* and *living*, he would see at once that language was being used in an improper way. Many political words are similarly abused. The word *Fascism* has now no meaning except in so far as it signifies "something not desirable." The words *democracy*, *socialism freedom*, *patriotic*, *realistic*, *justice*, have each of them several different meanings which cannot be reconciled with one another. In the case of a word like *democracy*, not only is there no agreed definition, but the attempt to make one is resisted from all sides. It is almost universally felt that when we call a country democratic we are praising it: consequently the defenders of every kind of régime claim that it is a democracy, and fear that they might have to stop using the word if it were tied down to any one meaning. Words of this kind are often used in a consciously dishonest way. That is, the person who uses them has his own private definition, but allows his hearer to think he means something quite different. Statements like *Marshal Pétain was a true patriot*, *The Soviet*

[2] Example: "Comfort's catholicity of perception and image, strangely Whitmanesque in range, almost the exact opposite in aesthetic compulsion, continues to evoke that trembling atmospheric accumulative hinting at a cruel, an inexorably serene timelessness. . . . Wrey Gardiner scores by aiming at simple bull's-eyes with precision. Only they are not so simple, and through this contented sadness runs more than the surface bitter-sweet of resignation." (Poetry Quarterly.)

Press is the freest in the world, The Catholic Church is opposed to persecution, are almost always made with intent to deceive. Other words used in variable meanings, in most cases more or less dishonestly, are: *class, totalitarian, science, progressive, reactionary, bourgeois, equality.*

Now that I have made this catalogue of swindles and perversions, let me give another example of the kind of writing that they lead to. This time it must of its nature be an imaginary one. I am going to translate a passage of good English into modern English of the worst sort. Here is a well-known verse from *Ecclesiastes:*

"I returned and saw under the sun, that the race is not to the swift, nor the battle to the strong, neither yet bread to the wise, nor yet riches to men of understanding, nor yet favour to men of skill; but time and chance happeneth to them all."

Here it is in modern English:

"Objective consideration of contemporary phenomena compels the conclusion that success or failure in competitive activities exhibits no tendency to be commensurate with innate capacity, but that a considerable element of the unpredictable must invariably be taken into account."

This is a parody, but not a very gross one. Exhibit (3), above, for instance, contains several patches of the same kind of English. It will be seen that I have not made a full translation. The beginning and ending of the sentence follow the original meaning fairly closely, but in the middle the concrete illustrations—race, battle, bread—dissolve into the vague phrase "success or failure in competitive activities." This had to be so, because no modern writer of the kind I am discussing—no one capable of using phrases like "objective consideration of contemporary phenomena"—would ever tabulate his thoughts in that precise and detailed way. The whole tendency of modern prose is away from concreteness. Now analyse these two sentences a little more closely. The first contains forty-nine words but only sixty syllables, and all its words are those of everyday life. The second contains thirty-eight words of ninety syllables: eighteen of its words are from Latin roots, and one from Greek. The first sentence contains six vivid images, and only one phrase ("time and chance") that could be called vague. The second contains not a single fresh, arresting phrase, and in spite of its ninety syllables it gives only a shortened version of the meaning contained in the first. Yet without a doubt it is the second kind of sentence that is gaining ground in modern English. I do not want to exaggerate. This kind of writing is not yet universal, and outcrops of simplicity will occur here and there in the worst-written page. Still, if you or I were told to write a few lines on the uncertainty of human fortunes, we should probably come much nearer to my imaginary sentence than to the one from *Ecclesiastes.*

As I have tried to show, modern writing at its worst does not consist in picking out words for the sake of their meaning and inventing images in order to make the meaning clearer. It consists in gumming together long strips of words which have already been set in order by someone else, and making the results presentable by sheer humbug. The attraction of this way of writing is that it is easy. It is easier—even quicker, once you have the habit—to say *In my opinion it is not an unjustifiable assumption that* than to say *I think.* If you use ready-made phrases, you not only don't have to hunt about for words; you also don't have to bother with the rhythms of your sentences, since these phrases are generally so arranged as to be more or less euphonious. When you are composing in a hurry—when you are dictating to a stenographer, for instance, or making a public speech—it is natural to fall into a pretentious, Latinized style. Tags like *a consideration which we should do well to bear in mind* or *a conclusion to which all of us would readily assent* will save many a sentence from coming down with a bump. By using stale metaphors, similes and idioms, you save much mental effort, at the cost of leaving your meaning vague, not only for your reader but for yourself. This is the significance of mixed metaphors. The sole aim of a metaphor is to call up a visual image. When these images clash—as in *The Fascist octopus has sung its swan song, the jackboot is thrown into the melting pot*—it can be taken as certain that the writer is not seeing a mental image of the objects he is naming; in other words he is not really thinking. Look again at the examples I gave at the beginning of this essay. Professor Laski (1) uses five negatives in fifty-three words. One of these is superfluous, making nonsense of the whole passage, and in addition there is the slip *alien* for akin, making further nonsense, and several avoidable pieces of clumsiness which increase the general vagueness. Professor Hogben (2) plays ducks and drakes with a battery which is able to write prescriptions, and, while disapproving of the everyday phrase *put up with,* is unwilling to look *egregious* up in the dictionary and see what it means;

(3), if one takes an uncharitable attitude towards it, is simply meaningless: probably one could work out its intended meaning by reading the whole of the article in which it occurs. In (4), the writer knows more or less what he wants to say, but an accumulation of stale phrases chokes him like tea leaves blocking a sink. In (5), words and meaning have almost parted company. People who write in this manner usually have a general emotional meaning—they dislike one thing and want to express solidarity with another—but they are not interested in the detail of what they are saying. A scrupulous writer, in every sentence that he writes, will ask himself at least four questions, thus: What am I trying to say? What words will express it? What image or idiom will make it clearer? Is this image fresh enough to have an effect? And he will probably ask himself two more: Could I put it more shortly? Have I said anything that is avoidably ugly? But you are not obliged to go to all this trouble. You can shirk it by simply throwing your mind open and letting the ready-made phrases come crowding in. They will construct your sentences for you—even think your thoughts for you, to a certain extent—and at need they will perform the important service of partially concealing your meaning even from yourself. It is at this point that the special connection between politics and the debasement of language becomes clear.

In our time it is broadly true that political writing is bad writing. Where it is not true, it will generally be found that the writer is some kind of rebel, expressing his private opinions and not a "party line." Orthodoxy, of whatever color, seems to demand a lifeless, imitative style. The political dialects to be found in pamphlets, leading articles, manifestos, White Papers and the speeches of under-secretaries do, of course, vary from party to party, but they are all alike in that one almost never finds in them a fresh, vivid home-made turn of speech. When one watches some tired hack on the platform mechanically repeating the familiar phrases—*bestial atrocities, iron heel, bloodstained tyranny, free peoples of the world, stand shoulder to shoulder*—one often has a curious feeling that one is not watching a live human being but some kind of dummy: a feeling which suddenly becomes stronger at moments when the light catches the speaker's spectacles and turns them into blank discs which seem to have no eyes behind them. And this is not altogether fanciful. A speaker who uses that kind of phraseology has gone some distance towards turning himself into a machine. The appropriate noises are coming out of his larynx, but his brain is not involved as it would be if he were choosing his words for himself. If the speech he is making is one that he is accustomed to make over and over again, he may be almost unconscious of what he is saying, as one is when one utters the responses in church. And this reduced state of consciousness, if not indispensable, is at any rate favorable to political conformity.

In our time, political speech and writing are largely the defense of the indefensible. Things like the continuance of British rule in India, the Russian purges and deportations, the dropping of the atom bombs on Japan, can indeed be defended, but only by arguments which are too brutal for most people to face, and which do not square with the professed aims of political parties. Thus political language has to consist largely of euphemism, question-begging and sheer cloudy vagueness. Defenceless villages are bombarded from the air, the inhabitants driven out into the countryside, the cattle machine-gunned, the huts set on fire with incendiary bullets: this is called *pacification.* Millions of peasants are robbed of their farms and sent trudging along the roads with no more than they can carry: this is called *transfer of population* or *rectification of frontiers.* People are imprisoned for years without trial, or shot in the back of the neck or sent to die of scurvy in Arctic lumber camps: this is called *elimination of unreliable elements.* Such phraseology is needed if one wants to name things without calling up mental pictures of them. Consider for instance some comfortable English professor defending Russian totalitarianism. He cannot say outright, "I believe in killing off your opponents when you can get good results by doing so." Probably, therefore, he will say something like this:

"While freely conceding that the Soviet régime exhibits certain features which the humanitarian may be inclined to deplore, we must, I think, agree that a certain curtailment of the right to political opposition is an unavoidable concomitant of transitional periods, and that the rigors which the Russian people have been called upon to undergo have been amply justified in the sphere of concrete achievement."

The inflated style is itself a kind of euphemism. A mass of Latin words falls upon the facts like soft snow, blurring the outlines and covering up all the details. The great enemy of clear language is insincerity. When there is a gap between one's real and one's declared aims, one turns as it were instinctively to long words and exhausted idioms, like a cuttlefish squirting out ink. In our age there is no such thing as "keeping out of politics." All issues are political issues, and politics itself is a mass of lies, evasions, folly, hatred and schizophrenia. When the general atmosphere is bad, language must suffer. I should expect to find—this is a guess which I have not sufficient knowledge to verify—that the German, Russian and Italian languages have all deteriorated in the last ten or fifteen years, as a result of dictatorship.

But if thought corrupts language, language can also corrupt thought. A bad usage can spread by tradition and imitation, even among people who should and do know better. The debased language that I have been discussing is in some ways very convenient. Phrases like *a not unjustifiable assumption, leaves much to be desired, would serve no good purpose, a consideration which we should do well to bear in mind,* are a continuous temptation, a packet of aspirins always at one's elbow. Look back through this essay, and for certain you will find that I have again and again committed the very faults I am protesting against. By this morning's post I have received a pamphlet dealing with conditions in Germany. The author tells me that he "felt impelled" to write it. I opened it at random and here is almost the first sentence that I see: "[The Allies] have an opportunity not only of achieving a radical transformation of Germany's social and political structure in such a way as to avoid a nationalistic reaction in Germany itself, but at the same time of laying the foundations of a co-operative and unified Europe." You see, he "feels impelled" to write—feels, presumably, that he has something new to say—and yet his words, like cavalry horses answering the bugle, group themselves automatically into the familiar dreary pattern. This invasion of one's mind by ready-made phrases (*lay the foundations, achieve a radical transformation*) can only be prevented if one is constantly on guard against them, and every such phrase anaesthetizes a portion of one's brain.

I said earlier that the decadence of our language is probably curable. Those who deny this would argue, if they produced an argument at all, that language merely reflects existing social conditions, and that we cannot influence its development by any direct tinkering with words and constructions. So far as the general tone or spirit of a language goes, this may be true, but it is not true in detail. Silly words and expressions have often disappeared, not through any evolutionary process but owing to the conscious action of a minority. Two recent examples were *explore every avenue* and *leave no stone unturned,* which were killed by the jeers of a few journalists. There is a long list of flyblown metaphors which could similarly be got rid of if enough people would interest themselves in the job; and it should also be possible to laugh the *not un-* formation out of existence,[3] to reduce the amount of Latin and Greek in the average sentence, to drive out foreign phrases and strayed scientific words, and, in general, to make pretentiousness unfashionable. But all these are minor points. The defence of the English language implies more than this, and perhaps it is best to start by saying what it does *not* imply.

To begin with it has nothing to do with archaism, with the salvaging of obsolete words and turns of speech, or with the setting up of a "standard English" which much never be departed from. On the contrary, it is especially concerned with the scrapping of every word or idiom which has outworn its usefulness. It has nothing to do with correct grammar and syntax, which are of no importance so long as one makes one's meaning clear, or with the avoidance of Americanisms, or with having what is called a "good prose style." On the other hand it is not concerned with fake simplicity and the attempt to make written English colloquial. Nor does it even imply in every case preferring the Saxon word to the Latin one, though it does imply using the fewest and shortest words that will cover one's meaning. What is above all needed is to let the meaning choose the word, and not the other way about. In prose, the worst thing one can do with words is to surrender to them. When you think of a concrete object, you think wordlessly, and then, if you want to describe the thing you have been visualizing you probably hunt about till you find the exact words that seem to fit it. When you think of something abstract you are more inclined to use words from the start, and unless you make a conscious effort to prevent it, the existing dialect will come rushing in and do the job for you, at the expense of blurring or even changing your meaning. Probably it is better to put off using words as long as possible and get one's meaning as clear as one can though pictures or sensations. Afterwards one can choose—not simply *accept*—the phrases that will best cover the meaning, and then switch round and decide what impression one's words are likely to make on another person. This last effort of the mind cuts out all stale or mixed images, all prefabricated phrases, needless repetitions, and humbug and vagueness generally. But one can often be in doubt about the effect of a word or a phrase, and one needs

[3] One can cure oneself of the *not un-* formation by memorizing this sentence: *A not unblack dog was chasing a not unsmall rabbit across a not ungreen field.*

rules that one can rely on when instinct fails. I think the following rules will cover most cases:

(i) Never use a metaphor, simile or other figure of speech which you are used to seeing in print.

(ii) Never use a long word where a short one will do.

(iii) If it is possible to cut a word out, always cut it out.

(iv) Never use the passive where you can use the active.

(v) Never use a foreign phrase, a scientific word or a jargon word if you can think of an everyday English equivalent.

(vi) Break any of these rules sooner than say anything outright barbarous.

These rules sound elementary, and so they are, but they demand a deep change of attitude in anyone who has grown used to writing in the style now fashionable. One could keep all of them and still write bad English, but one could not write the kind of stuff that I quoted in those five specimens at the beginning of this article.

I have not here been considering the literary use of language, but merely language as an instrument for expressing and not for concealing or preventing thought. Stuart Chase and others have come near to claiming that all abstract words are meaningless, and have used this as a pretext for advocating a kind of political quietism. Since you don't know what Fascism is, how can you struggle against Fascism? One need not swallow such absurdities as this, but one ought to recognize that the present political chaos is connected with the decay of language, and that one can probably bring about some improvement by starting at the verbal end. If you simplify your English, you are freed from the worst follies of orthodoxy. You cannot speak any of the necessary dialects, and when you make a stupid remark its stupidity will be obvious, even to yourself. Political language—and with variations this is true of all political parties, from Conservatives to Anarchists—is designed to make lies sound truthful and murder respectable, and to give an appearance of solidity to pure wind. One cannot change this all in a moment, but one can at least change one's own habits, and from time to time one can even, if one jeers loudly enough, send some worn-out and useless phrase—some *jackboot, Achilles' heel, hotbed, melting pot, acid test, veritable inferno* or other lump of verbal refuse—into the dustbin where it belongs.

Shooting an Elephant

This essay was written some time between 1931 and 1936.

In Moulmein, in Lower Burma, I was hated by large numbers of people —the only time in my life that I have been important enough for this to happen to me. I was sub-divisional police officer of the town, and in an aimless, petty kind of way anti-European feeling was very bitter. No one had the guts to raise a riot, but if a European woman went through the bazaars alone somebody would probably spit betel juice over her dress. As a police officer I was an obvious target and was baited whenever it seemed safe to do so. When a nimble Burman tripped me up on the football field and the referee (another Burman) looked the other way, the crowd yelled with hideous laughter. This happened more than once. In the end the sneering yellow faces of young men that met me everywhere, the insults hooted after me when I was at a safe distance, got badly on my nerves. The young Buddhist priests were the worst of all. There were several thousands of them in the town and none of them seemed to have anything to do except stand on street corners and jeer at Europeans.

All this was preplexing and upsetting. For at that time I had already made up my mind that imperialism was an evil thing and the sooner I chucked up my job and got out of it the better. Theoretically—and secretly, of course—I was all for the Burmese and all against their oppressors, the British. As for the job I was doing, I hated it more bitterly than I can perhaps make clear. In a job like that you see the dirty work of Empire at close quarters. The wretched prisoners huddling in the stinking cages of the lock-ups, the grey, cowed faces of the long-term convicts, the scarred buttocks of the men who had been flogged with bamboos—all these oppressed me with an intolerable sense of guilt. But I could get nothing into perspective. I was young and ill-educated and I had had to think out my problems in the utter silence that is imposed on every Englishman in the East. I did not even know that the British Empire is dying, still less did I know that it is a great deal better than the younger empires that are going to supplant it. All I knew was that I was stuck between my hatred of the empire I served and my rage against the evil-spirited little beasts who tried to make my job impossible. With one part of my mind I thought of the British Raj as an unbreakable tyranny, as something clamped down, in *saecula saeculorum,* upon the will of prostrate peoples; with another part I thought that the greatest joy in the world would be to drive a bayonet into a Buddhist priest's guts. Feelings like these are the normal by-products of imperialism; ask any Anglo-Indian official, if you can catch him off duty.

One day something happened which in a roundabout way was enlightening. It was a tiny incident in itself, but it gave me a better glimpse than I had had before of the real nature of imperialism—the real motives for which despotic governments act. Early one morning the sub-inspector at a police station the other end of the town rang me up on the 'phone and said that an elephant was ravaging the bazaar. Would I please come and do something about it? I did not know what I could do, but I wanted to see what was happening and I got on to a pony and started out. I took my rifle, an old .44 Winchester and much too small to kill an elephant, but I thought the noise might be useful *in terrorem.* Various Burmans stopped me on the way and told me about the elephant's doings. It was not, of course, a wild elephant, but a tame one which had gone "must." It had been chained up, as tame elephants always are when their attack of "must" is due, but on the previous night it had broken its chain and escaped. Its mahout, the only person who could manage it when it was in that state, had set out in pursuit, but had taken the wrong direction and was now twelve hours' journey away, and in the morning the elephant had suddenly reappeared in the town. The Burmese population had no weapons and were quite helpless against it. It had already destroyed somebody's bamboo hut, killed a cow and raided some fruit-stalls and devoured the stock; also it had met the municipal rubbish van and, when the driver jumped out and took to his heels, had turned the van over and inflicted violences upon it.

The Burmese sub-inspector and some Indian constables were waiting for me in the quarter where the elephant had been seen. It was a very poor quarter, a labyrinth of squalid bamboo huts, thatched with palm-leaf, winding all over a steep hillside. I remember that it was a cloudy, stuffy morning at the beginning of the rains. We began questioning the people as to where the elephant had gone and, as usual, failed to get any definite information. That is invariably the case in the East; a story always sounds clear enough at a distance, but the nearer you get to the scene of events the vaguer it becomes. Some of the people said that the elephant had gone in one direction, some said that he had gone in another, some professed not even to have heard of any elephant. I had almost made up my mind that the whole story was a pack of lies, when we heard yells a little distance away. There was a loud, scandalized cry of "Go away, child! Go away this instant!" and an old woman with a switch in her hand came round the corner of a hut, violently shooing away a crowd of naked children. Some more women followed, clicking their tongues and exclaiming; evidently there was something that the children ought not to have seen. I rounded the hut and saw a man's dead body sprawling in the mud. He was an Indian, a black Dravidian coolie, almost naked, and he could not have been dead many minutes. The people said that the elephant had come suddenly upon him round the corner of the hut, caught him with its trunk, put its foot on his back and ground him into the earth. This was the rainy season and the ground was soft, and his face had scored a trench a foot deep and a couple of yards long. He was lying on his belly with arms crucified and head sharply twisted to one side. His face was coated with mud, the eyes wide open, the teeth bared and grinning with an expression of unendurable agony. (Never tell me, by the way, that the dead look peaceful. Most of the corpses I have seen looked devilish.) The friction of the great beast's foot had stripped the skin from his back as neatly as one skins a rabbit. As soon as I saw the dead man I sent an orderly to a friend's house nearby to borrow an elephant rifle. I had already sent back the pony, not wanting it to go mad with fright and throw me if it smelt the elephant.

The orderly came back in a few minutes with a rifle and five cartridges, and meanwhile some Burmans had arrived and told us that the elephant was in the paddy fields below, only a few hundred yards away. As I started forward practically the whole population of the quarter flocked out of the houses and followed me. They had seen the rifle and were all shouting excitedly that I was going to shoot the elephant. They had not shown much interest in the elephant when he was merely ravaging their homes, but it was different now that he was going to be shot. It was a bit of fun to them, as it would be to an English crowd; besides they wanted the meat. It made me vaguely uneasy. I had no intention of shooting the elephant—I had merely sent for the rifle to defend myself if necessary—and it is always unnerving to have a crowd following you. I marched down the hill, looking and feeling a fool, with the rifle over my shoulder and an ever-growing army of people jostling at my heels. At the bottom, when you got away from the huts, there was a metalled road and beyond that a miry waste of paddy fields a thousand yards across, not yet ploughed but soggy from the first rains and dotted with coarse grass. The elephant was standing eight yards from the road, his left side towards us. He took not the slightest notice of the crowd's approach. He was tearing up bunches of grass, beating them against his knees to clean them and stuffing them into his mouth.

I had halted on the road. As soon as I saw the elephant I knew with perfect certainty that I ought not to shoot him. It is a serious matter to shoot a working elephant—it is comparable to destroying a huge and costly piece of machinery—and obviously one ought not to do it if it can possibly be avoided. And at that distance, peacefully eating, the elephant looked no more dangerous than a cow. I thought then and I think now that his attack of "must" was already passing off; in which case he would merely wander harmlessly about until the mahout came back and caught him. Moreover, I did not in the least want to shoot him. I decided that I would watch him for a little while to make sure that he did not turn savage again, and then go home.

But at that moment I glanced round at the crowd that had followed me. It was an immense crowd, two thousand at the least and growing every minute. It blocked the road for a long distance on either side. I looked at the sea of yellow faces above the garish clothes—faces all happy and excited over this bit of fun, all certain that the elephant was going to be shot. They were watching me as they would watch a conjurer about to perform a trick. They did not like me, but with the magical rifle in my hands I was momentarily worth watching. And suddenly I realized that I should have to shoot the elephant after all. The people expected it of me and I had got to do it; I could feel their two thousand wills pressing me forward, irresistibly. And it was at this moment, as I stood there with the rifle in my hands, that I first grasped the hollowness, the futility of the white man's dominion in the East. Here was I, the white man with his gun, standing in front of the unarmed native crowd—seemingly the leading actor of the piece; but in reality I was only an absurd puppet pushed to and fro by the will of those yellow faces behind. I perceived in this moment that when the white man turns tyrant it is his own freedom that he destroys. He becomes a sort of hollow, posing dummy, the conventionalized figure of a sahib. For it is the condition of his rule that he shall spend his life in trying to impress the "natives," and so in every crisis he has got to do what the "natives" expect of him. He wears a mask, and his face grows to fit it. I had got to shoot the elephant. I had committed myself to doing it when I sent for the rifle. A sahib has got to act like a sahib; he has got to appear resolute, to know his own mind and do definite things. To come all that way, rifle in hand, with two thousand people marching at my heels, and then to trail feebly away, having done nothing—no, that was impossible. The crowd would laugh at me. And my whole life, every white man's life in the East, was one long struggle not to be laughed at.

But I did not want to shoot the elephant. I watched him beating his bunch of grass against his knees, with that preoccupied grandmotherly air that elephants have. It seemed to me that it would be murder to shoot him. At that age I was not squeamish about killing animals, but I had never shot an elephant and never wanted to. (Somehow it always seems worse to kill a *large* animal.) Besides, there was the beast's owner to be considered. Alive, the elphant was worth at last a hundred pounds; dead, he would only be worth the value of his tusks, five pounds, possibly. But I had got to act quickly. I turned to some experienced-looking Burmans who had been there when we arrived, and asked them how the elephant had been behaving. They all said the same thing: he took no notice of you if you left him alone, but he might charge if you went too close to him.

It was perfectly clear to me what I ought to do. I ought to walk up to within, say, twenty-five yards of the elephant and test his behavior.

If he charged, I could shoot; if he took no notice of me, it would be safe to leave him until the mahout came back. But also I knew that I was going to do no such thing. I was a poor shot with a rifle and the ground was soft mud into which one would sink at every step. If the elephant charged and I missed him, I should have about as much chance as a toad under a steam-roller. But even then I was not thinking particularly of my own skin, only of the watchful yellow faces behind. For at that moment, with the crowd watching me, I was not afraid in the ordinary sense, as I would have been if I had been alone. A white man mustn't be frightened in front of "natives"; and so, in general, he isn't frightened. The sole thought in my mind was that if anything went wrong those two thousand Burmans would see me pursued, caught, trampled on and reduced to a grinning corpse like that Indian up the hill. And if that happened it was quite probable that some of them would laugh. That would never do. There was only one alternative. I shoved the cartridges into the magazine and lay down on the road to get a better aim.

The crowd grew very still, and a deep, low, happy sigh, as of people who see the theatre curtain go up at last, breathed from innumerable throats. They were going to have their bit of fun after all. The rifle was a beautiful German thing with cross-hair sights. I did not then know that in shooting an elephant one would shoot to cut an imaginary bar running from ear-hole to ear-hole. I ought, therefore, as the elephant was sideways on, to have aimed straight at his ear-hole; actually I aimed several inches in front of this, thinking the brain would be further forward.

When I pulled the trigger I did not hear the bang or feel the kick —one never does when a shot goes home—but I heard the devilish roar of glee that went up from the crowd. In that instant, in too short a time, one would have thought, even for the bullet to get there, a mysterious, terrible change had come over the elephant. He neither stirred nor fell, but every line of his body had altered. He looked suddenly stricken, shrunken, immensely old, as though the frightful impact of the bullet had paralysed him without knocking him down. At last, after what seemed a long time—it might have been five seconds, I dare say—he sagged flabbily to his knees. His mouth slobbered. An enormous senility seemed to have settled upon him. One could have imagined him thousands of years old. I fired again into the same spot. At the second shot he did not collapse but climbed with desperate slowness to his feet and stood weakily upright, with legs sagging and head drooping. I fired a third time. That was the shot that did for him. You could see the agony of it jolt his whole body and knock the last remnant of strength from his legs. But in falling he seemed for a moment to rise, for as his hind legs collapsed beneath him he seemed to tower upward like a huge rock toppling, his trunk reaching skywards like a tree. He trumpeted, for the first and only time. And then down he came, his belly towards me, with a crash that seemed to shake the ground even where I lay.

I got up. The Burmans were already racing past me across the mud. It was obvious that the elephant would never rise again, but he was not dead. He was breathing very rhythmically with long rattling gasps, his great mound of a side painfully rising and falling. His mouth was wide open—I could see far down into caverns of pale pink throat. I waited a long time for him to die, but his breathing did not weaken. Finally I fired my two remaining shots into the spot where I thought his heart must be. The thick blood welled out of him like red velvet, but still he did not die. His body did not even jerk when the shots hit him, the tortured breathing continued without a pause. He was dying, very slowly and in great agony, but in some world remote from me where not even a bullet could damage him further. I felt that I had got to put an end to that dreadful noise. It seemed dreadful to see the great beast lying there, powerless to move and yet powerless to die, and not even to be able to finish him. I sent back for my small rifle and poured shot after shot into his heart and down his throat. They seemed to make no impression. The tortured gasps continued as steadily as the ticking of a clock.

In the end I could not stand it any longer and went away. I heard later that it took him half an hour to die. Burmans were bringing dahs and baskets even before I left, and I was told they had stripped his body almost to the bones by the afternoon.

Afterwards, of course, there were endless discussions about the shooting of the elephant. The owner was furious, but he was only an Indian and could do nothing. Besides, legally I had done the right thing, for a mad elephant has to be killed, like a mad dog, if its owner fails to control it. Among the Europeans opinion was divided. The older men said I was right, the younger men said it was a damn shame to shoot an elephant for killing a coolie, because an elephant was worth more than any damn Coringhee coolie. And afterwards I was very glad that the coolie had been killed; it put me legally in the right and it gave me a sufficient pretext for shooting the elephant. I often wondered whether any of the others grasped that I had done it solely to avoid looking a fool.

Life in an Industrial Town

This is the first chapter in The Road to Wigan Pier. *The title used here has been supplied by the editor.*

The first sound in the mornings was the clumping of the mill-girls' clogs down the cobbled street. Earlier than that, I suppose, there were factory whistles which I was never awake to hear.

There were generally four of us in the bedroom, and a beastly place it was, with that defiled impermanent look of rooms that are not serving their rightful purpose. Years earlier the house had been an ordinary dwelling-house, and when the Brookers had taken it and fitted it out as a tripe-shop and lodging-house, they had inherited some of the more useless pieces of furniture and had never had the energy to remove them. We were therefore sleeping in what was still recognisably a drawing-room. Hanging from the ceiling there was a heavy glass chandelier on which the dust was so thick that it was like fur. And covering most of one wall there was a huge hideous piece of junk, something between a sideboard and a hall-stand, with lots of carving and little drawers and strips of looking-glass, and there was a once-gaudy carpet ringed by the slop-pails of years, and two gilt chairs with burst seats, and one of those old-fashioned horsehair armchairs which you slide off when you try to sit on them. The room had been turned into a bedroom by thrusting four squalid beds in among this other wreckage.

My bed was in the right-hand corner on the side nearest the door. There was another bed across the foot of it and jammed hard against it (it had to be in that position to allow the door to open) so that I had to sleep with my legs doubled up; if I straightened them out I kicked the occupant of the other bed in the small of the back. He was an elderly man named Mr. Reilly, a mechanic of sorts and employed "on top" at one of the coal-pits. Luckily he had to go to work at five in the morning, so I could uncoil my legs and have a couple of hours' proper sleep after he was gone. In the bed opposite there was a Scotch miner who had been injured in a pit accident (a huge chunk of stone pinned him to the ground and it was a couple of hours before they could lever it off), and had received five hundred pounds compensation. He was a big handsome man of forty, with grizzled hair and a clipped moustache, more like a sergeant-major than a miner, and he would lie in bed till late in the day, smoking a short pipe. The other bed was occupied by a succession of commercial travellers, newspaper-canvassers and hire-purchase touts who generally stayed for a couple of nights. It was a double bed and much the best in the room. I had slept in it myself my first night there, but had been manœuvred out of it to make room for another lodger. I believe all newcomers spent their first night in the double bed, which was used, so to speak, as bait. All the windows were kept tight shut, with a red sandbag jammed in the bottom, and in the morning the room stank like a ferret's cage. You did not notice it when you got up, but if you went out of the room and came back, the smell hit you in the face with a smack.

I never discovered how many bedrooms the house contained, but strange to say there was a bathroom, dating from before the Brookers' time. Downstairs there was the usual kitchen living-room with its huge open range burning night and day. It was lighted only by a skylight, for on one side of it was the shop and on the other the larder, which opened into some dark subterranean place where the tripe was stored. Partly blocking the door of the larder there was a shapeless sofa upon which Mrs. Brooker, our landlady, lay permanently ill, festooned in grimy blankets. She had a big, pale yellow, anxious face. No one knew for certain what was the matter with her; I suspect that her only real trouble was over-eating. In front of the fire there was almost always a line of damp washing, and in the middle of the room was the big kitchen table at which the family and all the lodgers ate. I never saw this table completely uncovered, but I saw its various wrappings at different times. At the bottom there was a layer of old newspapers stained by Worcester Sauce; above that a sheet of sticky white oilcloth; above that a green serge cloth; above that a coarse linen cloth, never changed and seldom taken off. Generally the crumbs from breakfast were still on the table at supper. I used to get to know individual crumbs by sight and watch their progress up and down the table from day to day.

The shop was a narrow, cold sort of room. On the outside of the window a few white letters, relics of ancient chocolate advertisements, were scattered like stars. Inside there was a slab upon which lay the great white folds of tripe, and the grey flocculent stuff known as "black tripe," and the ghostly translucent feet of pigs, ready boiled. It was the ordinary "tripe and pea" shop, and not much else was stocked except bread, cigarettes and tinned stuff. "Teas" were advertised in the window, but if a customer demanded a cup of tea he was usually put off with excuses. Mr. Brooker, though out of work for two years, was a miner by trade, but he and his wife had been keeping shops of various kinds as a side-line all their lives. At one time they had had a pub, but they had lost their licence for allowing gambling on the premises. I doubt whether any of their businesses had ever paid; they were the kind of people who ran a business chiefly in order to have something to grumble about. Mr. Brooker was a dark, small-boned, sour, Irish-looking man, and astonishingly dirty. I don't think I ever once saw his hands clean. As Mrs. Brooker was now an invalid he prepared most of the food, and like all people with permanently dirty hands he had a peculiarly intimate lingering manner of handling things. If he gave you a slice of bread-and-butter there was always a black thumb-print on it. Even in the early morning when he descended into the mysterious den behind Mrs. Brooker's sofa and fished out the tripe, his hands were already black. I heard dreadful stories from the other lodgers about the place where the tripe was kept. Blackbeetles were said to swarm there. I do not know how often fresh consignments of tripe were ordered, but it was at long intervals, for Mrs. Brooker used to date events by it. "Let me see now, I've had in three lots of froze (frozen tripe) since that happened," etc., etc. We lodgers were never given tripe to eat. At the time I imagined that this was because tripe was too expensive; I have since thought that it was merely because we knew too much about it. The Brookers never ate tripe themselves, I noticed.

The only permanent lodgers were the Scotch miner, Mr. Reilly, two old-age pensioners and an unemployed man on the P.A.C. named Joe—he was the kind of person who has no surname. The Scotch miner was a bore when you got to know him. Like so many unemployed men he spent too much time reading newspapers, and if you did not head him off he would discourse for hours about such things as the Yellow Peril, trunk murders, astrology, and the conflict between religion and science. The old-age pensioners had, as usual, been driven from their homes by the Means Test. They handed their weekly ten shillings over to the Brookers and in return got the kind of accommodation you would expect for ten shillings; that is, a bed in the attic and meals chiefly of bread-and-butter. One of them was of "superior" type and was dying of some malignant disease—cancer, I believe. He only got out of bed on the days when he went to draw his pension. The other, called by everyone Old Jack, was an ex-miner aged seventy-eight who had worked well over fifty years in the pits. He was alert and intelligent, but curiously enough he seemed only to remember his boyhood experiences and to have forgotten all about the modern mining machinery and improvements. He used to tell me tales of fights with savage horses in the narrow galleries underground. When he heard that I was arranging to go down several coal mines he was contemptuous and declared that a man of my size (six feet two and a half) would never manage the "travelling"; it was no use telling him that the "travelling" was better than it used to be. But he was friendly to everyone and used to give us all a fine shout of "Good night, boys!" as he crawled up the stairs to his bed somewhere under the rafters. What I most admired about Old Jack was that he never cadged; he was generally out of tobacco towards the end of the week, but he always refused to smoke anyone else's. The Brookers had insured the lives of both old-age pensioners with one of the tanner-a-week companies. It was said that they were overheard anxiously asking the insurance-tout "how long people lived when they'd got cancer."

Joe, like the Scotchman, was a great reader of newspapers and spent almost his entire day in the public library. He was the typical unmarried unemployed man, a derelict-looking, frankly ragged creature with a round, almost childish face on which there was a naïvely naughty expression. He looked more like a neglected little boy than a grown-up man. I suppose it is the complete lack of responsibility that makes so many of these men look younger than their ages. From Joe's appearance I took him to be about twenty-eight, and was amazed to learn that he was forty-three. He had a love of resounding phrases and was very proud of the astuteness with which he had avoided getting married. He often said to me, "Matrimonial chains is a big item," evidently feeling this to be a very subtle and portentous remark. His total income was fifteen shillings a week, and he paid out six or seven to the Brookers for his bed. I sometimes used to see him making himself a cup of tea over the kitchen fire, but for the rest he got his meals somewhere out of doors; it was mostly slices of bread-and-marg and packets of fish and chips, I suppose.

Besides these there was a floating clientele of commercial travellers of the poorer sort, travelling actors—always common in the North because most of the larger pubs hire variety artists at the week-ends—and newspaper-canvassers. The newspaper-canvassers were a type I had never met before. Their job seemed to me so hopeless, so appalling that I wondered how anyone could put up with such a thing when prison was a possible alternative. They were employed mostly by weekly or Sunday papers, and they were sent from town to town, provided with maps and given a list of streets which they had to "work" each day. If they failed to secure a minimum of twenty orders a day, they got the sack. So long as they kept up their twenty orders a day they received a small salary—two pounds a week, I think; on any order over the twenty they drew a tiny commission. The thing is not so impossible as it sounds, because in working-class districts every family takes in a twopenny weekly paper and changes it every few weeks; but I doubt whether anyone keeps a job of that kind long. The newspapers engage poor desperate wretches, out-of-work clerks and commercial travellers and the like, who for a while make frantic efforts and keep their sales up to the minimum; then as the deadly work wears them down they are sacked and fresh men are taken on. I got to know two who were employed by one of the more notorious weeklies. Both of them were middle-aged men with families to support, and one of them was a grandfather. They were on their feet ten hours a day, "working" their appointed streets, and then busy late into the night filling in blank forms for some swindle their paper was running—one of those schemes by which you are "given" a set of crockery if you take out a six weeks' subscription and send a two-shilling postal order as well. The fat one, the grandfather, used to fall asleep with his head on a pile of forms. Neither of them could afford the pound a week which the Brookers charged for full board. They used to pay a small sum for their beds and make shame-faced meals in a corner of the kitchen off bacon and bread-and-margarine which they stored in their suitcases.

The Brookers had large numbers of sons and daughters, most of whom had long since fled from home. Some were in Canada—"at Canada," as Mrs. Brooker used to put it. There was only one son living near by, a large pig-like young man employed in a garage, who frequently came to the house for his meals. His wife was there all day with the two children, and most of the cooking and laundering was done by her and by Emmie, the fiancée of another son who was in London. Emmie was a fair-haired, sharp-nosed, unhappy-looking girl who worked at one of the mills for some starvation wage, but nevertheless spent all her evenings in bondage at the Brookers' house. I gathered that the marriage was constantly being postponed and would probably never take place, but Mrs. Brooker had already appropriated Emmie as a daughter-in-law, and nagged her in that peculiar watchful, loving way that invalids have. The rest of the housework was done, or not done, by Mr. Brooker. Mrs. Brooker seldom rose from her sofa in the kitchen (she spent the night there as well as the day) and was too ill to do anything except eat stupendous meals. It was Mr. Brooker who attended to the shop, gave the lodgers their food and "did out" the bedrooms. He was always moving with incredible slowness from one hated job to another. Often the beds were still unmade at six in the evening, and at any hour of the day you were liable to meet Mr. Brooker on the stairs, carrying a full chamber-pot which he gripped with his thumb well over the rim. In the mornings he sat by the fire with a tub of filthy water, peeling potatoes at the speed of a slow-motion picture. I never saw anyone who could peel potatoes with quite such an air of brooding resentment. You could see the hatred of this "bloody woman's work," as he called it, fermenting inside him, a kind of bitter juice. He was one of those people who can chew their grievances like a cud.

Of course, as I was indoors a good deal, I heard all about the Brookers' woes, and how everyone swindled them and was ungrateful to them, and how the shop did not pay and the lodging-house hardly paid. By local standards they were not so badly off, for, in some way I did not understand, Mr. Brooker was dodging the Means Test and drawing an allowance from the P.A.C., but their chief pleasure was talking about their grievances to anyone who would listen. Mrs. Brooker used to lament by the hour, lying on her sofa, a soft mound of fat and self-pity, saying the same things over and over again. "We don't seem to get no customers nowadays. I don't know 'ow it is. The tripe's just a-laying there day after day—such beautiful tripe it is, too! It does seem 'ard don't it now?" etc., etc., etc. All Mrs. Brooker's laments ended with "It does seem 'ard, don't it now?" like the refrain of a ballade. Certainly it was true that the shop did not pay. The whole place had the unmistakable dusty, flyblown air of a business that is going down. But it would have been quite useless to explain to them *why* nobody came to the shop, even if one had had the face to do it; neither was capable of understanding that last year's dead blue-bottles supine in the shop window are not good for trade.

But the thing that really tormented them was the thought of those two old-age pensioners living in their house, usurping floor-space, devouring food and paying only ten shillings a week. I doubt whether they were really losing money over the old-age pensioners, though certainly the profit on ten shillings a week must have been very small. But in their eyes the two old men were a kind of dreadful parasite who had fastened on them and were living on their charity. Old Jack they could just tolerate, because he kept out-of-doors most of the day, but they really hated the bedridden one, Hooker by name. Mr. Brooker had a queer way of pronouncing his name, without the H and with a long U—"Uker." What tales I heard about old Hooker and his fractiousness, the nuisance of making his bed, the way he "wouldn't eat" this and "wouldn't eat" that, his endless ingratitude and, above all, the selfish obstinacy with which he refused to die! The Brookers were quite openly pining for him to die. When that happened they could at least draw the insurance money. They seemed to feel him there, eating their substance day after day, as though he had been a living worm in their bowels. Sometimes Mr. Brooker would look up from his potato-peeling, catch my eye and jerk his head with a look of inexpressible bitterness towards the ceiling, towards old Hooker's room. "It's a b——, ain't it?" he would say. There was no need to say more; I had heard all about old Hooker's ways already. But the Brookers had grievances of one kind and another against all their lodgers, myself included, no doubt. Joe, being on the P.A.C., was practically in the same category as the old-age pensioners. The Scotchman paid a pound a week, but he was indoors most of the day and they "didn't like him always hanging round the place," as they put it. The newspaper-canvassers were out all day, but the Brookers bore them a grudge for bringing in their own food, and even Mr. Reilly, their best lodger, was in disgrace because Mrs. Brooker said that he woke her up when he came downstairs in the mornings. They couldn't, they complained perpetually, get the kind of lodgers they wanted—good-class "commercial gentlemen" who paid full board and were out all day. Their ideal lodger would have been somebody who paid thirty shillings a week and never came indoors except to sleep. I have noticed that people who let lodgings nearly always hate their lodgers. They want their money but they look on them as intruders and have a curiously watchful, jealous attitude which at bottom is a determination not to let the lodger make himself too much at home. It is an inevitable result of the bad system by which the lodger has to live in somebody else's house without being one of the family.

The meals at the Brookers' house were uniformly disgusting. For breakfast you got two rashers of bacon and a pale fried egg, and bread-and-butter which had often been cut overnight and always had thumb-marks on it. However tactfully I tried, I could never induce Mr. Brooker to let me cut my own bread-and-butter; he *would* hand it to me slice by slice, each slice gripped firmly under that broad black thumb. For dinner there were generally those threepenny steak puddings which are sold ready-made in tins—these were part of the stock of the shop, I think—and boiled potatoes and rice pudding. For tea there was more bread-and-butter and frayed-looking sweet cakes which were probably bought as "stales" from the baker. For supper there was the pale flabby Lancashire cheese and biscuits. The Brookers never called these biscuits biscuits. They always referred to them reverently as "cream crackers"—"Have another cream cracker, Mr. Reilly. You'll like a cream cracker with your cheese"—thus glozing over the fact that there was only cheese for supper. Several bottles of Worcester Sauce and a half-full jar of marmalade lived permanently on the table. It was usual to souse everything, even a piece of cheese, with Worcester Sauce, but I never saw anyone brave the marmalade jar, which was an unspeakable mass of stickiness and dust. Mrs. Brooker had her meals separately but also took snacks from any meal that happened to be going, and manœuvred with great skill for what she called "the bottom of the pot," meaning the strongest cup of tea. She had a habit of constantly wiping her mouth on one of her blankets. Towards the end of my stay she took to tearing off strips of newspaper for this purpose, and in the morning the floor was often littered with crumpled-up balls of slimy paper which lay there for hours. The smell of the kitchen was dreadful, but, as with that of the bedroom, you ceased to notice it after a while.

It struck me that this place must be fairly normal as lodging-houses in the industrial areas go, for on the whole the lodgers did not complain. The only one who ever did so to my knowledge was a little black-haired, sharp-nosed Cockney, a traveller for a cigarette firm. He had never been in the North before, and I think that till recently he had been in better employ and was used to staying in commercial hotels. This was his first glimpse of really low-class lodgings, the kind of place in which the poor tribe of touts and canvassers have to shelter upon their endless journeys. In the morning as we were dressing (he had slept in the double bed, of course) I saw him look round the desolate room with a sort of wondering aversion. He caught my eye and suddenly divined that I was a fellow-Southerner.

"The filthy bloody bastards!" he said feelingly.

After that he packed his suit-case, went downstairs and, with great strength of mind, told the Brookers that this was not the kind of house he was accustomed to and that he was leaving immediately. The Brookers could never understand why. They were astonished and hurt. The ingratitude of it! Leaving them like that for no reason after a single night! Afterwards they discussed it over and over again, in all its bearings. It was added to their store of grievances.

On the day when there was a full chamber-pot under the breakfast table I decided to leave. The place was beginning to depress me. It was not only the dirt, the smells and the vile food, but the feeling of stagnant meaningless decay, of having got down into some subterranean place where people go creeping round and round, just like blackbeetles, in an endless muddle of slovened jobs and mean grievances. The most dreadful thing about people like the Brookers is the way they say the same things over and over again. It gives you the feeling that they are not real people at all, but a kind of ghost for ever rehearsing the same futile rigmarole. In the end Mrs. Brooker's self-pitying talk—always the same complaints, over and over, and always ending with the tremulous whine of "It does seem 'ard, don't it now?"—revolted me even more than her habit of wiping her mouth with bits of newspaper. But it is no use saying that people like the Brookers are just disgusting and trying to put them out of mind. For they exist in tens and hundreds of thousands; they are one of the characteristic by-products of the modern world. You cannot disregard them if you accept the civilisation that produced them. For this is part at least of what industrialism has done for us. Columbus sailed the Atlantic, the first steam engines tottered into motion, the British squares stood firm under the French guns at Waterloo, the one-eyed scoundrels of the nineteenth century praised God and filled their pockets; and this is where it all led—to labyrinthine slums and dark back kitchens with sickly, ageing people creeping round and round them like blackbeetles. It is a kind of duty to see and smell such places now and again, especially smell them, lest you should forget that they exist; though perhaps it is better not to stay there too long.

The train bore me away, through the monstrous scenery of slag-heaps, chimneys, piled scrap-iron, foul canals, paths of cindery mud criss-crossed by the prints of clogs. This was March, but the weather had been horribly cold and everywhere there were mounds of blackened snow. As we moved slowly through the outskirts of the town we passed row after row of little grey slum houses running at right angles to the embankment. At the back of one of the houses a young woman was kneeling on the stones, poking a stick up the leaden waste-pipe which ran from the sink inside and which I suppose was blocked. I had time to see everything about her—her sacking apron, her clumsy clogs, her arms reddened by the cold. She looked up as the train passed, and I was almost near enough to catch her eye. She had a round pale face, the usual exhausted face of the slum girl who is twenty-five and looks forty, thanks to miscarriages and drudgery; and it wore, for the second in which I saw it, the most desolate, hopeless expression I have ever seen. It struck me then that we are mistaken when we say that "It isn't the same for them as it would be for us," and that people bred in the slums can imagine nothing but the slums. For what I saw in her face was not the ignorant suffering of an animal. She knew well enough what was happening to her—understood as well as I did how dreadful a destiny it was to be kneeling there in the bitter cold, on the slimy stones of a slum backyard, poking a stick up a foul drain-pipe.

But quite soon the train drew away into open country, and that seemed strange, almost unnatural, as though the open country had been a kind of park; for in the industrial areas one always feels that the smoke and filth must go on for ever and that no part of the earth's surface can escape them. In a crowded, dirty little country like ours one takes defilement almost for granted. Slag-heaps and chimneys seem a more normal, probable landscape than grass and trees, and even in the depths of the country when you drive your fork into the ground you half expect to lever up a broken bottle or a rusty can. But out here the snow was untrodden and lay so deep that only the tops of the stone boundary-walls were showing, winding over the hills like black paths. I remembered that D. H. Lawrence, writing of this same landscape or another near by, said that the snow covered hills rippled away into the distance "like muscle." It was not the simile that would have occurred to me. To my eye the snow and the black walls were more like a white dress with black piping running across it.

Although the snow was hardly broken the sun was shining brightly, and behind the shut windows of the carriage it seemed warm. According to the almanac this was spring, and a few of the birds seemed to believe it. For the first time in my life, in a bare patch beside the line, I saw rooks treading. They did it on the ground and not, as I should have expected, in a tree. The manner of courtship was curious. The female stood with her beak open and the male walked round her and appeared to be feeding her. I had hardly been in the train half an hour, but it seemed a very long way from the Brookers' back-kitchen to the empty slopes of snow, the bright sunshine and the big gleaming birds.

The whole of the industrial districts are really one enormous town, of about the same population as Greater London but, fortunately, of much larger area; so that even in the middle of them there is still room for patches of cleanness and decency. That is an encouraging thought. In spite of hard trying, man has not yet succeeded in doing his dirt everywhere. The earth is so vast and still so empty that even in the filthy heart of civilisation you find fields where the grass is green instead of grey; perhaps if you looked for them you might even find streams with live fish in them instead of salmon tins. For quite a long time, perhaps another twenty minutes, the train was rolling through open country before the villa-civilisation began to close in upon us again, and then the outer slums, and then the slag-heaps, belching chimneys, blast-furnaces, canals and gasometers of another industrial town.

The Ministry of Love

The following work is a self-contained unit taken from the novel, 1984. *The title used here has been supplied by the editor.*

He was lying on something that felt like a camp bed, except that it was higher off the ground and that he was fixed down in some way so that he could not move. Light that seemed stronger than usual was falling on his face. O'Brien was standing at his side, looking down at him intently. At the other side of him stood a man in a white coat, holding a hypodermic syringe.

Even after his eyes were open he took in his surroundings only gradually. He had the impression of swimming up into this room from some quite different world, a sort of underwater world far beneath it. How long he had been down there he did not know. Since the moment when they arrested him he had not seen darkness or daylight. Besides, his memories were not continuous. There had been times when consciousness, even the sort of consciousness that one has in sleep, had stopped dead and started again after a blank interval. But whether the intervals were of days or weeks or only seconds, there was no way of knowing.

With that first blow on the elbow the nightmare had started. Later he was to realize that all that then happened was merely a preliminary, a routine interrogation to which nearly all prisoners were subjected.

There was a long range of crimes—espionage, sabotage, and the like—to which everyone had to confess as a matter of course. The confession was a formality, though the torture was real. How many times he had been beaten, how long the beatings had continued, he could not remember. Always there were five or six men in black uniforms at him simultaneously. Sometimes it was fists, sometimes it was truncheons, sometimes it was steel rods, sometimes it was boots. There were times when he rolled about the floor, as shameless as an animal, writhing his body this way and that in an endless, hopeless effort to dodge the kicks, and simply inviting more and yet more kicks, in his ribs, in his belly, on his elbows, on his shins, in his groin, in his testicles, on the bone at the base of his spine. There were times when it went on and on until the cruel, wicked, unforgivable thing seemed to him not that the guards continued to beat him but that he could not force himself into losing consciousness. There were times when his nerve so forsook him that he began shouting for mercy even before the beating began, when the mere sight of a fist drawn back for a blow was enough to make him pour forth a confession of real and imaginary crimes. There were other times when he started out with the resolve of confessing nothing, when every word had to be forced out of him between gasps of pain, and there were times when he feebly tried to compromise, when he said to himself: "I will confess, but not yet. I must hold out till the pain becomes unbearable. Three more kicks, two more kicks, and then I will tell them what they want." Sometimes he was beaten till he could hardly stand, then flung like a sack of potatoes onto the stone floor of a cell, left to recuperate for a few hours, and then taken out and beaten again. There were also longer periods of recovery. He remembered them dimly, because they were spent chiefly in sleep or stupor. He remembered a cell with a plank bed, a sort of shelf sticking out from the wall, and a tin washbasin, and meals of hot soup and bread and sometimes coffee. He remembered a surly barber arriving to scrape his chin and crop his hair, and businesslike, unsympathetic men in white coats feeling his pulse, tapping his reflexes, turning up his eyelids, running harsh fingers over him in search of broken bones, and shooting needles into his arm to make him sleep.

The beatings grew less frequent, and became mainly a threat, a horror to which he could be sent back at any moment when his answers were unsatisfactory. His questioners now were not ruffians in black uniforms but Party intellectuals, little rotund men with quick movements and flashing spectacles, who worked on him in relays over periods which lasted—he thought, he could not be sure—ten or twelve hours at a stretch. These other questioners saw to it that he was in constant slight pain, but it was not chiefly pain that they relied on. They slapped his face, wrung his ears, pulled his hair, made him stand on one leg, refused him leave to urinate, shone glaring lights in his face until his eyes ran with water; but the aim of this was simply to humiliate him and destroy his power of arguing and reasoning. Their real weapon was the merciless questioning that went on and on hour after hour, tripping him up, laying traps for him, twisting everything that he said, convicting him at every step of lies and self-contradiction, until he began weeping as much from shame as from nervous fatigue. Sometimes he would weep half a dozen times in a single session. Most of the time they screamed abuse at him and threatened at every hesitation to deliver him over to the guards again; but sometimes they would suddenly change their tune, call him comrade, appeal to him in the name of Ingsoc and Big Brother, and ask him sorrowfully whether even now he had not enough loyalty to the Party left to make him wish to undo the evil he had done. When his nerves were in rags after hours of questioning, even this appeal could reduce him to sniveling tears. In the end the nagging voices broke him down more completely than the boots and fists of the guards. He became simply a mouth that uttered, a hand that signed whatever was demanded of him. His sole concern was to find out what they wanted him to confess, and then confess it quickly, before the bullying started anew. He confessed to the assassination of eminent Party members, the distribution of seditious pamphlets, embezzlement of public funds, sale of military secrets, sabotage of every kind. He confessed that he had been a spy in the pay of the Eastasian government as far back as 1968. He confessed that he was a religious believer, an admirer of capitalism, and a sexual pervert. He confessed that he had murdered his wife, although he knew, and his questioners must have known, that his wife was still alive. He confessed that for years he had been in personal touch with Goldstein and had been a member of an underground organization which had included almost every human being he had ever known. It was easier to confess everything and implicate everybody. Besides, in a sense it was all true. It was true that he had been the enemy of the Party, and in the eyes of the Party there was no distinction between the thought and the deed.

There were also memories of another kind. They stood out in his mind disconnectedly, like pictures with blackness all round them.

He was in a cell which might have been either dark or light, because he could see nothing except a pair of eyes. Near at hand some kind of instrument was ticking slowly and regularly. The eyes grew larger and more luminous. Suddenly he floated out of his seat, dived into the eyes, and was swallowed up.

He was strapped into a chair surrounded by dials, under dazzling lights. A man in a white coat was reading the dials. There was a tramp of heavy boots outside. The door clanged open. The waxen-faced officer marched in, followed by two guards.

"Room 101," said the officer.

The man in the white coat did not turn round. He did not look at Winston either; he was looking only at the dials.

He was rolling down a mighty corridor, a kilometer wide, full of glorious, golden light, roaring with laughter and shouting out confessions at the top of his voice. He was confessing everything, even the things he had succeeded in holding back under the torture. He was relating the entire history of his life to an audience who knew it already. With him were the guards, the other questioners, the men in white coats, O'Brien, Julia, Mr. Charrington, all rolling down the corridor together and shouting with laughter. Some dreadful thing which had lain embedded in the future had somehow been skipped over and had not happened. Everything was all right, there was no more pain, the last detail of his life was laid bare, understood, forgiven.

He was starting up from the plank bed in the half-certainty that he had heard O'Brien's voice. All through his interrogation, although he had never seen him, he had had the feeling that O'Brien was at his elbow, just out of sight. It was O'Brien who was directing everything. It was he who set the guards onto Winston and who prevented them from killing him. It was he who decided when Winston should scream with pain, when he should have a respite, when he should be fed, when he should sleep, when the drugs should be pumped into his arm. It was he who asked the questions and suggested the answers. He was the tormentor, he was the protector, he was the inquisitor, he was the friend. And once—Winston could not remember whether it was in drugged sleep, or in normal sleep, or even in a moment of wakefulness—a voice murmured in his ear: "Don't worry, Winston; you are in my keeping.

For seven years I have watched over you. Now the turning point has come. I shall save you, I shall make you perfect." He was not sure whether it was O'Brien's voice; but it was the same voice that had said to him, "We shall meet in the place where there is no darkness," in that other dream, seven years ago.

He did not remember any ending to his interrogation. There was a period of blackness and then the cell, or room, in which he now was had gradually materialized round him. He was almost flat on his back, and unable to move. His body was held down at every essential point. Even the back of his head was gripped in some manner. O'Brien was looking down at him gravely and rather sadly. His face, seen from below, looked coarse and worn, with pouches under the eyes and tired lines from nose to chin. He was older than Winston had thought him; he was perhaps forty-eight or fifty. Under his hand there was a dial with a lever on top and figures running round the face.

"I told you," said O'Brien, "that if we met again it would be here."

"Yes," said Winston.

Without any warning except a slight movement of O'Brien's hand, a wave of pain flooded his body. It was a frightening pain, because he could not see what was happening, and he had the feeling that some mortal injury was being done to him. He did not know whether the thing was really happening, or whether the effect was electrically produced; but his body was being wrenched out of shape, the joints were being slowly torn apart. Although the pain had brought the sweat out on his forehead, the worst of all was the fear that his backbone was about to snap. He set his teeth and breathed hard through his nose, trying to keep silent as long as possible.

"You are afraid," said O'Brien, watching his face, "that in another moment something is going to break. Your especial fear is that it will be your backbone. You have a vivid mental picture of the vertebrae snapping apart and the spinal fluid dripping out of them. That is what you are thinking, is it not, Winston?"

Winston did not answer. O'Brien drew back the lever on the dial. The wave of pain receded almost as quickly as it had come.

"That was forty," said O'Brien. "You can see that the numbers on this dial run up to a hundred. Will you please remember, throughout our conversation, that I have it in my power to inflict pain on you at any moment and to whatever degree I choose. If you tell me any lies, or attempt to prevaricate in any way, or even fall below your usual level of intelligence, you will cry out with pain, instantly. Do you understand that?"

"Yes," said Winston.

O'Brien's manner became less severe. He resettled his spectacles thoughtfully, and took a pace or two up and down. When he spoke his voice was gentle and patient. He had the air of a doctor, a teacher, even a priest, anxious to explain and persuade rather than to punish.

"I am taking trouble with you, Winston," he said, "because you are worth trouble. You know perfectly well what is the matter with you. You have known it for years, though you have fought against the knowledge. You are mentally deranged. You suffer from a defective memory. You are unable to remember real events, and you persuade yourself that you remember other events which never happened. Fortunately it is curable. You have never cured yourself of it, because you did not choose to. There was a small effort of the will that you were not ready to make. Even now, I am well aware, you are clinging to your disease under the impression that it is a virtue. Now we will take an example. At this moment, which power is Oceania at war with?"

"When I was arrested, Oceania was at war with Eastasia."

"With Eastasia. Good. And Oceania has always been at war with Eastasia, has it not?"

Winston drew in his breath. He opened his mouth to speak and then did not speak. He could not take his eyes away from the dial.

"The truth, please, Winston. *Your* truth. Tell me what you think you remember."

"I remember that until only a week before I was arrested, we were not at war with Eastasia at all. We were in alliance with them. The war was against Eurasia. That had lasted for four years. Before that—"

O'Brien stopped him with a movement of the hand.

"Another example," he said. "Some years ago you had a very serious delusion indeed. You believed that three men, three one-time Party members named Jones, Aaronson, and Rutherford—men who were executed for treachery and sabotage after making the fullest possible confession—were not guilty of the crimes they were charged with. You believed that you had seen unmistakable documentary evidence proving that their confessions were false. There was a certain photograph about which you had a hallucination. You believed that you had actually held it in your hands. It was a photograph something like this."

An oblong slip of newspaper had appeared between O'Brien's fingers. For perhaps five seconds it was within the angle of Winston's vision. It was a photograph, and there was no question of its identity. It was *the* photograph. It was another copy of the photograph of Jones, Aaronson, and Rutherford at the Party function in New York, which he had chanced upon eleven years ago and promptly destroyed. For only an instant it was before his eyes, then it was out of sight again. But he had seen it, unquestionably he had seen it! He made a desperate, agonizing effort to wrench the top half of his body free. It was impossible to move so much as a centimeter in any direction. For the moment he had even forgotten the dial. All he wanted was to hold the photograph in his fingers again, or at least to see it.

"It exists!" he cried.

"No," said O'Brien.

He stepped across the room. There was a memory hole in the opposite wall. O'Brien lifted the grating. Unseen, the frail slip of paper was whirling away on the current of warm air; it was vanishing in a flash of flame. O'Brien turned away from the wall.

"Ashes," he said. "Not even identifiable ashes. Dust. It does not exist. It never existed."

"But it did exist! It does exist! It exists in memory. I remember it. You remember it."

"I do not remember it," said O'Brien.

"Winston's heart sank. That was doublethink. He had a feeling of deadly helplessness. If he could have been certain that O'Brien was lying, it would not have seemed to matter. But it was perfectly possible that O'Brien had really forgotten the photograph. And if so, then already he would have forgotten his denial of remembering it, and forgotten the act of forgetting. How could one be sure that it was simply trickery? Perhaps that lunatic dislocation in the mind could really happen: that was the thought that defeated him.

O'Brien was looking down at him speculatively. More than ever he had the air of a teacher taking pains with a wayward but promising child.

"There is a Party slogan dealing with the control of the past," he said. "Repeat it, if you please."

" 'Who controls the past controls the future; who controls the present controls the past,' " repeated Winston obediently.

" 'Who controls the present controls the past,' " said O'Brien, nodding his head with slow approval. "Is it your opinion, Winston, that the past has real existence?"

Again the feeling of helplessness descended upon Winston. His eyes flitted toward the dial. He not only did not know whether "yes" or "no" was the answer that would save him from pain; he did not even know which answer he believed to be the true one.

O'Brien smiled faintly. "You are no metaphysician, Winston," he said. "Until this moment you had never considered what is meant by existence. I will put it more precisely. Does the past exist concretely, in space? Is there somewhere or other a place, a world of solid objects, where the past is still happening?"

"No."

"Then where does the past exist, if at all?"

"In records. It is written down."

"In records. And—?"

"In the mind. In human memories."

"In memory. Very well, then. We, the Party, control all records, and we control all memories. Then we control the past, do we not?"

"But how can you stop people remembering things?" cried Winston, again momentarily forgetting the dial. "It is involuntary. It is outside oneself. How can you control memory? You have not controlled mine!"

O'Brien's manner grew stern again. He laid his hand on the dial.

"On the contrary," he said, "*you* have not controlled it. That is what has brought you here. You are here because you have failed in humility, in self-discipline. You would not make the act of submission which is the price of sanity. You preferred to be a lunatic, a minority of one. Only the disciplined mind can see reality, Winston. You believe that reality is something objective, external, existing in its own right. You also believe that the nature of reality is self-evident. When you delude yourself into thinking that you see something, you assume that everyone else sees the same thing as you. But I tell you, Winston, that reality is not external. Reality exists in the human mind, and nowhere else. Not in the individual mind, which can make mistakes, and in any case soon perishes; only in the mind of the Party, which is collective and immortal. Whatever the Party holds to be truth *is* truth. It is impossible to see reality except by looking through the eyes of the Party. That is the fact that you have got to relearn, Winston. It needs an act of self-destruction, an effort of the will. You must humble yourself before you can become sane."

He paused for a few moments, as though to allow what he had been saying to sink in.

"Do you remember," he went on, "writing in your diary, 'Freedom is the freedom to say that two plus two make four'?"

"Yes," said Winston.

O'Brien held up his left hand, its back toward Winston, with the thumb hidden and the four fingers extended.

"How many fingers am I holding up, Winston?"

"Four."

"And if the Party says that it is not four but five—then how many?"

"Four."

The word ended in a gasp of pain. The needle of the dial had shot up to fifty-five. The sweat had sprung out all over Winston's body. The air tore into his lungs and issued again in deep groans which even by clenching his teeth he could not stop. O'Brien watched him, the four fingers still extended. He drew back the lever. This time the pain was only slightly eased.

"How many fingers, Winston?"

"Four."

The needle went up to sixty.

"How many fingers, Winston?"

"Four! Four! What else can I say? Four!"

The needle must have risen again, but he did not look at it. The heavy, stern face and the four fingers filled his vision. The fingers stood up before his eyes like pillars, enormous, blurry, and seeming to vibrate, but unmistakably four.

"How many fingers, Winston?"

"Four! Stop it, stop it! How can you go on? Four! Four!"

"How many fingers, Winston?"

"Five! Five! Five!"

"No, Winston, that is no use. You are lying. You still think there are four. How many fingers, please?"

"Four! Five! Four! Anything you like. Only stop it, stop the pain!"

Abruptly he was sitting up with O'Brien's arm round his shoulders. He had perhaps lost consciousness for a few seconds. The bonds that had held his body down were loosened. He felt very cold, he was shaking uncontrollably, his teeth were chattering, the tears were rolling down his cheeks. For a moment he clung to O'Brien like a baby, curiously comforted by the heavy arm round his shoulders. He had the feeling that O'Brien was his protector, that the pain was something that came from outside, from some other source, and that it was O'Brien who would save him from it.

"You are a slow learner, Winston," said O'Brien gently.

"How can I help it?" he blubbered. "How can I help seeing what is in front of my eyes? Two and two are four."

"Sometimes, Winston. Sometimes they are five. Sometimes they are three. Sometimes they are all of them at once. You must try harder. It is not easy to become sane."

He laid Winston down on the bed. The grip on his limbs tightened again, but the pain had ebbed away and the trembling had stopped, leaving him merely weak and cold. O'Brien motioned with his head to the man in the white coat, who had stood immobile throughout the proceedings. The man in the white coat bent down and looked closely into Winston's eyes, felt his pulse, laid an ear against his chest, tapped here and there; then he nodded to O'Brien.

"Again," said O'Brien.

The pain flowed into Winston's body. The needle must be at seventy, seventy-five. He had shut his eyes this time. He knew that the fingers were still there, and still four. All that mattered was somehow to stay alive until the spasm was over. He had ceased to notice whether he was crying out or not. The pain lessened again. He opened his eyes. O'Brien had drawn back the lever.

"How many fingers, Winston?"

"Four. I suppose there are four. I would see five if I could. I am trying to see five."

"Which do you wish: to persuade me that you see five, or really to see them?"

"Really to see them."

"Again," said O'Brien.

Perhaps the needle was at eighty—ninety. Winston could only intermittently remember why the pain was happening. Behind his screwed-up eyelids a forest of fingers seemed to be moving in a sort of dance, weaving in and out, disappearing behind one another and reappearing again. He was trying to count them, he could not remember why. He knew only that it was impossible to count them, and that this was somehow due to the mysterious identity between five and four. The pain died down again. When he opened his eyes it was to find that he was still seeing the same thing. Innumerable fingers, like moving trees, were still streaming past in either direction, crossing and recrossing. He shut his eyes again.

"How many fingers am I holding up, Winston?"

"I don't know. I don't know. You will kill me if you do that again. Four, five, six—in all honesty I don't know."

"Better," said O'Brien.

A needle slid into Winston's arm. Almost in the same instant a blissful, healing warmth spread all through his body. The pain was already half-forgotten. He opened his eyes and looked up gratefully at O'Brien. At sight of the heavy, lined face, so ugly and so intelligent, his heart seemed to turn over. If he could have moved he would have stretched out a hand and laid it on O'Brien's arm. He had never loved him so deeply as at this moment, and not merely because he had stopped the pain. The old feeling, that at bottom it did not matter whether O'Brien was a friend or an enemy, had come back. O'Brien was a person who could be talked to. Perhaps one did not want to be loved so much as to be understood. O'Brien had tortured him to the edge of lunacy, and in a little while, it was certain, he would send him to his death. It made no difference. In some sense that went deeper than friendship, they were intimates; somewhere or other, although the actual words might never be spoken, there was a place where they could meet and talk. O'Brien was looking down at him with an expression which suggested that the same thought might be in his own mind. When he spoke it was in an easy, conversational tone.

"Do you know where you are, Winston?" he said.

"I don't know. I can guess. In the Ministry of Love."

"Do you know how long you have been here?"

"I don't know. Days, weeks, months—I think it is months."

"And why do you imagine that we bring people to this place?"

"To make them confess."

"No, that is not the reason. Try again."

"To punish them."

"No!" exclaimed O'Brien. His voice had changed extraordinarily, and his face had suddenly become both stern and animated. "No! Not merely to extract your confession, nor to punish you. Shall I tell you why we have brought you here? To cure you! To make you sane! Will you understand, Winston, that no one whom we bring to this place ever leaves our hands uncured? We are not interested in those stupid crimes that you have committed. The Party is not interested in the overt act; the thought is all we care about. We do not merely destroy our enemies; we change them. Do you understand what I mean by that?"

He was bending over Winston. His face looked enormous because of its nearness, and hideously ugly because it was seen from below. Moreover it was filled with a sort of exaltation, a lunatic intensity. Again Winston's heart shrank. If it had been possible he would have cowered deeper into the bed. He felt certain that O'Brien was about to twist the dial out of sheer wantonness. At this moment, however, O'Brien turned away. He took a pace or two up and down. Then he continued less vehemently:

"The first thing for you to understand is that in this place there are no martyrdoms. You have read of the religious persecutions of the past. In the Middle Ages there was the Inquisition. It was a failure. It set out to eradicate heresy, and ended by perpetuating it. For every heretic it burned at the stake, thousands of others rose up. Why was that? Because the Inquisition killed its enemies in the open, and killed them while they were still unrepentant; in fact, it killed them because they were unrepentant. Men were dying because they would not abandon their true beliefs. Naturally all the glory belonged to the victim and all the shame to the Inquisitor who burned him. Later, in the twentieth century, there were the totalitarians, as they were called. There were the German Nazis and the Russian Communists. The Russians persecuted heresy more cruelly than the Inquisition had done. And they imagined that they had learned from the mistakes of the past; they knew, at any rate, that one must not make martyrs. Before they exposed their victims to public trial, they deliberately set themselves to destroy their dignity. They wore them down by torture and solitude until they were despicable, cringing wretches, confessing whatever was put into their mouths, covering themselves with abuse, accusing and sheltering behind one another, whimpering for mercy. And yet after only a few years the same thing had happened over again. The dead men had become martyrs and their degradation was forgotten. Once again, why was it? In the first place, because the confessions that they had made were obviously extorted and untrue. We do not make mistakes of that kind. All the confessions that are uttered here are true. We make them true. And, above all, we do not allow the dead to rise up against us. You must stop imagining that posterity will vindicate you, Winston. Posterity will never hear of you. You will be lifted clean out from the stream of history. We shall turn you into gas and pour you into the stratosphere. Nothing will remain of you: not a name in a register, not a memory in a living brain. You will be annihilated in the past as well as in the future. You will never have existed."

Then why bother to torture me? thought Winston, with a momentary bitterness. O'Brien checked his step as though Winston had uttered the thought aloud. His large ugly face came nearer, with the eyes a little narrowed.

"You are thinking," he said, "that since we intend to destroy you utterly, so that nothing that you say or do can make the smallest difference—in that case, why do we go to the trouble of interrogating you first? That is what you were thinking, was it not?"

"Yes," said Winston.

O'Brien smiled slightly. "You are a flaw in the pattern, Winston. You are a stain that must be wiped out. Did I not tell you just now that we are different from the persecutors of the past? We are not content with negative obedience, nor even with the most abject submission. When finally you surrender to us, it must be of your own free will. We do not destroy the heretic because he resists us; so long as he resists us we never destroy him. We convert him, we capture his inner mind, we reshape him. We burn all evil and all illusion out of him; we bring him over to our side, not in appearance, but genuinely, heart and soul. We make him one of ourselves before we kill him. It is intolerable to us that an erroneous thought should exist anywhere in the world, however secret and powerless it may be. Even in the instant of death we cannot permit any deviation. In the old days the heretic walked to the stake still a heretic, proclaiming his heresy, exulting in it. Even the victim of the Russian purges could carry rebellion locked up in his skull as he walked down the passage waiting for the bullet. But we make the brain perfect before we blow it out. The command of the old despotisms was 'Thou shalt not.' The command of the totalitarians was 'Thou shalt.' Our command is '*Thou art.*' No one whom we bring to this place ever stands out against us. Everyone is washed clean. Even those three miserable traitors in whose innocence you once believed—

Jones, Aaronson, and Rutherford—in the end we broke them down. I took part in their interrogation myself. I saw them gradually worn down, whimpering, groveling, weeping—and in the end it was not with pain or fear, only with penitence. By the time we had finished with them they were only the shells of men. There was nothing left in them except sorrow for what they had done, and love of Big Brother. It was touching to see how they loved him. They begged to be shot quickly, so that they could die while their minds were still clean."

His voice had grown almost dreamy. The exaltation, the lunatic enthusiasm, was still in his face. He is not pretending, thought Winston; he is not a hypocrite; he believes every word he says. What most oppressed him was the consciousness of his own intellectual inferiority. He watched the heavy yet graceful form strolling to and fro, in and out of the range of his vision. O'Brien was a being in all ways larger than himself. There was no idea that he had ever had, or could have, that O'Brien had not long ago known, examined, and rejected. His mind *contained* Winston's mind. But in that case how could it be true that O'Brien was mad? It must be he, Winston, who was mad. O'Brien halted and looked down at him. His voice had grown stern again.

"Do not imagine that you will save yourself, Winston, however completely you surrender to us. No one who has once gone astray is ever spared. And even if we chose to let you live out the natural term of your life, still you would never escape from us. What happens to you here is forever. Understand that in advance. We shall crush you down to the point from which there is no coming back. Things will happen to you from which you could not recover, if you lived a thousand years. Never again will you be capable of ordinary human feeling. Everything will be dead inside you. Never again will you be capable of love, or friendship, or joy of living, or laughter, or curiosity, or courage, or integrity. You will be hollow. We shall squeeze you empty, and then we shall fill you with ourselves."

He paused and signed to the man in the white coat. Winston was aware of some heavy piece of apparatus being pushed into place behind his head. O'Brien had sat down beside the bed, so that his face was almost on a level with Winston's.

"Three thousand," he said, speaking over Winston's head to the man in the white coat.

Two soft pads, which felt slightly moist, clamped themselves against

Winston's temples. He quailed. There was pain coming, a new kind of pain. O'Brien laid a hand reassuringly, almost kindly, on his.

"This time it will not hurt," he said. "Keep your eyes fixed on mine."

At this moment there was a devastating explosion, or what seemed like an explosion, though it was not certain whether there was any noise. There was undoubtedly a blinding flash of light. Winston was not hurt, only prostrated. Although he had already been lying on his back when the thing happened, he had a curious feeling that he had been knocked into that position. A terrific, painless blow had flattened him out. Also something had happened inside his head. As his eyes regained their focus he remembered who he was, and where he was, and recognized the face that was gazing into his own; but somewhere or other there was a large patch of emptiness, as though a piece had been taken out of his brain.

"It will not last," said O'Brien. "Look me in the eyes. What country is Oceania at war with?"

Winston thought. He knew what was meant by Oceania, and that he himself was a citizen of Oceania. He also remembered Eurasia and Eastasia; but who was at war with whom he did not know. In fact he had not been aware that there was any war.

"I don't remember."

"Oceania is at war with Eastasia. Do you remember that now?"

"Yes."

"Oceania has always been at war with Eastasia. Since the beginning of your life, since the beginning of the Party, since the beginning of history, the war has continued without a break, always the same war. Do you remember that?"

"Yes."

"Eleven years ago you created a legend about three men who had been condemned to death for treachery. You pretended that you had seen a piece of paper which proved them innocent. No such piece of paper ever existed. You invented it, and later you grew to believe in it. You remember now the very moment at which you first invented it. Do you remember that?"

"Yes."

"Just now I held up the fingers of my hand to you. You saw five fingers. Do you remember that?"

"Yes."

O'Brien held up the fingers of his left hand, with the thumb concealed.

"There are five fingers there. Do you see five fingers?"

"Yes."

And he did see them, for a fleeting instant, before the scenery of his mind changed. He saw five fingers, and there was no deformity. Then everything was normal again, and the old fear, the hatred, and the bewilderment came crowding back again. But there had been a moment—he did not know how long, thirty seconds, perhaps—of luminous certainty, when each new suggestion of O'Brien's had filled up a patch of emptiness and become absolute truth, and when two and two could have been three as easily as five, if that were what was needed. It had faded out before O'Brien had dropped his hand; but though he could not recapture it, he could remember it, as one remembers a vivid experience at some remote period of one's life when one was in effect a different person.

"You see now," said O'Brien, "that it is at any rate possible."

"Yes," said Winston.

O'Brien stood up with a satisfied air. Over to his left Winston saw the man in the white coat break an ampoule and draw back the plunger of a syringe. O'Brien turned to Winston with a smile. In almost the old manner he resettled his spectacles on his nose.

"Do you remember writing in your diary," he said, "that it did not matter whether I was a friend or an enemy, since I was at least a person who understood you and could be talked to? You were right. I enjoy talking to you. Your mind appeals to me. It resembles my own mind except that you happen to be insane. Before we bring the session to an end you can ask me a few questions, if you choose."

"Any question I like?"

"Anything." He saw that Winston's eyes were upon the dial. "It is switched off. What is your first question?"

"What have you done with Julia?" said Winston.

O'Brien smiled again. "She betrayed you, Winston. Immediately—unreservedly. I have seldom seen anyone come over to us so promptly. You would hardly recognize her if you saw her. All her rebelliousness, her deceit, her folly, her dirty-mindedness—everything has been burned out of her. It was a perfect conversion, a textbook case."

"You tortured her."

O'Brien left this unanswered. "Next question," he said.

"Does Big Brother exist?"

"Of course he exists. The Party exists. Big Brother is the embodiment of the Party."

"Does he exist in the same way as I exist?"

"You do not exist," said O'Brien.

Once again the sense of helplessness assailed him. He knew, or he could imagine, the arguments which proved his own nonexistence; but they were nonsense, they were only a play on words. Did not the statement, "You do not exist," contain a logical absurdity? But what use was it to say so? His mind shriveled as he thought of the unanswerable, mad arguments with which O'Brien would demolish him.

"I think I exist," he said wearily. "I am conscious of my own identity. I was born, and I shall die. I have arms and legs. I occupy a particular point in space. No other solid object can occupy the same point simultaneously. In that sense, does Big Brother exist?"

"It is of no importance. He exists."

"Will Big Brother ever die?"

"Of course not. How could he die? Next question."

"Does the Brotherhood exist?"

"That, Winston, you will never know. If we choose to set you free when we have finished with you, and if you live to be ninety years old, still you will never learn whether the answer to that question is Yes or No. As long as you live, it will be an unsolved riddle in your mind."

Winston lay silent. His breast rose and fell a little faster. He still had not asked the question that had come into his mind the first. He had got to ask it, and yet it was as though his tongue would not utter it. There was a trace of amusement in O'Brien's face. Even his spectacles seemed to wear an ironical gleam. He knows, thought Winston suddenly, he knows what I am going to ask! At the thought the words burst out of him:

"What is in Room 101?"

The expression on O'Brien's face did not change. He answered drily:

"You know what is in Room 101, Winston. Everyone knows what is in Room 101."

He raised a finger to the man in the white coat. Evidently the session was at an end. A needle jerked into Winston's arm. He sank almost instantly into deep sleep.

II

"There are three stages in your reintegration," said O'Brien. "There is learning, there is understanding, and there is acceptance. It is time for you to enter upon the second stage."

As always, Winston was lying flat on his back. But of late his bonds were looser. They still held him to the bed, but he could move his knees a little and could turn his head from side to side and raise his arms from the elbow. The dial, also, had grown to be less of a terror. He could evade its pangs if he was quick-witted enough; it was chiefly when he showed stupidity that O'Brien pulled the lever. Sometimes they got through a whole session without use of the dial. He could not remember how many sessions there had been. The whole process seemed to stretch out over a long, indefinite time—weeks, possibly—and the intervals between the sessions might sometimes have been days, sometimes only an hour or two.

"As you lie there," said O'Brien, "you have often wondered—you have even asked me—why the Ministry of Love should expend so much time and trouble on you. And when you were free you were puzzled by what was essentially the same question. You could grasp the mechanics of the society you lived in, but not its underlying motives. Do you remember writing in your diary, 'I understand *how;* I do not understand *why*'*?* It was when you thought about 'why' that you doubted your own sanity. You have read *the book,* Goldstein's book, or parts of it, at least. Did it tell you anything that you did not know already?"

"You have read it?" said Winston.

"I wrote it. That is to say, I collaborated in writing it. No book is produced individually, as you know."

"Is it true, what it says?"

"As description, yes. The program it sets forth is nonsense. The secret accumulation of knowledge—a gradual spread of enlightenment—ultimately a proletarian rebellion—the overthrow of the Party. You foresaw yourself that that was what it would say. It is all nonsense. The proletarians will never revolt, not in a thousand years or a million. They cannot. I do not have to tell you the reason; you know it already. If you have ever cherished any dreams of violent insurrection, you must abandon them. There is no way in which the Party can be overthrown. The rule of the Party is forever. Make that the starting point of your thoughts."

He came closer to the bed. "Forever!" he repeated. "And now let us get back to the question of 'how' and 'why.' You understand well enough *how* the Party maintains itself in power. Now tell me *why* we cling to power. What is our motive? Why should we want power? Go on, speak," he added as Winston remained silent.

Nevertheless Winston did not speak for another moment or two. A feeling of weariness had overwhelmed him. The faint, mad gleam of enthusiasm had come back into O'Brien's face. He knew in advance what O'Brien would say: that the Party did not seek power for its own ends, but only for the good of the majority. That it sought power because men in the mass were frail, cowardly creatures who could not endure liberty or face the truth, and must be ruled over and systematically deceived by others who were stronger than themselves. That the choice for mankind lay between freedom and happiness, and that, for the great bulk of mankind, happiness was better. That the Party was the eternal guardian of the weak, a dedicated sect doing evil that good might come, sacrificing its own happiness to that of others. The terrible thing, thought Winston, the terrible thing was that when O'Brien said this he would believe it. You could see it in his face. O'Brien knew everything. A thousand times better than Winston, he knew what the world was really like, in what degradation the mass of human beings lived and by what lies and barbarities the Party kept them there. He had understood it all, weighed it all, and it made no difference: all was justified by the ultimate purpose. What can you do, thought Winston, against the lunatic who is more intelligent than yourself, who gives your arguments a fair hearing and then simply persists in his lunacy?

"You are ruling over us for our own good," he said feebly. "You believe that human beings are not fit to govern themselves, and therefore—"

He started and almost cried out. A pang of pain had shot through his body. O'Brien had pushed the lever of the dial up to thirty-five.

"That was stupid, Winston, stupid!" he said. "You should know better than to say a thing like that."

He pulled the lever back and continued:

"Now I will tell you the answer to my question. It is this. The Party seeks power entirely for its own sake. We are not interested in the good of others; we are interested solely in power. Not wealth or luxury or long life or happiness; only power, pure power. What pure power means you will understand presently. We are different from all the oligarchies of the past in that we know what we are doing. All the others, even those who resembled ourselves, were cowards and hypocrites. The German Nazis and the Russian Communists came very close to us in their methods, but they never had the courage to recognize their own motives. They pretended, perhaps they even believed, that they had seized power unwillingly and for a limited time, and that just round the corner there lay a paradise where human beings would be free and equal. We are not like that. We know that no one ever seizes power with the intention of relinquishing it. Power is not a means; it is an end. One does not establish a dictatorship in order to safeguard a revolution; one makes the revolution in order to establish the dictatorship. The object of persecution is persecution. The object of torture is torture. The object of power is power. Now do you begin to understand me?"

Winston was struck, as he had been struck before, by the tiredness of O'Brien's face. It was strong and fleshy and brutal, it was full of intelligence and a sort of controlled passion before which he felt himself helpless; but it was tired. There were pouches under the eyes, the skin sagged from the cheekbones. O'Brien leaned over him, deliberately bringing the worn face nearer.

"You are thinking," he said, "that my face is old and tired. You are thinking that I talk of power, and yet I am not even able to prevent the decay of my own body. Can you not understand, Winston, that the individual is only a cell? The weariness of the cell is the vigor of the organism. Do you die when you cut your fingernails?"

He turned away from the bed and began strolling up and down again, one hand in his pocket.

"We are the priests of power," he said. "God is power. But at present power is only a word so far as you are concerned. It is time for you to gather some idea of what power means. The first thing you must realize is that power is collective. The individual only has power in so far as he ceases to be an individual. You know the Party slogan: 'Freedom is Slavery.' Has it ever occurred to you that it is reversible? Slavery is freedom. Alone—free—the human being is always defeated. It must be so, because every human being is doomed to die, which is the greatest of all failures. But if he can make complete, utter submission, if he can escape from his identity, if he can merge himself in the Party so that he *is* the Party, then he is all-powerful and immortal. The second thing for you to realize is that power is power over human beings. Over the body—but, above all, over the mind. Power over matter—external reality, as you would call it—is not important. Already our control over matter is absolute."

For a moment Winston ignored the dial. He made a violent effort to raise himself into a sitting position, and merely succeeded in wrenching his body painfully.

"But how can you control matter?" he burst out. "You don't even control the climate or the law of gravity. And there are disease, pain, death—"

O'Brien silenced him by a movement of the hand. "We control matter because we control the mind. Reality is inside the skull. You will learn by degrees, Winston. There is nothing that we could not do. Invisibility, levitation—anything. I could float off this floor like a soap bubble if I wished to. I do not wish to, because the Party does not wish it. You must get rid of those nineteenth-century ideas about the laws of nature. We make the laws of nature."

"But you do not! You are not even masters of this planet. What about Eurasia and Eastasia? You have not conquered them yet."

"Unimportant. We shall conquer them when it suits us. And if we did not, what difference would it make? We can shut them out of existence. Oceania is the world."

"But the world itself is only a speck of dust. And man is tiny—helpless! How long has he been in existence? For millions of years the earth was uninhabited."

"Nonsense. The earth is as old as we are, no older. How could it be older? Nothing exists except through human consciousness."

"But the rocks are full of the bones of extinct animals—mammoths and mastodons and enormous reptiles which lived here long before man was ever heard of."

"Have you ever seen those bones, Winston? Of course not. Nineteenth-century biologists invented them. Before man there was nothing.

After man, if he could come to an end, there would be nothing. Outside man there is nothing."

"But the whole universe is outside us. Look at the stars! Some of them are a million light-years away. They are out of our reach forever."

"What are the stars?" said O'Brien indifferently. "They are bits of fire a few kilometers away. We could reach them if we wanted to. Or we could blot them out. The earth is the center of the universe. The sun and the stars go round it."

Winston made another convulsive movement. This time he did not say anything. O'Brien continued as though answering a spoken objection:

"For certain purposes, of course, that is not true. When we navigate the ocean, or when we predict an eclipse, we often find it convenient to assume that the earth goes round the sun and that the stars are millions upon millions of kilometers away. But what of it? Do you suppose it is beyond us to produce a dual system of astronomy? The stars can be near or distant, according as we need them. Do you suppose our mathematicians are unequal to that? Have you forgotten doublethink?"

Winston shrank back upon the bed. Whatever he said, the swift answer crushed him like a bludgeon. And yet he knew, he *knew*, that he was in the right. The belief that nothing exists outside your own mind—surely there must be some way of demonstrating that it was false. Had it not been exposed long ago as a fallacy? There was even a name for it, which he had forgotten. A faint smile twitched the corners of O'Brien's mouth as he looked down at him.

"I told you, Winston," he said, "that metaphysics is not your strong point. The word you are trying to think of is solipsism. But you are mistaken. This is not solipsism. Collective solipsism, if you like. But that is a different thing; in fact, the opposite thing. All this is a digression," he added in a different tone. "The real power, the power we have to fight for night and day, is not power over things, but over men." He paused, and for a moment assumed again his air of a schoolmaster questioning a promising pupil: "How does one man assert his power over another, Winston?"

Winston thought. "By making him suffer," he said.

"Exactly. By making him suffer. Obedience is not enough. Unless he is suffering, how can you be sure that he is obeying your will and not his own? Power is in inflicting pain and humiliation. Power is in tearing human minds to pieces and putting them together again in new shapes of your own choosing. Do you begin to see, then, what kind of world we are creating? It is the exact opposite of the stupid hedonistic Utopias that the old reformers imagined. A world of fear and treachery and torment, a world of trampling and being trampled upon, a world which will grow not less but *more* merciless as it refines itself. Progress in our world will be progress toward more pain. The old civilizations claimed that they were founded on love or justice. Ours is founded upon hatred. In our world there will be no emotions except fear, rage, triumph, and self-abasement. Everything else we shall destroy—everything. Already we are breaking down the habits of thought which have survived from before the Revolution. We have cut the links between child and parent, and between man and man, and between man and woman. No one dares trust a wife or a child or a friend any longer. But in the future there will be no wives and no friends. Children will be taken from their mothers at birth, as one takes eggs from a hen. The sex instinct will be eradicated. Procreation will be an annual formality like the renewal of a ration card. We shall abolish the orgasm. Our neurologists are at work upon it now. There will be no loyalty, except loyalty toward the Party. There will be no love, except the love of Big Brother. There will be no laughter, except the laugh of triumph over a defeated enemy. There will be no art, no literature, no science. When we are omnipotent we shall have no more need of science. There will be no distinction between beauty and ugliness. There will be no curiosity, no enjoyment of the process of life. All competing pleasures will be destroyed. But always—do not forget this, Winston—always there will be the intoxication of power, constantly increasing and constantly growing subtler. Always, at every moment, there will be the thrill of victory, the sensation of trampling on an enemy who is helpless. If you want a picture of the future, imagine a boot stamping on a human face—forever."

He paused as though he expected Winston to speak. Winston had tried to shrink back into the surface of the bed again. He could not say anything. His heart seemed to be frozen. O'Brien went on:

"And remember that it is forever. The face will always be there to be stamped upon. The heretic, the enemy of society, will always be there, so that he can be defeated and humiliated over again. Everything that you have undergone since you have been in our hands—all that will continue, and worse. The espionage, the betrayals, the arrests, the tortures, the executions, the disappearances will never cease. It will be a world of terror as much as a world of triumph. The more the

Party is powerful, the less it will be tolerant; the weaker the opposition, the tighter the despotism. Goldstein and his heresies will live forever. Every day, at every moment, they will be defeated, discredited, ridiculed, spat upon—and yet they will always survive. This drama that I have played out with you during seven years will be played out over and over again, generation after generation, always in subtler forms. Always we shall have the heretic here at our mercy, screaming with pain, broken up, contemptible—and in the end utterly penitent, saved from himself, crawling to our feet of his own accord. That is the world that we are preparing, Winston. A world of victory after victory, triumph after triumph after triumph: an endless pressing, pressing, pressing upon the nerve of power. You are beginning, I can see, to realize what that world will be like. But in the end you will do more than understand it. You will accept it, welcome it, become part of it."

Winston had recovered himself sufficiently to speak. "You can't!" he said weakly.

"What do you mean by that remark, Winston?"

"You could not create such a world as you have just described. It is a dream. It is impossible."

"Why?"

"It is impossible to found a civilization on fear and hatred and cruelty. It would never endure."

"Why not?"

"It would have no vitality. It would disintegrate. It would commit suicide."

"Nonsense. You are under the impression that hatred is more exhausting than love. Why should it be? And if it were, what difference would that make? Suppose that we choose to wear ourselves out faster. Suppose that we quicken the tempo of human life till men are senile at thirty. Still what difference would it make? Can you not understand that the death of the individual is not death? The Party is immortal."

As usual, the voice had battered Winston into helplessness. Moreover he was in dread that if he persisted in his disagreement O'Brien would twist the dial again. And yet he could not keep silent. Feebly, without arguments, with nothing to support him except his inarticulate horror of what O'Brien had said, he returned to the attack.

"I don't know—I don't care. Somehow you will fail. Something will defeat you. Life will defeat you."

"We control life, Winston, at all its levels. You are imagining that there is something called human nature which will be outraged by what we do and will turn against us. But we create human nature. Men are infinitely malleable. Or perhaps you have returned to your old idea that the proletarians or the slaves will arise and overthrow us. Put it out of your mind. They are helpless, like the animals. Humanity is the Party. The others are outside—irrelevant."

"I don't care. In the end they will beat you. Sooner or later they will see you for what you are, and then they will tear you to pieces."

"Do you see any evidence that that is happening? Or any reason why it should?"

"No. I believe it. I *know* that you will fail. There is something in the universe—I don't know, some spirit, some principle—that you will never overcome."

"Do you believe in God, Winston?"

"No."

"Then what is it, this principle that will defeat us?"

"I don't know. The spirit of Man."

"And do you consider yourself a man?"

"Yes."

"If you are a man, Winston, you are the last man. Your kind is extinct; we are the inheritors. Do you understand that you are *alone?* You are outside history, you are nonexistent." His manner changed and he said more harshly: "And you consider yourself morally superior to us, with our lies and our cruelty?"

"Yes, I consider myself superior."

O'Brien did not speak. Two other voices were speaking. After a moment Winston recognized one of them as his own. It was a sound track of the conversation he had had with O'Brien, on the night when he had enrolled himself in the Brotherhood. He heard himself promising to lie, to steal, to forge, to murder, to encourage drug taking and prostitution, to disseminate venereal diseases, to throw vitriol in a child's face. O'Brien made a small impatient gesture, as though to say that the demonstration was hardly worth making. Then he turned a switch and the voices stopped.

"Get up from that bed," he said.

The bonds had loosened themselves. Winston lowered himself to the floor and stood up unsteadily.

"You are the last man," said O'Brien. "You are the guardian of the human spirit. You shall see yourself as you are. Take off your clothes."

Winston undid the bit of string that held his overalls together. The zip fastener had long since been wrenched out of them. He could not remember whether at any time since his arrest he had taken off all his clothes at one time. Beneath the overalls his body was looped with filthy yellowish rags, just recognizable as the remnants of underclothes. As he slid them to the ground he saw that there was a three-sided mirror at the far end of the room. He approached it, then stopped short. An involuntary cry had broken out of him.

"Go on," said O'Brien. "Stand between the wings of the mirror. You shall see the side view as well."

He had stopped because he was frightened. A bowed, gray-colored, skeletonlike thing was coming toward him. Its actual appearance was frightening, and not merely the fact that he knew it to be himself. He moved closer to the glass. The creature's face seemed to be protruded, because of its bent carriage. A forlorn, jailbird's face with a nobby forehead running back into a bald scalp, a crooked nose and battered-looking cheekbones above which the eyes were fierce and watchful. The cheeks were seamed, the mouth had a drawn-in look. Certainly it was his own face, but it seemed to him that it had changed more than he had changed inside. The emotions it registered would be different from the ones he felt. He had gone partially bald. For the first moment he had thought that he had gone gray as well, but it was only the scalp that was gray. Except for his hands and a circle of his face, his body was gray all over with ancient, ingrained dirt. Here and there under the dirt there were the red scars of wounds, and near the ankle the varicose ulcer was an inflamed mass with flakes of skin peeling off it. But the truly frightening thing was the emaciation of his body. The barrel of the ribs was as narrow as that of a skeleton; the legs had shrunk so that the knees were thicker than the thighs. He saw now what O'Brien had meant about seeing the side view. The curvature of the spine was astonishing. The thin shoulders were hunched forward so as to make a cavity of the chest, the scraggy neck seemed to be bending double under the weight of the skull. At a guess he would have said that it was the body of a man of sixty, suffering from some malignant disease.

"You have thought sometimes," said O'Brien, "that my face—the face of a member of the Inner Party—looks old and worn. What do you think of your own face?"

He seized Winston's shoulder and spun him round so that he was facing him.

"Look at the condition you are in!" he said. "Look at this filthy grime all over your body. Look at the dirt between your toes. Look at that disgusting running sore on your leg. Do you know that you stink like a goat? Probably you have ceased to notice it. Look at your emaciation. Do you see? I can make my thumb and forefinger meet around your bicep. I could snap your neck like a carrot. Do you know that you have lost twenty-five kilograms since you have been in our hands? Even your hair is coming out in handfuls. Look!" He plucked at Winston's head and brought away a tuft of hair. "Open your mouth. Nine, ten, eleven teeth left. How many had you when you came to us? And the few you have left are dropping out your head. Look here!"

He seized one of Winston's remaining front teeth between his powerful thumb and forefinger. A twinge of pain shot through Winston's jaw. O'Brien had wrenched the loose tooth out by the roots. He tossed it across the cell.

"You are rotting away," he said; "you are falling to pieces. What are you? A bag of filth. Now turn round and look into that mirror again. Do you see that thing facing you? That is the last man. If you are human, that is humanity. Now put your clothes on again."

Winston began to dress himself with slow stiff movements. Until now he had not seemed to notice how thin and weak he was. Only one thought stirred in his mind: that he must have been in this place longer than he had imagined. Then suddenly as he fixed the miserable rags round himself a feeling of pity for his ruined body overcame him. Before he knew what he was doing he had collapsed onto a small stool that stood beside the bed and burst into tears. He was aware of his ugliness, his gracelessness, a bundle of bones in filthy underclothes sitting weeping in the harsh white light; but he could not stop himself. O'Brien laid a hand on his shoulder, almost kindly.

"It will not last forever," he said. "You can escape from it whenever you choose. Everything depends on yourself."

"You did it!" sobbed Winston. "You reduced me to this state."

"No, Winston, you reduced yourself to it. This is what you accepted when you set yourself up against the Party. It was all contained in that first act. Nothing has happened that you did not foresee."

He paused, and then went on:

"We have beaten you, Winston. We have broken you up. You

have seen what your body is like. Your mind is in the same state. I do not think there can be much pride left in you. You have been kicked and flogged and insulted, you have screamed with pain, you have rolled on the floor in your own blood and vomit. You have whimpered for mercy, you have betrayed everybody and everything. Can you think of a single degradation that has not happened to you?"

Winston had stopped weeping, though the tears were still oozing out of his eyes. He looked up at O'Brien.

"I have not betrayed Julia," he said.

O'Brien looked down at him thoughtfully. "No," he said, "no; that is perfectly true. You have not betrayed Julia."

The peculiar reverence for O'Brien, which nothing seemed able to destroy, flooded Winston's heart again. How intelligent, he thought, how intelligent! Never did O'Brien fail to understand what was said to him. Anyone else on earth would have answered promptly that he *had* betrayed Julia. For what was there that they had not screwed out of him under the torture? He had told them everything he knew about her, her habits, her character, her past life; he had confessed in the most trivial detail everything that had happened at their meetings, all that he had said to her and she to him, their black-market meals, their adulteries, their vague plottings against the Party—everything. And yet, in the sense in which he intended the word, he had not betrayed her. He had not stopped loving her; his feeling toward her had remained the same. O'Brien had seen what he meant without the need for explanation.

"Tell me," he said, "how soon will they shoot me?"

"It might be a long time," said O'Brien. "You are a difficult case. But don't give up hope. Everyone is cured sooner or later. In the end we shall shoot you."

III

He was much better. He was growing fatter and stronger every day, if it was proper to speak of days.

The white light and the humming sound were the same as ever, but the cell was a little more comfortable than the others he had been in. There were a pillow and a mattress on the plank bed, and a stool to sit on. They had given him a bath, and they allowed him to wash himself fairly frequently in a tin basin. They even gave him warm water to wash with. They had given him new underclothes and a clean suit of overalls. They had dressed his varicose ulcer with soothing ointment. They had pulled out the remnants of his teeth and given him a new set of dentures.

Weeks or months must have passed. It would have been possible now to keep count of the passage of time, if he had felt any interest in doing so, since he was being fed at what appeared to be regular intervals. He was getting, he judged, three meals in the twenty-four hours; sometimes he wondered dimly whether he was getting them by night or by day. The food was surprisingly good, with meat at every third meal. Once there was even a packet of cigarettes. He had no matches, but the never-speaking guard who brought his food would give him a light. The first time he tried to smoke it made him sick, but he persevered, and spun the packet out for a long time, smoking half a cigarette after each meal.

They had given him a white slate with a stump of pencil tied to the corner. At first he made no use of it. Even when he was awake he was completely torpid. Often he would lie from one meal to the next almost without stirring, sometimes asleep, sometimes waking into vague reveries in which it was too much trouble to open his eyes. He had long grown used to sleeping with a strong light on his face. It seemed to make no difference, except that one's dreams were more coherent. He dreamed a great deal all through this time, and they were always happy dreams. He was in the Golden Country, or he was sitting among enormous, glorious, sunlit ruins, with his mother, with Julia, with O'Brien—not doing anything, merely sitting in the sun, talking of peaceful things. Such thoughts as he had when he was awake were mostly about his dreams. He seemed to have lost the power of intellectual effort, now that the stimulus of pain had been removed. He was not bored; he had no desire for conversation or distraction. Merely to be alone, not to be beaten or questioned, to have enough to eat, and to be clean all over, was completely satisfying.

By degrees he came to spend less time in sleep, but he still felt no impulse to get off the bed. All he cared for was to lie quiet and feel the strength gathering in his body. He would finger himself here and there, trying to make sure that it was not an illusion that his muscles were growing rounder and his skin tauter. Finally it was established beyond a doubt that he was growing fatter; his thighs were now definitely thicker than his knees. After that, reluctantly at first, he began exercising himself regularly. In a little while he could walk three kilometers, measured by pacing the cell, and his bowed shoulders were growing straighter. He attempted more elaborate exercises, and was astonished and humiliated to find what things he could not do. He could not move out of a walk, he could not hold his stool out at arm's length, he could not stand on one leg without falling over. He squatted down on his heels, and found that with agonizing pains in thigh and calf he could just lift himself to a standing position. He lay flat on his belly and tried to lift his weight by his hands. It was hopeless; he could not raise himself a centimeter. But after a few more days—a few more mealtimes—even that feat was accomplished. A time came when he could do it six times running. He began to grow actually proud of his body, and to cherish an intermittent belief that his face also was growing back to normal. Only when he chanced to put his hand on his bald scalp did he remember the seamed, ruined face that had looked back at him out of the mirror.

His mind grew more active. He sat down on the plank bed, his back against the wall and the slate on his knees, and set to work deliberately at the task of re-educating himself.

He had capitulated; that was agreed. In reality, as he saw now, he had been ready to capitulate long before he had taken the decision. From the moment when he was inside the Ministry of Love—and yes, even during those minutes when he and Julia had stood helpless while the iron voice from the telescreen told them what to do—he had grasped the frivolity, the shallowness of his attempt to set himself up against the power of the Party. He knew now that for seven years the Thought Police had watched him like a beetle under a magnifying glass. There was no physical act, no word spoken aloud, that they had not noticed, no train of thought that they had not been able to infer. Even the speck of whitish dust on the cover of his diary they had carefully replaced. They had played sound tracks to him, shown him photographs. Some of them were photographs of Julia and himself. Yes, even . . . He could not fight against the Party any longer. Besides, the Party was in the right. It must be so: how could the immortal, collective brain be mistaken? By what external standard could you check its judgments? Sanity was statistical. It was merely a question of learning to think as they thought. Only—!

The pencil felt thick and awkward in his fingers. He began to write down the thoughts that came into his head. He wrote first in large clumsy capitals:

FREEDOM IS SLAVERY.

Then almost without a pause he wrote beneath it:

TWO AND TWO MAKE FIVE.

But then there came a sort of check. His mind, as though shying away from something, seemed unable to concentrate. He knew that he knew what came next, but for the moment he could not recall it. When he did recall it, it was only by consciously reasoning out what it must be; it did not come of its own accord. He wrote:

GOD IS POWER.

He accepted everything. The past was alterable. The past never had been altered. Oceania was at war with Eastasia. Oceania had always been at war with Eastasia. Jones, Aaronson, and Rutherford were guilty of the crimes they were charged with. He had never seen the photograph that disproved their guilt. It had never existed; he had invented it. He remembered remembering contrary things, but those were false memories, products of self-deception. How easy it all was! Only surrender, and everything else followed. It was like swimming against a current that swept you backwards however hard you struggled, and then suddenly deciding to turn round and go with the current instead of opposing it. Nothing had changed except your own attitude; the predestined thing happened in any case. He hardly knew why he had ever rebelled. Everything was easy, except—!

Anything could be true. The so-called laws of nature were nonsense. The law of gravity was nonsense. "If I wished," O'Brien had said, "I could float off this floor like a soap bubble." Winston worked it out. "If he *thinks* he floats off the floor, and if I simultaneously *think* I see him do it, then the thing happens." Suddenly, like a lump of submerged wreckage breaking the surface of water, the thought burst into his mind: "It doesn't really happen. We imagine it. It is hallucination." He pushed the thought under instantly. The fallacy was obvious. It presupposed that somewhere or other, outside oneself, there was a "real" world where "real" things happened. But how could there be such a world? What knowledge have we of anything, save through our own minds? All happenings are in the mind. Whatever happens in all minds, truly happens.

He had no difficulty in disposing of the fallacy, and he was in no danger of succumbing to it. He realized, nevertheless, that it ought never to have occurred to him. The mind should develop a blind spot whenever a dangerous thought presented itself. The process should be automatic, instinctive. *Crimestop,* they called it in Newspeak.

He set to work to exercise himself in crimestop. He presented himself with propositions—"the Party says the earth is flat," "the Party says that ice is heavier than water"—and trained himself in not seeing or not understanding the arguments that contradicted them. It was not easy. It needed great powers of reasoning and improvisation. The arithmetical problems raised, for instance, by such a statement as "two and two make five" were beyond his intellectual grasp. It needed also a sort of athleticism of mind, an ability at one moment to make the most delicate use of logic and at the next to be unconscious of the crudest logical errors. Stupidity was as necessary as intelligence, and as difficult to attain.

All the while, with one part of his mind, he wondered how soon they would shoot him. "Everything depends on yourself," O'Brien had said; but he knew that there was no conscious act by which he could bring it nearer. It might be ten minutes hence, or ten years. They might keep him for years in solitary confinement; they might send him to a labor camp; they might release him for a while, as they sometimes did. It was perfectly possible that before he was shot the whole drama of his arrest and interrogation would be enacted all over again. The one certain thing was that death never came at an expected moment. The tradition—the unspoken tradition: somehow you knew it, though you never heard it said—was that they shot you from behind, always in the back of the head, without warning, as you walked down a corridor from cell to cell.

One day—but "one day" was not the right expression; just as probably it was in the middle of the night: once—he fell into a strange, blissful reverie. He was walking down the corridor, waiting for the bullet. He knew that it was coming in another moment. Everything was settled, smoothed out, reconciled. There were no more doubts, no more arguments, no more pain, no more fear. His body was healthy and strong. He walked easily, with a joy of movement and with a feeling of walking in sunlight. He was not any longer in the narrow white corridors of the Ministry of Love; he was in the enormous sunlit passage, a kilometer wide, down which he had seemed to walk in the delirium induced by drugs. He was in the Golden Country, following the foot track across the old rabbit-cropped pasture. He could feel the short springy turf under his feet and the gentle sunshine on his face. At the edge of the field were the elm trees, faintly stirring, and somewhere beyond that was the stream where the dace lay in the green pools under the willows.

Suddenly he started up with a shock of horror. The sweat broke out on his backbone. He had heard himself cry aloud:

"Julia! Julia! Julia, my love! Julia!"

For a moment he had had an overwhelming hallucination of her presence. She had seemed to be not merely with him, but inside him. It was as though she had got into the texture of his skin. In that moment he had loved her far more than he had ever done when they were together and free. Also he knew that somewhere or other she was still alive and needed his help.

He lay back on the bed and tried to compose himself. What had he done? How many years had he added to his servitude by that moment of weakness?

In another moment he would hear the tramp of boots outside. They could not let such an outburst go unpunished. They would know now, if they had not known before, that he was breaking the agreement he had made with them. He obeyed the Party, but he still hated the Party. In the old days he had hidden a heretical mind beneath an appearance of conformity. Now he had retreated a step further: in the mind he had surrendered, but he had hoped to keep the inner heart inviolate. He knew that he was in the wrong, but he preferred to be in the wrong. They would understand that—O'Brien would understand it. It was all confessed in that single foolish cry.

He would have to start all over again. It might take years. He ran a hand over his face, trying to familiarize himself with the new shape. There were deep furrows in the cheeks, the cheekbones felt sharp, the nose flattened. Besides, since last seeing himself in the glass he had been given a complete new set of teeth. It was not easy to preserve inscrutability when you did not know what your face looked like. In any case, mere control of the features was not enough. For the first time he perceived that if you want to keep a secret you must also hide it from yourself. You must know all the while that it is there, but until it is needed you must never let it emerge into your consciousness in any shape that could be given a name. From now onwards he must not only think right; he must feel right, dream right. And all the while he must keep his hatred locked up inside him like a ball of matter which was part of himself and yet unconnected with the rest of him, a kind of cyst.

One day they would decide to shoot him. You could not tell when it would happen, but a few seconds beforehand it should be possible to guess. It was always from behind, walking down a corridor. Ten seconds would be enough. In that time the world inside him could turn over. And then suddenly, without a word uttered, without a check in his step, without the changing of a line in his face—suddenly the camouflage would be down and bang! would go the batteries of his hatred. Hatred would fill him like an enormous roaring flame. And almost in the same instant bang! would go the bullet, too late, or too early. They would have blown his brain to pieces before they could reclaim it. The heretical thought would be unpunished, unrepented, out of their reach forever. They would have blown a hole in their own perfection. To die hating them, that was freedom.

He shut his eyes. It was more difficult than accepting an intellectual discipline. It was a question of degrading himself, mutilating himself. He had got to plunge into the filthiest of filth. What was the most horrible, sickening thing of all? He thought of Big Brother. The enormous face (because of constantly seeing it on posters he always thought of it as being a meter wide), with its heavy black mustache and the eyes that followed you to and fro, seemed to float into his mind of its own accord. What were his true feelings toward Big Brother?

There was a heavy tramp of boots in the passage. The steel door swung open with a clang. O'Brien walked into the cell. Behind him were the waxen-faced officer and the black-uniformed guards.

"Get up," said O'Brien. "Come here."

Winston stood opposite him. O'Brien took Winston's shoulders between his strong hands and looked at him closely.

"You have had thoughts of deceiving me," he said. "That was stupid. Stand up straighter. Look me in the face."

He paused, and went on in a gentler tone:

"You are improving. Intellectually there is very little wrong with you. It is only emotionally that you have failed to make progress. Tell me, Winston—and remember, no lies; you know that I am always able to detect a lie—tell me, what are your true feelings toward Big Brother?"

"I hate him."

"You hate him. Good. Then the time has come for you to take the last step. You must love Big Brother. It is not enough to obey him; you must love him."

He released Winston with a little push toward the guards.

"Room 101," he said.

IV

At each stage of his imprisonment he had known, or seemed to know, whereabouts he was in the windowless building. Possibly there were slight differences in the air pressure. The cells where the guards had beaten him were below ground level. The room where he had been interrogated by O'Brien was high up near the roof. This place was many meters underground, as deep down as it was possible to go.

It was bigger than most of the cells he had been in. But he hardly noticed his surroundings. All he noticed was that there were two small tables straight in front of him, each covered with green baize. One was only a meter or two from him; the other was further away, near the door. He was strapped upright in a chair, so tightly that he could move nothing, not even his head. A sort of pad gripped his head from behind, forcing him to look straight in front of him.

For a moment he was alone, then the door opened and O'Brien came in.

"You asked me once," said O'Brien, "what was in Room 101. I told you that you knew the answer already. Everyone knows it. The thing that is in Room 101 is the worst thing in the world."

The door opened again. A guard came in, carrying something made of wire, a box or basket of some kind. He set it down on the further table. Because of the position in which O'Brien was standing, Winston could not see what the thing was.

"The worst thing in the world," said O'Brien, "varies from individual to individual. It may be burial alive, or death by fire, or by drowning, or by impalement, or fifty other deaths. There are cases where it is some quite trivial thing, not even fatal."

He had moved a little to one side, so that Winston had a better view of the thing on the table. It was an oblong wire cage with a handle on top for carrying it by. Fixed to the front of it was something that looked like a fencing mask, with the concave side outwards. Although it was three or four meters away from him, he could see that the cage was divided lengthways into two compartments, and that there was some kind of creature in each. They were rats.

"In your case," said O'Brien, "the worst thing in the world happens to be rats."

A sort of premonitory tremor, a fear of he was not certain what, had passed through Winston as soon as he caught his first glimpse of the cage. But at this moment the meaning of the masklike attachment in front of it suddenly sank into him. His bowels seemed to turn to water.

"You can't do that!" he cried out in a high cracked voice. "You couldn't, you couldn't! It's impossible."

"Do you remember," said O'Brien, "the moment of panic that used to occur in your dreams? There was a wall of blackness in front of you, and a roaring sound in your ears. There was something terrible on the other side of the wall. You knew that you knew what it was, but you dared not drag it into the open. It was the rats that were on the other side of the wall."

"O'Brien!" said Winston, making an effort to control his voice. "You know this is not necessary. What is it that you want me to do?"

O'Brien made no direct answer. When he spoke it was in the schoolmasterish manner that he sometimes affected. He looked thoughtfully into the distance, as though he were addressing an audience somewhere behind Winston's back.

"By itself," he said, "pain is not always enough. There are occasions when a human being will stand out against pain, even to the point of death. But for everyone there is something unendurable—something that cannot be contemplated. Courage and cowardice are not involved. If you are falling from a height it is not cowardly to clutch at a rope. If you have come up from deep water it is not cowardly to fill your lungs with air. It is merely an instinct which cannot be disobeyed. It is the same with the rats. For you, they are unendurable. They are a form of pressure that you cannot withstand, even if you wished to. You will do what is required of you."

"But what is it, what is it? How can I do it if I don't know what it is?"

O'Brien picked up the cage and brought it across to the nearer table.

He set it down carefully on the baize cloth. Winston could hear the blood singing in his ears. He had the feeling of sitting in utter loneliness. He was in the middle of a great empty plain, a flat desert drenched with sunlight, across which all sounds came to him out of immense distances. Yet the cage with the rats was not two meters away from him. They were enormous rats. They were at the age when a rat's muzzle grows blunt and fierce and his fur brown instead of gray.

"The rat," said O'Brien, still addressing his invisible audience, "although a rodent, is carnivorous. You are aware of that. You will have heard of the things that happen in the poor quarters of this town. In some streets a woman dare not leave her baby alone in the house, even for five minutes. The rats are certain to attack it. Within quite a small time they will strip it to the bones. They also attack sick or dying people. They show astonishing intelligence in knowing when a human being is helpless."

There was an outburst of squeals from the cage. It seemed to reach Winston from far away. The rats were fighting; they were trying to get at each other through the partition. He heard also a deep groan of despair. That, too, seemed to come from outside himself.

O'Brien picked up the cage, and, as he did so, pressed something in it. There was a sharp click. Winston made a frantic effort to tear himself loose from the chair. It was hopeless: every part of him, even his head, was held immovably. O'Brien moved the cage nearer. It was less than a meter from Winston's face.

"I have pressed the first lever," said O'Brien. "You understand the construction of this cage. The mask will fit over your head, leaving no exit. When I press this other lever, the door of the cage will slide up. These starving brutes will shoot out of it like bullets. Have you ever seen a rat leap through the air? They will leap onto your face and bore straight into it. Sometimes they attack the eyes first. Sometimes they burrow through the cheeks and devour the tongue."

The cage was nearer; it was closing in. Winston heard a succession of shrill cries which appeared to be occurring in the air above his head. But he fought furiously against his panic. To think, to think, even with a split second left—to think was the only hope. Suddenly the foul musty odor of the brutes struck his nostrils. There was a violent convulsion of nausea inside him, and he almost lost consciousness. Everything had gone black. For an instant he was insane, a screaming animal. Yet he came out of the blackness clutching an idea. There was one and only one way to save himself. He must interpose another human being, the *body* of another human being, between himself and the rats.

The circle of the mask was large enough now to shut out the vision of anything else. The wire door was a couple of hand-spans from his face. The rats knew what was coming now. One of them was leaping up and down; the other, an old scaly grandfather of the sewers, stood up, with his pink hands against the bars, and fiercely snuffed the air. Winston could see the whiskers and the yellow teeth. Again the black panic took hold of him. He was blind, helpless, mindless.

"It was a common punishment in Imperial China," said O'Brien as didactically as ever.

The mask was closing on his face. The wire brushed his cheek. And then—no, it was not relief, only hope, a tiny fragment of hope. Too late, perhaps too late. But he had suddenly understood that in the whole world there was just *one* person to whom he could transfer his punishment—*one* body that he could thrust between himself and the rats. And he was shouting frantically, over and over:

"Do it to Julia! Do it to Julia! Not me! Julia! I don't care what you do to her. Tear her face off, strip her to the bones. Not me! Julia! Not me!"

He was falling backwards, into enormous depths, away from the rats. He was still strapped in the chair, but he had fallen through the floor, through the walls of the building, through the earth, through the oceans, through the atmosphere, into outer space, into the gulfs between the stars—always away, away, away from the rats. He was light-years distant, but O'Brien was still standing at his side. There was still the cold touch of a wire against his cheek. But through the darkness that enveloped him he heard another metallic click, and knew that the cage door had clicked shut and not open.

WILLIAM FAULKNER

William Harrison Faulkner was born in Union County, Mississippi, in 1897. His family had been important in the political, economic, and cultural life of northern Mississippi for three generations, but their power and influence were declining, and for a time it looked as if young William might be its least distinguished member. As a school-boy he spent most of his time hunting, fishing, and playing baseball. But he was gifted at drawing and telling stories, and maintained from an early age that he wanted to be a writer like his great-grandfather, William Cuthbert Faulkner, whose White Rose of Memphis *had gone through thirty-five editions after its publication in 1880.*

During World War I Faulkner was turned down by the U. S. Army Air Corps because of his short stature but got accepted for flight training in the Royal Canadian Air Force. He wanted to fly in combat, but the war ended too soon, and he was injured when he and a friend celebrated Armistice Day by stunting over the field and crashing through a hangar roof.

Returning to Oxford, Mississippi, he continued to read and write with the encouragement and guidance of an older friend, Phil Stone. He also took courses at the University of Mississippi at this time, but he was neither a regular nor a successful student. Nor was he having any luck trying to place his fiction and poetry with magazines. Finally, Stone subsidized a private printing of a volume of Faulkner's poetry, The Marble Faun, *in 1924. In later life Faulkner spoke of himself as a "failed poet," who had turned to fiction only because his poetry was not good enough.*

In 1925 he moved to New Orleans, where he was admitted to the circle of writers that gathered around Sherwood Anderson. At this time he began to publish sketches in the Sunday feature section of the New Orleans Times-Picayune. *Then, with the help of Anderson, he was able to get his first novel,* Soldier's Pay, *published in 1926. In his third novel,* Sartoris *(1929), he began to find his proper material and realize his strength as a writer. With this work he began his immense chronicle of an imaginary Mississippi county, based on the history of the area around his home in Oxford, Mississippi. His Yoknapatawpha County has become a permanent feature in the international literary landscape. Of the six writers represented in this book, he is the one who has stayed closest to home. But one could paraphrase Thoreau in his case and say that he "travelled much" in Mississippi.*

The Sound and the Fury *(1929) established him as an important writer of fiction.* Sanctuary *(1930) brought him success and notoriety because of its "scandalous" picture of the South. Among his most highly regarded works are* Light in August *(1932) and* Absalom, Absalom! *(1936), and two collections of short fiction which have novelistic shape and movement:* The Unvanquished *(1938) and* Go Down, Moses *(1942). He continued writing fiction, much of it less admired by critics but all with flashes of his unique skill, until his death in 1962. In 1950 he received the Nobel Prize for literature.*

The student interested in extending his knowledge of Faulkner would do well to begin with the Viking Portable Faulkner, *which has an excellent critical introduction by Malcolm Cowley and an inspired selection and arrangement of Faulkner's short fiction. At this moment (January 1970) Joseph Blotner's authorized biography of Faulkner has not yet been published. Meanwhile, Robert Coughlan's* The Private World of William Faulkner *(Harper, 1954) provides some basic facts and anecdotes about Faulkner's life. Cleanth Brooks's* William Faulkner *(Yale, 1963) is a thorough and sensible guide through Faulkner's work.*

On Writing

Under this title (supplied by the editor) are collected an essay that appeared as the Foreword to The Faulkner Reader *(Random House, 1954) and the speech given in acceptance of the Nobel Prize in Stockholm 10 December 1950.*

My grandfather had a moderate though reasonably diffuse and catholic library; I realize now that I got most of my early education in it. It was a little limited in its fiction content, since his taste was for simple straightforward romantic excitement like Scott or Dumas. But there was a heterogeneous scattering of other volumes, chosen apparently at random and by my grandmother, since the flyleaves bore her name and the dates in the 1880's and '90's of that time when even in a town as big as Memphis, Tennessee, ladies stopped in their carriages in the street in front of the stores and shops, and clerks and even proprietors came out to receive their commands—that time when women did most of the book-buying and the reading too, naming their children Byron and Clarissa and St. Elmo and Lothair after the romantic and tragic heroes and heroines and the even more romantic creators of them.

One of these books was by a Pole, Sienkiewicz—a story of the time of King John Sobieski, when the Poles, almost single-handed, kept the Turks from overrunning Central Europe. This one, like all books of that period, at least the ones my grandfather owned, had a preface, a foreword. I never read any of them; I was too eager to get on to what the people themselves were doing and anguishing and triumphing over. But I did read the foreword in this one, the first one I ever took time to read; I don't know why now. It went something like this:

This book was written at the expense of considerable effort, to uplift men's hearts, and I thought: *What a nice thing to have thought to say*. But no more than that. I didn't even think, *Maybe some day I will write a book too and what a shame I didn't think of that first so I could put it on the front page of mine*. Because I hadn't thought of writing books then. The future didn't extend that far. This was 1915 and '16; I had seen an aeroplane and my mind was filled with names: Ball, and Immelman and Boelcke, and Guynemer and Bishop, and I was waiting, biding, until I would be old enough or free enough or anyway could get to France and become glorious and beribboned too.

Then that had passed. It was 1923 and I wrote a book and discovered that my doom, fate, was to keep on writing books: not for any exterior or ulterior purpose: just writing the books for the sake of writing the books; obviously, since the publisher considered them worth the financial risk of being printed, someone would read them. But that was unimportant too as measured against the need to get them written, though naturally one hopes that who read them would find them true and honest and even perhaps moving. Because one was too busy writing the books during the time while the demon which drove him still considered him worthy of, deserving of, the anguish of being driven, while the blood and glands and flesh still remained strong and potent, the heart and the imagination still remained undulled to follies and lusts and heroisms of men and women; still writing the books because they had to be written after the blood and glands began to slow and cool a little and the heart began to tell him, *You don't know the answer either and you will never find it*, but still writing the books because the demon was still kind; only a little more severe and unpitying: until suddenly one day he saw that that old half-forgotten Pole had had the answer all the time.

To uplift man's heart; the same for all of us: for the ones who are trying to be artists, the ones who are trying to write simple entertainment, the ones who write to shock, and the ones who are simply escaping themselves and their own private anguishes.

Some of us don't know that this is what we are writing for. Some of us will know it and deny it, lest we be accused and self-convicted and condemned of sentimentality, which people nowadays for some reason are ashamed to be tainted with; some of us seem to have curious ideas of just where the heart is located, confusing it with other and baser glands and organs and activities. But we all write for this one purpose.

This does not mean that we are trying to change man, improve him, though this is the hope—maybe even the intention—of some of us. On the contrary, in its last analysis, this hope and desire to uplift man's heart is completely selfish, completely personal. He would lift up man's heart for his own benefit because in that way he can say No to death. He is saying No to death for himself by means of the hearts which he has hoped to uplift, or even by means of the mere base glands which he has disturbed to that extent where they can say No to death on their own account by knowing, realizing, having been told and believing it: *At least we are not vegetables because the hearts and glands capable of partaking in this excitement are not those of vegetables, and will, must, endure.*

So he who, from the isolation of cold impersonal print, can engender this excitement, himself partakes of the immortality which he has engendered. Some day he will be no more, which will not matter then, because isolated and itself invulnerable in the cold print remains that which is capable of engendering still the old deathless excitement in hearts and glands whose owners and custodians are generations from even the air he breathed and anguished in; if it was capable once, he knows that it will be capable and potent still long after there remains of him only a dead and fading name.

II

I feel that this award was not made to me as a man, but to my work—a life's work in the agony and sweat of the human spirit, not for glory and least of all for profit, but to create out of the materials of the human spirit something which did not exist before. So this award is only mine in trust. It will not be difficult to find a dedication for the money part of it commensurate with the purpose and significance of its origin. But I would like to do the same with the acclaim too, by using this moment as a pinnacle from which I might be listened to by the young men and women already dedicated to the same anguish and travail, among whom is already that one who will some day stand here where I am standing.

Our tragedy today is a general and universal physical fear so long sustained by now that we can even bear it. There are no longer problems of the spirit. There is only the question: When will I be blown up? Because of this, the young man or woman writing today has forgotten the problems of the human heart in conflict with itself which alone can make good writing because only that is worth writing about, worth the agony and the sweat.

He must learn them again. He must teach himself that the basest of all things is to be afraid; and, teaching himself that, forget it forever, leaving no room in his workshop for anything but the old verities and truths of the heart, the old universal truths lacking which any story is ephemeral and doomed—love and honor and pity and pride and compassion and sacrifice. Until he does so, he labors under a curse. He writes not of love but of lust, of defeats in which nobody loses anything of value, of victories without hope and, worst of all, without pity or compassion. His griefs grieve on no universal bones, leaving no scars. He writes not of the heart but of the glands.

Until he relearns these things, he will write as though he stood among and watched the end of man. I decline to accept the end of man. It is easy enough to say that man is immortal simply because he will endure: that when the last ding-dong of doom has clanged and faded from the last worthless rock hanging tideless in the last red and dying evening, that even then there will still be one more sound: that of his puny inexhaustible voice, still talking. I refuse to accept this. I believe that man will not merely endure: he will prevail. He is immortal, not because he alone among creatures has an inexhaustible voice, but because he has a soul, a spirit capable of compassion and sacrifice and endurance. The poet's, the writer's, duty is to write about these things. It is his privilege to help man endure by lifting his heart, by reminding him of the courage and honor and hope and pride and compassion and pity and sacrifice which have been the glory of his past. The poet's voice need not merely be the record of man, it can be one of the props, the pillars to help him endure and prevail.

Sunset

This piece first appeared as a sketch in the New Orleans Times-Picayune *for 24 May 1925.*

BLACK DESPERADO SLAIN

The negro who has terrorized this locality for two days, killing three men, two whites and a negro, was killed last night with machine gun fire by a detachment of the –th Regiment, State National Guard. The troopers set up their gun before the copse in which the black was hiding and when there was no reply to their fire, Captain Wallace entered the place and found the negro dead. No reason has been ascertained for the black's running amuck, though it is believed he was insane. He has not been identified.
—The Clarion-Eagle.

He came part of the way on or in or beneath freight cars, but mostly he walked. It took him two days to come from Carrollton avenue to Canal street, because he was afraid of the traffic; and on Canal street at last, carrying his shotgun and his bundle, he stood frightened and dazed. Pushed and shoved, ridiculed by his own race and cursed by policemen, he did not know what to do save that he must cross the street.

So at last, taking his courage in both hands and shutting his eyes, he dashed blindly across in the middle of the block. Cars were about him, a taxi driver screamed horrid imprecations at him, but, clutching his gun and bundle, he made it. And then a kind white man directed him to the river which he sought.

And here was a boat, all tied up to the bank, waiting for him. In climbing down a pile and leaping six feet of water to get on it, he nearly lost his gun; and then another white man, cursing, drove him from the boat.

"But, cap'n," he protested, "I jest wants to go to Af'ica. I kin pay my way."

"Africa, hell," said the white man. "Get to hell off this boat. If you ever try to get on here again that way I'll shoot you. Get on up yonder and get a ticket, if you want to ride."

"Yes, suh. 'Scuse me, cap'n."

"What?" repeated the ticket seller, in amazement.

"Lemme have a ticket to Af'ica, please um."

"Do you mean Algiers?"

"No'm; Af'ica."

"Do you want a ferry ticket?"

"Yassum, I expec' so: so I kin ride dat boat waitin' yonder."

"Come on, come on, up there," said a voice from the waiting queue behind him, so he took his ticket and was hustled through the gate and was once more on board the ferry.

To his surprise the boat, instead of going down the river, in which direction he vaguely supposed Africa to be, held straight across the stream, and he was herded ashore like a sheep. Clinging to his gun he stared about him helplessly. At last he diffidently approached a policeman.

"Cap'n, suh, is dis Af'ica?"

"Huh?" said the startled officer.

"Ah'm tryin' to get to Af'ica, please suh. Is dis de right way?"

"Africa, hell," said this white man, just as the steamboat man had done. "Look here, what are you up to?"

"Ah wants to go back home, whar de preacher say us come fum."

"Where do you live, nigger?"

"Back up yonder ways, in de country."

"What town?"

"Ain't no town, suh, 'ceptin' Mist' Bob and de fambly and his niggers."

"Mississippi or Louisana?"

"Yessuh, I 'speck so."

"Well, lemme tell you something. You go back there on the first train you can catch. This ain't no place for you."

"But, cap'n, I wants to go to Af'ica."

"You forget about Africa, and go buy yourself the longest railroad ticket you can, do you hear?"

"But, cap'n—"

"Beat it, now. Do you want me to take you up?"

At the foot of Canal street again, he looked about him in perplexity. How did one get to Africa? He was hustled and shoved this way and that, and he allowed destiny to carry him along the river front. Here was another boat tied up to the wharf, with niggers carrying things up a plank and dumping them down upon the floor. A coatless white man was evident, loudly.

Niggers pushing trucks rattled and banged, singing, about him. He was still thrust around, leaping from the path of one truck only to find another bearing down upon him. "Look out, black man!"

Suddenly the boss whirled upon him.

"What in hell are you doing? Grab aholt of something there, or get off this job. I don't have no spectators on this job at all. You hear me."

"Yas suh, cap'n," he returned equably; and soon he was throwing sacks onto a truck. His blood warmed with activity, he began to sweat and to sing. This was where he was at home—for the first time in how long? He had forgotten. "Af'ica, where is you?" he said.

Quitting time: the sun hung redly in the west and the long shadows were still and flat, waiting for dark. The spinning golden motes spun slower in the last sunlight; and the other hands gathered up coats and lunch pails and moved away toward the flashing street lights, and supper. He picked up his gun and bundle and went aboard the boat.

Among soft, bulky sacks he lay down to munch the loaf of bread he had bought. Darkness came down completely, the lapping of water against the hull and the pungently sweet smell of the sacked grain soon put him to sleep.

Motion waked him, a smooth lift and fall and a steady drumming of engines. Light was about him and he lay in a dullness of comfort, not even thinking. Then he found that he was hungry, and wondering mildly where he was, he got up.

As soon as he appeared on deck another mad white man fell upon him.

"Ah wants to go to Af'ica, cap'n," he protested, "when I holp dem niggers loadin' yestiddy Ah thought us was all goin' on dis boat."

The white man bore him down with tides of profanity. "God in heaven, you niggers will drive me crazy. Don't you know where this boat is going? It's going to Natchez."

"Dat suit me all right, jes' so she pass Af'ica. You jes' tell me when we gits dar and if she don't stop I kin jump off and swim to de bank."

The man looked at him for a long minute quite in amazement.

"En don't worry about de fare neither, suh," his passenger hastened to reassure him. "I got money: I kin pay it."

"How much you got?"

"Plenty, cap'n," he replied grandly, digging in his overalls. His out-thrust hand held four silver dollars, and some smaller coins. The white man took the four dollars.

"Well, I'll take you as far as Africa for this. And you get on up there and help them niggers shift cargo until we get there."

"Yas suh!" he said with alacrity. He paused again. "But you'll sho' tell me at de right station, won't you, cap'n?"

"Yeh, sure. But beat it now, and help them other boys. G'on, now."

He helped the other boys while they passed under the perfect day from one shimmering reach of the river to another; and again the sun hung redly in the west. Bells rang somewhere and the boat sheered in toward the shore. More bells, the boat lost speed and nosed easily into the mud beneath a row of barrels. The white cap'n, the mad one, leaned down from the front porch above his head.

"All right, Jack," he roared, "here you are. Help put them barrels on board, and Africa is about a mile across them fields yonder."

He stood to watch the boat draw away from the shore, trailing black smoke from its tall funnels across the evening; then he shouldered his gun and struck inland. He had not gone far when he thought of the lions and bears he would probably meet, so he stopped and loaded his gun.

After walking until all the light was gone and the Dipper swung majestically down the west, he knew that he must be well into Africa, and that it was time to eat and sleep again. To eat he could not, so he decided to find a safe place to sleep. Tomorrow he could probably kill a rabbit. He suddenly found a fence beside him; across it loomed something that might be a haystack. He climbed the fence and something rose horribly from almost under his feet.

He knew stark and terrible fear. His gun leaped to his shoulder and roared and flamed in the darkness, and the lion or whatever it was plunged bellowing away into the night. He could feel sweat cold as copper pieces on his face and he ran toward the haystack and clawed madly at it, trying to climb it. His fear grew with his futile efforts, then cooled away, allowing him to mount the slippery thing. Once on top he felt safe, but he was cautious to place the shotgun close to his hand as he lay on his belly staring into the night. The thing he had shot was quiet now, but the night was filled with sound.

A light came twinkling along the ground and soon he could see legs criss-crossing it, and he heard voices in a language he could not understand. Savages, he thought, folks that eat you; and he crouched lower in his straw. The light and the voices passed on in the direction the beast he had shot had taken; soon the light stopped beside a blotched thing that swelled up from the ground, and the voices rose in imprecation.

"Gentlemen!" he breathed. "I mus' a shot dem folks' own private lion."

But a lion was a lion. And so he lay hidden while the light moved on away and was lost at last, and the stars swung over him, and he slept.

He was shaken into wakefulness. He threw an arm across his eyes. That strange language was in his ears again and he opened his eyes to see a small dark-skinned man kneeling over him with a pistol. The language he could not understand, but the language the pistol talked he could.

They are going to eat me! he thought. His leg gathered and sickled, the man toppled backward toward the ground, and as an animal leaps he flung himself bodily earthward. A pistol went off and something slapped him dully high in the shoulder. He replied, and a man flopped to the ground. He leaped to his feet and ran, while bullets whined past him. The fence was before him: he turned to follow it, seeking a gate.

His left arm was warm and wet, and there at the turn of the fence was a gate. The shooting behind him continued, he clutched his own gun as he saw a running figure, trying to cut him off at the gate. As they drew together he saw that this one was a member of his own race. "Out de way, nigger," he gasped at the other's waving arms; and he saw the expression of ludicrous amazement on the man's face as his gun crashed again.

His breath came in gulping lungsful. He must stop. Here was a ditch, and a long embankment. Just ahead, where another embankment intersected it, was a small copse. Into this he plunged, concealed, and lay on his back, panting. His heaving lungs at last breathed easier. Then he discovered the wound in his shoulder. He looked at his blood in surprise. "Now when you suppose dat happen?" he thought. "Whew! Dese Af'ikins shoots niggers jes' like white folks does."

He bound it crudely, then took stock of the situation. He had shelter, and that was all. There were still eighteen shells left. And he would need them: there was already one man about two hundred yards away, holding a rifle and watching his thicket. "Don't ack like he gwine bother me right soon," he decided. "I'll jes' rest here twell dark, and den I'm gwine back to Mist' Bob. Af'ica sho' ain't no place fer civilized folks—steppin' on lions, and bein' shot, and havin' to shoot folks yo'self. But I guess dese Af'icans is used to it."

His shoulder began to throb dully. He twisted and turned in his mounting fever. How thirsty he was! He had been hungry, but now he was only thirsty, and he thought of the cool brown creek at home, and the cold spring in the wood lot. He raised his sweating face, and saw the watchman had drawn closer in. He raised his gun, aiming the best he could with one hand, and fired. The watchman fell backward, leaped to his feet and ran dodging beyond range. "Jes' to skeer you," he muttered.

Things were beginning to look funny, and his shoulder hurt dreadfully. He dozed a moment and thought he was at home again; he waked to pain and dozed again. Dozing and waking, he passed the long day, crawling at intervals to sip the muddy, stinking water in the ditch. At last he waked to night, and lanterns and fires, and men walking in the firelight and talking.

He had dragged himself down the bank for water, and as he returned an automobile's lights were suddenly turned full on him. A voice screamed, and bullets whipped about him. He plunged back to his copse and fired blindly at the lights. A man shrieked and bullets ripped and tore at the thicket: the limbs were whipped as by a gale, tortured against the sky. He was seared as with hot irons, and he lowered his head, pressing his face into the muddy earth.

The firing suddenly ceased; the silence literally dragged him from the regions of oblivion. He thrust his gun forward, waiting. At last the darkness detached itself and became two things; and in the flash of his point-blank explosion he saw two men crouching. One of them fired a pistol almost in his face, and fled.

Again it was dawn. The sun rose, became hot, and marched above his head. He was at home, working in the fields; he was asleep, fighting his way from out a nightmare; he was a child again—no, he was a bird, a big one like a buzzard, drawing endless black circles on a blue sky.

Again the sun sank. The west was like blood: it was his own blood painted onto a wall. Supper in the pot, and night where there were no fires and people moving around them, and then all stopping as though they were waiting for something to happen.

He raised his face from the mud and looked at the circle of fires about him. It looked as though everybody had gathered at one place, directly in front of him, all watching or waiting for something. Let them wait: tomorrow he'll be at home, with Mr. Bob to curse him in his gentle voice, and regular folks to work and laugh and talk with.

Here was a wind coming up: the branches and bushes about him whipped suddenly to a gale fiercer than any yet; flattened and screamed, and melted away under it. And he, too, was a tree caught in that same wind: he felt the dull blows of it, and the rivening of himself into tattered and broken leaves.

The gale died away, and all broken things were still. His black, kind, dull, once-cheerful face was turned up to the sky and the cold, cold stars. Africa or Louisiana: what care they?

Dry September

This story was written in the early 1930's.

Through the bloody September twilight, aftermath of sixty-two rainless days, it had gone like a fire in dry grass—the rumor, the story, whatever it was. Something about Miss Minnie Cooper and a Negro. Attacked, insulted, frightened: none of them, gathered in the barber shop on that Saturday evening where the ceiling fan stirred, without freshening it, the vitiated air, sending back upon them, in recurrent surges of stale pomade and lotion, their own stale breath and odors, knew exactly what had happened.

"Except it wasn't Will Mayes," a barber said. He was a man of middle age; a thin, sand-colored man with a mild face, who was shaving a client. "I know Will Mayes. He's a good nigger. And I know Miss Minnie Cooper, too."

"What do you know about her?" a second barber said.

"Who is she?" the client said. "A young girl?"

"No," the barber said. "She's about forty, I reckon. She aint married. That's why I dont believe—"

"Believe, hell!" a hulking youth in a sweat-stained silk shirt said. "Wont you take a white woman's word before a nigger's?"

"I dont believe Will Mayes did it," the barber said. "I know Will Mayes."

"Maybe you know who did it, then. Maybe you already got him out of town, you damn niggerlover."

"I dont believe anybody did anything. I dont believe anything happened. I leave it to you fellows if them ladies that get old without getting married dont have notions that a man cant—"

"Then you are a hell of a white man," the client said. He moved under the cloth. The youth had sprung to his feet.

"You dont?" he said. "Do you accuse a white woman of lying?"

The barber held the razor poised above the half-risen client. He did not look around.

"It's this durn weather," another said. "It's enough to make a man do anything. Even to her."

Nobody laughed. The barber said in his mild, stubborn tone: "I aint accusing nobody of nothing. I just know and you fellows know how a woman that never—"

"You damn niggerlover!" the youth said.

"Shut up, Butch," another said. "We'll get the facts in plenty of time to act."

"Who is? Who's getting them?" the youth said. "Facts, hell! I—"

"You're a fine white man," the client said. "Aint you?" In his frothy beard he looked like a desert rat in the moving pictures. "You tell them, Jack," he said to the youth. "If there aint any white men in this town, you can count on me, even if I aint only a drummer and a stranger."

"That's right, boys," the barber said. "Find out the truth first. I know Will Mayes."

"Well, by God!" the youth shouted. "To think that a white man in this town—"

"Shut up, Butch," the second speaker said. "We got plenty of time."

The client sat up. He looked at the speaker. "Do you claim that anything excuses a nigger attacking a white woman? Do you mean to tell me you are a white man and you'll stand for it? You better go back North where you came from. The South dont want your kind here."

"North what?" the second said. "I was born and raised in this town."

"Well, by God!" the youth said. He looked about with a strained, baffled gaze, as if he was trying to remember what it was he wanted to say or to do. He drew his sleeve across his sweating face. "Damn if I'm going to let a white woman—"

"You tell them, Jack," the drummer said. "By God, if they—"

The screen door crashed open. A man stood in the floor, his feet apart and his heavy-set body poised easily. His white shirt was open at the throat; he wore a felt hat. His hot, bold glance swept the group. His name was McLendon. He had commanded troops at the front in France and had been decorated for valor.

"Well," he said, "are you going to sit there and let a black son rape a white woman on the streets of Jefferson?"

Butch sprang up again. The silk of his shirt clung flat to his heavy shoulders. At each armpit was a dark halfmoon. "That's what I been telling them! That's what I—"

"Did it really happen?" a third said. "This aint the first man scare she ever had, like Hawkshaw says. Wasn't there something about a man on the kitchen roof, watching her undress, about a year ago?"

"What?" the client said. "What's that?" The barber had been slowly forcing him back into the chair; he arrested himself reclining, his head lifted, the barber still pressing him down.

McLendon whirled on the third speaker. "Happen? What the hell difference does it make? Are you going to let the black sons get away with it until one really does it?"

"That's what I'm telling them!" Butch shouted. He cursed, long and steady, pointless.

"Here, here," a fourth said. "Not so loud. Dont talk so loud."

"Sure," McLendon said; "no talking necessary at all. I've done my talking. Who's with me?" He poised on the balls of his feet, roving his gaze.

The barber held the drummer's face down, the razor poised. "Find out the facts first, boys. I know Willy Mayes. It wasn't him. Let's get the sheriff and do this thing right."

McLendon whirled upon him his furious, rigid face. The barber did not look away. They looked like men of different races. The other barbers had ceased also above their prone clients. "You mean to tell me," McLendon said, "that you'd take a nigger's word before a white woman's? Why, you damn niggerloving—"

The third speaker rose and grasped McLendon's arm; he too had been a soldier. "Now, now. Let's figure this thing out. Who knows anything about what really happened?"

"Figure out hell!" McLendon jerked his arm free. "All that're with me get up from there. The ones that aint—" He roved his gaze, dragging his sleeve across his face.

Three men rose. The drummer in the chair sat up. "Here," he said, jerking at the cloth about his neck; "get this rag off me. I'm with him. I dont live here, but by God, if our mothers and wives and sisters—" He smeared the cloth over his face and flung it to the floor. McLendon stood in the floor and cursed the others. Another rose and moved toward him. The remainder sat uncomfortable, not looking at one another, then one by one they rose and joined him.

The barber picked the cloth from the floor. He began to fold it neatly. "Boys, dont do that. Will Mayes never done it. I know."

"Come on," McLendon said. He whirled. From his hip pocket protruded the butt of a heavy automatic pistol. They went out. The screen door crashed behind them reverberant in the dead air.

The barber wiped the razor carefully and swiftly, and put it away, and ran to the rear, and took his hat from the wall. "I'll be back as soon as I can," he said to the other barbers. "I cant let—" He went out, running. The two other barbers followed him to the door and caught it on the rebound, leaning out and looking up the street after him. The air was flat and dead. It had a metallic taste at the base of tongue.

"What can he do?" the first said. The second one was saying "Jees Christ, Jees Christ" under his breath. "I'd just as lief be Will Mayes as Hawk, if he gets McLendon riled."

"Jees Christ, Jees Christ," the second whispered.

"You reckon he really done it to her?" the first said.

II

She was thirty-eight or thirty-nine. She lived in a small frame house with her invalid mother and a thin, sallow, unflagging aunt, where each morning between ten and eleven she would appear on the porch in a lace-trimmed boudoir cap, to sit swinging in the porch swing until noon. After dinner she lay down for a while, until the afternoon began to cool. Then, in one of the three or four new voile dresses which she had each summer, she would go downtown to spend the afternoon in the stores with the other ladies, where they would handle the goods and haggle over the prices in cold, immediate voices, without any intention of buying.

She was of comfortable people—not the best in Jefferson, but good people enough—and she was still on the slender side of ordinary looking, with a bright, faintly haggard manner and dress. When she was young she had had a slender, nervous body and a sort of hard vivacity which had enabled her for a time to ride upon the crest of the town's social life as exemplified by the high school party and church social period of her contemporaries while still children enough to be unclassconscious.

She was the last to realize that she was losing ground; that those among whom she had been a little brighter and louder flame than any other were beginning to learn the pleasure of snobbery—male—and retaliation—female. That was when her face began to wear that bright, haggard look. She still carried it to parties on shadowy porticoes and summer lawns, like a mask or a flag, with that bafflement of furious repudiation of truth in her eyes. One evening at a party she heard a boy and two girls, all schoolmates, talking. She never accepted another invitation.

She watched the girls with whom she had grown up as they married and got homes and children, but no man ever called on her steadily until the children of the other girls had been calling her "aunty" for several years, the while their mothers told them in bright voices about how popular Aunt Minnie had been as a girl. Then the town began to see her driving on Sunday afternoons with the cashier in the bank. He was a widower of about forty—a high-colored man, smelling always faintly of the barber shop or of whisky. He owned the first automobile in town, a red runabout; Minnie had the first motoring bonnet and veil the town ever saw. Then the town began to say: "Poor Minnie." "But she is old enough to take care of herself," others said. That was when she began to ask her old schoolmates that their children call her "cousin" instead of "aunty."

It was twelve years now since she had been relegated into adultery by public opinion, and eight years since the cashier had gone to a Memphis bank, returning for one day each Christmas, which he spent at an annual bachelors' party at a hunting club on the river. From behind their curtains the neighbors would see the party pass, and during the over-the-way Christmas day visiting they would tell her about him, about how well he looked, and how they heard that he was prospering in the city, watching with bright, secret eyes her haggard, bright face. Usually by that hour there would be the scent of whisky on her breath. It was supplied her by a youth, a clerk at the soda fountain: "Sure; I buy it for the old gal. I reckon she's entitled to a little fun."

Her mother kept to her room altogether now; the gaunt aunt ran the house. Against that background Minnie's bright dresses, her idle and empty days, had a quality of furious unreality. She went out in the evenings only with women now, neighbors, to the moving pictures. Each afternoon she dressed in one of the new dresses and went downtown alone, where her young "cousins" were already strolling in the late afternoons with their delicate, silken heads and thin, awkward arms and conscious hips, clinging to one another or shrieking and giggling with paired boys in the soda fountain when she passed and went on along the serried store fronts, in the doors of which the sitting and lounging men did not even follow her with their eyes any more.

III

The barber went swiftly up the street where the sparse lights, insect-swirled, glared in rigid and violent suspension in the lifeless air. The day had died in a pall of dust; above the darkened square, shrouded by the spent dust, the sky was as clear as the inside of a brass bell. Below the east was a rumor of the twice-waxed moon.

When he overtook them McLendon and three others were getting into a car parked in an alley. McLendon stooped his thick head, peering out beneath the top. "Changed your mind, did you?" he said. "Damn good thing; by God, tomorrow when this town hears about how you talked tonight—"

"Now, now," the other ex-soldier said. "Hawkshaw's all right. Come on, Hawk; jump in."

"Will Mayes never done it, boys," the barber said. "If anybody done it. Why, you all know well as I do there aint any town where they got better niggers than us. And you know how a lady will kind of think things about men when there aint any reason to, and Miss Minnie anyway—"

"Sure, sure," the soldier said. "We're just going to talk to him a little; that's all."

"Talk hell!" Butch said. "When we're through with the—"

"Shut up, for God's sake!" the soldier said. "Do you want everybody in town—"

"Tell them, by God!" McLendon said. "Tell every one of the sons that'll let a white woman—"

"Let's go; let's go: here's the other car." The second car slid squealing out of a cloud of dust at the alley mouth. McLendon started his car and took the lead. Dust lay like fog in the street. The street lights hung nimbused as in water. They drove on out of town.

A rutted lane turned at right angles. Dust hung above it too, and above all the land. The dark bulk of the ice plant, where the Negro Mayes was night watchman, rose against the sky. "Better stop here, hadn't we?" the soldier said. McLendon did not reply. He hurled the car up and slammed to a stop, the headlights glaring on the blank wall.

"Listen here, boys," the barber said; "if he's here, dont that prove he never done it? Dont it? If it was him, he would run. Dont you see he would?" The second car came up and stopped. McLendon got down; Butch sprang down beside him. "Listen, boys," the barber said.

"Cut the lights off!" McLendon said. The breathless dark rushed down. There was no sound in it save their lungs as they sought air in the parched dust in which for two months they had lived; then the diminishing crunch of McLendon's and Butch's feet, and a moment later McLendon's voice:

"Will! . . . Will!"

Below the east the wan hemorrhage of the moon increased. It heaved above the ridge, silvering the air, the dust, so that they seemed to breathe, live, in a bowl of molten lead. There was no sound of nightbird nor insect, no sound save their breathing and a faint ticking of contracting metal about the cars. Where their bodies touched one another they seemed to sweat dryly, for no more moisture came. "Christ!" a voice said; "let's get out of here."

But they didn't move until vague noises began to grow out of the darkness ahead; then they got out and waited tensely in the breathless dark. There was another sound: a blow, a hissing expulsion of breath and McLendon cursing in undertone. They stood a moment longer, then they ran forward. They ran in a stumbling clump, as though they were fleeing something. "Kill him, kill the son," a voice whispered. McLendon flung them back.

"Not here," he said. "Get him into the car." "Kill him, kill the black son!" the voice murmured. They dragged the Negro to the car.

The barber had waited beside the car. He could feel himself sweating and he knew he was going to be sick at the stomach.

"What is it, captains?" the Negro said. "I aint done nothing. 'Fore God, Mr John." Someone produced handcuffs. They worked busily about the Negro as though he were a post, quiet, intent, getting in one another's way. He submitted to the handcuffs, looking swiftly and constantly from dim face to dim face. "Who's here, captains?" he said, leaning to peer into the faces until they could feel his breath and smell his sweaty reek. He spoke a name or two. "What you all say I done, Mr John?"

McLendon jerked the car door open. "Get in!" he said.

The Negro did not move. "What you all going to do with me, Mr John? I aint done nothing. White folks, captains, I aint done nothing: I swear 'fore God." He called another name.

"Get in!" McLendon said. He struck the Negro. The others expelled their breath in a dry hissing and struck him with random blows and he whirled and cursed them, and swept his manacled hands across their faces and slashed the barber upon the mouth, and the barber struck him also. "Get him in there," McLendon said. They pushed at him. He ceased struggling and got in and sat quietly as the others took their places. He sat between the barber and the soldier, drawing his limbs in so as not to touch them, his eyes going swiftly and constantly from face to face. Butch clung to the running board. The car moved on. The barber nursed his mouth with his handkerchief.

"What's the matter, Hawk?" the soldier said.

"Nothing," the barber said. They regained the highroad and turned away from town. The second car dropped back out of the dust. They went on, gaining speed; the final fringe of houses dropped behind.

"Goddamn, he stinks!" the soldier said.

"We'll fix that," the drummer in front beside McLendon said. On the running board Butch cursed into the hot rush of air. The barber leaned suddenly forward and touched McLendon's arm.

"Let me out John," he said.

"Jump out, niggerlover," McLendon said without turning his head. He drove swiftly. Behind them the sourceless lights of the second car glared in the dust. Presently McLendon turned into a narrow road. It was rutted with disuse. It led back to an abandoned brick kiln—a series of reddish mounds and weed- and vine-choked vats without bottom. It had been used for pasture once, until one day the owner missed one of his mules. Although he prodded carefully in the vats with a long pole, he could not even find the bottom of them.

"John," the barber said.

"Jump out, then," McLendon said, hurling the car along the ruts. Beside the barber the Negro spoke:

"Mr Henry."

The barber sat forward. The narrow tunnel of the road rushed up and past. Their motion was like an extinct furnace blast: cooler, but utterly dead. The car bounded from rut to rut.

"Mr Henry," the Negro said.

The barber began to tug furiously at the door, "Look out, there!" the soldier said, but the barber had already kicked the door open and swung onto the running board. The soldier leaned across the Negro and grasped at him, but he had already jumped. The car went on without checking speed.

The impetus hurled him crashing through dust-sheathed weeds, into the ditch. Dust puffed about him, and in a thin, vicious crackling of sapless stems he lay choking and retching until the second car passed and died away. Then he rose and limped on until he reached the highroad and turned toward town, brushing at his clothes with his hands. The moon was higher, riding high and clear of the dust at last, and after a while the town began to glare beneath the dust. He went on, limping. Presently he heard cars and the glow of them grew in the dust behind him and he left the road and crouched again in the weeds until they passed. McLendon's car came last now. There were four people in it and Butch was not on the running board.

They went on; the dust swallowed them; the glare and the sound died away. The dust of them hung for a while, but soon the eternal dust absorbed it again. The barber climbed back onto the road and limped on toward town.

IV

As she dressed for supper on that Saturday evening, her own flesh felt like fever. Her hands trembled among the hooks and eyes, and her eyes had a feverish look, and her hair swirled crisp and crackling under the comb. While she was still dressing the friends called for her and sat while she donned her sheerest underthings and stockings and a new voile dress. "Do you feel strong enough to go out?" they said, their eyes bright too, with a dark glitter. "When you have had time to get over the shock, you must tell us what happened. What he said and did; everything."

In the leafed darkness, as they walked toward the square, she began to breathe deeply, something like a swimmer preparing to dive, until she ceased trembling, the four of them walking slowly because of the terrible heat and out of solicitude for her. But as they neared the square she began to tremble again, walking with her head up, her hands clenched at her sides, their voices about her murmurous, also with that feverish, glittering quality of their eyes.

They entered the square, she in the center of the group, fragile in her fresh dress. She was trembling worse. She walked slower and slower, as children eat ice cream, her head up and her eyes bright in the haggard banner of her face, passing the hotel and the coatless drummers in chairs along the curb looking around at her: "That's the one: see? The one in pink in the middle." "Is that her? What did they do with the nigger? Did they—?" "Sure. He's all right." "All right, is he?" "Sure. We went on a little trip." Then the drug store, where even the young men lounging in the doorway tipped their hats and followed with their eyes the motion of her hips and legs when she passed.

They went on, passing the lifted hats of the gentlemen, the suddenly ceased voices, deferent, protective. "Do you see?" the friends said. Their voice sounded like long, hovering sighs of hissing exultation. "There's not a Negro on the square. Not one."

They reached the picture show. It was like a miniature fairyland with its lighted lobby and colored lithographs of life caught in its terrible and beautiful mutations. Her lips began to tingle. In the dark, when the picture began, it would be all right; she could hold back the laughing so it would not waste away so fast and so soon. So she hurried on before the turning faces, the undertones of low astonishment, and they took their accustomed places where she could see the aisle against the silver glare and the young men and girls coming in two and two against it.

The lights flicked away; the screen glowed silver, and soon life began to unfold, beautiful and passionate and sad, while still the young men and girls entered, scented and sibilant in the half dark, their paired backs in silhouette delicate and sleek, their slim, quick bodies awkward, divinely young, while beyond them the silver dream accumulated, inevitably on and on. She began to laugh. In trying to suppress it, it made more noise than ever; heads began to turn. Still laughing, her friends raised her and led her out, and she stood at the curb, laughing on a high, sustained note, until the taxi came up and they helped her in.

They removed the pink voile and the sheer underthings and the stockings, and put her to bed, and cracked ice for her temples, and sent for the doctor. He was hard to locate, so they ministered to her with hushed ejaculations, renewing the ice and fanning her. While the ice was fresh and cold she stopped laughing and lay still for a time, moaning only a little. But soon the laughing welled again and her voice rose screaming.

"Shhhhhhhhhhh! Shhhhhhhhhhhhhh!" they said, freshening the icepack, smoothing her hair, examining it for gray; "poor girl!" Then to one another: "Do you suppose anything really happened?" their eyes darkly aglitter, secret and passionate. "Shhhhhhhhhh! Poor girl! Poor Minnie!"

V

It was midnight when McLendon drove up to his neat new house. It was trim and fresh as a birdcage and almost as small, with its clean, green-and-white paint. He locked the car and mounted the porch and entered. His wife rose from a chair beside the reading lamp. McLendon stopped in the floor and stared at her until she looked down.

"Look at that clock," he said, lifting his arm, pointing. She stood before him, her face lowered, a magazine in her hands. Her face was pale, strained, and weary-looking. "Haven't I told you about sitting up like this, waiting to see when I come in?"

"John," she said. She laid the magazine down. Poised on the balls of his feet, he glared at her with his hot eyes, his sweating face.

"Didn't I tell you?" He went toward her. She looked up then. He caught her shoulder. She stood passive, looking at him.

"Don't, John. I couldn't sleep . . . The heat; something. Please, John. You're hurting me."

"Didn't I tell you?" He released her and half struck, half flung her across the chair, and she lay there and watched him quietly as he left the room.

He went on through the house, ripping off his shirt, and on the dark, screened porch at the rear he stood and mopped his head and shoulders with the shirt and flung it away. He took the pistol from his hip and laid it on the table beside the bed, and sat on the bed and removed his shoes, and rose and slipped his trousers off. He was sweating again already, and he stooped and hunted furiously for the shirt. At last he found it and wiped his body again, and, with his body pressed against the dusty screen, he stood panting. There was no movement, no sound, not even an insect. The dark world seemed to lie stricken beneath the cold moon and the lidless stars.

The Old People

This story has a place in the sequence of stories that make up Go Down, Moses, *but it is complete in itself.*

At first there was nothing. There was the faint, cold, steady rain, the gray and constant light of the late November dawn, with the voices of the hounds converging somewhere in it and toward them. Then Sam Fathers, standing just behind the boy as he had been standing when the boy shot his first running rabbit with his first gun and almost with the first load it ever carried, touched his shoulder and he began to shake, not with any cold. Then the buck was there. He did not come into sight; he was just there, looking not like a ghost but as if all of light were condensed in him and he were the source of it, not only moving in it but disseminating it, already running, seen first as you always see the deer, in that split second after he has already seen you, already slanting away in that first soaring bound, the antlers even in that dim light looking like a small rocking-chair balanced on his head.

"Now," Sam Fathers said, "shoot quick, and slow."

The boy did not remember that shot at all. He would live to be eighty, as his father and his father's twin brother and their father in his turn had lived to be, but he would never hear that shot nor remember even the shock of the gun-butt. He didn't even remember what he did with the gun afterward. He was running. Then he was standing over the buck where it lay on the wet earth still in the attitude of speed and not looking at all dead, standing over it shaking and jerking, with Sam Fathers beside him again, extending the knife. "Dont walk up to him in front," Sam said. "If he aint dead, he will cut you all to pieces with his feet. Walk up to him from behind and take him by the horn first, so you can hold his head down until you can jump away. Then slip your other hand down and hook your fingers in his nostrils."

The boy did that—drew the head back and the throat taut and drew Sam Fathers' knife across the throat and Sam stooped and dipped his hands in the hot smoking blood and wiped them back and forth across the boy's face. Then Sam's horn rang in the wet gray woods and again and again; there was a boiling wave of dogs about them, with Tennie's Jim and Boon Hogganbeck whipping them back after each had had a taste of the blood, then the men, the true hunters—Walter Ewell whose rifle never missed, and Major de Spain and old General Compson and the boy's cousin, McCaslin Edmonds, grandson of his father's sister, sixteen years his senior and, since both he and McCaslin were only children and the boy's father had been nearing seventy when he was born, more his brother than his cousin and more his father than either—sitting their horses and looking down at them: at the old man of seventy who had been a negro for two generations now but whose face and bearing were still those of the Chickasaw chief who had been his father; and the white boy of twelve with the prints of the bloody hands on his face, who had nothing to do now but stand straight and not let the trembling show.

"Did he do all right, Sam?" his cousin McCaslin said.

"He done all right," Sam Fathers said.

They were the white boy, marked forever, and the old dark man sired on both sides by savage kings, who had marked him, whose bloody hands had merely formally consecrated him to that which, under the man's tutelage, he had already accepted, humbly and joyfully, with abnegation and with pride too; the hands, the touch, the first worthy blood which he had been found at last worthy to draw, joining him and the man forever, so that the man would continue to live past the boy's seventy years and then eighty years, long after the man himself had entered the earth as chiefs and kings entered it;—the child, not yet a man, whose grandfather had lived in the same country and in almost the same manner as the boy himself would grow up to live, leaving his descendants in the land in his turn as his grandfather had done, and the old man past seventy whose grandfathers had owned the land long before the white men ever saw it and who had vanished from it now with all their kind, what of blood they left behind them running now in another race and for a while even in bondage and now drawing toward the end of its alien and irrevocable course, barren, since Sam Fathers had no children.

His father was Ikkemotubbe himself, who had named himself Doom. Sam told the boy about that—how Ikkemotubbe, old Issetibbeha's sister's son, had run away to New Orleans in his youth and returned seven years later with a French companion calling himself the Chevalier Soeur-Blonde de Vitry, who must have been the Ikkemotubbe of his family too and who was already addressing Ikkemotubbe as *Du Homme;*—returned, came home again, with his foreign Aramis and the quadroon slave woman who was to be Sam's mother, and a gold-laced hat and coat and a wicker wine-hamper containing a litter of month-old puppies and a gold snuff-box filled with a white powder resembling fine sugar. And how he was met at the River landing by three or four companions of his bachelor youth, and while the light of a smoking torch gleamed on the glittering braid of the hat and coat Doom squatted in the mud of the land and took one of the puppies from the hamper and put a pinch of the white powder on its tongue and the puppy died before the one who was holding it could cast it away. And how they returned to the Plantation where Issetibbeha, dead now, had been succeeded by his son, Doom's fat cousin Moketubbe, and the next day Moketubbe's eight-year-old son died suddenly and that afternoon, in the presence of Moketubbe and most of the others (the People, Sam Fathers called them) Doom produced another puppy from the wine-hamper and put a pinch of the white powder on its tongue and Moketubbe abdicated and Doom became in fact The Man which his French friend already called him. And how on the day after that, during the ceremony of accession, Doom pronounced a marriage between the pregnant quadroon and one of the slave men which he had just inherited (that was how Sam Fathers got his name, which in Chickasaw had been Had-Two-Fathers) and two years later sold the man and woman and the child who was his own son to his white neighbor, Carothers McCaslin.

That was seventy years ago. The Sam Fathers whom the boy knew was already sixty—a man not tall, squat rather, almost sedentary, flabby-looking though he actually was not, with hair like a horse's mane which even at seventy showed no trace of white and a face which showed no age until he smiled, whose only visible trace of negro blood was a slight dullness of the hair and the fingernails, and something else which you did notice about the eyes, which you noticed because it was not always there, only in response and not always then—something not in their shape nor pigment but in their expression, and the boy's cousin McCaslin told him what that was: not the heritage of Ham, not the mark of servitude but of bondage; the knowledge that for a while that part of his blood had been the blood of slaves. "Like an old lion or a bear in a cage," McCaslin said. "He was born in the cage and has been in it all his life; he knows nothing else. Then he smells something. It might be anything, any breeze blowing past anything and then into his nostrils. But there for a second was the hot sand or the cane-brake that he never even saw himself, might not even know if he did see it and probably does know he couldn't hold his own with it if he got back to it. But that's not what he smells then. It was the cage he smelled. He hadn't smelled the cage until that minute. Then the hot sand or the brake blew into his nostrils and blew away, and all he could smell was the cage. That's what makes his eyes look like that."

"Then let him go!" the boy cried. "Let him go!"

His cousin laughed shortly. Then he stopped laughing, making the sound that is. It had never been laughing. "His cage aint McCaslins," he said. "He was a wild man. When he was born, all his blood on both sides, except the little white part, knew things that had been tamed out of our blood so long ago that we have not only forgotten them, we have to live together in herds to protect ourselves from our own sources. He was the direct son not only of a warrior but of a chief. Then he grew up and began to learn things, and all of a sudden one day he found out that he had been betrayed, the blood of the warriors and chiefs had been betrayed. Not by his father," he added quickly. "He probably never held it against old Doom for selling him and his mother into slavery, because he probably believed the damage was already done before then and it was the same warriors' and chiefs' blood in him and Doom both that was betrayed through the black blood which his mother gave him. Not betrayed by the black blood and not wilfully betrayed by his mother, but betrayed by her all the same, who had bequeathed him not only the blood of slaves but even a little of the very blood which had enslaved it; himself his own battleground, the scene of his own vanquishment and the mausoleum of his defeat. His cage ain't us," McCaslin said. "Did you ever know anybody yet, even your father and Uncle Buddy, that ever told him to do or not do anything that he ever paid any attention to?"

That was true. The boy first remembered him as sitting in the door of the plantation blacksmith-shop, where he sharpened plow-points and mended tools and even did rough carpenter-work when he was not in the woods. And sometimes, even when the woods had not drawn him, even with the shop cluttered with work which the farm waited on, Sam would sit there, doing nothing at all for half a day or a whole one, and no man, neither the boy's father and twin uncle in their day nor his cousin McCaslin after he became practical though not yet titular master, ever to say to him, "I want this finished by sundown" or "why wasn't this done yesterday?" And once each year, in the late fall, in November, the boy would watch the wagon, the hooped canvas top erected now, being loaded—the food, hams and sausage from the smokehouse, coffee and flour and molasses from the commissary, a whole beef killed just last night for the dogs until there would be meat in camp, the crate containing the dogs themselves, then the bedding, the guns, the horns and lanterns and axes, and his cousin McCaslin and Sam Fathers in their hunting clothes would mount to the seat and with Tennie's Jim sitting on the dog-crate they would drive away to Jefferson, to join Major de Spain and General Compson and Boon Hogganbeck and Walter Ewell and go on into the big bottom of the Tallahatchie where the deer and bear were, to be gone two weeks. But before the wagon was even loaded the boy would find that he could watch no longer. He would go away, running almost, to stand behind the corner where he could not see the wagon and nobody could see him, not crying, holding himself rigid except for the trembling, whispering to himself: "Soon now. Soon now. Just three more years" (or two more or one more) "and I will be ten. Then Cass said I can go."

White man's work, when Sam did work. Because he did nothing else: farmed no alloted acres of his own, as the other ex-slaves of old Carothers McCaslin did, performed no field-work for daily wages as the younger and newer negroes did—and the boy never knew just how that had been settled between Sam and old Carothers, or perhaps with old Carothers' twin sons after him. For, although Sam lived among the negroes, in a cabin among the other cabins in the quarters, and consorted with negroes (what of consorting with anyone Sam did after the boy got big enough to walk alone from the house to the blacksmith-shop and then to carry a gun) and dressed like them and talked like them and even went with them to the negro church now and then, he was still the son of that Chickasaw chief and the negroes knew it. And, it seemed to the boy, not only negroes. Boon Hogganbeck's grandmother had been a Chickasaw woman too, and although the blood had run white since and Boon was a white man, it was not chief's blood. To the boy at least, the difference was apparent immediately you saw Boon and Sam together, and even Boon seemed to know it was there —even Boon, to whom in his tradition it had never occurred that anyone might be better born than himself. A man might be smarter, he admitted that, or richer (luckier, he called it) but not better born. Boon was a mastiff, absolutely faithful, dividing his fidelity equally between Major de Spain and the boy's cousin McCaslin, absolutely dependent for his very bread and dividing that impartially too between Major de Spain and McCaslin, hardy, generous, courageous enough, a slave to all the appetites and almost unratiocinative. In the boy's eyes at least it was Sam Fathers, the negro, who bore himself not only toward his cousin McCaslin and Major de Spain but toward all white men, with gravity and dignity and without servility or recourse to that impenetrable wall of ready and easy mirth which negroes sustain between themselves and white men, bearing himself toward his cousin McCaslin not only as one man to another but as an older man to a younger.

He taught the boy the woods, to hunt, when to shoot and when not to shoot, when to kill and when not to kill, and better, what to do with it afterward. Then he would talk to the boy, the two of them sitting beneath the close fierce stars on a summer hilltop while they waited for the hounds to bring the fox back within hearing, or beside a fire in the November or December woods while the dogs worked out a coon's trail along the creek, or fireless in the pitch dark and heavy dew of April mornings while they squatted beneath a turkey-roost. The boy would never question him; Sam did not react to questions. The boy would just wait and then listen and Sam would begin, talking about the old days and the People whom he had not had time ever to know and so could not remember (he did not remember ever having seen his father's face), and in place of whom the other race into which his blood had run supplied him with no substitute.

And as he talked about those old times and those dead and vanished men of another race from either that the boy knew, gradually to the boy those old times would cease to be old times and would become a part of the boy's present, not only as if they had happened yesterday but as if they were still happening, the men who walked through them actually walking in breath and air and casting an actual shadow on the earth they had not quitted. And more: as if some of them had not happened yet but would occur tomorrow, until at last it would seem to the boy that he himself had not come into existence yet, that none of his race nor the other subject race which his people had brought with them into the land had come here yet; that although it had been his grandfather's and then his father's and uncle's and was now his cousin's and someday would be his own land which he and Sam hunted over, their hold upon it actually was as trivial and without reality as the now faded and archaic script in the chancery book in Jefferson which allocated it to them and that it was he, the boy, who was the guest here and Sam Father's voice the mouthpiece of the host.

Until three years ago there had been two of them, the other a full-blood Chickasaw, in a sense even more incredibly lost than Sam Fathers. He called himself Jobaker, as if it were one word. Nobody knew his history at all. He was a hermit, living in a foul little shack at the forks of the creek five miles from the plantation and about that far from any other habitation. He was a market hunter and fisherman and he consorted with nobody, black or white; no negro would even cross his path and no man dared approach his hut except Sam. And perhaps once a month the boy would find them in Sam's shop—two old men squatting on their heels on the dirt floor, talking in a mixture of negroid English and flat hill dialect and now and then a phrase of that old tongue which as time went on and the boy squatted there too listening, he began to learn. Then Jobaker died. That is, nobody had seen him in some time. Then one morning Sam was missing, nobody, not even the boy, knew when nor where, until that night when some negroes hunting in the creek bottom saw the sudden burst of flame and approached. It was Jobaker's hut, but before they got anywhere near it, someone shot at them from the shadows beyond it. It was Sam who fired, but nobody ever found Jobaker's grave.

The next morning, sitting at breakfast with his cousin, the boy saw Sam pass the dining-room window and he remembered then that never in his life before had he seen Sam nearer the house than the blacksmith-shop. He stopped eating even; he sat there and he and his cousin both heard the voices from beyond the pantry door, then the door opened and Sam entered, carrying his hat in his hand but without knocking as anyone else on the place except a house servant would have done, entered just far enough for the door to close behind him and stood looking at neither of them—the Indian face above the nigger clothes, looking at something over their heads or at something not even in the room.

"I want to go," he said. "I want to go to the Big Bottom to live."

"To live?" the boy's cousin said.

"At Major de Spain's and your camp, where you go to hunt," Sam said. "I could take care of it for you all while you aint there. I will build me a little house in the woods, if you rather I didn't stay in the big one."

"What about Isaac here?" his cousin said. "How will you get away from him? Are you going to take him with you?" But still Sam looked at neither of them, standing just inside the room with that face which showed nothing, which showed that he was an old man only when it smiled.

"I want to go," he said. "Let me go."

"Yes," the cousin said quietly. "Of course. I'll fix it with Major de Spain. You want to go soon?"

"I'm going now," Sam said. He went out. And that was all. The boy was nine then; it seemed perfectly natural that nobody, not even his cousin McCaslin, should argue with Sam. Also, since he was nine now, he could understand that Sam could leave him and their days and nights in the woods together without any wrench. He believed that he and Sam both knew that this was not only temporary but that the exigencies of his maturing, of that for which Sam had been training him all his life some day to dedicate himself, required it. They had settled that one night last summer while they listened to the hounds bringing a fox back up the creek valley; now the boy discerned in that very talk under the high, fierce August stars a presage, a warning, of this moment today. "I done taught you all there is of this settled country," Sam said. "You can hunt it good as I can now. You are ready for the Big Bottom now, for bear and deer. Hunter's meat," he said. "Next year you will be ten. You will write your age in two numbers and you will be ready to become a man. Your pa" (Sam always referred to the boy's cousin as his father, establishing even before the boy's orphanhood did that relation between them not of the ward to his guardian and kinsman and chief and head of his blood, but of the child to the man who sired his flesh and his thinking too.) "promised you can go with us then." So the boy could understand Sam's going. But he couldn't understand why now, in March, six months before the moon for hunting.

"If Jobaker's dead like they say," he said, "and Sam hasn't got anybody but us at all kin to him, why does he want to go to the Big Bottom now, when it will be six months before we get there?"

"Maybe that's what he wants," McCaslin said. "Maybe he wants to get away from you a little while."

But that was all right. McCaslin and other grown people often said things like that and he paid no attention to them, just as he paid no attention to Sam saying he wanted to go to the Big Bottom to live. After all, he would have to live there for six months, because there would be no use in going at all if he was going to turn right around and come back. And, as Sam himself had told him, he already knew all about hunting in this settled country that Sam or anybody else could teach him. So it would be all right. Summer, then the bright days after the first frost, then the cold and himself on the wagon with McCaslin this time and the moment would come and he would draw the blood, the big blood which would make him a man, a hunter, and Sam would come back home with them and he too would have outgrown the child's pursuit of rabbits and 'possums. Then he too would make one before the winter fire, talking of the old hunts and the hunts to come as hunters talked.

So Sam departed. He owned so little that he could carry it. He walked. He would neither let McCaslin send him in the wagon, nor take a mule to ride. No one saw him go even. He was just gone one morning, the cabin which had never had very much in it, vacant and empty, the shop in which there never had been very much done, standing idle. Then November came at last, and now the boy made one—himself and his cousin McCaslin and Tennie's Jim, and Major de Spain and General Compson and Walter Ewell and Boon and old Uncle Ash to do the cooking, waiting for them in Jefferson with the other wagon, and the surrey in which he and McCaslin and General Compson and Major de Spain would ride.

Sam was waiting at the camp to meet them. If he was glad to see them, he did not show it. And if, when they broke camp two weeks later to return home, he was sorry to see them go, he did not show that either. Because he did not come back with them. It was only the boy who returned, returning solitary and alone to the settled familiar land, to follow for eleven months the childish business of rabbits and such while he waited to go back, having brought with him, even from his brief first sojourn, an unforgettable sense of the big woods—not a quality dangerous or particularly inimical, but profound, sentient, gigantic and brooding, amid which he had been permitted to go to and fro at will, unscathed, why he knew not, but dwarfed and, until he had drawn honorably blood worthy of being drawn, alien.

Then November, and they would come back. Each morning Sam would take the boy out to the stand allotted him. It would be one of the poorer stands of course, since he was only ten and eleven and twelve and he had never even seen a deer running yet. But they would stand there, Sam a little behind him and without a gun himself, as he had been standing when the boy shot the running rabbit when he was eight years old. They would stand there in the November dawns, and after a while they would hear the dogs. Sometimes the chase would sweep up and past quite close, belling and invisible; once they heard the two heavy reports of Boon Hogganbeck's old gun with which he had never killed anything larger than a squirrel and that sitting, and twice they heard the flat unreverberant clap of Walter Ewell's rifle, following which you did not even wait to hear his horn.

"I'll never get a shot," the boy said. "I'll never kill one."

"Yes you will," Sam said. "You wait. You'll be a hunter. You'll be a man."

But Sam wouldn't come out. They would leave him there. He would come as far as the road where the surrey waited, to take the riding horses back, and that was all. The men would ride the horses and Uncle Ash and Tennie's Jim and the boy would follow in the wagon with Sam, with the camp equipment and the trophies, the meat, the heads, the antlers, the good ones, the wagon winding on among the tremendous gums and cypresses and oaks where no axe save that of the hunter had ever sounded, between the impenetrable walls of cane and brier—the two changing yet constant walls just beyond which the wilderness whose mark he had brought away forever on his spirit even from that first two weeks seemed to lean, stooping a little, watching them and listening, not quite inimical because they were too small, even those such as Walter and Major de Spain and old General Compson who had killed many deer and bear, their sojourn too brief and too harmless to excite to that, but just brooding, secret, tremendous, almost inattentive.

Then they would emerge, they would be out of it, the line as sharp as the demarcation of a doored wall. Suddenly skeleton cotton- and corn-fields would flow away on either hand, gaunt and motionless beneat the gray rain; there would be a house, barns, fences, where the hand of man had clawed for an instant, holding, the wall of the wilderness behind them now, tremendous and still and seemingly impenetrable in the gray and fading light, the very tiny orifice through which they had emerged apparently swallowed up. The surrey would be waiting, his cousin McCaslin and Major de Spain and General Compson and Walter and Boon dismounted beside it. Then Sam would get down from the wagon and mount one of the horses and, with the others on a rope behind him, he would turn back. The boy would watch him for a while against that tall and secret wall, growing smaller and smaller against it, never looking back. Then he would enter it, returning to what the boy believed, and thought that his cousin McCaslin believed, was his loneliness and solitude.

II

So the instant came. He pulled trigger and Sam Fathers marked his face with the hot blood which he had spilled and he ceased to be a child and became a hunter and a man. It was the last day. They broke camp that afternoon and went out, his cousin and Major de Spain and General Compson and Boon on the horses, Walter Ewell and the negroes in the wagon with him and Sam and his hide and antlers. There could have been (and were) other trophies in the wagon. But for him they did not exist, just as for all practical purposes he and Sam Fathers were still alone together as they had been that morning. The wagon wound and jolted between the slow and shifting yet constant walls from beyond and above which the wilderness watched them pass, less than inimical now and never to be inimical again since the buck still and forever leaped, the shaking gun-barrels coming constantly and forever steady at last, crashing, and still out of his instant of immortality the buck sprang, forever immortal;—the wagon jolting and bouncing on, the moment of the buck, the shot, Sam Fathers and himself and the blood with which Sam had marked him forever one with the wilderness which had accepted him since Sam said that he had done all right, when suddenly Sam reined back and stopped the wagon and they all heard the unmistakable and unforgettable sound of a deer breaking cover.

Then Boon shouted from beyond the bend of the trail and while they sat motionless in the halted wagon, Walter and the boy already reaching for their guns, Boon came galloping back, flogging his mule with his hat, his face wild and amazed as he shouted down at them. Then the other riders came around the bend, also spurring.

"Get the dogs!" Boon cried. "Get the dogs! If he had a nub on his head, he had fourteen points! Laying right there by the road in the pawpaw thicket! If I'd a knowed he was there, I could have cut his throat with my pocket knife!"

"Maybe that's why he run," Walter said. "He saw you never had your gun." He was already out of the wagon with his rifle. Then the boy was out too with his gun, and the other riders came up and Boon got off his mule somehow and was scrabbling and clawing among the duffel in the wagon, still shouting, "Get the dogs! Get the dogs!" And it seemed to the boy too that it would take them forever to decide what to do—the old men in whom the blood ran cold and slow, in whom during the intervening years between them and himself the blood had become a different and colder substance from that which ran in him and even in Boon and Walter.

"What about it, Sam?" Major de Spain said. "Could the dogs bring him back?"

"We wont need the dogs," Sam said. "If he dont hear the dogs behind him, he will circle back in here about sundown to bed."

"All right," Major de Spain said. "You boys take the horses. We'll go on out to the road in the wagon and wait there." He and General Compson and McCaslin got into the wagon and Boon and Walter and Sam and the boy mounted the horses and turned back and out of the trail. Sam led them for an hour through the gray and unmarked afternoon whose light was little different from what it had been at dawn and which would become darkness without any graduation between. The Sam stopped them.

"This is far enough," he said. "He'll be coming upwind, and he dont want to smell the mules." They tied the mounts in a thicket. Sam led them on foot now, unpathed through the markless afternoon, the boy pressing close behind him, the two others, or so it seemed to the boy, on his heels. But they were not. Twice Sam turned his head slightly and spoke back to him across his shoulder, still walking: "You got time. We'll get there fore he does."

So he tried to go slower. He tried deliberately to decelerate the dizzy rushing of time in which the buck which he had not even seen was moving, which it seemed to him must be carrying the buck farther and farther and more and more irretrievably away from them even though there were no dogs behind him now to make him run, even though, according to Sam, he must have completed his circle now and was heading back toward them. They went on; it could have been another hour or twice that or less than half, the boy could not have said. Then they were on a ridge. He had never been in here before and he could not see that it was a ridge. He just knew that the earth had risen slightly because the underbrush had thinned a little, the ground sloping invisibly away toward a dense wall of cane. Sam stopped. "This is it," he said. He spoke to Walter and Boon: "Follow this ridge and you will come to two crossings. You will see the tracks. If he crosses, it will be at one of these three."

Walter looked about for a moment. "I know it," he said. "I've even seen your deer. I was in here last Monday. He aint nothing but a yearling."

"A yearling?" Boon said. He was panting from the walking. His face still looked a little wild. "If the one I saw was any yearling, I'm still in kindergarden."

"Then I must have seen a rabbit," Walter said. "I always heard you quit school altogether two years before the first grade."

Boon glared at Walter. "If you dont want to shoot him, get out of the way," he said. "Set down somewhere. By God, I——"

"Aint nobody going to shoot him standing here," Sam said quietly.

"Sam's right," Walter said. He moved, slanting the worn, silver-colored barrel of his rifle downward to walk with it again. "A little more moving and a little more quiet too. Five miles is still Hogganbeck range, even if we wasn't downwind." They went on. The boy could still hear Boon talking, though presently that ceased too. Then once more he and Sam stood motionless together against a tremendous pin oak in a little thicket, and again there was nothing. There was only the soaring and sombre solitude in the dim light, there was the thin murmur of the faint cold rain which had not ceased all day. Then, as if it had waited for them to find their positions and become still, the wilderness breathed again. It seemed to lean inward above them, above himself and Sam and Walter and Boon in their separate lurking-places, tremendous, attentive, impartial and omniscient, the buck moving in it somewhere, not running yet since he had not been pursued, not frightened yet and never fearsome but just alert also as they were alert, perhaps already circling back, perhaps quite near, perhaps conscious also of the eye of the ancient immortal Umpire. Because he was just twelve then, and that morning something had happened to him: in less than a second he had ceased forever to be the child he was yesterday. Or perhaps that made no difference, perhaps even a city-bred man, let alone a child, could not have understood it; perhaps only a country-bred one could comprehend loving the life he spills. He began to shake again.

"I'm glad it's started now," he whispered. He did not move to speak; only his lips shaped the expiring words: "Then it will be gone when I raise the gun——"

Nor did Sam. "Hush," he said.

"Is he that near?" the boy whispered. "Do you think——"

"Hush," Sam said. So he hushed. But he could not stop the shaking. He did not try, because he knew it would go away when he needed the steadiness—had not Sam Fathers already consecrated and absolved him from weakness and regret too?—not from love and pity for all which lived and ran and then ceased to live in a second in the very midst of splendor and speed, but from weakness and regret. So they stood motionless, breathing deep and quiet and steady. If there had been any sun, it would be near to setting now; there was a condensing, a densifying, of what he had thought was the gray and unchanging light until he realised suddenly that it was his own breathing, his heart, his blood —something, all things, and that Sam Fathers had marked him indeed, not as a mere hunter, but with something Sam had had in his turn of his vanished and forgotten people. He stopped breathing then; there was only his heart, his blood, and in the following silence the wilderness ceased to breathe also, leaning, stooping overhead with its breath held, tremendous and impartial and waiting. Then the shaking stopped too, as he had known it would, and he drew back the two heavy hammers of the gun.

Then it had passed. It was over. The solitude did not breathe again yet; it had merely stopped watching him and was looking somewhere else, even turning its back on him, looking on away up the ridge at another point, and the boy knew as well as if he had seen him that the buck had come to the edge of the cane and had either seen or scented them and faded back into it. But the solitude did not breathe again. It should have suspired again then but it did not. It was still facing, watching, what it had been watching and it was not here, not where he and Sam stood; rigid, not breathing himself, he thought, cried *No! No!*, knowing already that it was too late, thinking with the old despair of two and three years ago: *I'll never get a shot.* Then he heard it—the flat single clap of Walter Ewell's rifle which never missed. Then the mellow sound of the horn came down the ridge and something went out of him and he knew then he had never expected to get the shot at all.

"I reckon that's it," he said. "Walter got him." He had raised the gun slightly without knowing it. He lowered it again and had lowered one of the hammers and was already moving out of the thicket when Sam spoke.

"Wait."

"Wait?" the boy cried. And he would remember that—how he turned upon Sam in the truculence of a boy's grief over the missed opportunity, the missed luck. "What for? Dont you hear that horn?"

And he would remember how Sam was standing. Sam had not moved. He was not tall, squat rather and broad, and the boy had been growing fast for the past year or so and there was not much difference between them in height, yet Sam was looking over the boy's head and up the ridge toward the sound of the horn and the boy knew that Sam did not even see him; that Sam knew he was still there beside him but he did not see the boy. Then the boy saw the buck. It was coming down the ridge, as if it were walking out of the very sound of the horn which related its death. It was not running, it was walking, tremendous, unhurried, slanting and tilting its head to pass the antlers through the undergrowth, and the boy standing with Sam beside him now instead of behind him as Sam always stood, and the gun still partly aimed and one of the hammers still cocked.

Then it saw them. And still it did not begin to run. It just stopped for an instant, taller than any man, looking at them; then its muscles suppled, gathered. It did not even alter its course, not fleeing, not even running, just moving with that winged and effortless ease with which deer move, passing within twenty feet of them, its head high and the eye not proud and not haughty but just full and wild and unafraid, and Sam standing beside the boy now, his right arm raised at full length, palm-outward, speaking in that tongue which the boy had learned from listening to him and Joe Baker in the blacksmith shop, while up the ridge Walter Ewell's horn was still blowing them in to a dead buck.

"Oleh, Chief," Sam said. "Grandfather."

When they reached Walter, he was standing with his back toward them, quite still, bemused almost, looking down at his feet. He didn't look up at all.

"Come here, Sam," he said quietly. When they reached him he still did not look up, standing above a little spike buck which had still been a fawn last spring. "He was so little I pretty near let him go," Walter said. "But just look at the track he was making. It's pretty near big as a cow's. If there were any more tracks here besides the ones he is laying in, I would swear there was another buck here that I never even saw."

III

It was dark when they reached the road where the surrey waited. It was turning cold, the rain had stopped, and the sky was beginning to blow clear. His cousin and Major de Spain and General Compson had a fire going. "Did you get him?" Major de Spain said.

"Got a good-sized swamp-rabbit with spike horns," Walter said. He slid the little buck down from his mule. The boy's cousin McCaslin looked at it.

"Nobody saw the big one?" he said.

"I dont even believe Boon saw it," Walter said. "He probably jumped somebody's stray cow in that thicket." Boon started cursing, swearing at Walter and at Sam for not getting the dogs in the first place and at the buck and all.

"Never mind," Major de Spain said. "He'll be here for us next fall. Let's get started home."

It was after midnight when they let Walter out at his gate two miles from Jefferson and later still when they took General Compson to his house and then returned to Major de Spain's, where he and McCaslin would spend the rest of the night, since it was still seventeen miles home. It was cold, the sky was clear now; there would be a heavy frost by sunup and the ground was already frozen beneath the horses' feet and the wheels and beneath their own feet as they crossed Major de Spain's yard and entered the house, the warm dark house, feeling their way up the dark stairs until Major de Spain found a candle and lit it, and into the strange room and the big deep bed, the still cold sheets until they began to warm to their bodies and at last the shaking stopped and suddenly he was telling McCaslin about it while McCaslin listened, quietly until he had finished. "You dont believe it," the boy said. "I know you dont——"

"Why not?" McCaslin said. "Think of all that has happened here, on this earth. All the blood hot and strong for living, pleasuring, that has soaked back into it. For grieving and suffering too, of course, but still getting something out of it for all that, getting a lot out of it, because after all you dont have to continue to bear what you believe is suffering; you can always choose to stop that, put an end to that. And even suffering and grieving is better than nothing; there is only one thing worse than not being alive, and that's shame. But you cant be alive forever, and you always wear out life long before you have exhausted the possibilities of living. And all that must be somewhere; all that could not have been invented and created just to be thrown away. And the earth is shallow; there is not a great deal of it before you come to the rock. And the earth dont want to just keep things, hoard them; it wants to use them again. Look at the seed, the acorns, at what happens even to carrion when you try to bury it: it refuses too, seethes and struggles too until it reaches light and air again, hunting the sun still. And they—" the boy saw his hand in silhouette for a moment against the window beyond which, accustomed to the darkness now, he could see sky where the scoured and icy stars glittered "—they dont want it, need it. Besides, what would it want, itself, knocking around out there, when it never had enough time about the earth as it was, when there is plenty of room about the earth, plenty of places still unchanged from what they were when the blood used and pleasured in them while it was still blood?"

"But we want them," the boy said. "We want them too. There is plenty of room for us and them too."

"That's right," McCaslin said. "Suppose they don't have substance, cant cast a shadow——"

"But I saw it!" the boy cried. "I saw him!"

"Steady" McCaslin said. For an instant his hand touched the boy's flank beneath the covers. "Steady. I know you did. So did I. Sam took me in there once after I killed my first deer."

RALPH ELLISON

Ralph Waldo Ellison was born in Oklahoma City in 1914. He is the only writer among the six included here who is still living, and the only one of African descent. It is presumptuous to write a biographical sketch of a living author, and in this case most of the important biographical material can be found in his own essays printed below. Ellison's first novel Invisible Man, *was published in 1952 and received the National Book Award for that year. In the nearly twenty years since then its reputation has grown steadily, while many another award winner has been forgotten. In 1964 Ellison's collection of essays,* Shadow and Act, *was published. Both books are available in Signet editions.*

Brave Words for a Startling Occasion

This essay was first given as Ellison's acceptance speech for the National Book Award. It is among those collected in Shadow and Act.

First, as I express my gratitude for this honor which you have bestowed on me, let me say that I take it that you are rewarding my efforts rather than my not quite fully achieved attempt at a major novel. Indeed, if I were asked in all seriousness just what I considered to be the chief significance of *Invisible Man* as a fiction, I would reply: Its experimental attitude, and its attempt to return to the mood of personal moral responsibility for democracy which typified the best of our nineteenth-century fiction. That my first novel should win this most coveted prize must certainly indicate that there is a crisis in the American novel. You as critics have told us so, and current fiction sales would indicate that the reading public agrees. Certainly the younger novelists concur. The explosive nature of events mocks our brightest efforts. And the very "facts" which the naturalists assumed would make us free have lost the power to protect us from despair. Controversy now rages over just what aspects of American experience are suitable for novelistic treatment. The prestige of the theorists of the so-called novel of manners has been challenged. Thus after a long period of stability we find our assumptions concerning the novel being called into question. And though I was only vaguely aware, it was this growing crisis which shaped the writing of *Invisible Man*.

After the usual apprenticeship of imitation and seeking with delight to examine my experience through the discipline of the novel, I became gradually aware that the forms of so many of the works which impressed me were too restricted to contain the experience which I knew. The diversity of American life with its extreme fluidity and openness seemed too vital and alive to be caught for more than the briefest instant in the tight well-made Jamesian novel, which was, for all its artistic perfection, too concerned with "good taste" and stable areas. Nor could I safely use the forms of the "hard-boiled" novel, with its dedication to physical violence, social cynicism and understatement. Understatement depends, after all, upon commonly held assumptions and my minority status rendered all such assumptions questionable. There was also a problem of language, and even dialogue, which, with its hard-boiled stance and its monosyllabic utterance, is one of the shining achievements of twentieth-century American writing. For despite the notion that its rhythms were those of everyday speech, I found that when compared with the rich babel of idiomatic expression around me, a language full of imagery and gesture and rhetorical canniness, it was embarrassingly austere. Our speech I found resounding with an alive language swirling with over three hundred years of American living, a mixture of the folk, the Biblical, the scientific and the political. Slangy in one instance, academic in another, loaded poetically with imagery at one moment, mathematically bare of imagery in the next. As for the rather rigid concepts of reality which informed a number of the works which impressed me and to which I owe a great deal, I was forced to conclude that reality was far more mysterious and uncertain, and more exciting, and still, despite its raw violence and capriciousness, more promising. To attempt to express that American experience which has carried one back and forth and up and down the land and across, and across again the great river, from freight train to Pullman car, from contact with slavery to contact with a world of advanced scholarship, art and science, is simply to burst such neatly understated forms of the novel asunder.

A novel whose range was both broader and deeper was needed. And in my search I found myself turning to our classical nineteenth-century novelists. I felt that except for the work of William Faulkner something vital had gone out of American prose after Mark Twain. I came to believe that the writers of that period took a much greater responsibility for the condition of democracy and, indeed, their works were imaginative projections of the conflicts within the human heart which arose when the sacred principles of the Constitution and the Bill of Rights clashed with the practical exigencies of human greed and fear, hate and love. Naturally I was attracted to these writers as a Negro. Whatever they thought of my people per se, in their imaginative economy the Negro symbolized both the man lowest down and the mysterious, underground aspect of human personality. In a sense the Negro was the gauge of the human condition as it waxed and waned in our democracy. These writers were willing to confront the broad complexities of American life and we are the richer for their having done so.

Thus to see America with an awareness of its rich diversity and its almost magical fluidity and freedom, I was forced to conceive of a novel unburdened by the narrow naturalism which has led, after so many triumphs, to the final and unrelieved despair which marks so much of our current fiction. I was to dream of a prose which was flexible, and swift as American change is swift, confronting the inequalities and brutalities of our society forthrightly, but yet thrusting forth its images of hope, human fraternity and individual self-realization. It would use the richness of our speech, the idiomatic expression and the rhetorical flourishes from past periods which are still alive among us. And despite my personal failures, there must be possible a fiction which, leaving sociology to the scientists, can arrive at the truth about the human condition, here and now, with all the bright magic of a fairy tale.

What has been missing from so much experimental writing has been the passionate will to dominate reality as well as the laws of art. This will is the true source of the experimental attitude. We who struggle with form and with America should remember Eidothea's advice to Menelaus when in the *Odyssey* he and his friends are seeking their way home. She tells him to seize her father, Proteus, and to hold him fast "however he may struggle and fight. He will turn into all sorts of shapes to try you," she says, "into all the creatures that live and move upon the earth, into water, into blazing fire; but you must hold him fast and press him all the harder. When he is himself, and questions you in the same shape that he was when you saw him in his bed, let the old man go; and then, sir, ask which god it is who is angry, and how you shall make your way homewards over the fish-giving sea."

For the novelist, Proteus stands for both America and the inheritance of illusion through which all men must fight to achieve reality; the offended god stands for our sins against those principles we all hold sacred. The way home we seek is that condition of man's being at home in the world, which is called love, and which we term democracy. Our task then is always to challenge the apparent forms of reality—that is, the fixed manners and values of the few, and to struggle with it until it reveals its mad, vari-implicated chaos, its false faces, and on until it surrenders its insight, its truth. We are fortunate as American writers in that with our variety of racial and national traditions, idioms and manners, we are yet one. On its profoundest level American experience is of a whole. Its truth lies in its diversity and swiftness of change. Through forging forms of the novel worthy of it, we achieve not only the promise of our lives, but we anticipate the resolution of those world problems of humanity which for a moment seem to those who are in awe of statistics completely insoluble.

Whenever we as Americans have faced serious crises we have returned to fundamentals; this, in brief, is what I have tried to do.

Hidden Name and Complex Fate

This essay was given as a talk at the Library of Congress in 1964 before its appearance in Shadow and Act.

A WRITER'S EXPERIENCE IN THE UNITED STATES

In *Green Hills of Africa* Ernest Hemingway reminds us that both Tolstoy and Stendhal had seen war, that Flaubert had seen a revolution and the Commune, that Dostoievsky had been sent to Siberia and that such experiences were important in shaping the art of these great masters. And he goes on to observe that "writers are forged in injustice as a sword is forged." He declined to describe the many personal forms which injustice may take in this chaotic world—who would be so mad as to try?—nor does he go into the personal wounds which each of these writers sustained. Now, however, thanks to his brother and sister, we do know something of the injustice in which he himself was forged, and this knowledge has been added to what we have long known of Hemingway's artistic temper.

In the end, however, it is the quality of his art which is primary. It is the art which allows the wars and revolutions which he knew, and the personal and social injustice which he suffered, to lay claims upon our attention; for it was through his art that they achieved their most enduring meaning. It is a matter of outrageous irony, perhaps, but in literature the great social clashes of history no less than the painful experience of the individual are secondary to the meaning which they take on through the skill, the talent, the imagination and personal vision of the writer who transforms them into art. Here they are reduced to more manageable proportions; here they are imbued with humane values; here, injustice and catastrophe become less important in themselves than what the writer makes of them. This is *not* true, however, of the writer's struggle with that recalcitrant angel called Art; and it was through *this* specific struggle that Ernest Hemingway became *Hemingway* (now refined to a total body of transcendent work, after forty years of being endlessly dismembered and resurrected, as it continues to be, in the styles, the themes, the sense of life and literature of countless other writers). And it was through this struggle with form that he became the master, the culture hero, whom we have come to know and admire.

It was suggested that it might be of interest if I discussed here this evening some of my notions of the writer's experience in the United States, hence I have evoked the name of Hemingway, not by way of inviting farfetched comparisons but in order to establish a perspective, a set of assumptions from which I may speak, and in an attempt to avoid boring you by emphasizing those details of racial hardship which for some forty years now have been evoked whenever writers of my own cultural background have essayed their experience in public.

I do this *not* by way of denying totally the validity of these by now stylized recitals, for I have shared and still share many of their detailed injustices—what Negro can escape them?—but by way of suggesting that they are, at least in a discussion of a writer's experience, as *writer*, as artist, somewhat beside the point.

For we select neither our parents, our race nor our nation; these occur to us out of the love, the hate, the circumstances, the fate, of others. But we *do* become writers out of an act of will, out of an act of choice; a dim, confused and ofttimes regrettable choice, perhaps, but choice nevertheless. And what happens therefore causes all those experiences which occurred before we began to function as writers to take on a special quality of uniqueness. If this does not happen then as far as writing goes, the experiences have been misused. If we do not make of them a value, if we do not transform them into forms and images of meaning which they did not possess before, then we have failed as artists.

Thus for a writer to insist that his personal suffering is of special interest in itself, or simply because he belongs to a particular racial or religious group, is to advance a claim for special privileges which members of his group who are not writers would be ashamed to demand. The kindest judgment one can make of this point of view is that it reveals a sad misunderstanding of the relationship between suffering and art. Thomas Mann and André Gide have told us much of this and there are critics, like Edmund Wilson, who have told of the connection between the wound and the bow.

As I see it, it is through the process of making artistic forms—plays, poems, novels—out of one's experience that one becomes a writer, and it is through this process, this struggle, that the writer helps give meaning to the experience of the group. And it is the process of mastering the discipline, the techniques, the fortitude, the culture, through which this is made possible that constitutes the writer's real experience as *writer*, as artist. If this sounds like an argument for the artist's withdrawal from social struggles, I would recall to you W. H. Auden's comment to the effect that:

> In our age, the mere making of a work of art is itself a political act. So long as artists exist, making what they please, and think they ought to make, even if it is not terribly good, even if it appeals to only a handful of people, they remind the Management of something managers need to be reminded of, namely, that the managed are people with faces, not anonymous members, that *Homo Laborans* is also *Homo Ludens*. . . .

Without doubt, even the most *engagé* writer—and I refer to true artists, not to artists *manqués*—begin their careers in play and puzzlement, in dreaming over the details of the world in which they become conscious of themselves.

Let Tar Baby, that enigmatic figure from Negro folklore, stand for the world. He leans, black and gleaming, against the wall of life utterly noncommittal under our scrutiny, our questioning, starkly unmoving before our naïve attempts at intimidation. Then we touch him playfully and before we can say *Sonny Liston!* we find ourselves stuck. Our playful investigations become a labor, a fearful struggle, an *agon*. Slowly we perceive that our task is to learn the proper way of freeing ourselves to develop, in other words, technique.

Sensing this, we give him our sharpest attention, we question him carefully, we struggle with more subtlety; while he, in his silent way, holds on, demanding that we perceive the necessity of calling him by his true name as the price of our freedom. It is unfortunate that he has so many, many "true names"—all spelling chaos; and in order to discover even one of these we must first come into the possession of our own names. For it is through our names that we first place ourselves in the world. Our names, being the gift of others, must be made our own.

Once while listening to the play of a two-year-old girl who did not know she was under observation, I heard her saying over and over again, at first with questioning and then with sounds of growing satisfaction, "I am Mimi Livisay? . . . *I* am Mimi Livisay. I *am* Mimi Livisay . . . I am *Mimi* Li-vi-say! I am Mimi . . ."

And in deed and in fact she was—or became so soon thereafter, by working playfully to establish the unit between herself and her name.

For many of us this is far from easy. We must learn to wear our names within all the noise and confusion of the environment in which we find ourselves; make them the center of all of our associations with the world, with man and with nature. We must charge them with all our emotions, our hopes, hates, loves, aspirations. They must become our masks and our shields and the containers of all those values and traditions which we learn and/or imagine as being the meaning of our familial past.

And when we are reminded so constantly that we bear, as Negroes, names originally possessed by those who owned our enslaved grandparents, we are apt, especially if we are potential writers, to be more than ordinarily concerned with the veiled and mysterious events, the fusions of blood, the furtive couplings, the business transactions, the violations of faith and loyalty, the assaults; yes, and the unrecognized and unrecognizable loves through which our names were handed down unto us.

So charged with emotion does this concern become for some of us, that we have, earlier, the example of the followers of Father Divine and, now, the Black Muslims, discarding their original names in rejection of the bloodstained, the brutal, the sinful images of the past. Thus they would declare new identities, would clarify a new program of intention and destroy the verbal evidence of a willed and ritualized discontinuity of blood and human intercourse.

Not all of us, actually only a few, seek to deal with our names in this manner. We take what we have and make of them what we can. And there are even those who know where the old broken connections lie, who recognize their relatives across the chasm of historical denial and the artificial barriers of society, and who see themselves as bearers of many of the qualities which were admirable in the original sources of their common line (Faulkner has made much of this); and I speak here not of mere forgiveness, nor of obsequious insensitivity to the outrages symbolized by the denial and the division, but of the conscious acceptance of the harsh realities of the human condition, of the ambiguities and hypocrisies of human history as they have played themselves out in the United States.

Perhaps, taken in aggregate, these European names which (sometimes with irony, sometimes with pride, but always with personal investment) represent a certain triumph of the spirit, speaking to us of those who rallied, reassembled and transformed themselves and who under dismembering pressures refused to die. "Brothers and sisters," I once heard a Negro preacher exhort, "let us make up our faces before the world, and our names shall sound throughout the land with honor! For we ourselves are our *true* names, not their epithets! So let us, I say, Make Up Our Faces and Our Minds!"

Perhaps my preacher had read T. S. Eliot, although I doubt it. And in actuality, it was unnecessary that he do so, for a concern with names and naming was very much part of that special area of American culture from which I come, and it is precisely for this reason that this example should come to mind in a discussion of my own experience as a writer.

Undoubtedly, writers begin their *conditioning* as manipulators of words long before they become aware of literature—certain Freudians would say at the breast. Perhaps. But if so, that is far too early to be of use at this moment. Of this, though, I am certain: that despite the misconceptions of those educators who trace the reading difficulties experienced by large numbers of Negro children in Northern schools to their Southern background, these children are, in *their* familiar South, facile manipulators of words. I know, too, that the Negro community is deadly in its ability to create nicknames and to spot all that is ludicrous in an unlikely name or that which is incongruous in conduct. Names are not qualities; nor are words, in their particular sense, actions. To assume that they are could cost one his life many times a day. Language skills depend to a large extent upon a knowledge of the details, the manners, the objects, the folkways, the psychological patterns, of a given environment. Humor and wit depend upon much the same awareness, and so does the suggestive power of names.

"A small brown bowlegged Negro with the name 'Franklin D. Roosevelt Jones' might sound like a clown to someone who looks at him from the outside," said my friend Albert Murray, "but on the other hand he just might turn out to be a hell of a fireside operator. He might just lie back in all of that comic juxtaposition of names and manipulate you deaf, dumb and blind—and you not even suspecting it, because you're thrown out of stance by his name! There you are, so dazzled by the F.D.R. image—which you *know* you can't see—and so delighted with your own superior position that you don't realize that it's *Jones* who must be confronted."

Well, as you must suspect, all of this speculation on the matter of names has a purpose, and now, because it is tied up so ironically with my own experience as a writer, I must turn to my own name.

For in the dim beginnings, before I ever thought consciously of writing, there was my own name, and there was, doubtless, a certain magic in it. From the start I was uncomfortable with it, and in my earliest years it caused me much puzzlement. Neither could I understand what a poet was, nor why, exactly, my father had chosen to name me after one. Perhaps I could have understood it perfectly well had he named me after his own father, but that name had been given to an older brother who died and thus was out of the question. But why hadn't he named me after a hero, such as Jack Johnson, or a soldier like Colonel Charles Young, or a great seaman like Admiral Dewey, or an educator like Booker T. Washington, or a great orator and abolitionist like Frederick Douglass? Or again, why hadn't he named me (as so many Negro parents had done) after President Teddy Roosevelt?

Instead, he named me after someone called Ralph Waldo Emerson, and then, when I was three, he died. It was too early for me to have understood his choice, although I'm sure he must have explained it many times, and it was also too soon for me to have made the connection between my name and my father's love for reading. Much later, after I began to write and work with words, I came to suspect that he was aware of the suggestive powers of names and of the magic involved in naming.

I recall an odd conversation with my mother during my early teens in which she mentioned their interest in, of all things, prenatal culture! But for a long time I actually knew only that my father read a lot, and that he admired this remote Mr. Emerson, who was something called a "poet and philosopher"—so much so that he named his second son after him.

I knew, also, that whatever his motives, the combination of names he'd given me caused me no end of trouble from the moment when I could talk well enough to respond to the ritualized question which grownups put to very young children. Emerson's name was quite familiar to Negroes in Oklahoma during those days when World War I was brewing, and adults, eager to show off their knowledge of literary figures, and obviously amused by the joke implicit in such a small brown nubbin of a boy carrying around such a heavy moniker, would invariably repeat my first two names and then to my great annoyance, they'd add "Emerson."

And I, in my confusion, would reply, "No, *no*, I'm not Emerson, he's the little boy who lives next door." Which only made them laugh all the louder. "Oh no," they'd say, "*you're* Ralph Waldo Emerson," while I had fantasies of blue murder.

For a while the presence next door of my little friend, Emerson, made it unnecessary for me to puzzle too often over this peculiar adult confusion. And since there were other Negro boys named Ralph in the city, I came to suspect that there was something about the combination of names which produced their laughter. Even today I know of only one other Ralph who had as much comedy made out of his name, a campus politician and deep-voiced orator whom I knew at Tuskegee, who was called in friendly ribbing, *Ralph Waldo Emerson Edgar Allan Poe*, spelled Powe. This must have been quite a trial for him, but I had been initiated much earlier.

During my early school years the name continued to puzzle me, for it constantly evoked in the faces of others some secret. It was as though I possessed some treasure or some defect, which was invisible to my own eyes and ears; something which I had but did not *possess*, like a piece of property in South Carolina, which was mine but which I could not have until some future time. I recall finding, about this time, while seeking adventure in back alleys—which possess for boys a superiority over playgrounds like that which kitchen utensils possess over toys designed for infants—a large photographic lens. I remember nothing of its optical qualities, of its speed or color correction, but it gleamed with crystal mystery and it was beautiful.

Mounted handsomely in a tube of shiny brass, it spoke to me of distant worlds of possibility. I played with it, looking through it with squinted eyes, holding it in shafts of sunlight, and tried to use it for a magic lantern. But most of this was as unrewarding as my attempts to make the music come from a phonograph record by holding the needle in my fingers.

I could burn holes through newspapers with it, or I could pretend that it was a telescope, the barrel of a cannon, or the third eye of a monster—*I* being the monster—but I could do nothing at all about its proper function of making images, nothing to make it yield its secret. But I could not discard it.

Older boys sought to get it away from me by offering knives or tops, agate marbles or whole zoos of grass snakes and horned toads in trade, but I held on to it. No one, not even the white boys I knew, had such a lens, and it was my own good luck to have found it. Thus I would hold on to it until such time as I could acquire the parts needed to make it function. Finally I put it aside and it remained buried in my box of treasures, dusty and dull, to be lost and forgotten as I grew older and became interested in music.

I had reached by now the grades where it was necessary to learn something about Mr. Emerson and what he had written, such as the "Concord Hymn" and the essay "Self-Reliance," and in following his advice, I reduced the "Waldo" to a simple and, I hoped, mysterious "W," and in my own reading I avoided his works like the plague. I could no more deal with my name—I shall never really master it—than I could find a creative use for my lens. Fortunately there were other problems to occupy my mind. Not that I forgot my fascination with names, but more about that later.

Negro Oklahoma City was starkly lacking in writers. In fact, there was only Roscoe Dungee, the editor of the local Negro newspaper and a very fine editorialist in that valuable tradition of personal journalism which is now rapidly disappearing; a writer who in his emphasis upon the possibilities for justice offered by the Constitution anticipated the anti-segregation struggle by decades. There were also a few reporters who drifted in and out, but these were about all. On the level of *conscious* culture the Negro community was biased in the direction of music.

These were the middle and late twenties, remember, and the state was still a new frontier state. The capital city was one of the great centers for southwestern jazz, along with Dallas and Kansas City. Orchestras which were to become famous within a few years were constantly coming and going. As were the blues singers—Ma Rainey and Ida Cox, and the old bands like that of King Oliver. But best of all, thanks to Mrs. Zelia N. Breaux, there was an active and enthusiastic school music program through which any child who had the interest and the talent could learn to play an instrument and take part in the band, the orchestra, the brass quartet. And there was a yearly operetta and a chorus and a glee club. Harmony was taught for four years and the music appreciation program was imperative. European folk dances were taught throughout the Negro school system, and we were also taught complicated patterns of military drill.

I tell you this to point out that although there were no incentives to write, there was ample opportunity to receive an artistic discipline. Indeed, once one picked up an instrument it was difficult to escape. If you chafed at the many rehearsals of the school band or orchestra and were drawn to the many small jazz groups, you were likely to discover that the jazzmen were apt to rehearse far more than the school band, it was only that they seemed to enjoy themselves better and to possess a freedom of imagination which we were denied at school. And one soon learned that the wild, transcendent moments which occurred at dances or "battles of music," moments in which memorable improvisations were ignited, depended upon a dedication to a discipline which was observed even when rehearsals had to take place in the crowded quarters of Halley Richardson's shoeshine parlor. It was not the place which counted, although a large hall with good acoustics was preferred, but what one did to perfect one's performance.

If this talk of musical discipline gives the impression that there were no forces working to nourish one who would one day blunder, after many a twist and turn, into writing, I am misleading you. And here I might give you a longish lecture on the Ironies and Uses of Segregation. When I was a small child there was no library for Negroes in our city, and not until a Negro minister invaded the main library did we get one. For it was discovered that there was no law, only custom, which held that we could not use these public facilities. The results were the quick renting of two large rooms in a Negro office building (the recent site of a pool hall), the hiring of a young Negro librarian, the installation of shelves and a hurried stocking of the walls with any and every book possible. It was, in those first days, something of a literary chaos.

But how fortunate for a boy who loved to read! I started with the fairy tales and quickly went through the junior fiction; then through the Westerns and the detective novels, and very soon I was reading the classics—only I didn't know it. There were also the Haldeman Julius Blue Books, which seem to have floated on the air down from Girard, Kansas; the syndicated columns of O. O. McIntyre, and the copies of *Vanity Fair* and the *Literary Digest* which my mother brought home from work—how could I ever join uncritically in the heavy-handed attacks on the so-called Big Media which have become so common today?

There were also the pulp magazines and, more important, that other library which I visited when I went to help my adopted grandfather, J. D. Randolph (my parents had been living in his rooming house when I was born), at his work as custodian of the law library of the Oklahoma State Capitol. Mr. Randolph had been one of the first teachers in what became Oklahoma City, and he'd also been one of the leaders of a group who walked from Gallatin, Tennessee, to the Oklahoma Territory. He was a tall man, as brown as smoked leather, who looked like the Indians with whom he'd herded horses in the early days.

And while his status was merely the custodian of the law library, I was to see the white legislators come down on many occasions to question him on points of law, and often I was to hear him answer without recourse to the uniform rows of books on the shelves. This was a thing to marvel at in itself, and the white lawmakers did so, but even more marvelous, ironic, intriguing, haunting—call it what you will—is the fact that the Negro who knew the answers was named after Jefferson Davis. What Tennessee lost, Oklahoma was to gain, and after gaining it (a gift of courage, intelligence, fortitude and grace), used it only in concealment and, one hopes, with embarrassment.

So, let us, I say, make up our faces and our minds!

In the loosely structured community of that time, knowledge, news of other ways of living, ancient wisdom, the latest literary fads, hate literature—for years I kept a card warning Negroes away from the polls, which had been dropped by the thousands from a plane which circled over the Negro community—information of all kinds, found its level, catch-as-catch can, in the minds of those who were receptive to it. Not that there was no conscious structuring—I read my first Shaw and Maupassant, my first Harvard Classics in the home of a friend whose parents were products of that stream of New England education which had been brought to Negroes by the young and enthusiastic white teachers who staffed the schools set up for the freedmen after the Civil War. These parents were both teachers and there were others like them in our town.

But the places where a rich oral literature was truly functional were the churches, the schoolyards, the barbershops, the cotton-picking camps; places where folklore and gossip thrived. The drug store where I worked was such a place, where on days of bad weather the older men would sit with their pipes and tell tall tales, hunting yarns and homely versions of the classics. It was here that I heard stories of searching for buried treasure and of headless horsemen, which I was told were my own father's versions told long before. There were even recitals of popular verse, "The Shooting of Dan McGrew," and, along with these, stories of Jesse James, of Negro outlaws and black United States marshals, of slaves who became the chiefs of Indian tribes and of the exploits of Negro cowboys. There was both truth and fantasy in this, intermingled in the mysterious fashion of literature.

Writers, in their formative period, absorb into their consciousness much that has no special value until much later, and often much which is of no special value even then—perhaps, beyond the fact that it throbs with affect and mystery and in it "time and pain and royalty in the blood" are suspended in imagery. So, long before I thought of writing, I was claimed by weather, by speech rhythms, by Negro voices and their different idioms, by husky male voices and by the high shrill singing voices of certain Negro women, by music, by tight spaces and by wide spaces in which the eyes could wander, by death, by newly born babies, by manners of various kinds, company manners and street manners, the manners of white society and those of our own high society, and by interracial manners; by street fights, circuses and minstrel shows, by vaudeville and moving pictures, by prize fights and foot races, baseball games and football matches. By spring floods and blizzards, catalpa worms and jack rabbits, honeysuckle and snapdragons (which smelled like old cigar butts); by sunflowers and hollyhocks, raw sugar cane and baked yams; pigs' feet, chili and blue haw ice cream. By parades, public dances and jam sessions, Easter sunrise ceremonies and large funerals. By contests between fire-and-brimstone preachers and by presiding elders who got "laughing-happy" when moved by the spirit of God.

I was impressed by expert players of the "dozens" and certain notorious bootleggers of corn whiskey. By jazz musicians and fortune-tellers and by men who did anything well; by strange sicknesses and by interesting brick or razor scars; by expert cursing vocabularies as well as by exalted praying and terrifying shouting, and by transcendent playing or singing of the blues. I was fascinated by old ladies, those who had seen slavery and those who were defiant of white folk and black alike; by the enticing walks of prostitutes and by the limping walks affected by Negro hustlers, especially those who wore Stetson hats, expensive shoes with well-starched overalls, usually with a diamond stickpin (when not in hock) in their tieless collars as their gambling uniforms.

And there were the blind men who preached on corners, and the blind men who sang the blues to the accompaniment of washboard and guitar; and the white junkmen who sang mountain music and the famous hucksters of fruit and vegetables.

And there was the Indian-Negro confusion. There were Negroes who were part Indian and who lived on reservations, and Indians who had children who lived in towns as Negroes, and Negroes who were Indians and traveled back and forth between the groups with no trouble. And Indians who were wild as wild Negroes and others who were as solid and steady as bankers. There were the teachers, too, inspiring teachers and villainous teachers who chased after the girl students, and certain female teachers who one wished would chase after young male students. And a handsome old principal of military bearing who had been blemished by his classmates at West Point when they discovered on the eve of the graduation that he was a Negro. There were certain Jews, Mexicans, Chinese cooks, a German orchestra conductor and an English grocer who owned a Franklin touring car. And certain Negro mechanics—"Cadillac Slim," "Sticks" Walker, Buddy Bunn and Oscar Pitman—who had so assimilated the automobile that they seemed to be behind a steering wheel even as they walked the streets or danced with girls. And there were the whites who despised us and the others who shared our hardships and joys.

There is much more, but this is sufficient to indicate some of what was present even in a segregated community to form the background of my work, my sense of life.

And now comes the next step. I went to Tuskegee to study music, hoping to become a composer of symphonies and there, during my second year, I read *The Waste Land* and that, although I was then unaware of it, was the real transition to writing.

Mrs. L. C. McFarland had taught us much of Negro history in grade school and from her I'd learned of the New Negro Movement of the twenties, of Langston Hughes, Countee Cullen, Claude McKay, James Weldon Johnson and the others. They had inspired pride and had given me a closer identification with poetry (by now, oddly enough, I seldom thought of my hidden name), but with music so much on my mind it never occurred to me to try to imitate them. Still I read their work and was excited by the glamour of the Harlem which emerged from their poems and it was good to know that there were Negro writers.—Then came *The Waste Land.*

I was much more under the spell of literature than I realized at the time. *Wuthering Heights* had caused me an agony of unexpressible emotion and the same was true of *Jude the Obscure*, but *The Waste Land* seized my mind. I was intrigued by its power to move me while eluding my understanding. Somehow its rhythms were often closer to those of jazz than were those of the Negro poets, and even though I could not understand then, its range of allusion was as mixed and as varied as that of Louis Armstrong. Yet there were its discontinuities, its changes of pace and its hidden system of organization which escaped me.

There was nothing to do but look up the references in the footnotes to the poem, and thus began my conscious education in literature.

For this, the library at Tuskegee was quite adequate and I used it. Soon I was reading a whole range of subjects drawn upon by the poet, and this led, in turn, to criticism and to Pound and Ford Madox Ford, Sherwood Anderson and Getrude Stein, Hemingway and Fitzgerald and "round about 'til I was come" back to Melville and Twain —the writers who are taught and doubtlessly overtaught today. Perhaps it was my good luck that they were not taught at Tuskegee, I wouldn't know. But at the time I was playing, having an intellectually interesting good time.

Having given so much attention to the techniques of music, the process of learning something of the craft and intention of modern poetry and fiction seemed quite familiar. Besides, it was absolutely painless because it involved no deadlines or credits. Even then, however, a process which I described earlier had begun to operate. The more I learned of literature in this conscious way, the more the details of my background became transformed. I heard undertones in remembered conversations which had escaped me before, local customs took on a more universal meaning, values which I hadn't understood were revealed; some of the people whom I had known were diminished while others were elevated in stature. More important, I began to see my own possibilities with more objective, and in some ways, more hopeful eyes.

The following summer I went to New York seeking work, which I did not find, and remained there, but the personal transformation continued. Reading had become a conscious process of growth and discovery, a method of reordering the world. And that world had widened considerably.

At Tuskegee I had handled manuscripts which Prokofiev had given to Hazel Harrison, a Negro concert pianist who taught there and who had known him in Europe, and through Miss Harrison I had become aware of Prokofiev's symphonies. I had also become aware of the radical movement in politics and art, and in New York had begun reading the work of André Malraux, not only the fiction but chapters published from his *Psychology of Art.* And in my search for an expression of modern sensibility in the works of Negro writers I discovered Richard Wright. Shortly thereafter I was to meet Wright, and it was at his suggestion that I wrote both my first book review and my first short story. These were fatal suggestions.

For although I had tried my hand at poetry while at Tuskegee, it hadn't occurred to me that I might write fiction, but once he suggested it, it seemed the most natural thing to try. Fortunately for me, Wright, then on the verge of his first success, was eager to talk with a beginner and I was able to save valuable time in searching out those works in which writing was discussed as a craft. He guided me to Henry James' prefaces, to Conrad, to Joseph Warren Beach and to the letters of Dostoievsky. There were other advisers and other books involved, of course, but what is important here is that I was consciously concerned with the art of fiction, that almost from the beginning I was grappling quite consciously with the art through which I wished to realize myself. And this was not done in isolation; the Spanish Civil War was now in progress and the Depression was still on. The world was being shaken up, and through one of those odd instances which occur to young provincials in New York, I was to hear Malraux make an appeal for the Spanish Loyalists at the same party where I first heard the folk singer Leadbelly perform. Wright and I were there seeking money for the magazine which he had come to New York to edit.

Art and politics; a great French novelist and a Negro folk singer; a young writer who was soon to publish *Uncle Tom's Children;* and I who had barely begun to study his craft. It is such accidents, such fortuitous meetings, which count for so much in our lives. I had never dreamed that I would be in the presence of Malraux, of whose work I became aware on my second day in Harlem when Langston Hughes suggested that I read *Man's Fate* and *Days of Wrath* before returning them to a friend of his. And it is this fortuitous circumstance which led to my selecting Malraux as a literary "ancestor," whom, unlike a relative, the artist is permitted to choose. There was in progress at the time all the agitation over the Scottsboro boys and the Herndon Case, and I was aware of both. I had to be; I myself had been taken off a freight train at Decatur, Alabama, only three years before while on my way to Tuskegee. But while I joined in the agitation for their release, my main energies went into learning to write.

I began to publish enough, and not too slowly, to justify my hopes for success, and as I continued, I made a most perplexing discovery; namely, that for all his conscious concern with technique, a writer did not so much create the novel as he was created *by* the novel. That is, one did not make an arbitrary gesture when one sought to write. And when I say that the novelist is created by the novel, I mean to remind you that fictional techniques are not a mere set of objective tools, but something much more intimate: a way of feeling, of seeing and of expressing one's sense of life. And the process of *acquiring* technique is a process of modifying one's responses, of learning to see and feel, to hear and observe, to evoke and evaluate the images of memory and of summoning up and directing the imagination; of learning to conceive of human values in the ways which have been established by the great writers who have developed and extended the art. And perhaps the writer's greatest freedom, as artist, lies precisely in his possession of technique; for it is through technique that he comes to possess and express the meaning of his life.

Perhaps at this point it would be useful to recapitulate the route—perhaps as mazelike as those of *Finnegans Wake*—which I have been trying to describe, that which leads from the writer's discovery of a sense of purpose, which is that of becoming a writer, and then the involvement in the passionate struggle required to master a bit of technique, and then, as this begins to take shape, the disconcerting discovery that it is *technique* which transforms the individual before he is able in turn to transform it. And in that personal transformation he discovers something else: he discovers that he has taken on certain obligations, that he must not embarrass his choosen forms, and that in order to avoid this he must develop taste. He learns—and this is most discouraging—that he is involved with values which turn in their *own* way, and not in the ways of politics, upon the central issues affecting his nation and his time. He learns that the American novel, from its first consciousness of itself as a literary form, has grappled with the meaning of the American experience, that it has been aware and has sought to define the nature of that experience by addressing itself to the specific details, the moods, the landscapes, the cityscapes, the tempo of American change. And that it has borne, at its best, the full weight of that burden of conscience and consciousness which Americans inherit as one of the results of the revolutionary circumstances of our national beginnings.

We began as a nation not through the accidents of race or religion or geography (Robert Penn Warren has dwelled on these circumstances) but when a group of men, *some* of them political philosophers, put down, upon what we now recognize as being quite sacred papers, their conception of the nation which they intended to establish on these shores. They described, as we know, the obligations of the state to the citizen, of the citizen to the state; they committed themselves to certain ideas of justice, just as they committed us to a system which would guarantee all of its citizens equality of opportunity.

I need not describe the problems which have arisen from these beginnings. I need only remind you that the contradiction between these noble ideals and the actualities of our conduct generated a guilt, an unease of spirit, from the very beginning, and that the American novel at its best has always been concerned with this basic moral predicament. During Melville's time and Twain's, it was an implict aspect of their major themes, by the twentieth century and after the discouraging and traumatic effect of the Civil War and the Reconstruction it had gone underground, had become *understated.* Nevertheless it did not disappear completely and it is to be found operating in the work of Henry James as well as in that of Hemingway and Fitzgerald. And then (and as one who believes in the impelling moral function of the novel and who believes in the moral seriousness of the form) it pleases me no end that it comes into explicit statement again in the works of Richard Wright and William Faulkner, writers who lived close to moral and political problems which would not stay put underground.

I go into these details not to recapitulate the history of the American novel but to indicate the trend of thought which was set into motion when I began to discover the nature of that process with which I was actually involved. Whatever the opinions and decisions of critics, a novelist must arrive at his own conclusions as to the meaning and function of the form with which he is engaged, and these are, in all modesty, some of mine.

In order to orient myself I also began to learn that the American novel had long concerned itself with the puzzle of the one-and-the-many; the mystery of how each of us, despite his origin in diverse regions, with our diverse racial, cultural, religious backgrounds, speaking his own diverse idiom of the American in his own accent, is, nevertheless, American. And with this concern with the implicit pluralism of the country and with the composite nature of the ideal character called "the American," there goes a concern with gauging the health of the American promise, with depicting the extent to which it was being achieved, being made manifest in our daily conduct.

And with all of this there still remained the specific concerns of literature. Among these is the need to keep literary standards high, the necessity of exploring new possibilities of language which would allow it to retain that flexibility and fidelity to the common speech which has been its glory since Mark Twain. For me this meant learning to add to it the wonderful resources of Negro American speech and idiom and to bring into range as fully and eloquently as possible the complex reality of the American experience as it shaped and was shaped by the lives of my own people.

Notice that I stress as "fully" as possible, because I would no more strive to write great novels by leaving out the complexity of circumstances which go to make up the Negro experience and which alone go to make the obvious injustice bearable, than I would think of preparing myself to become President of the United States simply by studying Negro American history or confining myself to studying those laws affecting civil rights.

For it seems to me that one of the obligations I took on when I committed myself to the art and form of the novel was that of striving for the broadest range, the discovery and articulation of the most exalted values. And I must squeeze these from the life which I know best. (A highly truncated impression of that life I attempted to convey to you earlier.)

If all this sounds a bit heady, remember that I did not destroy that troublesome middle name of mine, I only suppressed it. Sometimes it reminds me of my obligations to the man who named me.

It is our fate as human beings always to give up some good things for other good things, to throw off certain bad circumstances only to create others. Thus there is a value for the writer in trying to give as thorough a report of social reality as possible. Only by doing so may we grasp and convey the cost of change. Only by considering the broadest accumulation of data may we make choices that are based upon our own hard-earned sense of reality. Speaking from my own special area of American culture, I feel that to embrace uncritically values which are extended to us by others is to reject the validity, even the sacredness, of our own experience. It is also to forget that the small share of reality which each of our diverse groups is able to snatch from the whirling chaos of history belongs not to the group alone, but to all of us. It is a property and a witness which can be ignored only to the danger of the entire nation.

I could suppress the name of my namesake out of respect for the achievements of its original bearer but I cannot escape the obligation of attempting to achieve some of the things which he asked of the American writer. As Henry James suggested, being an American is an arduous task, and for most of us, I suspect, the difficulty begins with the name.

The Invisible Man

This is the prologue to Invisible Man. (*Title supplied by the editor.*)

I am an invisible man. No, I am not a spook like those who haunted Edgar Allan Poe; nor am I one of your Hollywood-movie ectoplasms. I am a man of substance, of flesh and bone, fiber and liquids—and I might even be said to possess a mind. I am invisible, understand, simply because people refuse to see me. Like the bodiless heads you see sometimes in circus sideshows, it is as though I have been surrounded by mirrors of hard, distorting glass. When they approach me they see only my surroundings, themselves, or figments of their imagination—indeed, everything and anything except me.

Nor is my invisibility exactly a matter of a bio-chemical accident to my epidermis. That invisibility to which I refer occurs because of a peculiar disposition of the eyes of those with whom I come in contact. A matter of the construction of their *inner* eyes, those eyes with which they look through their physical eyes upon reality. I am not complaining, nor am I protesting either. It is sometimes advantageous to be unseen, although it is most often rather wearing on the nerves. Then too, you're constantly being bumped against by those of poor vision. Or again, you often doubt if you really exist. You wonder whether you aren't simply a phantom in other people's minds. Say, a figure in a nightmare which the sleeper tries with all his strength to destroy. It's when you feel like this that, out of resentment, you begin to bump people back. And, let me confess, you feel that way most of the time. You ache with the need to convince yourself that you do exist in the real world, that you're a part of all the sound and anguish, and you strike out with your fists, you curse and you swear to make them recognize you. And, alas, it's seldom successful.

One night I accidentally bumped into a man, and perhaps because of the near darkness he saw me and called me an insulting name. I sprang at him, seized his coat lapels and demanded that he apologize. He was a tall blond man, and as my face came close to his he looked insolently out of his blue eyes and cursed me, his breath hot in my face as he struggled. I pulled his chin down sharp upon the crown of my head, butting him as I had seen the West Indians do, and I felt his flesh tear and the blood gush out, and I yelled, "Apologize! Apologize!" But he continued to curse and struggle, and I butted him again and again until he went down heavily, on his knees, profusely bleeding. I kicked him repeatedly, in a frenzy because he still uttered insults though his lips were frothy with blood. Oh yes, I kicked him! And in my outrage I got out my knife and prepared to slit his throat, right there beneath the lamplight in the deserted street, holding him by the collar with one hand, and opening the knife with my teeth—when it occurred to me that the man had not *seen* me, actually; that he, as far as he knew, was in the midst of a walking nightmare! And I stopped the blade, slicing the air as I pushed him away, letting him fall back to the street. I stared at him hard as the lights of a car stabbed through the darkness. He lay there, moaning on the asphalt; a man almost killed by a phantom. It unnerved me. I was both disgusted and ashamed. I was like a drunken man myself, wavering about on weakened legs. Then I was amused. Something in this man's thick head had sprung out and beaten him within an inch of his life. I began to laugh at this crazy discovery. Would he have awakened at the point of death? Would Death himself have freed him for wakeful living? But I didn't linger. I ran away into the dark, laughing so hard I feared I might rupture myself. The next day I saw his picture in the *Daily News*, beneath a caption stating that he had been "mugged." Poor fool, poor blind fool, I thought with sincere compassion, mugged by an invisible man!

Most of the time (although I do not choose as I once did to deny the violence of my days by ignoring it) I am not so overtly violent. I remember that I am invisible and walk softly so as not to awaken the sleeping ones. Sometimes it is best not to awaken them; there are few things in the world as dangerous as sleepwalkers. I learned in time though that it is possible to carry on a fight against them without their realizing it. For instance, I have been carrying on a fight with Monopolated Light & Power for some time now. I use their service and pay them nothing at all, and they don't know it. Oh, they suspect that power is being drained off, but they don't know where. All they know is that according to the master meter back there in their power station a hell of a lot of free current is disappearing somewhere into the jungle of Harlem. The joke, of course, is that I don't live in Harlem but in a border area. Several years ago (before I discovered the advantage of being invisible) I went through the routine process of buying service and paying their outrageous rates. But no more. I gave up all that, along with my apartment, and my old way of life: That way based upon the fallacious assumption that I, like other men, was visible. Now, aware of my invisibility, I live rent-free in a building rented strictly to whites, in a section of the basement that was shut off and forgotten during the nineteenth century, which I discovered when I was trying to escape in the night from Ras the Destroyer. But that's gettting too far ahead of the story, almost to the end, although the end is in the beginning and lies far ahead.

The point now is that I found a home—or a hole in the ground, as you will. Now don't jump to the conclusion that because I call my home a "hole" it is damp and cold like a grave; there are cold holes and warm holes. Mine is a warm hole. And remember, a bear retires to his hole for the winter and lives until spring; then he comes strolling out like the Easter chick breaking from its shell. I say all this to assure you that it is incorrect to assume that, because I'm invisible and live in a hole, I am dead. I am neither dead nor in a state of suspended animation. Call me Jack-the-Bear, for I am in a state of hibernation.

My hole is warm and full of light. Yes, *full* of light. I doubt if there is a brighter spot in all New York than this hole of mine, and I do not exclude Broadway. Or the Empire State Building on a photographer's dream night. But that is taking advantage of you. Those two spots are among the darkest of our whole civilization—pardon me, our whole *culture* (an important distinction, I've heard)—which might sound like a hoax, or a contradiction, but that (by contradiction, I mean) is how the world moves: Not like an arrow, but a boomerang. (Beware of those who speak of the *spiral* of history; they are preparing a boomerang. Keep a steel helmet handy.) I know; I have been boomeranged across my head so much that I now can see the darkness of lightness. And I love light. Perhaps you'll think it strange that an invisible man should need light, desire light, love light. But maybe it is exactly because I *am* invisible. Light confirms my reality, gives birth to my form. A beautiful girl once told me of a recurring nightmare in which she lay in the center of a large dark room and felt her face expand until it filled the whole room, becoming a formless mass while her eyes ran in bilious jelly up the chimney. And so it is with me. Without light I am not only invisible, but formless as well; and to be unaware of one's form is to live a death. I myself, after existing some twenty years, did not become alive until I discovered my invisibility.

That is why I fight my battle with Monopolated Light & Power. The deeper reason, I mean: it allows me to feel my vital aliveness. I also fight them for taking so much of my money before I learned to protect myself. In my hole in the basement there are exactly 1,369 lights. I've wired the entire ceiling, every inch of it. And not with fluorescent bulbs, but with the older, more-expensive-to-operate kind, the filament type. An act of sabotage, you know. I've already begun to wire the wall. A junk man I know, a man of vision, has supplied me with wire and sockets. Nothing, storm or flood, must get in the way of our need for light and ever more and brighter light. The truth is the light and light is the truth. When I finish all four walls, then I'll start on the floor. Just how that will go, I don't know. Yet when you have lived invisible as long as I have you develop a certain ingenuity. I'll solve the problem. And maybe I'll invent a gadget to place my coffee-pot on the fire while I lie in bed, and even invent a gadget to warm my bed—like the fellow I saw in one of the picture magazines who made himself a gadget to warm his shoes! Though invisible, I am in the great American tradition of tinkers. That makes me kin to Ford, Edison and Franklin. Call me, since I have a theory and a concept, a "thinker-tinker." Yes, I'll warm my shoes; they need it, they're usually full of holes. I'll do that and more.

Now I have one radio-phonograph; I plan to have five. There is a certain acoustical deadness in my hole, and when I have music I want to *feel* its vibration, not only with my ear but with my whole body. I'd like to hear five recordings of Louis Armstrong playing and singing "What Did I Do to Be so Black and Blue"—all at the same time. Sometimes now I listen to Louis while I have my favorite dessert of vanilla ice cream and sloe gin. I pour the red liquid over the white mound, watching it glisten and the vapor rising as Louis bends that military instrument into a beam of lyrical sound. Perhaps I like Louis Armstrong because he's made poetry out of being invisible. I think it must be because he's unaware that he *is* invisible. And my own grasp of invisibility aids me to understand his music. Once when I asked for a cigarette, some jokers gave me a reefer, which I lighted when I got home and sat listening to my phonograph. It was a strange evening. Invisibility, let me explain, gives one a slightly different sense of time, you're never quite on the beat. Sometimes you're ahead and sometimes behind. Instead of the swift and imperceptible flowing of time, you are aware of its nodes, those points where time stands still or from which it leaps ahead. And you slip into the breaks and look around. That's what you hear vaguely in Louis' music.

Once I saw a prizefighter boxing a yokel. The fighter was swift and amazingly scientific. His body was one violent flow of rapid rhythmic action. He hit the yokel a hundred times while the yokel held up his arms in stunned surprise. But suddenly the yokel, rolling about in the gale of boxing gloves, struck one blow and knocked science, speed and footwork as cold as a well-digger's posterior. The smart money hit the canvas. The long shot got the nod. The yokel had simply stepped inside of his opponent's sense of time. So under the spell of the reefer I discovered a new analytical way of listening to music. The unheard sounds came through, and each melodic line existed of itself, stood out clearly from all the rest, said its piece, and waited patiently for the other voices to speak. That night I found myself hearing not only in time, but in space as well. I not only entered the music but descended, like Dante, into its depths. And *beneath the swiftness of the hot tempo there was a slower tempo and a cave and I entered it and looked around and heard an old woman singing a spiritual as full of Weltschmerz as flamenco, and beneath that lay a still lower level on which I saw a beautiful girl the color of ivory pleading in a voice like my mother's as she stood before a group of slave owners who bid for her naked body, and below that I found a lower level and a more rapid tempo and I heard someone shout:*

"Brothers and sisters, my text this morning is the 'Blackness of Blackness.' "

And a congregation of voices answered: "That blackness is most black, brother, most black . . ."

"In the beginning . . ."

"At the very start," they cried.

". . . there was blackness . . ."

"Preach it . . ."

". . . and the sun . . ."

"The sun, Lawd . . ."

". . . was bloody red . . ."

"Red . . ."

"Now black is . . ." the preacher shouted.

"Bloody . . ."

"I said black is . . ."

"Preach it, brother . . ."

". . . an' black ain't . . ."

"Red, Lawd, red: He said it's red!"

"Amen, brother . . ."

"Black will git you . . ."

"Yes, it will . . ."

" . . . an' black won't . . ."

"Naw, it won't!"

"It do . . ."

"It do, Lawd . . ."

". . . an' it don't."

"Halleluiah . . ."

". . . It'll put you, glory, glory, Oh my Lawd, in the WHALE'S BELLY."

"Preach it, dear brother . . ."

". . . an' make you tempt . . ."

"Good God a-mighty!"

"Old Aunt Nelly!"

"Black will make you . . ."

"Black . . ."

". . . or black will un-make you."

"Ain't it the truth, Lawd?"

And at that point a voice of trombone timbre screamed at me, "Git out of here, you fool! Is you ready to commit treason?"

And I tore myself away, hearing the old singer of spirituals moaning, "Go curse your God, boy, and die."

I stopped and questioned her, asked her what was wrong.

"I dearly loved my master, son," she said.

"You should have hated him," I said.

"He gave me several sons," she said, "and because I loved my sons I learned to love their father though I hated him too."

"I too have become acquainted with ambivalence," I said. "That's why I'm here."

"What's that?"

"Nothing, a word that doesn't explain it. Why do you moan?"

"I moan this way 'cause he's dead," she said.

"Then tell me, who is that laughing upstairs?"

"Them's my sons. They glad."

"Yes, I can understand that too," I said.

"I laughs too, but I moans too. He promised to set us free but he never could bring hisself to do it. Still I loved him . . ."

"Loved him? You mean . . ."

"Oh yes, but I loved something else even more."

"What more?"

"Freedom."

"Freedom," I said. "Maybe freedom lies in hating."

"Naw, son, it's in loving. I loved him and give him the poison and he withered away like a frost-bit apple. Them boys woulda tore him to pieces with they homemake knives."

"A mistake was made somewhere," I said, "I'm confused." And I wished to say other things, but the laughter upstairs became too loud and moan-like for me and I tried to break out of it, but I couldn't. Just as I was leaving I felt an urgent desire to ask her what freedom was and went back. She sat with her head in her hands, moaning softly; her leather-brown face was filled with sadness.

"Old woman, what is this freedom you love so well?" I asked around a corner of my mind.

She looked surprised, then thoughtful, then baffled. "I done forgot, son. It's all mixed up. First I think it's one thing, then I think it's another. It gits my head to spinning. I guess now it ain't nothing but knowing how to say what I got up in my head. But it's a hard job, son. Too much is done happen to me in too short a time. Hit's like I have a fever. Ever' time I starts to walk my head gits to swirling and I falls down. Or if it ain't that, it's the boys; they gits to laughing and wants to kill up the white folks. They bitter, that's what they is . . ."

"But what about freedom?"

"Leave me 'lone, boy; my head aches!"

I left her, feeling dizzy myself. I didn't get far.

Suddenly one of the sons, a big fellow six feet tall, appeared out of nowhere and struck me with his fist.

"What's the matter, man?" I cried.

"You made Ma cry!"

"But how?" I said, dodging a blow.

"Askin' her them questions, that's how. Git outa here and stay, and next time you got questions like that, ask yourself!"

He held me in a grip like cold stone, his fingers fastening upon my windpipe until I thought I would suffocate before he finally allowed me to go. I stumbled about dazed, the music beating hysterically in my ears. It was dark. My head cleared and I wandered down a dark narrow passage, thinking I heard his footsteps hurrying behind me. I was sore, and into my being had come a profound craving for tranquillity, for peace and quiet, a state I felt I could never achieve. For one thing, the trumpet was blaring and the rhythm was too hectic. A tom-tom beating like heart-thuds began drowning out the trumpet, filling my ears. I longed for water and I heard it rushing through the cold mains my fingers touched as I felt my way, but I couldn't stop to search because of the footsteps behind me.

"Hey, Ras," I called. "Is it you, Destroyer? Rinehart?"

No answer, only the rhythmic footsteps behind me. Once I tried crossing the road, but a speeding machine struck me, scraping the skin from my leg as it roared past.

Then somehow I came out of it, ascending hastily from this underworld of sound to hear Louis Armstrong innocently asking,

What did I do
To be so black
And blue?

At first I was afraid; this familiar music had demanded action, the kind of which I was incapable, and yet had I lingered there beneath the surface I might have attempted to act. Nevertheless, I know now that few really listen to this music. I sat on the chair's edge in a soaking sweat, as though each of my 1,369 bulbs had everyone become a klieg light in an individual setting for a third degree with Ras and Rinehart in charge. It was exhausting—as though I had held my breath continuously for an hour under the terrifying serenity that comes from days of intense hunger. And yet, it was a strangely satisfying experience for an invisible man to hear the silence of sound. I had discovered unrecognized compulsions of my being—even though I could not answer "yes" to their promptings. I haven't smoked a reefer since, however; not because they're illegal, but because to *see* around corners is enough (that is not unusual when you are invisible). But to hear around them is too much; it inhibits action. And despite Brother Jack and all that sad, lost period of the Brotherhood, I believe in nothing if not in action.

Please, a definition: A hibernation is a covert preparation for a more overt action.

Besides, the drug destroys one's sense of time completely. If that happened, I might forget to dodge some bright morning and some cluck would run me down with an orange and yellow street car, or a bilious bus! Or I might forget to leave my hole when the moment for action presents itself.

Meanwhile I enjoy my life with the compliments of Monopolated Light and Power. Since you never recognize me even when in closest contact with me, and since, no doubt, you'll hardly believe that I exist, it won't matter if you know that I tapped a power line leading into the building and ran it into my hole in the ground. Before that I lived in the darkness into which I was chased, but now I see. I've illuminated the blackness of my invisibility—and vice versa. And so I play the invisible music of my isolation. The last statement doesn't seem just right, does it? But it is; you hear this music simply because music is heard and seldom seen, except by musicians. Could this compulsion to put invisibility down in black and white be thus an urge to make music of invisibilty? But I am an orator, a rabble rouser—Am? I *was*, and perhaps shall be again. Who knows? All sickness is not unto death, neither is invisibility.

I can hear you say, "What a horrible, irresponsible bastard!" And you're right. I leap to agree with you. I am one of the most irresponsible beings that ever lived. Irresponsibility is part of my invisibility; any way you face it, it is a denial. But to whom can I be responsible, and why should I be, when you refuse to see me? And wait until I reveal how truly irresponsible I am. Responsibility rests upon recognition, and recognition is a form of agreement. Take the man whom I almost killed: Who was responsible for that near murder—I? I don't think so, and I refuse it. I won't buy it. You can't give it to me. *He* bumped *me, he* insulted *me*. Shouldn't he, for his own personal safety, have recognized my hysteria, my "danger potential"? He, let us say, was lost in a dream world. But didn't *he* control that dream world—which, alas, is only too real!—and didn't *he* rule me out of it? And if he had yelled for a policeman, wouldn't *I* have been taken for the offending one? Yes, yes, yes! Let me agree with you, I was the irresponsible one; for I should have used my knife to protect the higher interests of society. Some day that kind of foolishness will cause us tragic trouble. All dreamers and sleepwalkers must pay the price, and even the invisible victim is responsible for the fate of all. But I shirked that responsibility; I became too snarled in the incompatible notions that buzzed within my brain. I was a coward . . .

But what did *I* do to be so blue? Bear with me.

Battle Royal

This is the first chapter of Invisible Man. *The title supplied here has been used by Ellison to refer to this chapter and has been given to this episode in separate publication as a short story.*

It goes a long way back, some twenty years. All my life I had been looking for something, and everywhere I turned someone tried to tell me what it was. I accepted their answers too, though they were often in contradiction and even self-contradictory. I was naïve. I was looking for myself and asking everyone except myself questions which I, and only I, could answer. It took me a long time and much painful boomeranging of my expectations to achieve a realization everyone else appears to have been born with: That I am nobody but myself. But first I had to discover that I am an invisible man!

And yet I am no freak of nature, nor of history. I was in the cards, other things having been equal (or unequal) eighty-five years ago. I am not ashamed of my grandparents for having been slaves. I am only ashamed of myself for having at one time been ashamed. About eighty-five years ago they were told that they were free, united with others of our country in everything pertaining to the common good, and, in everything social, separate like the fingers of the hand. And they believed it. They exulted in it. They stayed in their place, worked hard, and brought up my father to do the same. But my grandfather is the one. He was an odd old guy, my grandfather, and I am told I take after him. It was he who caused the trouble. On his deathbed he called my father to him and said, "Son, after I'm gone I want you to keep up the good fight. I never told you, but our life is a war and I have been a traitor all my born days, a spy in the enemy's country ever since I give up my gun back in the Reconstruction. Live with your head in the lion's mouth. I want you to overcome 'em with yeses, undermine 'em with grins, agree 'em to death and destruction, let 'em swoller you till they vomit or bust wide open." They thought the old man had gone out of his mind. He had been the meekest of men. The younger children were rushed from the room, the shades drawn and the flame of the lamp turned so low that it sputtered on the wick like the old man's breathing. "Learn it to the younguns," he whispered fiercely; then he died.

But my folks were more alarmed over his last words than over his dying. It was as though he had not died at all, his words caused so much anxiety. I was warned emphatically to forget what he had said and, indeed, this is the first time it has been mentioned outside the family circle. It had a tremendous effect upon me, however. I could never be sure of what he meant. Grandfather had been a quiet old man who never made any trouble, yet on his deathbed he had called himself a traitor and a spy, and he had spoken of his meekness as a dangerous activity. It became a constant puzzle which lay unanswered in the back of my mind. And whenever things went well for me I remembered my grandfather and felt guilty and uncomfortable. It was as though I was carrying out his advice in spite of myself. And to make it worse, everyone loved me for it. I was praised by the most lily-white men of the town. I was considered an example of desirable conduct—just as my grandfather had been. And what puzzled me was that the old man had defined it as *treachery*. When I was praised for my conduct I felt a guilt that in some way I was doing something that was really against the wishes of the white folks, that if they had understood they would have desired me to act just the opposite, that I should have been sulky and mean, and that that really would have been what they wanted, even though they were fooled and thought they wanted me to act as I did. It made me afraid that some day they would look upon me as a traitor and I would be lost. Still I was more afraid to act any other way because they didn't like that at all. The old man's words were like a curse. On my graduation day I delivered an oration in which I showed that humility was the secret, indeed, the very essence of progress. (Not that I believed this—how could I, remembering my grandfather?—I only believed that it worked.) It was a great success. Everyone praised me and I was invited to give the speech at a gathering of the town's leading white citizens. It was a triumph for our whole community.

It was the main ballroom of the leading hotel. When I got there I discovered that it was on the occasion of a smoker, and I was told that since I was to be there anyway I might as well take part in the battle royal to be fought by some of my schoolmates as part of the entertainment. The battle royal came first.

All of the town's big shots were there in their tuxedoes, wolfing down the buffet foods, drinking beer and whiskey and smoking black cigars. It was a large room with a high ceiling. Chairs were arranged in neat rows around three sides of a portable boxing ring. The fourth side was clear, revealing a gleaming space of polished floor. I had some misgivings over the battle royal, by the way. Not from a distaste for fighting, but because I didn't care too much for the other fellows who were to take part. They were tough guys who seemed to have no grandfather's curse worrying their minds. No one could mistake their toughness. And besides, I suspected that fighting a battle royal might detract from the dignity of my speech. In those pre-invisible days I visualized myself as a potential Booker T. Washington. But the other fellows didn't care too much for me either, and there were nine of them. I felt superior to them in my way, and I didn't like the manner in which we were all crowded together into the servants' elevator. Nor did they like my being there. In fact, as the warmly lighted floors flashed past the elevator we had words over the fact that I, by taking part in the fight, had knocked one of their friends out of a night's work.

We were led out of the elevator through a rococo hall into an anteroom and told to get into our fighting togs. Each of us was issued a pair of boxing gloves and ushered out into the big mirrored hall, which we entered looking cautiously about us and whispering, lest we might accidentally be heard above the noise of the room. It was foggy with cigar smoke. And already the whiskey was taking effect. I was shocked to see some of the most important men of the town quite tipsy. They were all there—bankers, lawyers, judges, doctors, fire chiefs, teachers, merchants. Even one of the more fashionable pastors.

Something we could not see was going on up front. A clarinet was vibrating sensuously and the men were standing up and moving eagerly forward. We were a small tight group, clustered together, our bare upper bodies touching and shining with anticipatory sweat; while up front the big shots were becoming increasingly excited over something we still could not see. Suddenly I heard the school superintendent, who had told me to come, yell, "Bring up the shines, gentlemen! Bring up the little shines!"

We were rushed up to the front of the ballroom, where it smelled even more strongly of tobacco and whiskey. Then we were pushed into place. I almost wet my pants. A sea of faces, some hostile, some amused, ringed around us, and in the center, facing us, stood a magnificent blond—stark naked. There was dead silence. I felt a blast of cold air chill me. I tried to back away, but they were behind me and around me. Some of the boys stood with lowered heads, trembling. I felt a wave of irrational guilt and fear. My teeth chattered, my skin turned to goose flesh, my knees knocked. Yet I was strongly attracted and looked in spite of myself. Had the price of looking been blindness, I would have looked. The hair was yellow like that of a circus kewpie doll, the face heavily powdered and rouged, as though to form an abstract mask, the eyes hollow and smeared a cool blue, the color of a baboon's butt. I felt a desire to spit upon her as my eyes brushed slowly over her body. Her breasts were firm and round as the domes of East Indian temples, and I stood so close as to see the fine skin texture and beads of pearly perspiration glistening like dew around the pink and erected buds of her nipples. I wanted at one and the same time to run from the room, to sink through the floor, or go to her and cover her from my eyes and the eyes of the others with my body; to feel the soft thighs, to caress her and destroy her, to love her and murder her, to hide from her, and yet to stroke where below the small American flag tattooed upon her belly her thighs formed a capital V. I had a notion that of all in the room she saw only me with her impersonal eyes.

And then she began to dance, a slow sensuous movement; the smoke of a hundred cigars clinging to her like the thinnest of veils. She seemed like a fair bird-girl girdled in veils calling to me from the angry surface of some gray and threatening sea. I was transported. Then I became aware of the clarinet playing and the big shots yelling at us. Some threatened us if we looked and others if we did not. On my right I saw one boy faint. And now a man grabbed a silver pitcher from a table and stepped close as he dashed ice water upon him and stood him up and forced two of us to support him as his head hung and moans issued from his thick bluish lips. Another boy began to plead to go home. He was the largest of the group, wearing dark red fighting trunks much too small to conceal the erection which projected from him as though in answer to the insinuating low-registered moaning of the clarinet. He tried to hide himself with his boxing gloves.

And all the while the blonde continued dancing, smiling faintly at the big shots who watched her with fascination, and faintly smiling at our fear. I noticed a certain merchant who followed her hungrily, his lips loose and drooling. He was a large man who wore diamond studs in a shirtfront which swelled with the ample paunch underneath, and each time the blonde swayed her undulating hips he ran his hand through the thin hair of his bald head and, with his arms upheld, his posture clumsy like that of an intoxicated panda, wound his belly in a slow and obscene grind. This creature was completely hypnotized. The music had quickened. As the dancer flung herself about with a detached expression on her face, the men began reaching out to touch her. I could see their beefy fingers sink into the soft flesh. Some of the others tried to stop them and she began to move around the floor in graceful circles, as they gave chase, slipping and sliding over the polished floor. It was mad. Chairs went crashing, drinks were spilt, as they ran laughing and howling after her. They caught her just as she reached the door, raised her from the floor, and tossed her as college boys are tossed at a hazing, and above her red, fixed-smiling lips I saw the terror and disgust in her eyes, almost like my own terror and that which I saw in some of the other boys. As I watched, they tossed her twice and her soft breasts seemed to flatten against the air and her legs flung wildly as she spun. Some of the more sober ones helped her to escape. And I started off the floor, heading for the anteroom with the rest of the boys.

Some were still crying and in hysteria. But as we tried to leave we were stopped and ordered to get into the ring. There was nothing to do but what we were told. All ten of us climbed under the ropes and allowed ourselves to be blindfolded with broad bands of white cloth. One of the men seemed to feel a bit sympathetic and tried to cheer us up as we stood with our backs against the ropes. Some of us tried to grin. "See that boy over there?" one of the men said. "I want you to run across at the bell and give it to him right in the belly. If you don't get him, I'm going to get you. I don't like his looks." Each of us was told the same. The blindfolds were put on. Yet even then I had been going over my speech. In my mind each word was as bright as flame. I felt the cloth pressed into place, and frowned so that it would be loosened when I relaxed.

But now I felt a sudden fit of blind terror. I was unused to darkness. It was as though I had suddenly found myself in a dark room filled with poisonous cottonmouths. I could hear the bleary voices yelling insistently for the battle royal to begin.

"Get going in there!"

"Let me at that big nigger!"

I strained to pick up the school superintendent's voice, as though to squeeze some security out of that slightly more familiar sound.

"Let me at those black sonsabitches!" someone yelled.

"No, Jackson, no!" another voice yelled. "Here, somebody, help me hold Jack."

"I want to get at that ginger-colored nigger. Tear him limb from limb," the first voice yelled.

I stood against the ropes trembling. For in those days I was what they called ginger-colored, and he sounded as though he might crunch me between his teeth like a crisp ginger cookie.

Quite a struggle was going on. Chairs were being kicked about and I could hear voices grunting as with a terrific effort. I wanted to see, to see more desperately than ever before. But the blindfold was as tight as a thick skin-puckering scab and when I raised my gloved hands to push the layers of white aside a voice yelled, "Oh, no you don't, black bastard! Leave that alone!"

"Ring the bell before Jackson kills him a coon!" someone boomed in the sudden silence. And I heard the bell clang and the sound of feet scuffling forward.

A glove smacked against my head. I pivoted, striking out stiffly as someone went past, and felt the jar ripple along the length of my arm to my shoulder. Then it seemed as though all nine of the boys had turned upon me at once. Blows pounded me from all sides while I struck out as best I could. So many blows landed upon me that I wondered if I were not the only blindfolded fighter in the ring, or if the man called Jackson hadn't succeeded in getting me after all.

Blindfolded, I could no longer control my motions. I had no dignity. I stumbled about like a baby or a drunken man. The smoke had become thicker and with each new blow it seemed to sear and further restrict my lungs. My saliva became like hot bitter glue. A glove connected with my head, filling my mouth with warm blood. It was everywhere. I could not tell if the moisture I felt upon my body was sweat or blood. A blow landed hard against the nape of my neck. I felt myself going over, my head hitting the floor. Streaks of blue light filled the black world behind the blindfold. I lay prone, pretending that I was knocked out, but felt myself seized by hands and yanked to my feet. "Get going, black boy! Mix it up!" My arms were like lead, my head smarting from blows. I managed to feel my way to the ropes and held on, trying to catch my breath. A glove landed in my mid-section and I went over again, feeling as though the smoke had become a knife jabbed into my guts. Pushed this way and that by the legs milling around me I finally pulled erect and discovered that I could see the black, sweat-washed forms weaving in the smoky-blue atmosphere like drunken dancers weaving to the rapid drum-like thuds of blows.

Everyone fought hysterically. It was complete anarchy. Everybody fought everybody else. No group fought together for long. Two, three, four, fought one, then turned to fight each other, were themselves attacked. Blows landed below the belt and in the kidney, with the gloves open as well as closed, and with my eye partly opened now there was not so much terror. I moved carefully, avoiding blows, although not too many to attract attention, fighting from group to group. The boys groped about like blind, cautious crabs crouching to protect their mid-sections, their heads pulled in short against their shoulders, their arms stretched nervously before them, with their fists testing the smoke-filled air like the knobbed feelers of hypersensitive snails. In one corner I glimpsed a boy violently punching the air and heard him scream in pain as he smashed his hand against a ring post. For a second I saw him bent over holding his hand, then going down as a blow caught his unprotected head. I played one group against the other, slipping in and throwing a punch then stepping out of range while pushing the others into the melee to take the blows blindly aimed at me. The smoke was agonizing and there were no rounds, no bells at three minute intervals to relieve our exhaustion. The room spun round me, a swirl of lights, smoke, sweating bodies surrounded by tense white faces. I bled from both nose and mouth, the blood spattering upon my chest.

The men kept yelling, "Slug him, black boy! Knock his guts out!"

"Uppercut him! Kill him! Kill that big boy!"

Taking a fake fall, I saw a boy going down heavily beside me as though we were felled by a single blow, saw a sneaker-clad foot shoot into his groin as the two who had knocked him down stumbled upon him. I rolled out of range, feeling a twinge of nausea.

The harder we fought the more threatening the men became. And yet, I had begun to worry about my speech again. How would it go? Would they recognize my ability? What would they give me?

I was fighting automatically when suddenly I noticed that one after another of the boys was leaving the ring. I was surprised, filled with panic, as though I had been left alone with an unknown danger. Then I understood. The boys had arranged it among themselves. It was the custom for the two men left in the ring to slug it out for the winner's prize. I discovered this too late. When the bell sounded two men in tuxedoes leaped into the ring and removed the blindfold. I found myself facing Tatlock, the biggest of the gang. I felt sick at my stomach. Hardly had the bell stopped ringing in my ears than it clanged again and I saw him moving swiftly toward me. Thinking of nothing else to do I hit him smash on the nose. He kept coming, bringing the rank sharp violence of stale sweat. His face was a black blank of a face, only his eyes alive—with hate of me and aglow with a feverish terror from what had happened to us all. I became anxious. I wanted to deliver my speech and he came at me as though he meant to beat it out of me. I smashed him again and again, taking his blows as they came. Then on a sudden impulse I struck him lightly and as we clinched, I whispered, "Fake like I knocked you out, you can have the prize."

"I'll break your behind," he whispered hoarsely.

"For *them?*"

"For *me*, sonofabitch!"

They were yelling for us to break it up and Tatlock spun me half around with a blow, and as a joggled camera sweeps in a reeling scene, I saw the howling red faces crouching tense beneath the cloud of blue-gray smoke. For a moment the world wavered, unraveled, flowed, then my head cleared and Tatlock bounced before me. That fluttering shadow before my eyes was his jabbing left hand. Then falling forward, my head against his damp shoulder, I whispered,

"I'll make it five dollars more."

"Go to hell!"

But his muscles relaxed a trifle beneath my pressure and I breathed, "Seven?"

"Give it to your ma," he said, ripping me beneath the heart.

And while I still held him I butted him and moved away. I felt myself bombarded with punches. I fought back with hopeless desperation. I wanted to deliver my speech more than anything else in the world, because I felt that only these men could judge truly my ability, and now this stupid clown was ruining my chances. I began fighting carefully now, moving in to punch him and out again with my greater speed. A lucky blow to his chin and I had him going too—until I heard a loud voice yell, "I got my money on the big boy."

Hearing this, I almost dropped my guard. I was confused: Should I try to win against the voice out there? Would not this go against my speech, and was not this a moment for humility, for nonresistance? A blow to my head as I danced about sent my right eye popping like a jack-in-the-box and settled my dilemma. The room went red as I fell. It was a dream fall, my body languid and fastidious as to where to land, until the floor became impatient and smashed up to meet me. A moment later I came to. An hypnotic voice said FIVE emphatically. And I lay there, hazily watching a dark red spot of my own blood shaping itself into a butterfly, glistening and soaking into the soiled gray world of the canvas.

When the voice drawled TEN I was lifted up and dragged to a chair. I sat dazed. My eye pained and swelled with each throb of my pounding heart and I wondered if now I would be allowed to speak. I was wringing wet, my mouth still bleeding. We were grouped along the wall now. The other boys ignored me as they congratulated Tatlock and speculated as to how much they would be paid. One boy whimpered over his smashed hand. Looking up front, I saw attendants in white jackets rolling the portable ring away and placing a small square rug in the vacant space surrounded by chairs. Perhaps, I thought, I will stand on the rug to deliver my speech.

Then the M.C. called to us, "Come on up here boys and get your money."

We ran forward to where the men laughed and talked in their chairs, waiting. Everyone seemed friendly now.

"There it is on the rug," the man said. I saw the rug covered with coins of all dimensions and a few crumpled bills. But what excited me, scattered here and there, were the gold pieces.

"Boys, it's all yours," the man said. "You get all you grab."

"That's right, Sambo," a blond man said, winking at me confidentially.

I trembled with excitement, forgetting my pain. I would get the gold and the bills, I thought. I would use both hands. I would throw my body against the boys nearest me to block them from the gold.

"Get down around the rug now," the man commanded, "and don't anyone touch it until I give the signal."

"This ought to be good," I heard.

As told, we got around the square rug on our knees. Slowly the man raised his freckled hand as we followed it upward with our eyes.

I heard, "These niggers look like they're about to pray!"

Then, "Ready," the man said. "Go!"

I lunged for a yellow coin lying on the blue design of the carpet, touching it and sending a surprised shriek to join those rising around me. I tried frantically to remove my hand but could not let go. A hot, violent force tore through my body, shaking me like a wet rat. The rug was electrified. The hair bristled up on my head as I shook myself free. My muscles jumped, my nerves jangled, writhed. But I saw that this was not stopping the other boys. Laughing in fear and embarrassment, some were holding back and scooping up the coins knocked off by the painful contortions of the others. The men roared above us as we struggled.

"Pick it up, goddammit, pick it up!" someone called like a bass-voiced parrot. "Go on, get it!"

I crawled rapidly around the floor, picking up the coins, trying to avoid the coppers and to get greenbacks and the gold. Ignoring the shock by laughing, as I brushed the coins off quickly, I discovered that I could contain the electricity—a contradiction, but it works. Then the men began to push us onto the rug. Laughing embarrassedly, we struggled out of their hands and kept after the coins. We were all wet and slippery and hard to hold. Suddenly I saw a boy lifted into the air, glistening with sweat like a circus seal, and dropped, his back landing flush upon the charged rug, heard him yell and saw him literally dance upon his back, his elbows beating a frenzied tattoo upon the floor, his muscles twitching like the flesh of a horse stung by many flies. When he finally rolled off, his face was gray and no one stopped him when he ran from the floor amid booming laughter.

"Get the money," the M.C. called. "That's good hard American cash!"

And we snatched and grabbed, snatched and grabbed. I was careful not to come too close to the rug now, and when I felt the hot whiskey breath descend upon me like a cloud of foul air I reached out and grabbed the leg of a chair. It was occupied and I held on desperately.

"Leggo, nigger! Leggo!"

The huge face wavered down to mine as he tried to push me free. But my body was slippery and he was too drunk. It was Mr. Colcord, who owned a chain of movie houses and "entertainment palaces." Each time he grabbed me I slipped out of his hands. It became a real struggle. I feared the rug more than I did the drunk, so I held on, surprising myself for a moment by trying to topple *him* upon the rug. It was such an enormous idea that I found myself actually carrying it out. I tried not to be obvious, yet when I grabbed his leg, trying to tumble him out of the chair, he raised up roaring with laughter, and, looking at me with soberness dead in the eye, kicked me viciously in the chest. The chair leg flew out of my hand and I felt myself going and rolled. It was as though I had rolled through a bed of hot coals. It seemed a whole century would pass before I would roll free, a century in which I was seared through the deepest levels of my body to the fearful breath within me and the breath seared and heated to the point of explosion. It'll all be over in a flash, I thought as I rolled clear. It'll all be over in a flash.

But not yet, the men on the other side were waiting, red faces swollen as though from apoplexy as they bent forward in their chairs. Seeing their fingers coming toward me I rolled away as a fumbled football rolls off the receiver's fingertips, back into the coals. That time I luckily sent the rug sliding out of place and heard the coins ringing against the floor and the boys scuffling to pick them up and the M.C. calling, "All right, boys, that's all. Go get dressed and get your money."

I was limp as a dish rag. My back felt as though it had been beaten with wires.

When we had dressed the M.C. came in and gave us each five dollars, except Tatlock, who got ten for being last in the ring. Then he told us to leave. I was not to get a chance to deliver my speech, I thought. I was going out into the dim alley in despair when I was stopped and told to go back. I returned to the ballroom, where the men were pushing back their chairs and gathering in groups to talk.

The M.C. knocked on a table for quiet. "Gentlemen," he said, "we almost forgot an important part of the program. A most serious part, gentlemen. This boy was brought here to deliver a speech which he made at his graduation yesterday . . ."

"Bravo!"

"I'm told that he is the smartest boy we've got out there in Greenwood. I'm told that he knows more big words than a pocket-sized dictionary."

Much applause and laughter.

"So now, gentlemen, I want you to give him your attention."

There was still laughter as I faced them, my mouth dry, my eye throbbing. I began slowly, but evidently my throat was tense, because they began shouting, "Louder! Louder!"

"We of the younger generation extol the wisdom of that great leader and educator," I shouted, "who first spoke these flaming words of wisdom: 'A ship lost at sea for many days suddenly sighted a friendly vessel. From the mast of the unfortunate vessel was seen a signal: "Water, water; we die of thirst!" The answer from the friendly vessel came back: "Cast down your bucket where you are." The captain of the distressed vessel, at last heeding, the injunction, cast down his bucket, and it came up full of fresh sparkling water from the mouth of the Amazon River.' And like him I say, and in his words, 'To those of my race who depend upon bettering their condition in a foreign land, or who underestimate the importance of cultivating friendly relations with the Southern white man, who is his next-door neighbor, I would say: "Cast down your bucket where you are"—cast it down in making friends in every manly way of the people of all races by whom we are surrounded . . .' "

I spoke automatically and with such fervor that I did not realize that the men were still talking and laughing until my dry mouth, filling up with blood from the cut, almost strangled me. I coughed, wanting to stop and go to one of the tall brass, sand-filled spittoons to relieve myself, but a few of the men, especially the superintendent, were listening and I was afraid. So I gulped it down, blood, saliva and all, and continued. (What powers of endurance I had during those days! What enthusiasm! What a belief in the rightness of things!) I spoke even louder in spite of the pain. But still they talked and still they laughed, as though deaf with cotton in dirty ears. So I spoke with greater emotional emphasis. I closed my ears and swallowed blood until I was nauseated. The speech seemed a hundred times as long as before, but I could not leave out a single word. All had to be said, each memorized nuance considered, rendered. Nor was that all. Whenever I uttered a word of three or more syllables a group of voices would yell for me to repeat it. I used the phrase "social responsibility" and they yelled:

"What's that word you say, boy?"

"Social responsibility," I said.

"What?"

"Social . . ."

"Louder."

". . . responsibility."

"More!"

"Respon—"

"Repeat!"

"—sibility."

The room filled with the uproar of laughter until, no doubt, distracted by having to gulp down my blood, I made a mistake and yelled a phrase I had often seen denounced in newspaper editorials, heard debated in private.

"Social . . ."

"What?" they yelled.

". . . equality—"

The laughter hung smokelike in the sudden stillness. I opened my eyes, puzzled. Sounds of displeasure filled the room. The M.C. rushed forward. They shouted hostile phrases at me. But I did not understand.

A small dry mustached man in the front row blared out, "Say that slowly, son!"

"What sir?"

"What you just said!"

"Social responsibility, sir," I said.

"You weren't being smart, were you, boy?" he said, not unkindly.

"No, sir!"

"You sure that about 'equality' was a mistake?"

"Oh, yes, sir," I said. "I was swallowing blood."

"Well, you had better speak more slowly so we can understand.

We mean to do right by you, but you've got to know your place at all times. All right, now, go on with your speech."

I was afraid. I wanted to leave but I wanted also to speak and I was afraid they'd snatch me down.

"Thank you, sir," I said, beginning where I had left off, and having them ignore me as before.

Yet when I finished there was a thunderous applause. I was surprised to see the superintendent come forth with a package wrapped in white tissue paper, and, gesturing for quiet, address the men.

"Gentlemen, you see that I did not overpraise this boy. He makes a good speech and some day he'll lead his people in the proper paths. And I don't have to tell you that that is important in these days and times. This is a good, smart boy, and so to encourage him in the right direction, in the name of the Board of Education I wish to present him a prize in the form of this . . ."

He paused, removing the tissue paper and revealing a gleaming calfskin brief case.

". . . in the form of this first-class article from Shad Whitmore's shop."

"Boy," he said, addressing me, "take this prize and keep it well. Consider it a badge of office. Prize it. Keep developing as you are and some day it will be filled with important papers that will help shape the destiny of your people."

I was so moved that I could hardly express my thanks. A rope of bloody saliva forming a shape like an undiscovered continent drooled upon the leather and I wiped it quickly away. I felt an importance that I had never dreamed.

"Open it and see what's inside," I was told.

My fingers a-tremble, I complied, smelling the fresh leather and finding an official-looking document inside. It was a scholarship to the state college for Negroes. My eyes filled with tears and I ran awkwardly off the floor.

I was overjoyed; I did not even mind when I discovered that the gold pieces I had scrambled for were brass pocket tokens advertising a certain make of automobile.

When I reached home everyone was excited. Next day the neighbors came to congratulate me. I even felt safe from grandfather, whose deathbed curse usually spoiled my triumphs. I stood beneath his photograph with my brief case in hand and smiled triumphantly into his stolid black peasant's face. It was a face that fascinated me. The eyes seemed to follow everywhere I went.

That night I dreamed I was at a circus with him and that he refused to laugh at the clowns no matter what they did. Then later he told me to open my brief case and read what was inside and I did, finding an official envelope stamped with the state seal; and inside the envelope I found another and another, endlessly, and I thought I would fall of weariness. "Them's years," he said. "Now open that one." And I did and in it I found an engraved document containing a short message in letters of gold. "Read it," my grandfather said. "Out loud."

"To Whom It May Concern," I intoned. "Keep This Nigger-Boy Running."

I awoke with the old man's laughter ringing in my ears.

(It was a dream I was to remember and dream again for many years after. But at that time I had no insight into its meaning. First I had to attend college.)

In the Paint Factory

This episode is Chapter 10 in Invisible Man.
(Title here supplied by the editor.)

The plant was in Long Island, and I crossed a bridge in the fog to get there and came down in a stream of workers. Ahead of me a huge electric sign announced its message through the drifting strands of fog:

KEEP AMERICA PURE
WITH
LIBERTY PAINTS

Flags were fluttering in the breeze from each of a maze of buildings below the sign, and for a moment it was like watching some vast patriotic ceremony from a distance. But no shots were fired and no bugles sounded. I hurried ahead with the others through the fog.

I was worried, since I had used Emerson's name without his permission, but when I found my way to the personnel office it worked like magic. I was interviewed by a little droopy-eyed man named Mr. MacDuffy and sent to work for a Mr. Kimbro. An office boy came along to direct me.

"If Kimbro needs him," MacDuffy told the boy, "come back and have his name entered on the shipping department's payroll."

"It's tremendous," I said as we left the building. "It looks like a small city."

"It's big all right," he said. "We're one of the biggest outfits in the business. Make a lot of paint for the government."

We entered one of the buildings now and started down a pure white hall.

"You better leave your things in the locker room," he said, opening a door through which I saw a room with low wooden benches and rows of green lockers. There were keys in several of the locks, and he selected one for me. "Put your stuff in there and take the key," he said. Dressing, I felt nervous. He sprawled with one foot on a bench, watching me closely as he chewed on a match stem. Did he suspect that Emerson hadn't sent me?

"They have a new racket around here," he said, twirling the match between his finger and thumb. There was a note of insinuation in his voice, and I looked up from tying my shoe, breathing with conscious evenness.

"What kind of racket?" I said.

"Oh, you know. The wise guys firing the regular guys and putting on you colored college boys. Pretty smart," he said. "That way they don't have to pay union wages."

"How did you know I went to college?" I said.

"Oh, there're about six of you guys out here already. Some up in the testing lab. Everybody knows about that."

"But I had no idea that was why I was hired," I said.

"Forget it, Mac," he said. "It's not your fault. You new guys don't know the score. Just like the union says, it's the wise guys in the office. They're the ones who make scabs out of you—Hey! we better hurry."

We entered a long, shed-like room in which I saw a series of overhead doors along one side and a row of small offices on the other. I followed the boy down an aisle between endless cans, buckets and drums labeled with the company's trademark, a screaming eagle. The paint was stacked in neatly pyramided lots along the concrete floor. Then, starting into one of the offices, the boy stopped short and grinned.

"Listen to that!"

Someone inside the office was swearing violently over a telephone.

"Who's that?" I asked.

He grinned. "Your boss, the terrible Mr. Kimbro. We call him 'Colonel,' but don't let him catch you."

I didn't like it. The voice was raving about some failure of the laboratory and I felt a swift uneasiness. I didn't like the idea of starting to work for a man who was in such a nasty mood. Perhaps he was angry at one of the men from the school, and that wouldn't make him feel too friendly toward me.

"Let's go in," the boy said. "I've got to get back."

As we entered, the man slammed down the phone and picked up some papers.

"Mr. MacDuffy wants to know if you can use this new man," the boy said.

"You damn right I can use him and . . ." the voice trailed off, the eyes above the stiff military mustache going hard.

"Well, can you use him?" the boy said. "I got to go make out his card."

"Okay," the man said finally. "I can use him. I gotta. What's his name?"

The boy read my name off a card.

"All right," he said, "you go right to work. And you," he said to the boy, "get the hell out of here before I give you a chance to earn some of the money wasted on you every payday!"

"Aw, gwan, you slave driver," the boy said, dashing from the room.

Reddening Kimbro turned to me, "Come along, let's get going."

I followed him into the long room where the lots of paint were stacked along the floor beneath numbered markers that hung from the ceiling. Toward the rear I could see two men unloading heavy buckets from a truck, stacking them neatly on a low loading platform.

"Now get this straight," Kimbro said gruffly. "This is a busy department and I don't have time to repeat things. You have to follow instructions and you're going to be doing things you don't understand, so get your orders the first time and get them right! I won't have time to stop and explain everything. You have to catch on by doing exactly what I tell you. You got that?"

I nodded, noting that his voice became louder when the men across the floor stopped to listen.

"All right," he said, picking up several tools. "Now come over here."

"He's Kimbro," one of the men said.

I watched him kneel and open one of the buckets, stirring a milky brown substance. A nauseating stench arose. I wanted to step away. But he stirred it vigorously until it became glossy white, holding the spatula like a delicate instrument and studying the paint as it laced off the blade, back into the bucket. Kimbro frowned.

"Damn those laboratory blubberheads to hell! There's got to be dope put in every single sonofabitching bucket. And that's what you're going to do, *and* it's got to be put in so it can be trucked out of here before 11:30." He handed me a white enamel graduate and what looked like a battery hydrometer.

"The idea is to open each bucket and put in ten drops of this stuff," he said. "Then you stir it 'til it disappears. After it's mixed you take this brush and paint out a sample on one of these." He produced a number of small rectangular boards and a small brush from his jacket pocket. "You understand?"

"Yes, sir." But when I looked into the white graduate I hesitated; the liquid inside was dead black. Was he trying to kid me?

"What's wrong?"

"I don't know, sir . . . I mean. Well, I don't want to start by asking a lot of stupid questions, but do you know what's in this graduate?"

His eyes snapped. "You damn right I know," he said. "You just do what you're told!"

"I just wanted to make sure, sir," I said.

"Look," he said, drawing in his breath with an exaggerated show of patience. "Take the dropper and fill it full . . . Go on, do it!"

I filled it.

"Now measure ten drops into the paint . . . There, that's it, not too goddamn fast. Now. You want no more than ten, and no less."

Slowly, I measured the glistening black drops, seeing them settle upon the surface and become blacker still, spreading suddenly out to the edges.

"That's it. That's all you have to do," he said. "Never mind how it looks. That's my worry. You just do what you're told and don't try to think about it. When you've done five or six buckets, come back and see if the samples are dry . . . And hurry, we've got to get this batch back off to Washington by 11:30 . . ."

I worked fast but carefully. With a man like this Kimbro the least thing done incorrectly would cause trouble. So I wasn't supposed to think! To hell with him. Just a flunkey, a northern redneck, a Yankee cracker! I mixed the paint thoroughly, then brushed it smoothly on one of the pieces of board, careful that the brush strokes were uniform.

Struggling to remove an especially difficult cover, I wondered if the same Liberty paint was used on the campus, or if this "Optic White" was something made exclusively for the government. Perhaps it was of a better quality, a special mix. And in my mind I could see the brightly trimmed and freshly decorated campus buildings as they appeared on spring mornings—after the fall painting and the light winter snows, with a cloud riding over and a darting bird above—framed by the trees and encircling vines. The buildings had always seemed more impressive because they were the only buildings to receive regular paintings; usually, the nearby houses and cabins were left untouched to become the dull grained gray of weathered wood. And I remembered how the splinters in some of the boards were raised from the grain by the wind, the sun and the rain until the clapboards shone with a satiny, silvery, silver-fish sheen. Like Trueblood's cabin, or the Golden Day . . . The Golden Day had once been painted white; now its paint was flaking away with the years, the scratch of a finger being enough to send it showering down. Damn that Golden Day! But it was strange how life connected up; because I had carried Mr. Norton to the old run-down building with rotting paint, I was here. If, I thought, one could slow down his heartbeats and memory to the tempo of the black drops falling so slowly into the bucket yet reacting so swiftly, it would seem like a sequence in a feverish dream . . . I was so deep in reverie that I failed to hear Kimbro approach.

"How's it coming?" he said, standing with hands on hips.

"All right, sir."

"Let's see," he said, selecting a sample and running his thumb across the board. "That's it, as white as George Washington's Sunday-go-to-meetin' wig and as sound as the all-mighty dollar! That's paint!" he said proudly. "That's paint that'll cover just about anything!"

He looked as though I had expressed a doubt and I hurried to say, "It's certainly white all right."

"White! It's the purest white that can be found. Nobody makes a paint any whiter. This batch right here is heading for a national monument!"

"I see," I said, quite impressed.

He looked at his watch. "Just keep it up," he said. "If I don't hurry I'll be late for that production conference! Say, you're nearly out of dope: you'd better go in the tank room and refill it . . . And don't waste any time! I've got to go."

He shot away without telling me where the tank room was. It was easy to find, but I wasn't prepared for so many tanks. There were seven; each with a puzzling code stenciled on it. It's just like Kimbro not to tell me, I thought. You can't trust any of them. Well, it doesn't matter, I'll pick the tank from the contents of the drip cans hanging from the spigots.

But while the first five tanks contained clear liquids that smelled like turpentine, the last two both contained something black like the dope, but with different codes. So I had to make a choice. Selecting the tank with the drip can that smelled most like the dope, I filled the graduate, congratulating myself for not having to waste time until Kimbro returned.

The work went faster now, the mixing easier. The pigment and heavy oils came free of the bottom much quicker, and when Kimbro returned I was going at top speed. "How many have you finished?" he asked.

"About seventy-five, I think, sir. I lost count."

"That's pretty good, but not fast enough. They've been putting pressure on me to get the stuff out. Here, I'll give you a hand."

They must have given him hell, I thought, as he got grunting to his knees and began removing covers from the buckets. But he had hardly started when he was called away.

When he left I took a look at the last bunch of samples and got a shock: Instead of the smooth, hard surface of the first, they were covered with a sticky goo through which I could see the grain of the wood. What on earth had happened? The paint was not as white and glossy as before; it had a gray tinge. I stirred it vigorously, then grabbed a rag, wiping each of the boards clean, then made a new sample of each bucket. I grew panicky lest Kimbro return before I finished. Working feverishly, I made it, but since the paint required a few minutes to dry I picked up two finished buckets and started lugging them over to the loading platform. I dropped them with a thump as the voice rang out behind me. It was Kimbro.

"What the hell!" he yelled, smearing his finger over one of the samples. "This stuff's still wet!"

I didn't know what to say. He snatched up several of the later samples, smearing them, and letting out a groan. "Of all the things to happen to me. First they take all my good men and then they send me you. What'd you do to it?"

"Nothing, sir. I followed your directions," I said defensively.

I watched him peer into the graduate, lifting the dropper and sniffing it, his face glowing with exasperation.

"Who the hell gave you this?"

"No one . . ."

"Then where'd you get it?"

"From the tank room."

Suddenly he dashed for the tank room, sloshing the liquid as he ran. I thought, Oh, hell, and before I could follow, he burst out of the door in a frenzy.

"You took the wrong tank," he shouted. "What the hell, you trying to sabotage the company? That stuff wouldn't work in a million years. It's remover, *concentrated* remover! Don't you know the difference?"

"No, sir, I don't. It looked the same to me. I didn't know what I was using and you didn't tell me. I was trying to save time and took what I thought was right."

"But why this one?"

"Because it smelled the same—" I began.

"*Smelled!*" he roared. "Goddamit, don't you know you can't smell shit around all those fumes? Come on to my office!"

I was torn between protesting and pleading for fairness. It was not all my fault and I didn't want the blame, but I did wish to finish out the day. Throbbing with anger I followed, listening as he called personnel.

"Hello? Mac? Mac, this is Kimbro. It's about this fellow you sent me this morning. I'm sending him in to pick up his pay . . . What did he do? He doesn't satisfy me, that's what. I don't like his work . . . So the old man has to have a report, so what? Make him one. Tell him goddamit this fellow ruined a batch of government stuff—Hey! No, don't tell him that . . . Listen, Mac, you got anyone else out there? . . . Okay, forget it."

He crashed down the phone and swung toward me. "I swear I don't know why they hire you fellows. You just don't belong in a paint plant. Come on."

Bewildered, I followed him into the tank room, yearning to quit and tell him to go to hell. But I needed the money, and even though this was the North I wasn't ready to fight unless I had to. Here I'd be one against how many?

I watched him empty the graduate back into the tank and noted carefully when he went to another marked SKA-3-69-T-Y and refilled it. Next time I would know.

"Now, for God's sake," he said, handing me the graduate, "be careful and try to do the job right. And if you don't know what to do, ask somebody. I'll be in my office."

I returned to the buckets, my emotions whirling. Kimbro had forgotten to say what was to be done with the spoiled paint. Seeing it there I was suddenly seized by an angry impulse, and, filling the dropper with fresh dope, I stirred ten drops into each bucket and pressed home the covers. Let the government worry about that, I thought, and started to work on the unopened buckets. I stirred until my arm ached and painted the samples as smoothly as I could, becoming more skillful as I went along.

When Kimbro came down the floor and watched I glanced up silently and continued stirring.

"How is it?" he said, frowning.

"I don't know," I said, picking up a sample and hesitating.

"Well?"

"It's nothing . . . a speck of dirt," I said, standing and holding out the sample, a tightness growing within me.

Holding it close to his face, he ran his fingers over the surface and squinted at the texture. "That's more like it," he said. "That's the way it oughta be."

I watched with a sense of unbelief as he rubbed his thumb over the sample, handed it back and left without a further word.

I looked at the painted slab. It appeared the same: a gray tinge glowed through the whiteness, and Kimbro had failed to detect it. I stared for about a minute, wondering if I were seeing things, inspected another and another. All were the same, a brilliant white diffused with gray, I closed my eyes for a moment and looked again and still no change. Well, I thought, as long as he's satisfied . . .

But I had a feeling that something had gone wrong, something far more important than the paint; that either I had played a trick on Kimbro or he, like the trustees and Bledsoe, was playing one on me . . .

When the truck backed up to the platform I was pressing the cover on the last bucket—and there stood Kimbro above me.

"Let's see your samples," he said.

I reached, trying to select the whitest, as the blue-shirted truckmen climbed through the loading door.

"How about it, Kimbro," one of them said, "can we get started?"

"Just a minute, now," he said, studying the sample, "just a minute . . ."

I watched him nervously, waiting for him to throw a fit over the gray tinge and hating myself for feeling nervous and afraid. What would I say? But now he was turning to the truckmen.

"All right, boys, get the hell out of here.

"And you," he said to me, "go see MacDuffy; you're through."

I stood there, staring at the back of his head, at the pink neck beneath the cloth cap and the iron-gray hair. So he'd let me stay only to finish the mixing. I turned away, there was nothing that I could do. I cursed him all the way to the personnel office. Should I write the owners about what had happened? Perhaps they didn't know that Kimbro was having so much to do with the quality of the paint. But upon reaching the office I changed my mind. Perhaps this is how things are done here, I thought, perhaps the real quality of the paint is *always* determined by the man who ships it rather than by those who mix it. To hell with the whole thing . . . I'll find another job.

But I wasn't fired. MacDuffy sent me to the basement of Building No. 2 on a new assignment.

"When you get down there just tell Brockway that Mr. Sparland insists that he have an assistant. You do whatever he tells you."

"What is that name again, sir?" I said.

"Lucius *Brockway*," he said. "He's in charge."

It was a deep basement. Three levels underground I pushed upon a heavy metal door marked "Danger" and descended into a noisy, dimly lit room. There was something familiar about the fumes that filled the air and I had just thought *pine*, when a high-pitched Negro voice rang out above the machine sounds.

"Who you looking for down here?"

"I'm looking for the man in charge," I called, straining to locate the voice.

"You talkin' to him. What you want?"

The man who moved out of the shadow and looked at me sullenly was small, wiry and very natty in his dirty overalls. And as I approached him I saw his drawn face and the cottony white hair showing beneath his tight, striped engineer's cap. His manner puzzled me. I couldn't tell whether he felt guilty about something himself, or thought I had committed some crime. I came closer, staring. He was barely five feet tall, his overalls looking now as though he had been dipped in pitch.

"All right," he said. "I'm a busy man. What you want?"

"I'm looking for Lucius," I said.

He frowned. "That's me—and don't come calling me by my first name. To you and all like you I'm *Mister* Brockway . . ."

"You . . . ?" I began.

"Yeah, me! Who sent you down here anyway?"

"The personnel office," I said. "I was told to tell you that Mr. Sparland said for you to be given an assistant."

"Assistant!" he said. "I don't need no damn assistant! Old Man Sparland must think I'm getting old as him. Here I been running things by myself all these years and now they keep trying to send me some assistant. You get on back up there and tell 'em that when I want an assistant I'll ask for one!"

I was so disgusted to find such a man in charge that I turned without a word and started back up the stairs. First Kimbro, I thought, and now this old . . .

"Hey! wait a minute!"

I turned, seeing him beckon.

"Come on back here a minute," he called, his voice cutting sharply through the roar of the furnaces.

I went back, seeing him remove a white cloth from his hip pocket and wipe the glass face of a pressure gauge, then bend close to squint at the position of the needle.

"Here," he said, straightening and handing me the cloth, "you can stay 'til I can get in touch with the Old Man. These here have to be kept clean so's I can see how much pressure I'm getting."

I took the cloth without a word and began rubbing the glasses. He watched me critically.

"What's your name?" he said.

I told him, shouting it in the roar of the furnaces.

"Wait a minute," he called, going over and turning a valve in an intricate network of pipes. I heard the noise rise to a higher, almost hysterical pitch, somehow making it possible to hear without yelling, our voices moving blurrily underneath.

Returning, he looked at me sharply, his withered face an animated black walnut with shrewd, reddish eyes.

"This here's the first time they ever sent me anybody like you," he said as though puzzled. "That's how come I called you back. Usually they sends down some young white fellow who thinks he's going to watch me a few days and ask me a heap of questions and then take over. Some folks is too damn simple to even talk about," he said, grimacing and waving his hand in a violent gesture of dismissal. "You an engineer?" he said, looking quickly at me.

"An *engineer?*"

"Yeah, that's what I asked you," he said challengingly.

"Why, no, sir, I'm no engineer."

"You sho?"

"Of course I'm sure. Why shouldn't I be?"

He seemed to relax. "That's all right then. I have to watch them personnel fellows. One of them thinks he's going to git me out of here, when he ought to know by now he's wasting his time. Lucius Brockway not only intends to protect hisself, he *knows how* to do it! Everybody knows I been here ever since there's been a here—even helped dig the first foundation. The Old Man hired me, nobody else; and, by God, it'll take the Old Man to fire me!"

I rubbed away at the gauges, wondering what had brought on this outburst, and was somewhat relieved that he seemed to hold nothing against me personally.

"Where you go to school?" he said.

I told him.

"Is that so? What you learning down there?"

"Just general subjects, a regular college course," I said.

"Mechanics?"

"Oh no, nothing like that, just a liberal arts course. No trades."

"Is that so?" he said doubtfully. Then suddenly, "How much pressure I got on that gauge right there?"

"Which?"

"You see it," he pointed. "That one right there!"

I looked, calling off, "Forty-three and two-tenths pounds."

"Uh huh, uh huh, that's right." He squinted at the gauge and back at me. "Where you learn to read a gauge so good?"

"In my high-school physics class. It's like reading a clock."

"They teach you that in *high* school?"

"That's right."

"Well, that's going to be one of your jobs. These here gauges have to be checked every fifteen minutes. You ought to be able to do that."

"I think I can," I said.

"Some kin, some caint. By the way, who hired you?"

"Mr. MacDuffy," I said, wondering why all the questions.

"Yeah, then where you been all morning?"

"I was working over in Building No. 1."

"That there's a heap of a building. Where'bouts?"

"For Mr. Kimbro."

"I see, I see. I knowed they oughtn't to be hiring anybody this late in the day. What Kimbro have you doing?"

"Putting dope in some paint that went bad," I said wearily, annoyed with all the questions.

His lips shot out belligerently. "What paint went bad?"

"I think it was some for the government . . ."

He cocked his head. "I wonder how come nobody said nothing to me about it," he said thoughtfully. "Was it in buckets or them little biddy cans?"

"Buckets."

"Oh, that ain't so bad, them little ones is a heap of work." He gave me a high dry laugh. "How you hear about this job?" he snapped suddenly, as though trying to catch me off guard.

"Look," I said slowly, "a man I know told me about the job; MacDuffy hired me; I worked this morning for Mr. Kimbro; and I was sent to you by Mr. MacDuffy."

His face tightened. "You friends to one of those colored fellows?"

"Who?"

"Up in the lab?"

"No," I said. "Anything else you want to know?"

He gave me a long, suspicious look and spat upon a hot pipe, causing it to steam furiously. I watched him remove a heavy engineer's watch from his breast pocket and squint at the dial importantly, then turn to check it with an electric clock that glowed from the wall. "You keep on wiping them gauges," he said. "I got to look at my soup. And look here." He pointed to one of the gauges. "I wants you to keep a 'specially sharp eye on this here sonofabitch. The last couple of days he's 'veloped a habit of building up too fast. Causes me a heap of trouble. You see him gitting past 75, you yell, and yell loud!"

He went back into the shadows and I saw a shaft of brightness mark the opening of a door.

Running the rag over a gauge I wondered how an apparently uneducated old man could gain such a responsible job. He certainly didn't sound like an engineer; yet he alone was on duty. And you could never be sure, for at home an old man employed as a janitor at the Water Works was the only one who knew the location of all of the water mains. He had been employed at the beginning, before any records were kept, and actually functioned as an engineer though he drew a janitor's pay. Perhaps this old Brockway was protecting himself from something. After all, there was antagonism to our being employed. Maybe he was dissimulating, like some of the teachers at the college, who, to avoid trouble when driving through the small surrounding towns, wore chauffeur caps and pretended that their cars belonged to white men. But why was he pretending with me? And what was his job?

I looked around me. It was not just an engine room; I knew, for I had been in several, the last at college. It was something more. For one thing, the furnaces were made differently and the flames that flared through the cracks of the fire chambers were too intense and too blue. And there were the odors. No, he was *making* something down here, something that had to do with paint, and probably something too filthy and dangerous for white men to be willing to do even for money. It was not paint bceause I had been told that the paint was made on the floors above, where, passing through, I had seen men in splattered aprons working over large vats filled with whirling pigment. One thing was certain: I had to be careful with this crazy Brockway; he didn't like my being here . . . And there he was, entering the room now from the stairs.

"How's it going?" he asked.

"All right," I said. "Only it seems to have gotten louder."

"Oh, it gets pretty loud down here, all right; this here's the uproar department and I'm in charge . . . Did she go over the mark?"

"No, it's holding steady," I said.

"That's good. I been having plenty trouble with it lately. Haveta bust it down and give it a good going over soon as I can get the tank clear."

Perhaps he *is* the engineer, I thought, watching him inspect the gauges and go to another part of the room to adjust a series of valves. Then he went and said a few words into a wall phone and called me, pointing to the valves.

"I'm fixing to shoot it to 'em upstairs," he said gravely. "When I give you the signal I want you to turn 'em wide open. 'N when I give you the second signal I want you to close 'em up again. Start with this here red one and work right straight across . . ."

I took my position and waited, as he took a stand near the gauge.

"Let her go," he called. I opened the valves, hearing the sound of liquids rushing through the huge pipes. At the sound of a buzzer I looked up . . .

"Start closing," he yelled. "What you looking at? Close them valves!

"What's wrong with you?" he asked when the last valve was closed.

"I expected you to call."

"I said I'd *signal* you. Caint you tell the difference between a signal and a call? Hell, I buzzed you. You don't want to do that no more. When I buzz you I want you to do something and do it quick!"

"You're the boss," I said sarcastically.

"You mighty right, I'm the boss, and don't forgit it. Now come on back here, we got work to do."

We came to a strange-looking machine consisting of a huge set of gears connecting a series of drum-like rollers. Brockway took a shovel and scooped up a load of brown crystals from a pile on the floor, pitching them skillfully into a receptacle on top of the machine.

"Grab a scoop and let's git going," he ordered briskly. "You ever done this before?" he asked as I scooped into the pile.

"It's been a long time," I said. "What is this material?"

He stopped shoveling and gave me a long, black stare, then returned to the pile, his scoop ringing on the floor. You'll have to remember not to ask this suspicious old bastard any questions, I thought, scooping into the brown pile.

Soon I was perspiring freely. My hands were sore and I began to tire. Brockway watched me out of the corner of his eye, snickering noiselessly.

"You don't want to overwork yourself, young feller," he said blandly.

"I'll get used to it," I said, scooping up a heavy load.

"Oh, sho, sho," he said. "Sho. But you better take a rest when you git tired."

I didn't stop. I piled on the material until he said, "That there's the scoop we been trying to find. That's what we want. You better stand back a little, 'cause I'm fixing to start her up."

I backed away, watching him go over and push a switch. Shuddering into motion, the machine gave a sudden scream like a circular saw, and sent a tattoo of sharp crystals against my face. I moved clumsily away, seeing Brockway grin like a dried prune. Then with the dying hum of the furiously whirling drums, I heard the grains sifting lazily in the sudden stillness, sliding sand-like down the chute into the pot underneath.

I watched him go over and open a valve. A sharp new smell of oil arose.

"Now she's all set to cook down; all we got to do is put the fire to her," he said, pressing a button on something that looked like the burner of an oil furnace. There was an angry hum, followed by a slight explosion that caused something to rattle, and I could hear a low roaring begin.

"Know what that's going to be when it's cooked?"

"No, sir," I said.

"Well that's going to be the guts, what they call the *vee*-hicle of the paint. Least it will be by time I git through putting other stuff with it."

"But I thought the paint was made upstairs . . ."

"Naw, they just mixes in the color, make it look pretty. Right down here is where the real paint is made. Without what I do they couldn't do nothing, they be making bricks without straw. An' not only do I make up the base, I fixes the varnishes and lots of the oils too . . ."

"So that's it," I said. "I was wondering what you did down here."

"A whole lots of folks wonders about that without gitting anywhere. But as I was saying, caint a single doggone drop of paint move out of the factory lessen it comes through Lucius Brockway's hands."

"How long have you been doing this?"

"Long enough to know what I'm doing," he said. "And I learned it without all that education that them what's been sent down here is suppose to have. I learned it by doing it. Them personnel fellows don't want to face the facts, but Liberty Paints wouldn't be worth a plugged nickel if they didn't have me here to see that it got a good strong base. Old Man Sparland know it though. I caint stop laughing over the time when I was down with a touch of pneumonia and they put one of them so-called engineers to pooting around down here. Why, they started to having so much paint go bad they didn't know what to do. Paint was bleeding and wrinkling, wouldn't cover or nothing—you know, a man could make hisself all kinds of money if he found out what makes paint bleed. Anyway, everything was going bad. Then word got to me that they done put that fellow in my place and when I got well I wouldn't come back. Here I been with 'em so long and loyal and everything. Shucks, I just sent 'em word that Lucius Brockway was retiring!

"Next thing you know here comes the Old Man. He so old hisself his chauffeur has to help him up them steep stairs at my place. Come in a-puffing and a-blowing, says, 'Lucius, what's this I hear 'bout you retiring?'

" 'Well, sir, Mr. Sparland, sir,' I says, 'I been pretty sick, as you well know, and I'm gitting kinder along in my years, as you well know, and I hear that this here Italian fellow you got in my place is doing so good I thought I'd might as well take it easy round the house.'

"Why, you'd a-thought I'd done cursed him or something. 'What kind of talk is that from you, Lucius Brockway,' he said, 'taking it easy round the house when we need you out to the plant? Don't you know the quickest way to die is to retire? Why, that fellow out at the plant don't know a thing about those furnaces. I'm so worried about what he's going to do, that he's liable to blow up the plant or something that I took out some extra insurance. He can't do your job,' he said. 'He don't have the touch. We haven't put out a first-class batch of paint since you been gone.' Now that was the Old Man hisself!" Lucius Brockway said.

"So what happened?" I said.

"What you mean, what happened?" he said, looking as though it were the most unreasonable question in the world. "Shucks, a few days later the Old Man had me back down here in full control. That engineer got so mad when he found out he had to take orders from me he quit the next day."

He spat on the floor and laughed. "Heh, heh, heh, he was a fool, that's what. A fool! He wanted to boss *me* and I know more about this basement than anybody, boilers and everything. I helped lay the pipes and everything, and what I mean is I knows the location of each and every pipe and switch and cable and wire and everything else—both in the floors and in the walls *and* out in the yard. Yes, sir! And what's more, I got it in my head so good I can trace it out on paper down to the last nut and bolt; and ain't never been to nobody's engineering school neither, ain't even passed by one, as far as I know. Now what you think about that?"

"I think it's remarkable," I said, thinking, I don't like this old man.

"Oh, I wouldn't call it that," he said. "It's just that I been round here so long. I been studying this machinery for over twenty-five years. Sho, and that fellow thinking 'cause he been to some school and learned how to read a blueprint and how to fire a boiler he knows more 'bout this plant than Lucius Brockway. That fool couldn't make no engineer 'cause he can't see what's staring him straight in the face . . . Say, you forgettin' to watch them gauges."

I hurried over, finding all the needles steady.

"They're okay," I called.

"All right, but I'm warning you to keep an eye on 'em. You caint forgit down here, 'cause if you do, you liable to blow up something. They got all this machinery, but that ain't everything; *we are the machines inside the machine.*

"You know the best selling paint we got, the one that *made* this here business?" he asked as I helped him fill a vat with a smelly substance.

"No, I don't."

"Our white, Optic White."

"Why the white rather than the others?"

" 'Cause we started stressing it from the first. We make the best white paint in the world, I don't give a damn what nobody says. Our white is so white you can paint a chunka coal and you'd have to crack it open with a sledge hammer to prove it wasn't white clear through!"

His eyes glinted with humorous conviction and I had to drop my head to hide my grin.

"You notice that sign on top of the building?"

"Oh, you can't miss that," I said.

"You read the slogan?"

"I don't remember, I was in such a hurry."

"Well, you might not believe it, but I helped the Old Man make up that slogan. 'If It's Optic White, It's the Right White,' " he quoted with an upraised finger, like a preacher quoting holy writ. "I got me a three-hundred-dollar bonus for helping to think that up. These newfangled advertising folks is been tryin' to work up something about the other colors, talking about rainbows or something, but hell, *they* caint get nowhere."

" 'If It's Optic White, It's the Right White,' " I repeated and suddenly had to repress a laugh as a childhood jingle rang through my mind:

" 'If you're white, you're right,' " I said.

"That's it," he said. "And that's another reason why the Old Man ain't goin' to let nobody come down here messing with me. *He* knows what a lot of them new fellers don't; *he* knows that the reason our paint is so good is because of the way Lucius Brockway puts the pressure on them oils and resins before they even leaves the tanks." He laughed maliciously. "They thinks 'cause everything down here is done by machinery, that's all there is to it. They crazy! Ain't a continental thing that happens down here that ain't as iffen I done put my black hands into it! Them machines just do the cooking, these here hands right here do the sweeting. Yes, sir! Lucius Brockway hit it square on the head! I dips my fingers in and sweets it! Come on, let's eat . . ."

"But what about the gauges?" I said, seeing him go over and take a thermos bottle from a shelf near one of the furnaces.

"Oh, we'll be here close enough to keep an eye on 'em. Don't you worry 'bout that."

"But I left my lunch in the locker room over at Building No. 1."

"Go on and git it and come back here and eat. Down here we have to always be on the job. A man don't need no more'n fifteen minutes to eat no-how; then I say let him git on back on the job."

Upon opening the door I thought I had made a mistake. Men dressed in splattered painters' caps and overalls sat about on benches, listening to a thin tubercular-looking man who was addressing them in a nasal voice. Everyone looked at me and I was starting out when the thin man called, "There's plenty of seats for late comers. Come in, brother . . ."

Brother? Even after my weeks in the North this was surprising. "I was looking for the locker room," I sputtered.

"You're in it, brother. Weren't you told about the meeting?"

"Meeting? Why, no, sir, I wasn't."

The chairman frowned. "You see, the bosses are not cooperating," he said to the others. "Brother, who's your foreman?"

"Mr. Brockway, sir," I said.

Suddenly the men began scraping their feet and cursing. I looked about me. What was wrong? Were they objecting to my referring to Brockway as *Mister?*

"Quiet brothers," the chairman said, leaning across his table, his hand cupped to his ear. "Now what was that, brother; who is your foreman?"

"Lucius Brockway, sir," I said, dropping the *Mister*.

But this seemed only to make them more hostile. "Get him the hell out of here," they shouted. I turned. A group on the far side of the room kicked over a bench, yelling, "Throw him out! Throw him out!"

I inched backwards, hearing the little man bang on the table for order. "Men, brothers! Give the brother a chance . . ."

"He looks like a dirty fink to me. A first-class enameled fink!"

The hoarsely voiced word grated my ears like "nigger" in an angry southern mouth . . .

"Brothers, *please!*" The chairman was waving his hands as I reached out behind me for the door and touched an arm, feeling it snatch violently away. I dropped my hand.

"Who sent this fink into the meeting, brother chairman? Ask him that!" a man demanded.

"No, wait," the chairman said. "Don't ride that word too hard . . ."

"Ask him, brother chairman!" another man said.

"Okay, but don't label a man a fink until you know for sure." The chairman turned to me. "How'd you happen in here, brother?"

The men quieted, listening.

"I left my lunch in my locker," I said, my mouth dry.

"You weren't *sent* into the meeting?"

"No, sir, I didn't know about any meeting."

"The hell he says. None of these finks ever knows!"

"Throw the lousy bastard out!"

"Now, wait," I said.

They became louder, threatening.

"Respect the chair!" the chairman shouted. "We're a democratic union here, following democratic—"

"Never mind, git rid of the fink!"

". . . procedures. It's our task to make friends with all the workers. And I mean *all*. That's how we build the union strong. Now let's hear what the brother's got to say. No more of that beefing and interrupting!"

I broke into a cold sweat, my eyes seeming to have become extremely sharp, causing each face to stand out vivid in its hostility.

I heard, "When were you hired, friend?"

"This morning," I said.

"See, brothers, he's a new man. We don't want to make the mistake of judging the worker by his foreman. Some of you also work for sonsabitches, remember?"

Suddenly the men began to laugh and curse. "Here's one right here," one of them yelled.

"Mine wants to marry the boss's daughter—a frigging eight-day wonder!"

This sudden change made me puzzled and angry, as though they were making me the butt of a joke.

"Order, brothers! Perhaps the brother would like to join the union. How about it, brother?"

"Sir . . . ?" I didn't know what to say. I knew very little about unions—but most of these men seemed hostile . . . And before I could answer a fat man with shaggy gray hair leaped to his feet, shouting angrily,

"I'm against it! Brothers, this fellow could be a fink, even if he was hired right this minute! Not that I aim to be unfair to anybody, either. Maybe he ain't a fink," he cried passionately, "but brothers, I want to remind you that nobody knows it; and it seems to me that anybody that would work under that sonofabitching, double-crossing Brockway for more than fifteen minutes is just as apt as not to be *naturally* fink-minded! Please, brothers!" he cried, waving his arms for quiet. "As some of you brothers have learned, to the sorrow of your wives and babies, a fink don't have to know about trade unionism to be a fink! Finkism? Hell, I've made a study of finkism! Finkism is *born* into some guys. It's born into some guys, just like a good eye for color is born into other guys. That's right, that's the honest, scientific truth! A fink don't even have to have heard of a union before," he cried in a frenzy of words. "All you have to do is bring him around the neighborhood of a union and next thing you know, why, zip! he's finking his finking ass off!"

He was drowned out by shouts of approval. Men turned violently to look at me. I felt choked. I wanted to drop my head but faced them as though facing them was itself a denial of his statements. Another voice ripped out of the shouts of approval, spilling with great urgency from the lips of a little fellow with glasses who spoke with the index finger of one hand upraised and the thumb of the other crooked in the suspender of his overalls:

"I want to put this brother's remarks in the form of a motion: I move that we determine through a thorough investigation whether the new worker is a fink or no; and if he is a fink, let us discover who he's finking for! And this, brother members, would give the worker time, if he *ain't* a fink, to become acquainted with the work of the union and its aims. After all, brothers, we don't want to forget that workers like him aren't so highly developed as some of us who've been in the labor movement for a long time. So *I* says, let's give him time to see what we've done to improve the condition of the workers, and then, if he *ain't* a fink, we can decide in a democratic way whether we want to accept this brother into the union. Brother union members, I thank you!" He sat down with a bump.

The room roared. Biting anger grew inside me. So I was not so highly developed as they! What did he mean? Were they all Ph.D.'s? I couldn't move; too much was happening to me. It was as though by entering the room I had automatically applied for membership—even though I had no idea that a union existed, and had come up simply to get a cold pork chop sandwich. I stood trembling, afraid that they would ask me to join but angry that so many rejected me on sight. And worst of all, I knew they were forcing me to accept things on their own terms, and I was unable to leave.

"All right, brothers. We'll take a vote," the chairman shouted. "All in favor of the motion, signify by saying 'Aye' . . ."

The ayes drowned him out.

"The ayes carried it," the chairman announced as several men turned to stare at me. At last I could move. I started out, forgetting why I had come.

"Come in, brother," the chairman called. "You can get your lunch now. Let him through, you brothers around the door!"

My face stung as though it has been slapped. They had made their decision without giving me a chance to speak for myself. I felt that every man present looked upon me with hostility; and though I had lived with hostility all my life, now for the first time it seemed to reach me, as though I had expected more of these men than of others—even though I had not known of their existence. Here in this room my defenses were negated, stripped away, checked at the door as the weapons, the knives and razors and owlhead pistols of the country boys were checked on Saturday night at the Golden Day. I kept my eyes lowered, mumbling "Pardon me, pardon me," all the way to the drab green locker, where I removed the sandwich, for which I no longer had an appetite, and stood fumbling with the bag, dreading to face the men on my way out. Then still hating myself for the apologies made coming over, I brushed past silently as I went back.

When I reached the door the chairman called, "Just a minute, brother, we want you to understand that this is nothing against you personally. What you see here is the results of certain conditions here at the plant. We want you to know that we are only trying to protect ourselves. Some day we hope to have you as a member in good standing."

From here and there came a half-hearted applause that quickly died. I swallowed and stared unseeing, the words spurting to me from a red, misty distance.

"Okay, brothers," the voice said, "let him pass."

I stumbled through the bright sunlight of the yard, past the office workers chatting on the grass, back to Building No. 2, to the basement. I stood on the stairs, feeling as though my bowels had been flooded with acid. Why hadn't I simply left, I thought with anguish. And since I had remained, why hadn't I *said* something, defended myself? Suddenly I snatched the wrapper off a sandwich and tore it violently with my teeth, hardly tasting the dry lumps that squeezed past my constricted throat when I swallowed. Dropping the remainder back into the bag, I held onto the handrail, my legs shaking as though I had just escaped a great danger. Finally, it went away and I pushed open the metal door.

"What kept you so long?" Brockway snapped from where he sat on a wheelbarrow. He had been drinking from a white mug now cupped in his grimy hands.

I looked at him abstractedly, seeing how the light caught on his wrinkled forehead, his snowy hair.

"*I said, what kept you so long!*"

What had he to do with it, I thought, looking at him through a kind of mist, knowing that I disliked him and that I was very tired.

"I say . . ." he began, and I heard my voice come quiet from my tensed throat as I noticed by the clock that I had been gone only twenty minutes.

"I ran into a union meeting—"

"*Union!*" I heard his white cup shatter against the floor as he uncrossed his legs, rising. "I knowed you belonged to that bunch of troublemaking foreigners! I knowed it! Git out!" he screamed. "Git out of my basement!"

He started toward me as in a dream, trembling like the needle of one of the gauges as he pointed toward the stairs, his voice shrieking. I stared; something seemed to have gone wrong, my reflexes were jammed.

"But what's the matter?" I stammered, my voice low and my mind understanding and yet failing exactly to understand. "What's wrong?"

"You heard me. Git out!"

"But I don't understand . . ."

"Shut up and git!"

"But, Mr. Brockway," I cried, fighting to hold something that was giving way.

"You two-bit, trouble-making union louse!"

"Look, man," I cried, urgently now, "I don't belong to any union."

"If you don't git outta here, you low-down skunk," he said, looking wildly about the floor, "I'm liable to kill you. The Lord being my witness, I'LL KILL YOU!"

It was incredible, things were speeding up. "You'll do what?" I stammered.

"I'LL KILL YOU, THAT'S WHAT!"

He had said it again and something fell away from me, and I seemed to be telling myself in a rush: *You were trained to accept the foolishness of such old men as this, even when you thought them clowns and fools; you were trained to pretend that you respected them and acknowledged in them the same quality of authority and power in your world as the white before whom they bowed and scraped and feared and loved and imitated, and you were even trained to accept it when, angered or spiteful, or drunk with power, they came at you with a stick or strap or cane and you made no effort to strike back, but only to escape unmarked.* But this was too much . . . he was not grandfather or uncle or father, nor preacher or teacher. Something uncoiled in my stomach and I was moving toward him, shouting, more at a black blur that irritated my eyes than at a clearly defined human face, "YOU'LL KILL WHO?"

"*YOU*, THAT'S WHO!"

"Listen here, you old fool, don't talk about killing me! Give me a chance to explain. I don't belong to anything—Go on, pick it up! Go on!" I yelled, seeing his eyes fasten upon a twisted iron bar.

"You're old enough to be my grandfather, but if you touch that bar, I swear I'll make you eat it!"

"I done tole you, GIT OUTTA MY BASEMENT! *You impudent son'bitch*," he screamed.

I moved forward, seeing him stoop and reach aside for the bar; and I was throwing myself forward, feeling him go over with a grunt, hard against the floor, rolling beneath the force of my lunge. It was as though I had landed upon a wiry rat. He scrambled beneath me, making angry sounds and striking my face as he tried to use the bar. I twisted it from his grasp, feeling a sharp pain stab through my shoulder. He's using a knife, flashed through my mind and I slashed out with my elbow, sharp against his face, feeling it land solid and seeing his head fly backwards and up and back again as I struck again, hearing something fly free and skitter across the floor, thinking, It's gone, the knife is gone . . . and struck again as he tried to choke me, jabbing at his bobbing head, feeling the bar come free and bringing it down at his head, missing, the metal clinking against the floor, and bringing it up for a second try and him yelling, "No, no! You the best, you the best!"

"I'm going to beat your brains out!" I said, my throat dry, "stabbing me . . ."

"No," he panted. "I got enough. Ain't you heard me say I got enough?"

"So when you can't win you want to stop! Damn you, if you've cut me bad, I'll tear your head off!"

Watching him warily, I got to my feet. I dropped the bar, as a flash of heat swept over me: His face was caved in.

"What's wrong with you, old man?" I yelled nervously. "Don't you know better than to attack a man a third your age?"

He blanched at being called old, and I repeated it, adding insults I'd heard my grandfather use. "Why, you old-fashioned, slavery-time, mammy-made, handkerchief-headed bastard, you should know better! What made you think you could threaten *my* life? You meant nothing to me, I came down here because I was sent. I didn't know anything about you or the union either. Why'd you start riding me the minute I came in? Are you people crazy? Does this paint go to your head? Are you drinking it?"

He glared, panting tiredly. Great tucks showed in his overalls where the folds were stuck together by the goo with which he was covered, and I thought, Tar Baby, and wanted to blot him out of my sight. But now my anger was flowing fast from action to words.

"I go to get my lunch and they ask me who I work for and when I tell them, they call me a fink. *A fink!* You people must be out of your minds. No sooner do I get back down here than *you* start yelling that you're going to kill me! What's going on? What have you got against me? What did I do?"

He glowered at me silently, then pointed to the floor.

"Reach and draw back a nub," I warned.

"Caint a man even git his teeth?" he mumbled, his voice strange.

"TEETH?"

With a shamed frown, he opened his mouth. I saw a blue flash of shrunken gums. The thing that had skittered across the floor was not a knife, but a plate of false teeth. For a fraction of a second I was desperate, feeling some of my justification for wanting to kill him slipping away. My fingers leaped to my shoulder, finding wet cloth but no blood. The old fool had *bitten* me. A wild flash of laughter struggled to rise from beneath my anger. He had bitten me! I looked on the floor, seeing the smashed mug and the teeth glinting dully across the room.

"Get them," I said, growing ashamed. Without his teeth, some of the hatefulness seemed to have gone out of him. But I stayed close as he got his teeth and went over to the tap and held them beneath a stream of water. A tooth fell away beneath the pressure of his thumb, and I heard him grumbling as he placed the plate in his mouth. Then, wiggling his chin, he became himself again.

"You was really trying to kill me," he said. He seemed unable to believe it.

"You started the killing. I don't go around fighting," I said. "Why didn't you let me explain? Is it against the law to belong to the union?"

"That damn union," he cried, almost in tears. "That *damn* union! They after my job! I know they after my job! For one of us to join one of them damn unions is like we was to bite the hand of the man who teached us to bathe in a bathtub! I hates it, and I mean to keep on doing all I can to chase it outta the plant. They after my job, the chickenshit bastards!"

Spittle formed at the corners of his mouth; he seemed to boil with hatred.

"But what have I to do with that?" I said, feeling suddenly the older.

" 'Cause them young colored fellas up in the lab is trying to join that outfit, that's what! Here the white man done give 'em jobs," he wheezed as though pleading a case. "He done give 'em *good* jobs too, and they so ungrateful they goes and joins up with that backbiting union! I never seen such a no-good ungrateful bunch. All they doing is making things bad for the rest of us!"

"Well, I'm sorry," I said, "I didn't know about all that. I came here to take a temporary job and I certainly didn't intend to get mixed up in any quarrels. But as for us, I'm ready to forget our disagreement—if you are . . ." I held out my hand, causing my shoulder to pain.

He gave me a gruff look. "You ought to have more self-respect than to fight an old man," he said. "I got grown boys older than you."

"I thought you were trying to kill me," I said, my hand still extended. "I thought you had stabbed me."

"Well, I don't like a lot of bickering and confusion myself," he said, avoiding my eyes. And it was as though the closing of his sticky hand over mine was a signal. I heard a shrill hissing from the boilers behind me and turned, hearing Brockway yell, "I tole you to watch them gauges. Git over to the big valves, quick!"

I dashed for where a series of valve wheels projected from the wall near the crusher, seeing Brockway scrambling away in the other direction, thinking, Where's he going? as I reached the valves, and hearing him yell, "Turn it! Turn it!"

"Which?" I yelled, reaching.

"The white one, fool, the white one!"

I jumped, catching it and pulling down with all my weight, feeling it give. But this only increased the noise and I seemed to hear Brockway laugh as I looked around to see him scrambling for the stairs, his hands clasping the back of his head, and his neck pulled in close, like a small boy who has thrown a brick into the air.

"Hey you! Hey you!" I yelled. "Hey!" But it was too late. All my movements seemed too slow, ran together. I felt the wheel resisting and tried vainly to reverse it and tried to let go, and it sticking to my palms and my fingers stiff and sticky, and I turned, running now, seeing the needle on one of the gauges swinging madly, like a beacon gone out of control, and trying to think clearly, my eyes darting here and there through the room of tanks and machines and up the stairs so far away and hearing the clear new note arising while I seemed to run swiftly up an incline and shot forward with sudden acceleration into a wet blast of black emptiness that was somehow a bath of whiteness.

It was a fall into space that seemed not a fall but a suspension. Then a great weight landed upon me and I seemed to sprawl in an interval of clarity beneath a pile of broken machinery, my head pressed back against a huge wheel, my body splattered with a stinking goo. Somewhere an engine ground in furious futility, grating loudly until a pain shot around the curve of my head and bounced me off into blackness for a distance, only to strike another pain that lobbed me back. And in that clear instant of consciousness I opened my eyes to a blinding flash.

Holding on grimly, I could hear the sound of someone wading, sloshing, nearby, and an old man's garrulous voice saying, "I tole 'em these here young Nineteen-Hundred boys ain't no good for the job. They ain't got the nerves. Naw, sir, they just ain't got the nerves."

I tried to speak, to answer, but something heavy moved again, and I was understanding something fully and trying again to answer but seemed to sink to the center of a lake of heavy water and pause, transfixed and numb with the sense that I had lost irrevocably an important victory.